For years, this has been "the Bible" for anyone planning a ski or snowboard vacation to Europe

"Facts, prices and advice on choosing a ski package, getting around Europe and finding friends to ski with."

—*New York Times*

"Everything skiers need to know but the weather forecast."

—*Robb Report*

"Tips and money-saving ideas for skiing in Europe."

—*San Francisco Examiner*

"Detailed information on lift ticket prices, cross-country facilities, nightlife and more."

—*Powder Magazine*

"The flavor, feel and personality of each resort." —*Boston Globe*

"It provides independent evaluation of the ski terrain and offers more extensive information than found in other guides."

—*Skier News*

"Start your planning with SkiSnowboard Europe. It includes everything needed to make an educated decision about which slopes to hit."

—*PhysiciansFinancial News*

"Get it before you ski off." —*Endless Vacations*

"I've been using SkiSnowboard Europe since the first edition appeared to select destinations for my club and then to organize the trips."

—RN, Washington DC

"We live about two hours from Chamonix and we love your SkiSnowboard Europe book."

—JM, Thoiry, France

Visit us online at www.skisnowboardeurope.com

or www.ss-eur.com

- find even more up-to-date information
- get more information than from most resort sites
- hotels, restaurants, dining and sightseeing
- examine resort trail maps
- get ski and snowboard headlines from around the world
- link to the latest weather and snow conditions
- link to many resorts in this book with a Web site
- buy guidebooks, technique books and gift books

visit www.skisnowboard.com for information about resorts in USA and Canada

SKI
SNOWBOARD
EUROPE

14th Edition

by Charles Leocha
with
Karen Cummings
James Kitfield
Hilary Nangle
Peggy McKay Shinn
Zahlen, Xtehn, Rohre & Vehro Titcomb
William Walker
Vanessa Reese

WORLD LEISURE CORPORATION
Hampstead, NH

Help us do a better job

Research for this book is an ongoing process. We have been at it for more than a decade. Each year we revisit many of these resorts, and every winter we speak with locals from every resort.

If you find a new restaurant, hotel, bar or disco that you feel we should include, please let us know. If you find anything in these pages that is misleading or has changed, please let us know. If we use your suggestion, we will send you a copy of next year's edition.

Send your suggestions and comments to:

Charlie Leocha, *Ski Europe,* World Leisure Corporation
P.O. Box 160, Hampstead NH 03841, USA
or send e-mail to leocha@worldleisure.com

Front cover photos by TVB St. Anton am Arlberg, Austria.
Back cover photos, Children ski school and lunch on deck, courtesy of French Ski International; Village scene and snowboarder, courtesy Le Grand Bornand, France; Skier courtesy, Les Menuires, France.

Chapter heading illustrations by Len Shalansky,
59 Darling St., Warwick, RI 02886, (401) 738-3215

Distributed to the trade in the U.S.A. by
Midpoint Trade Books, Inc., 27 W. 20th Street, Suite 1102,
New York, NY 10011, Tel. (212) 727-0190, fax (212) 727-0195.
Internet: www.midpt.com

Distributed to the trade in U.K. by
Portfolio, Unit 5, Perivale Industrial Park, Perivale, Middlesex, UB6 7RL
Tel. (020) 8997-9000, fax (020) 8997-9097.
Internet: www.portfoliobooks.com

Distributed to the trade in Canada by
Hushion House, 36 Northline Road, Toronto, Ontatio, M4B 3E2, Canada
Tel. (461) 287-3146 fax (416) 287-0081 Internet: www.hushion.com

Mail Order, Catalog, other International sales and rights, and Special Sales by
World Leisure Corporation, 177 Paris Street, Boston, MA 02128.
Tel. (617) 569-1966, fax (603) 947-0838
E-mail: leocha@worldleisure.com; Internet: www.worldleisure.com or skisnowboard.com

ISBN: 0-915009-80-3 ISSN: 1072-8996 LCCN: 93-643935

Contributors to Ski Europe (14th edition)

Charlie Leocha has been skiing worldwide for over two decades. In addition to *Ski Europe*, he is author of *Ski America & Canada,* an annually updated guidebook to North America's top ski resorts. He has skied, eaten, slept and partied at virtually every major international resort. He writes about travel and skiing for scores of magazines and newspapers.

Karen Cummings, whose skiing heritage began in North Conway, N.H., has had the good fortune to be shown around the slopes by St. Anton native, Herbert Schneider (son of Hannes Schneider, the father of modern skiing).

James Kitfield has been awarded the Gerald R. Ford prize twice for distinguished reporting, and the Jesse H. Neal award for excellence in reporting. His book, *Prodigal Soldiers*, was published by Simon & Schuster. He skis whenever and wherever he has a chance. He first met Charlie Leocha dancing in a conga line through a bar in Verbier.

Hilary Nangle, the Eastern editor of *Ski America & Canada*, normally skis in Maine, but will manage a foray into the Alps whenever the opportunity avails.

Peggy McKay Shinn who grew up in the West and now lives in Vermont still enjoys a few turns in European snow.

Zahlen Titcomb, Xtehn Titcomb, Vehro Titcomb and **Rohre Titcomb** are lucky enough to split living and skiing between the U.S.A., Italy and France. They are all accomplished snowboarders, skiers and ultimate Frisbee players. They write about snowboarding and skiing specializing on discovering the young, hip places to stay and play. They updated Verbier, Megève, Morzine/Avoriaz and Tignes in France.

William Walker is one of the founding co-authors of this book. A skiing journalist, he has been writing and living in Germany for almost 20 years. He was an editor with European *Stars and Stripes* and has written for many international publications.

Vanessa Reese, a virtual skier, pulls information from the corners of the Alps and the Pyrenees and makes sure this project and our Web site, www.skisnowboardeurope.com, stays up-to-date.

Peter Aiken, Andrew Bill, Cindy Bohl, Claudia Carbone, Christopher Elliott, Kari Haugeto, Steve Giordano, Glen Putman and **Lynn Rosen** all contributed updates to various chapters.

Contents

Contents

SKI SNOWBOARD EUROPE

Ski Europe

Getting the most out of this guidebook

Skiing in Europe is the dream of just about every American skier and for British skiers it is normally the most cost effective ski holiday available. Today, with easy flights across the Atlantic and the Channel, and tour packages to dozens of the resorts that nestle in the Alps, the dream is easy to fulfill. This book is designed to help give you the information you'll need to plan your trip and get the most out of it.

For Alpine veterans who return year after year, this book will help you to make your own arrangements, or at least to decide which resorts you want to visit. We believe that you won't find another guide with as many useful numbers and addresses for a European ski vacation. And this is a guidebook that is useful on the ground, with details about dining, nightlife, day care, ski schools and other activities that will help to make your European ski vacation a totally enjoyable experience.

Time and money

Unfortunately, too many Americans don't seriously consider skiing in Europe. They may seriously dream about it, but dismiss the idea as too costly or too time-consuming. Skiing in Europe is neither.

Consider the average urban skier in the United States: reaching the nearest destination resort will take him five, six or seven hours, and that travel is normally during daytime. Skiers and snowboarders heading to Europe, normally board a flight in the evening and land the next morning. Transfers to the Alps are only a couple of hours, and this puts you in the resort the following afternoon. Voilà!—on the average, you spend about the same travel time.

As far as money goes, European ski packages average about $1,200 to $1,400 for a week of skiing, including seven nights of first-class lodging, transatlantic airfare, transfers to resorts, breakfast and dinner every day, lift tickets in some cases and all taxes. This is about the same as you would spend taking a vacation to a Rocky Mountain resort from the East Coast or from California.

Even a one-week vacation within driving distance from home in the United States can end up costing more than $600. Some tours only cost $635 for a week in Innsbruck, Austria, for example, including air, breakfast, dinner and transfers from the East Coast.

Also, with the advent of direct flights from the West Coast to Europe and code sharing, time and expense are no longer the major factors they once were for people living in once non-gateway cities.

What's new in this edition

Prices for lift tickets, child care and ski school at virtually every resort have been updated to 2003/2004 winter prices. Where new lifts have been installed, descriptions of the skiing have been modified. This year we are once again focusing on the Alps, where, again, one of the big changes has been the addition of snowmaking at many of the resorts. Low-level slopes are now covered with limited snowmaking to insure that vacationers can ski back into the towns and villages even in poor snow years.

Several of Europe's largest resorts have installed new cable cars, gondolas and other lifts to connect them to nearby resorts. For example, in the French Alps, Les Arcs is now connected with La Plagne creating another monster of an interconnected ski area with lift-served access to two glaciers.

Over the past years, another significant change, especially for families, is the establishment of a Youth or Teenage lift ticket. Now many resorts have created a new ticketing category with prices between those of children and adults. This new pricing category affects youth from 13–18 years in most cases.

Where we have been able to get the internet and e-mail addresses of various resorts, we have included them in the Tourist Information section. We have also set up a web site at **www.skisnowboardeurope.com** or **www.ss-eur.com** that will provide updated information on many of these resorts as well and provide a means of sending us any messages, suggestions for future books and questions. Come visit the site and join our mailing list.

We have also included basic information on the ski chalets operated by many British ski tour organizers. This information will be an assistance to many of our British readers as well as an eyeopener to our American readers who have no clue about this money-saving concept.

Chapter organization

The resort chapters are in several sections. We begin by sketching the personality of the place, to give you a feel for the overall resort—is it old and quaint or modern and high-rise? Clustered at the base of the slopes, or a few miles down the road? Remote and isolated, or around the bend from another resort? Is it family-oriented or catering to singles, walkable with good shuttlebuses or requiring a car, filled with happy, friendly faces or with an aloof herd of "beautiful" skiers?

A detailed description of the mountain layout is next, followed by a mountain rating. We suggest an approach to exploring the mountain based on your abilities, and in the mountain rating we describe what the mountain has to offer for beginner, intermediate or expert; more importantly, this section also suggests which resorts the beginner looking for the mellow might try or the expert looking for the extreme may choose to avoid.

The major ski school programs are outlined, together with prices for group and private lessons.

Lift ticket prices are listed for adults, children and seniors. The price lists in most cases include single-day passes, as well as multiday tickets where available. Where possible we list the 2003/04 prices; where no date is noted, assume the prices are from the 2002/03 season.

Under Accommodations we list the most luxurious places to stay as well as many of the ski area bargains. In the Condos and flats section we have many private homes that are available for rent during the winter season.

The dining recommendations always include the best gourmet restaurants in town, where money is no object—but we don't leave out affordable places where a hungry family, or a broke college kid, can chow down and relax. There are also plenty of in-between restaurants suggested. These suggestions have been compiled from interviews with locals and tourists, gleaned from the top gourmet guidebooks, then combined with our own dining experiences.

Après-ski/nightlife describes places to go once the lifts begin to close, and where to find entertainment later in the evening. We discuss, for example, which bars are packed with celebrants for immediate après-ski, likewise where to find an inviting, cozy spot in front of a fireplace. We'll help you find pulsing disco on a packed dance floor, or soft music and quiet after-dinner talk.

Details on resort child care facilities are given with prices, times and ages of children accepted.

Activities and facilities, such as tennis and squash, fitness clubs, skating, sleigh rides, hot-air ballooning, curling and festivals, are included under other activities.

Finally, we give detailed getting there instructions on how to reach the resort either by plane, car or train and finish with the most important phone numbers and addresses for tourist information.

Skier ability levels

The level of skiing ability needed to negotiate a particular trail is regularly noted. Because resorts and ski schools use different rating systems, we provide ours to assist you in reading "Where to ski":

Never-evers are just what the name implies, and the term normally sticks with them for the first three to five days on skis.

Beginners have about a week of instruction and can turn and stop more or less when they choose, but still rely on uncertain wedge turns.

Lower intermediates can link easy looping turns and are beginning to make parallel turns.

Intermediates can negotiate any blue trail and can normally more-or-less parallel ski on the smooth stuff; they go back to survival rules when working their way down an expert trail, and definitely struggle in heavy powder and crud.

Advanced skiers can ski virtually any marked trail with carved turns, but are still intimidated by crud, deep heavy powder and super steeps.

Experts can always ski anything, anytime, anywhere. They are few and far between.

For our European and Australian readers

Most of the introduction chapters are written with our North American audience in mind. But the chapters describing the skiing, accommodation, dining and other facets of each resort are totally international. Prices are given in the Euros and most of our observations are cross-cultural (at least across the English-speaking cultures).

If we refer to anything, such as a product or service, that is not available in your country feel free to send us a fax, letter, or e-mail. We will do our best to get back to you with details on how to order it.

You can reach us at:

World Leisure Corporation
PO Box 160
Hampstead, NH 03841, USA
(617) 569-1966; fax (603) 947-0838;
Internet: www.worldleisure.com (corporate publishing site)
skisnowboardeurope.com (The Alps, Pyrenees, Sierra Nevada)
skisnowboard.com (U.S.A. and Canada)
xcskiresorts.com (cross-country skiing in North America)

Using the Internet

One of the most significant changes in making reservations at and gathering information about ski resorts has been the development of the Internet. Virtually every world-class resort now has an Internet site with basic information about the resort including latest snow conditions, statistics, lift tickets, ski school prices, some lodging and contact information.

This Internet information is an excellent addition to the material in this guidebook. If there are any changes to the pricing and scheduled events, they are normally posted on the skisnowboardeurope.com site.

Skisnowboardeurope.com (or ss-eur.com) provides the most detailed destination information available on the Internet for European winter resorts. It will include more up-to-the-minute snow condition and weather reports, snow cams and late-breaking bargains. The site is online with basic resort information contined in this book.

Skisnowboard.com presents the most comprehensive information on destination resorts in North America gleaned from the pages of *SkiSnowboard America and Canada*. Check out either site and join our mailing list for breaking news about ski and snowboard resorts in the USA, Canada and Europe.

You will notice that we have included the Web addresses for almost every resort listed in this book. Use them to get more information. Many are linked directly from skisnowboard.com or from skisnowboardeurope.com. Some of the resorts now include real-time camera shots of the slopes, so you can get an idea of snow coverage. Other sites allow skiers and snowboarders to make their reservations and make payment for their vacation right online.

Getting To Europe

The first step in planning a European ski vacation is to get across the Atlantic. Crossing the ocean and getting to the resort is the major cost to be borne: for example, while transportation to Aspen, Colorado, from New York City constitutes about 37 percent of a typical week's ski vacation budget, the travel segment of a similar ski trip to Austria represents about 50 percent of the total cost. But transatlantic air travel is also where a clever traveler can save the most money.

If you are a do-it-yourselfer, even the transfer from the airport to the resort can be used to save both time and money, if you plan ahead. Remember, though, that there are tradeoffs between cost and convenience: you want to go to Europe to ski and see as much as possible, not to spend endless hours in bus or train stations waiting for connections. It's worth doing a little homework to get the best deal, and a travel agent or tour operator can help out with the specifics.

After studying pricing at ski resorts and airlines, we feel that the best overall values are available through tour operators or when making arrangements through the Web. These "packages," whether organized by an operator or created dynamically on the Internet, are not group tours where everyone is herded onto a bus together, but rather tours which take advantage of group discounts and negotiated air and hotel rates. You will fly with friends you choose and will receive coupons or passes for transportation to the resorts. Some operators use buses, others trains, and some even provide rental cars, all for remarkably low prices.

Getting across the Atlantic

Transatlantic airfares have been at all-time lows for several years. There is plenty of capacity and service from almost every area of the country, which makes getting to Europe more convenient, easier and less expensive than ever. And, of course, winter air travel works to a skier's advantage, because prices are often 40 to 50 percent lower than in the peak summer months.

A travel agent and tour operator can be extremely helpful at this stage. But supplement the agent's information by doing some investigating on your own. Airline fare structures are complicated and seem to change daily—even with scheduled airlines. And when charters and group tour flights are included, the options can become phenomenally complex.

Tell your travel agent exactly what you are looking for and explain what you think you should have to pay, based on ads you have seen. The agent will either confirm your opinions or let you know what has changed since your last information. Try to find an agent who will guarantee the lowest possible fare.

These agents often will let you know exactly what is available and then you can make a decision, even if it's to take a more expensive flight based on convenience or better connections. A good travel agent can save both time and money.

Tour operators specializing in European ski and snowboard vacations make the process of making air and hotel reservations simple. Most of these organizations allow selection from dozens of hotels and chalets and work together with several airlines.

Online travel agencies, such as Expedia and Travelocity, also provide good sources of winter vacation arrangements. On the Web, travelers can create a "dynamic tour package" with very low prices. In some cases the prices created on the Web are just as low at those negotiated by tour operators, months before the winter season.

Scheduled airlines vs. charters

You have two basic choices for transatlantic air travel:

• Scheduled airlines — There are many advantages in taking a scheduled airline. For one, the airline must adhere to its general schedule. If there is a problem with the aircraft, passengers are normally transferred to a flight on another airline. In emergencies, a scheduled airline offers flexibility with additional flights and interline connections.

Another aspect of their flexibility is the option of landing in one city and leaving from another. Called "Open Jaw" in travel jargon, this type of ticket might let you land in Milan, ski the Italian side of the Matterhorn for a week, ski Austria for the second week, then fly home from Munich. You can also arrange limited stopovers for an additional charge, depending on your ticket, making it easy to squeeze in a few days in Amsterdam, Paris or London on your way to the slopes or on your way back.

It helps to plan your trip as far in advance as possible. You may have to book—and pay—in advance by as much as a month to get special fares that approach the lowest charter prices. Arrival and departure dates must be set in advance, and changes may bring additional charges.

Most tour packagers work with scheduled airlines who sell them blocks of seats at near-charter rates. This saving is passed on to you. By working with a reputable packager through your travel agent you get most of the benefits of the scheduled airline for charter prices.

• Charter flights — These flights are money-savers and in some cases offer excellent connections for skiers. There are some problems with charters. Often you are only guaranteed a flight date rather than a time. The charters also reserve the right to reschedule your flight, cancel it or add fuel charges. Your best protection is to fly with a charter airline that has been in business for some time, one with which your travel agent is familiar.

Try to get some form of flight cancellation insurance in case you don't leave on the planned date, and also get additional medical insurance to cover the cost of an emergency trip home in case of an accident.

Getting around Europe

Car rental

For the independent skier who wants to get the most out of a European ski vacation, a rental car offers the most flexibility and is a bargain—especially when two skiers share expenses. Rental cars can be picked up directly at the airport upon arrival. Aside from making it a breeze to get to the ski resort, a rental car gives you the freedom to explore the surrounding area or take a short side trip when ski conditions aren't perfect or you just want a break from skiing.

What license do you need?

The driver of the car usually must be at least 19 years old and must have a valid driver's license that has been in effect for at least one year. (The age requirement increases for some more luxurious automobiles.) It is not necessary to have an International Driving Permit when driving in Europe—your home state license is acceptable—but it is a good idea. The AAA issues them, and they are good for a year. Fill out an application and give them two passport-type portrait snapshots. By mail, start the process a month before your departure. If you live near an AAA office, you can accomplish the entire process there, including photos, in less than an hour. International Driving Permits cost $10. Call AAA for details and the location for the nearest office issuing International Driving Permits at (800) AAA-HELP. Remember, even with the International Driving Permit you will still need your U.S. state license as well. Canadians can call (800) 336-HELP for information on the nearest location to pick up an international license. You can get an application over the Web from www.aaa.com.

BEWARE: We checked out the Internet for International Driver's Licenses. Watch out! There are scores of sites claiming to issue international driver licenses, but none are as inexpensive as the AAA license deal. We found pricing for $34, $40 and $230.

NOTE: In Europe, especially in the Alpine countries, you need to have what is called a Green Card (carte verte) for insurance. This is provided by rental companies, but it is best to make a quick check of the documents when you pick up your car.

Getting the best rates

If you make reservations two to seven days in advance of your arrival with any of the major car rental companies, you qualify for special European vacation rates. These run about $200 to $250 a week, excluding taxes. (If you're comparing car rentals to possible train travel, this will mean that each person will pay about $400 for a full month's automobile use—plus gasoline, which even in an extreme case shouldn't run more than $200 apiece.) The only requirement for this rate is that you keep the car for at least five days. If you return it before that, you will be charged at the daily rate, which often can cost more than keeping the car the entire week.

While all car rental companies may offer reasonable rates throughout the year for tourism, only Auto Europe (800-223-5555) guarantees that they will find the lowest rate. Auto Europe also can organize camper van rentals, handicap vehicles and chauffeur services.

Another tip: If the need to rent a car comes up while traveling in Europe, it is normally less expensive to call back to the U.S.A. (or go on the Web) and make your reservations with the U.S.-based office. Auto Europe's rates require a minimum rental of three days, however, even the three-day rate from Auto Europe is often less expensive than renting a car through a European rental car office for a single day. Check the Auto Europe Web site at www.autoeurope.com for a list of toll-free numbers that will connect directly to the Auto Europe call stateside center.

Drop-off charges

Generally, there are no drop-off charges if a rental car is returned in the country where it was picked up. Some rental companies will allow rental cars to be dropped off in other countries for no drop-off charge if the rental is for at least 21 days. There are some companies that will allow one-way rentals, but only to a limited group of cities. Ask whether your case falls into one of these categories and if not, pick up and drop off in the same country.

Collision damage waiver/insurance

If you rent your car with a credit card which provides collision damage waiver (CDW) you have adequate protection. Diners Club, American Express, MasterCard Gold and Business and VISA Gold and Business all provide this coverage automatically **as long as you decline the CDW option on the rental contract.**

This credit card coverage covers the card holder and additional drivers as long as they are correctly signed up properly with the rental company and appear on the contract. Read the fine print. Some credit card companies do not cover your car if you were driving on a dirt road or in the case of hit and run accidents and so on. Check also to see whether this is primary or secondary coverage. Primary coverage is what you want. Secondary coverage only comes into play after your own insurance company pays for damages ... then the credit card company pays the difference. Most credit card collision damage is primary in Europe, while back in the U.S. it is normally secondary.

In the U.S. most collision insurance coverage applies to rental cars as well as to your own automobile, but in Europe most American coverage is not valid. You should have some form of collision damage insurance. According to Auto Europe the normal rental contract deductibles in Europe range from $2,000 to $5,000.

Even with your credit card coverage, your rental car company may demand a security deposit to cover the deductible until everything is settled. You must, in most cases, settle with your credit card company and then reimburse the rental company. Taking the European collision damage insurance allows you to walk away from any accident without mountains of follow-up paperwork.

If you are planning on renting a luxury or four-wheel-drive vehicle, check with the credit card to make sure that the car you are renting is insured under their CDW plan. Some makes and models of automobiles are excluded from coverage.

Rental car operators highly recommend the purchase of CDW for anywhere from €3 to €30 a day depending on the make of car. It makes your life easier in the event of an accident. If you can handle the hassles of doing some of your own accident paperwork during the settlement, credit card companies allow you to save money.

Theft insurance

Collision damage used to include other types of damage such as theft of the vehicle. These days, theft insurance has been separated from collision—you must purchase it separately.

According to Auto Europe many countries have made theft insurance mandatory. Where theft insurance is mandatory it is included in Auto Europe rental charges at a discounted rate.

When theft insurance is not required, we recommend purchasing it even if you are covered for collision through your credit card CDW.

Other charges

Most major airports now assess an airport pickup surcharge.

Additional driver charges of around €22 per rental or about €10 a day will be added to your bill if you need to have an extra driver listed on the contract.

Child seats cost approximately €35 per rental.

Heading into Eastern Europe

If you are planning to take a rental car into Eastern Europe make sure to inform the company. Many rental car companies will not allow cars to be brought into Eastern Europe because of high rates of theft. Auto Europe has the largest selection of vehicles available for travel into the former Soviet Bloc, however, rates are higher than regular rentals.

Ask for a ski rack and check your chains

When you make reservations, be sure to tell the agent that you will require a ski rack and chains. Chains are usually provided free when ordered in advance, however in Austria there will be an extra charge. Ski racks cost extra (for example €35 per rental in Austria) in some countries. When you pick up the car, the ski rack will be easy to see, but you'll have to check closer for the chains. Make sure the chains provided are the correct size for the car. You are the one who will be putting the blasted things on, so you should take a great interest in making sure they are the right size. Check the number on the box carefully against the size of the tires. There is nothing more disconcerting than finding out that the chains are one size too small when you are stuck only a few hundred meters from the top of a pass.

Special airline car-rental deals

Airlines often offer reduced price cars or "free" cars with many promotions to Europe. You may be able to take advantage of them.

- You normally must travel with another person for the deal.
- Your deal is only for one week, or three days in many cases, and then you begin paying the regular rates—either weekly or daily. These may be high enough to wipe out the original savings if you remain in Europe for a week or two.
- You will have to pay the insurance, taxes, gasoline, and any drop-off charges in most cases.
- Ski racks and snow tires are much harder to come by with these deals.

Autobahn tolls

The superhighway systems in Italy, Spain and France are simply put, expensive. However, the time they save is normally worth the money spent.

NOTE: In Switzerland cars must pay an annual autobahn toll to be permitted on the superhighways. If you rent a car outside of Switzerland and plan to drive on the superhighways, make sure your rental car has the appropriate up-to-date Swiss highway toll sticker before you drive on the Swiss superhighways. The police will not let transgressions go unfined. The hassles can easily ruin a vacation.

Germany has no tolls and no speed limits.

Austria charges about 75¢ per day for a toll sticker payable to the local rental car company. If your car does not have a highway sticker you may be fined if you are caught on the superhighways. You can purchase a temporary sticker good for the length of time you will be Austria at the border.

Taking the train

There are good train transfers from Munich to Garmisch and the Austrian resorts; from Zürich and Geneva to most of the Swiss resorts; and from Milan to some of the Italian resorts. The major problem with rail travel is the hassle of dragging equipment on and off the train, compounded by the usual need to change trains at least once on a trip to an out-of-the-way resort. The Swiss railways are the only ones with a workable luggage transportation system: baggage can be checked in at the train station at Geneva or Zürich airport and then delivered to your resort. The system works in reverse, with the luggage actually checked through to your final destination—New York, London or anywhere. Cost for the service is about SFr10 per piece of luggage.

Virtually every Swiss resort except Champéry, Cran-Montana and Flims are easily reached by train. If you plan to stay in your resort, you can be comfortable taking the train and finding your luggage at your hotel when you arrive.

Four people sharing a car always save money over a train and, in many cases, two people can save money, or they will find the price difference so small that car rental is the way to go. Renting a car provides much more freedom and allows side trips in case of bad weather on the mountain.

The Eurailpass and other national train passes are not much good for a ski vacation. It is better to purchase a second-class ticket to the resort; remember, since skiing is your object, you probably will not be on the train long enough to justify buying a long-term pass.

Accommodations and meals

Where you sleep, live and eat constitutes the most expensive part of your stay at a European ski resort. Lodging and meals vary widely, not only with the type of hotel or restaurant but also with the season.

Use this guide to select a hotel or apartment that is near the slopes and near the center of town. Or if you want a quiet spot on the outskirts of the village we'll help to point you in the right direction.

Choosing a hotel

If you take a package tour or make your arrangements on the Web, your decisions are made long before you arrive at the resort. Most of the popular hotels used by tour packagers and available on the Internet are included in this guide; the descriptions should help.

If you arrive in a resort without reservations, plan ample time to select a hotel. This means taking about a half hour to check out what the room situation is like.

The local tourist office will steer you in the right direction and will tell you which hotels have rooms available. Ask for three or four recommendations, then check out the rooms in person. In low season—January or April—don't be pressured into taking a room you don't want; in most cases, there are plenty available.

Many times rates at hotels and pensions vary significantly even within the same categories. After choosing where you want to stay, you'll need to decide whether to take full or half board, or only breakfast (see below). Make sure to ask if any reductions are available. You may get a special rate by staying a full week or by staying through Friday night and leaving on Saturday, the day most ski weeks turn over.

Make sure that you understand exactly what the room rate includes. Are the listed prices for the room or are they per person? Are the prices with breakfast only, half pension (see below) or full pension. If you insist on getting clear information at the start, it makes your trip much more pleasant.

Staying in British-style ski chalets

Ski Chalets have recently become one of the most popular ways for British skiers to stay and ski in style, without paying whopping hotel rates. What the rest of the skiers of the world haven't yet realized is that they can use them, too.

A chalet takes the convenience and informality of an apartment and the amenities and gourmet cuisine of a hotel and lumps them all into one fantastic package. Chalets are often converted private homes or small hotels, fully catered (breakfast, afternoon tea and snack and three-course dinner with wine), and run by professional hosts who cook, clean, and do the shopping. Many are ski-in/ski-out or near the slopes and even employ their own ski guides to get their guests acquainted with the mountain.

Chalets are best suited for young, sociable skiers looking for an easy way to form a group of friends to eat, ski, and party with (some chalets sleep up to 35 people!). Chalet-goers should be easy-going and not too squeamish about sharing bedrooms (there is a charge for unused beds or rooms), but in return you will stay in some of the nicest accommodations around with a group of people who may challenge even your apres-ski and nightlife stamina.

Staying in a chalet, you'll also be able to customize your own vacation. While the meals and service included in the basic price are first-rate, there are a number of extras for you to choose from if the basic package just isn't enough. When you book your vacation, be prepared to specify if you want vegetarian meals, premier service (with even more amenities and gourmet cuisine!), or even, packed lunches for the slopes, etc.

One thing to remember: chalets can be a great alternative for families (with discounts for children and nanny services at an extra charge); however, many of the chalets listed by various travel companies do not accept children under age 16 unless you book the entire chalet. If you are travelling with children, you will probably need to look for smaller chalets for your family or inquire about special family chalets that will cater to your needs.

Chalets are available at most major French resorts and at a few Austrian, Swiss, and Italian areas as well. There are a number of tour holiday operators to call or write to for information. Be aware that most prices they will quote include one-week's lodging, food, ski guides plus round-trip airfare from London (or snowtrain from Calais), so be sure to tell the sales agent if you are not travelling from the U.K. All companies below have discounts for large groups and for children. The major tour operators are as follows (individual resort chapters list which ones provide chalets in the area):

Crystal Holidays (Internet: http://www.crystalholidays.co.uk E-mail: travel@crystalholidays.co.ukor Phone: 0870 848 7000) claims to have the largest service, with chalets in almost all resorts in Europe.

Inghams (020 8780 4433; e-mail Travel@inghams.co.uk) has an impressively long list of chalets at major ski resorts in France, Austria, Switzerland, Italy and Andorra.

Thomas Cook/Neilson (08705 141414; e-mail sales@neilson.co.uk; Web site www.neilson.co.uk) has chalets in 11 of these resorts. Or contact your travel agent.

Simply Ski (020 8742 2541; e-mail ski@simply-travel.com), and **Chalet World** (01952 840 462) have chalets for rent at most French resorts and a very limited number in Switzerland and Austria. **First Choice** (0990 557755) also has chalets in France and Austria.

Thompson (0870 606 1470) has chalets in 15 of these resorts.

We mention Ski Chalet availability in each resort, however please refer back to these pages for phone, fax and internet connections.

Country by country

Hotels in different European countries are organized and run by different standards. These standards affect how the hotels are listed and what amenities you can expect within their various categories.

Accommodation in Italy, Spain and France is controlled by a government rating system which is too difficult to explain and often seems to make no sense. Hotels grouped within the same category with similar room rates often vary greatly. Some regulations produce confusion, such as a requirement in Italy that to be classified as first class, a hotel must have at least 40 rooms. Thus, some 36-room super-luxurious hotels with fabulous rooms and perfect service are listed as second class.

Hotels and other accommodations in the mountains are usually far cleaner and the service far superior to what you normally find in the rest of France and Italy.

Switzerland, Austria and Germany are no-nonsense countries. The hotels are clean and neat. The rating system is based on stars, with the highest rating being five stars, which means luxury class. The hotels tend to be accurately rated. In these countries it is actually hard to find a real dive.

One fact of life in the mountains during the winter season is the requirement to take at least two meals, or half pension (see below), in the hotel where you are staying. During high season this requirement is firm, and some hotels may even insist on full pension. The price is well worth it in most cases. In your hotel search, however, ask several locals which hotels or pensions have the best food. This research should also enter into your decision on where to spend your week in the resort.

Season by season

For the lowest prices, the best season to stay in any resort hotel—and to eat at any restaurant—is low season. This is normally from December 1 through the weekend before Christmas, then again from the weekend after New Year's through the first weekend in February, and again from the end of March through the month of April. The exact dates vary. Be sure to check to see when the low season starts and finishes.

The bargains in January are wonderful. Resorts are virtually guaranteed to have snow and facilities will not be crowded. In low season the resorts are not packed to capacity, so the kitchen and hotel staff have time to provide exceptional service. In addition, the on-site facilities, such as sauna, steamroom, pool or exercise room tend to be less crowded.

Early-season and late-season bargains are always a bit dicey in terms of finding good snow. Should anyone be making decisions on whether to visit the Alps before Christmas or after Easter, opt for a trip in the Spring. The experience is delightful and the certainty of snow is far highter than in December.

Pensions

Pensions are usually smaller, family-run affairs that cost significantly less than hotels. The pension guest in many cases feels a part of the family.

Some lodgings have a bath and toilet in the room, others have the bath and toilet down the hall or just next door. Most pensions recommended in this book have rooms available with private bath and toilet. If you do not mind a semi-private arrangement, you can request that type of room and save even more.

Many pensions, especially in the mountains, offer full restaurant service and will include all three meals in the price during the ski season. Many require that you take at least half board (see below) when staying for a week. It usually is well worth the price.

Bed & Breakfasts and Garni

Bed & Breakfast (B&B) and Garni mean the same thing. A B&B is what the name implies: room with breakfast only. Normally, you cannot take lunch or dinner there. This means heading out to discover local restaurants.

The Bed & Breakfast arrangement is often the least expensive in a mountain town, other than staying in private homes or apartments. Do not let yourself be fooled by the low price, though. Remember, you will have to pay for your meals in restaurants, which will add significantly to your costs. Although pensions and hotels may appear to cost more, when meal prices are taken into consideration, they may really be a bargain.

Garnis and Bed & Breakfasts do offer several advantages. First, you have a chance to try different restaurants and different styles of cooking during your stay. Second, you can often save money by eating less. Hotel menus include a full meal with all the trimmings and each is priced on the assumption that you eat everything on the daily menu. You may only want to eat a plate of spaghetti and be on your way. In other words, you pay only for what you eat.

"Full pension/full board" or "Half pension/half board" That is the question

Full pension, or full board, means that your hotel will provide breakfast, lunch and dinner each day of your stay.

The meals are served at set times in most hotels and pensions. If you miss the mealtime, the establishment is not required to provide an alternative meal (but some of the better hotels will offer you a meal in a smaller grill rather than in the main dining room).

When you agree to full pension, ask whether the hotel has either a box lunch to take with you or a coupon arrangement with a restaurant on the slopes. If the hotel does not have such an arrangement, you will be required to return to the hotel for every meal, which can really cut into skiing time. (Or, simply forgo the meal even though you are paying for it.) This could be an important consideration when deciding between hotels.

Half pension means that the hotel will offer breakfast, plus one additional meal, normally dinner, every day of your stay. Often referred to as half board, this is often the best arrangement. You are free to eat what you want and where you want during the day while on the slopes. If you plan to go out on the town to dine at a special restaurant, you can arrange to have lunch at the hotel that day and be free for dinner elsewhere.

In high season many hotels require you to take full pension. But in low season you can often get the room at half pension only, or with breakfast only.

The basic meal is all that is included in the full- or half-pension price. Any wine, water, extras, changes from the menu, coffee or liqueurs are billed as extra charges.

What is breakfast?

Depending on where they come from, it's called petit déjeuner, Frühstück, desayuno, or prima colazione. Here is a primer on what you can expect.

In Switzerland, Austria, Germany and Italy's Val Gardena region, breakfast means yogurt, cold cuts, cheese, jams and jellies, butter, rolls and endless coffee or tea. In some hotels, you get boiled eggs and juice—all included in the breakfast with the room.

In France, Spain and most of Italy, breakfast means a basket of rolls, sometimes a few sweet rolls, butter, jam and jelly with coffee or tea. Juice and eggs are almost always extras.

Staying in condos, flats or chalets

An economical alternative to staying in a hotel, pension or B&B is to take a condominium, flat (apartment) or chalet. They are often scattered through the town and offer reasonably priced accommodations.

Apartments (condos) are most popular in Switzerland and France, and the Italians are now beginning to get their condominium rental arrangements organized.

They come in all sizes. You can rent a studio, which is perfect for a couple, or an apartment for four, five, six or eight people. The price per person drops considerably as the size increases. These are fantastic bargains: the daily cost can be as low as €20 to €30 per person if two share an apartment.

Units are normally rented with a fully equipped kitchen, all utensils and a dishwasher. Bed linen and a clean-up are sometimes included; in other cases there are charges for them. Check also for a utility fee: it may be included, or you may pay for the electricity used at the end of the stay.

You can cook your own breakfast and as many meals as you want, which will save a lot of money. There is usually a supermarket nearby—often on the ground floor of the building. Grocery prices are about the same as, or slightly higher than, those in a large European city.

If you decide that you would like to stay in a flat or chalet, contact the resort tourist office and ask for a listing of the units that will be free when you're going to visit. The tourist office will send you a list; make your choice and return the information to the tourist office. You will usually have your confirming correspondence with the owners.

If you arrive with no arrangements, the tourist office will make several calls and send you off to see several apartments and speak with the owners.

The leading apartment and chalet rental firm in the world is Interhome—in some resorts it virtually controls the apartment rentals. Interhome has offices in Britain and in the U.S. In the U.K., contact Interhome Ltd., 383 Richmond Road, Twickenham TW1-2EF, United Kingdom; tel. 01-8911294. In the U.S., contact Interhome at 124 Little Falls Road, Fairfield, NJ 07004; tel. (800) 882-6864, fax (201) 808-1742.

Staying in a private home

Private homes at many resorts will rent out rooms. These rooms are normally very inexpensive, with prices ranging between those of a B&B and an apartment. If you are traveling alone, a private home is often the best bargain you can get.

Staying in a private home can give you a better feel for the local scene: you pick up hints on the best places to go on the slopes and in town, and in many cases you will find yourself treated like a friend of the family.

Start at the local tourist office. It has addresses and phone numbers of the families who rent out rooms. The tourist office often will call and make arrangements. Ask to see several rooms and then make your choice. These rooms normally do not have private bath and shower. You share with the family in many cases.

In some cases, the room price includes breakfast but the arrangements vary from house to house. Expect to pay €20 to €30 a night, depending on the resort and season.

Make sure that baths or showers are included in the price; if not, ask for the price and the best time of day to take a bath or shower. (Hot water can be at a premium just after the slopes close for the day.)

European skiing basics

What should a skier expect when arriving at a European resort? Culture shock aside, there shouldn't be too many surprises, because the U.S. ski industry has been modeled to a great extent on the long-established European resorts.

In most cases you will be able to ski into the town or village where you are staying. Of course, this doesn't apply if you are staying in a city such as Innsbruck, Salzburg or Interlaken.

The weather

A friend had just arrived in Switzerland from New England the week before Christmas and we were getting ready to go skiing. Her preparations amazed me. She began by putting on lots of bulky clothing: sweaters, a jacket and other Arctic-expedition paraphernalia.

"Whoa," I said. "What are you doing? You want to be able to move on the mountain, don't you?"

"I don't want to be cold," she replied.

"Well, you'll melt if you dress like that," I said.

After this argument she reluctantly agreed to take off half of the clothing and risked taking my advice to wear only a turtleneck, a sweater and a windbreaker.

The point is this: Skiing in Europe is not a freezing proposition. The weather is very mild in the mountain areas. Even in the coldest sections of the Alps, the winter daytime temperatures hover at around 20 degrees Fahrenheit. Windy days, few and far between, usually herald a coming snowstorm.

What to wear

Try to dress in layers, and because temperatures are relatively mild, you will rarely need more than a ski jacket over a turtleneck shirt. On most days, a turtleneck worn under a light sweater and a windbreaker will be more than enough. Don't underestimate the temperatures, though; they drop rapidly when you're sitting in the wind on a long chair lift ride. Europe's use of T-bar and platter lifts will help keep you warmer, although American skiers may swear at staying on their feet.

Protection from the sun

Europe's resorts are no different from any others when it comes to sun, especially in spring. Sunburn or snow blindness can ruin any vacation, so use sun screen and lip protection, and always wear glasses or goggles. The glasses do not have to be tinted; the glass itself stops most harmful ultraviolet rays. Goggles are even better, especially on overcast days when they help you find trail contours.

General snow conditions

Snow in Europe is not as dry as Utah or Colorado snow, owing to lower elevations and milder climate. Nor is it ice half the time as in New England, because of more constant temperatures.

Most of the trails are well above treeline and are only defined by grooming machine tracks and signs posted to help out in white-out conditions.

The best snowfall seems to take place in January, making both January and February good months for skiing. Plan to go in January, since February and March are also the most expensive times to ski or snowboard, except for the Christmas, New Year's and Easter holiday periods. The week before Christmas is normally a pretty good time to go, but chancy in terms of snow.

Spring skiing sees the Alps at their finest, with prices at most resorts again at low-season levels. If you want an adventure, head off-piste with an instructor for spring skiing. In his company you will learn the best times to ski different areas as the day progresses and the sun warms the snow. The secret is to get onto the run just before you begin breaking through the crust and then move to the next part of the mountain.

Insurance

Before you go, take a close look at your health insurance to be certain you are covered in case of an accident. Most policies provide worldwide coverage, some are limited in the case of skiing accidents, and others group skiing accidents under the broad category of "accidental injury," which may mean that your deductible will be waived. Know what coverage you have. If you do not have enough, arrange to buy special ski insurance. Your agent should be able to point you in the right direction.

Several companies offer this insurance and surprisingly (amazing what you can find in the fine print) some credit cards include similar insurance if you purchase your airline ticket or pay for your vacation with the card. In addition, you can purchase ski insurance once you arrive at the resort. *Carte Neige* in France is easy to purchase at most resorts. Local tourist offices have details—and it is often sold with lift tickets—buy it.

Photocopy important papers

Make a photocopy of your passport pages showing your photo and personal information, and write down your passport number. Also, make photocopies of your airline tickets and the credit cards you'll be taking.

Make two copies: Keep one with you, separate from your passport, tickets and credit cards, and leave the second copy with a friend or relative.

If you somehow lose everything, these backup records will be invaluable. The passport copy will help in getting a replacement at an overseas consulate or embassy. The ticket copy may help in getting a replacement and alerts the airline to look for a stolen ticket with that number. The credit card numbers will make reporting stolen cards and limiting your liability much easier.

Telephones in the Alps

The telephone system in Europe works well, especially in this section of the continent. At the end of each resort section we have included the local prefix for the resort, the equivalent of an area code in the U.S. If you see a number in parentheses preceding another phone number it is normally a town prefix.

The prefixes are normally noted as a zero followed by one to five digits, then after a closed parentheses or dash, the local number follows. When calling inside the same country, you must dial the entire prefix including the zero; however, when calling the resort from outside that country, normally, you would dial the country code, then the prefix without the zero, then the local number.

In Italy you still must always dial the complete phone number—it will start with a zero. When you call into Italy dial the country code 0039 followed by 0.... The old prefixes have been incorporated into the phone numbers.

In France you will notice that there is no city prefix. It is included in the eight digits which make up the number. Only Paris has an additional prefix. Most of our phone numbers are listed as xxx xx xx xx. When you call from outside of France dial the country code, 0033, then dial the number as we show it in the book. When calling within France you must always dial zero first.

In Switzerland the prefixes are part of the local number. Dial the full number noted when calling from within Switzerland. When outside of Switzerland add the country code.

If calling a resort from within Europe, just dial the country code as shown below, including the double zeros. If you are calling the resort from the U.S. you must dial 011, then the country code without the double zeros, then the prefix without the zero, then the local number (except in Italy where the zero must also be dialed).

Country codes are as follows:

Austria:	0043
France:	0033
Germany:	0049
Italy:	0039
Spain:	0034
Switzerland:	0041
Andorra	00376

If you see phone numbers of varying lengths even within the same resort, it is not necessarily a misprint. In the Alps the phone numbers are not all the same number of digits—in fact, the main number of a hotel often has a different number of digits than its fax number.

Calling from Europe to the U.S.

It is simple to direct-dial from any of these European countries to the U.S.A. The prefix for the U.S. is 001 in most countries. Then dial the area code and your local number.

Purchase a telephone card overseas. They are easy to use and charges for calls to the USA are often less than using a stateside telephone card.

Internet connections

There are scores of Internet cafés in Europe. They can be found at virtually every resort mentioned in this guidebook. Prices are amazingly inexpensive. If you are an email junky, you can rest assured that you will not have to bring your laptop along to access your messages.

Credit cards and travelers checks

Most large resorts and full-fledged hotels accept major credit cards, but don't expect the smaller pensions and hotels to accept them. The normally accepted cards are American Express, Diners Club, Visa and MasterCard (called "Eurocard" in Europe). You can leave store credit cards and Discover cards at home.

Some resorts allow skiers to pay for lift tickets with credit cards but they are few and far between. It is best to come prepared with adequate cash or travelers checks to cover your expenses. American Express offers the best-known travelers checks, but in the Alps almost all are easily exchanged.

In Germany, Switzerland and Austria credit cards are accepted by restaurants and hotels but not with the frequency they are taken in the U.S. In France, Italy and Spain, however, credit cards are accepted for virtually all transactions from car rentals to highway tolls to some taxi cabs.

Credit cards often have advantages you wouldn't think about. They offer toll-free numbers for assistance in finding doctors and lawyers should you need them. Most credit cards also have a buyers protection plan that may insure gifts you buy from theft and damage during your travels. And some cards will help with arrangements back home should you have an unfortunate accident. Read your fine print.

Changing money

The basic rule of changing money at a bank applies at ski resorts—even more so than in most places. Hotels and restaurants that accept travelers checks almost never give you a rate of exchange equal to the one you can get from a bank. Plan ahead and save yourself the difference. To change a small amount of money, it is often better to exchange it at your hotel, because there is no minimum exchange fee.

The most advantageous exchange rates are available when receiving a cash advance using a credit card, however, make sure the credit card does not charge an "overseas charge fee" or have an exhorbitant "cash advance fee." These fees can add up to seven percent. Normally, credit cards issued by credit unions and a handful of smaller banks do not assess cash-advance fees or overseas charge fees.

If your credit card charges a two percent overseas charge fee and a cash-advance fee, it is best to take travelers checks or cash and exchange them at a bank overseas.

That said, you can get cash advances in local currency with a MasterCard or Visa at most banks in the Alps. In France and Spain cash machines are the most convenient means of getting Euros and often provide the best exchange rates (if you ues a low-fee credit card). But plan ahead—there is a limit on daily withdrawals. Don't wait until the last day when you have to settle your bills to head to the cash machine.

The cash advance service is available from many banks and automatic bank machines as well. Use your low-fee credit cards for a cash advance or your bank card. Though you pay a service charge (which you pay to change money anyway), you will be getting the best interbank exchange rate with the credit card.

Again, beware the added charges many credit cards add for overseas charges and pay attention to your card's cash advance fee. If your card charges a two percent overseas fee, it will be no better bargain than using travelers checks or exchanging cash.

Dealing with the Euro

Almost all of Europe has switched to the Euro as a standard currency. The major holdout is the United Kingdom and for purposes of this book, Switzerland. All prices are listed here in Euros, even though the Swiss Franc is still legal tender in Switzerland. In most cases prices will be listed at resorts in Euros and Swiss Francs.

Taking your own equipment

Most airlines will allow you to check your ski equipment onto your flight for no additional charge. However, check with the airline for their policies. Most airlines consider skis, snowboards and ski/snowboard boots one piece of luggage and they become part of your three free pieces of luggage. Some airlines, such as Iberia, simply don't take skis.

Upon your arrival in Europe, have a word with the personnel in the baggage-claim area to find out where to pick up your equipment. Skis are often delivered to a separate part of the baggage area.

Renting equipment

Equipment rentals are available at your resort. Ski rentals—depending on the quality ski you want—range from about €6–€20, with discounts for periods of three days or more and weekly rentals running €33–€75. Bring your own boots, however, because these are extremely important to your comfort. We have yet to find rental boots that are comfortable. If you rent boots, expect to pay €5–€10 a day, or €18–€40 a week, depending on the quality of the boot.

Dealing with European lift lines...or lack of them

One major difference between skiing in Europe and the United States can be seen in lift-line etiquette. In the U.S., lift lines are relatively orderly: a line for singles is maintained along the far right or left, and nearly everyone takes pains to avoid stepping on or skiing over another skier's equipment. The result is that you almost never get jammed together as you move through the lift line.

Not so in Europe. Although the lift lines in various countries on the Continent differ as to the degree of pushy behavior, in general they are a free-for-all. Until you reach the point where barriers have been set up to funnel skiers into the lift, there are no controls. He who moves the fastest and shuffles forward the most aggressively is usually the first to get up the lift. While there is a mild effort not to blatantly trample over each other's skis, you may presume that your equipment will be stepped on no matter what you do or how angry you appear to be.

Here are some tips to handling lift lines:

- Before you enter the line, see whether it turns to the right; if so, go to the far outside left of the line. If the line turns to the left, go to the extreme right. If you have ever tried to turn a sharp corner with skis on, you will understand the wisdom of this. There is no mercy shown in the lift line. Once stuck on the inside of a sharp turn within the barriers, you are in trouble—there is no room to swing your skis. I've seen skiers snap out of their bindings to make the corner.
- If the line is almost straight, get on its outside edge. You will quickly see that the mass of skiers funnel down the narrow barriers on either side. Those who get caught in the middle get squeezed from both sides and move about half as fast as those on the outside of the crowd.
- Another solution is to follow a snowboarder, whose board cuts a wider swath.
- Maintain a sense of humor. It will be tested, especially on weekends and school holidays.
- The best time to ski and avoid crowds is during lunch time. You'll find clear slopes, shorter lift lines and fewer frustrations. In Italy, Spain and France, the lines all but disappear as everyone heads in for a big lunch. The noon-hour difference is not as great in Switzerland and Austria.

Cross-country

All European resorts are not equal as far as cross-country skiing is concerned. Although this book focuses on downhill resorts, nearly all have excellent, well-developed cross-country facilities, easily accessible.

There are several areas in Europe which are considered the *crème de la crème* of cross-country regions, as follows:

Seefeld, Austria: Our top choice in all Europe is Seefeld, which hosted the 1964 and 1976 Olympic cross-country competitions. Nearly 100 miles of cross-country trails are maintained and most of the circuits lead from the Olympic Sport and Convention Center. Accommodations are outstanding and reasonably priced. In addition, an international atmosphere makes foreign visitors feel welcome. A challenging 30 km. circuit, with 20 and 10-km. loops make up the heart of the trails.

For more information contact: Tourismusverband, A-6100 Seefeld, Austria; tel. 05212-2313.

St. Moritz, Switzerland: One of Europe's greatest. A paradise for the true cross-country fan. No one talks long about cross-country skiing without bringing up St. Moritz. This elegant resort has a remarkable network of 120-km. of trails in the immediate area, and there are more than 300 km. of cross-country circuits on the valley floor and frozen lakes in the region. St. Moritz also has a mile-long lighted trail for night-skiing fans. The course of the famed Engadiner Ski Marathon race is nearby. St. Moritz is a great place to vacation for the skier who seeks cross-country only and demands great variety.

The Jura, France: Europe's greatest cross-country ski adventure is a 200-km. trek across the highlands of the French Jura region, which stretches from Belfort along the Swiss border toward Geneva. Nearly 40 percent of this mountain region is wooded, and the connecting trail, called the GTJ (Grand Traverse du Jura) is a superb run. The trail sections are difficult, ranging from 3 to 29 km. each, as you make your way from Maise, near Belfort, nearly 200 km. to La Pesse, south of St. Claude. There are inns all along the trail.

For details on the Jura trek, write GTJ: Office du Tourisme Regional, Place de l'Armée Française, F-25000 Besancon, France.

For general information on cross-country all-inclusive trips in the Jura, write Accueil Montagnard-Chapelle-de-Bois, F-25240 Mouthe, France; or A.G.A.D.-La Pesse, F-39370 Les Bouchoux, France.

Kaiserwinkl, Austria: This is a cross-country skier's paradise in the Austrian Tyrol a few miles off the autobahn between Munich and Innsbruck. The towns of Schwedt, Kössen and Walchsee have combined their trails for nearly 140 km. of Nordic runs. Each town has its own cross-country center and the interconnected circuits branch out from the centers. For information: Fremdenverkehrsverband, Postfach 127, A-6345 Kössen, Austria; tel. 05375-6287.

The Black Forest: Germany's best-known cross-country area. The best circuits are around Titisee and up to the slopes of the Feldberg, the highest mountain in the region. Altogether there are about 1,000 km. of trails in the Black Forest with nearly 120 km. of loops near Feldberg. Perhaps the most challenging runs are from Neustadt, where organized cross-country groups kick and glide for nearly 100 km., with planned stops at hotels and guest houses along the way. We do not cover this region in detail — call the German tourist office for information.

Allgäu, Germany: An interesting network of cross-country trails is found in this region. The trails branch off from the ski towns of Oberstaufen and Immenstadt. Part of the network includes a great marathon-length, 40-km. loop. Contact the German tourist office for further information.

Kronplatz, Italy: Few resorts mix the pleasures of cross-country and downhill better than those in Italy's Pustertal. Here in the south Tyrolean region, Kronplatz resorts boast nearly 150 km. of cross-country trails branching out from the central town of Bruneck (Brunico, in Italian) below the Kronplatz plateau.

If you come in January, you can take part in the 50-km. cross-country race, which begins in Innichen (San Candido, in Italian) and ends in Antholz. The race course ends at Olang. Downhill skiers can try out the slopes from the 7,462-foot Kronplatz summit.

For more information contact: Crontour, I-39031, Bruneck, Italy; tel. 0474-84544.

The following descriptions will let you compare cross-country possiblities. For more details about individual resorts—hotel, restaurant, nightlife and other information—see the resort chapters. We provide a ✔ rating from one ✔ to five ✔s.

Austria

✔✔ **The Arlberg**: If you are only looking for occasional cross-country skiing, this will provide limited alternatives to the downhill religion in this region. The St. Anton/St. Christoph side of the mountain offers the best cross-country with 40 km. of trails. Lech and Zürs are extremely limited with only 17 km. of trails.

✔✔✔✔ **Badgastein**: There's more than enough variety in the Gasteiner Valley for cross-country enthusiasts: The resorts have a total of 90 km. of trails. The six trails from Bad Hofgastein offer the most variety. There's an added incentive for cross-country here because anyone who completes 75 km. earns a bronze medal. The gold is awarded for 1,000 km., but clearly is beyond the reach of the one week-vacationer.

✔✔✔✔✔ **Innsbruck**: Perhaps the second or third greatest cross-country area in all Europe, with over 60 miles of trails in the immediate area of the city. Instruction is excellent. And as an added bonus, the marvelous resort of Seefeld is only a short bus ride away. Plus there is excellent cross-country skiing on 130 km. of trails in the Stubaital which is part of the overall regional ski pass.

✔✔+ **Ischgl and Pasnaun Valley**: An average network with 50 km. of trails in Ischgl and another 40 km. in Galtür.

✔✔✔✔+ **Kitzbühel/Kirchberg**: Some of the best cross-country trails in Austria. Great variety and some 200 km. of trails.

✔✔✔ **Mayrhofen/Zillertal**: Mayrhofen has 20 km. of tracked trails which connect with the connecting valleys. Zillertal has a good variety with over 60 km. of track.

✔✔✔**Montafon**: When all 11 main resorts in the Montafon valley are considered, this is an excellent cross-country area. But you'll need a car to drive to the various areas—no single resort has enough variety for a vacation. Over a dozen trails total about 45 miles.

✔✔✔ **Saalbach-Hinterglemm**: Extensive cross-country in the Leogang sector with 40 km. of prepared trails. Saalbach itself has only 8 km. and Hinterglemm claims 10km. of cross-country trails.

✔✔✔✔+ **Schladming**: Excellent cross-country trails especially on the Ramsau side of the valley, where a wide-open plateau just below the Dachstein glacier offers perfect terrain. Plan to stay in Ramsau, because the other towns are a long trek away from the best cross-country areas.

✔✔✔ **Söll**: Average Austrian cross-country with some great connecting trails between Söll, Hapfgarten, Elmau and the Brixen Valley.

✔✔✔✔ **St. Johann in Tirol**: Excellent choice for cross-country vacation. Not as much variety as Innsbruck-Seefeld, but the nearly 100 km. of trails are maintained for the serious skier. Changing rooms, first aid and restaurant facilities are excellent on the loops. Also a great choice for the skier who wants to mix downhill with cross-country.

✔ **Oetztal**: Meager offerings. Less than 20 km. of trails.

✔✔✔✔✔ **Kaprun/Zell am See**: One of the best-kept secrets among cross-country devotees. A great network of hundreds of km. of trails and a connection to an additional 65 km. of trails in the neighboring valley. The ski school also has good courses.

France

✔✔ **Les Arcs**: Moderately interesting trails with only 20 km. up at the resort. More trails are in the valley with 40 km. at Peisey/Vallandry and 25 km. at Bourg-St-Maurice.

✔✔ **Chamonix**: Moderately interesting trails total about 43 km. in the valley. Best combined with downhill; not good cross-country on its own.

✔✔ **Les Clusaz**: Good cross-country possibilities with 42 km. of trails on Plateau des Confins ringing a frozen lake and another 19 km. on Plateau de Beauregard where kick-and-gliders share trails with downhillers. Trail fees are €5.50 a day for adults and €2.50 a day for children.

✔✔✔✔ **Megève**: Surprisingly good network of four main trails totaling nearly 100 km. in the Megève-Combloux area. The resort has excellent cross-country events such as night skiing. There is good variety and some good challenges on endurance. A long trail goes from the Mont d'Abois cable car to St.-Nicolas-de-Véroce.

✔✔✔✔ **Flaine and Le Grand Massif**: Flaine itself has not much to recommend it to cross country skiers, however the region is excellent. Virtually all trails are down in the valley between Samoëns and Sixt or at Les Carroz. Samoëons has a 50 km. loop, Les Carroz has 64 km. of trails with some limited night skiing.

✔✔✔ **La Plagne**: Champagny-le-Haut on the far side of the ski resort near the village of Champagny-en-Vanoise has excellent cross-country opportunities with 79 km. of marked and groomed trails. Stay there rather than in one of the La Plagne purpose-built resorts. There are also 12 km. of trails between the main villages and an additional 32 km. of trails near Montchavin and Montalbert.

✔✔✔✔**Morzine**: This resort has almost 100 km. of trails spread around five different areas. You can find other cross-country in the Portes du Soleil region at Morgins with 20 km., and Chapelle d'Abondance with 22 km.

✔ **Tignes/Val d'Isère**: Poor choice for real cross-country skiers. Only short trails with a total of 15 km. of prepared track.

✔✔✔ **Les Trois Vallées**: Above-average network of trails by French resort standards. Nearly 100 km. of prepared loops spread over the rolling valley countryside. Méribel has almost 35 km. around the altiport sector, Les Menuires has about 30 km. between the village and St. Martin de Belleville. Courchevel has night skiing. Val Thorens sticks pretty much to downhill pursuits.

Germany

✔✔✔✔ **Garmisch-Partenkirchen**: You'll discover long, exceptionally scenic trails with nearly 200 km. of loops in the Garmisch-Partenkirchen area when linked with the Isartal and Loisachtal. Above Garmisch, in the Graswang Valley, there is beautiful cross-country skiing that takes you near Linderhof, perhaps the most beautiful of Ludwig's Bavarian castles.

Italy

Italy has developed an extensive cross-country system in the shadow of Mont-Blanc as well as in the Madonna di Campiglio area and in parts of the Dolomites.

✔ **Cervinia**: Only has a total of 15 km. of trails. If you want to kick and glide go somewhere else.

✔✔✔ **Courmayeur**: Good and scenic cross-country skiing beneath the towering Monte Bianco in the Val Ferret only minutes from the town. There are four major itineraries with 35 km. of prepared trails. The nearby resort of La Thuile has a 10 km. loop in its valley.

✔✔✔ **Pinzolo**: Only a few kilometers, or a 20-minute drive, from Madonna di Campiglio, Pinzolo was the site of one of cross-country's major 24-hour endurance races. The area near Campo Carlo Magno, in the **Madonna di Campiglio** area, has an expert cross-country course with a 30 km. trail.

✔✔✔ **Cortina d'Ampezzo**: Good cross-country area with more than 75 km. of prepared trails. A good place to mix downhill with cross-country. This resort was once the site of the Olympics. Cross-country itineraries take skiers into Austria and from village to village in the Dolomites.

✔✔✔✔✔ **Val Gardena:** Kick and glide along high mountain plateaus such as the Alpi di Siusi. The trails, though scenic, are short. There are over 1,000 km. of trails in the Dolomiti Superski region with 100 in this valley.

Switzerland

✔✔ **Arosa**: The cross-country trails are modest (about 30 km. of prepared trails) but well maintained, and from the beginning of December into April you can count on a variety of trails through the countryside.

✔✔✔ **Champéry and Portes du Soleil**: There are 150 km. of trails in the Swiss Portes du Soleil area. The best will be above Champéry linking Champoussin, Les Crosets and Morgins. Night skiing is in the Grand Paradis area of Champéry.

✔✔✔ **Crans-Montana**: There are three main trails with a total of about 45 km. Your best cross-country adventures will probably be on the nearly seven-mile loop on Plaine-Morte glacier. A long trail traverses the resort from Aminona to Plan Mayens.

✔✔✔✔ **Davos**: Excellent cross-country trails in classic Alpine scenery. Altogether there are nearly 75 km. of prepared trails with seven main loops kept in top condition. Good choice for cross-country. There is also a 7.5 km. loop that is lighted for night skiing. The Davos trails link with Klosters.

✔ **Engelberg**: Low-rated for the cross-country with less than 25 km. of prepared trails. Auto-free Melchsee-Frutt has nine miles of trails.

✔✔✔✔ **Flims/Laax**: Good cross-country area with a total of nearly 70 km. of double-tracked trails in Flims, Laax and Falera areas. Cross-country adventure treks with guides are offered in this region.

✔✔✔✔✔ **Gstaad and Weisses Hochland**: When considered with Saanen and other areas of the Weisse Hochland, cross-country is one of the best in Switzerland with nearly 100 km. of trails, guided adventure treks and very good instruction.

✔ **Jungfrau Region**: Grindelwald, with about 30 km. of trails, is the best in the area. They have good instruction. Wengen and Mürren are both very limited. The most beautiful trail is a 10 km. circuit in the Lauterbach valley near Lauterbrunnen. There is also nearby cross-country in Bonigen near Interlaken.

✔✔✔ **Klosters**: Moderately interesting, with nearly 60 km. of tracks split between four prepared trails. Combined with the next-door town of Davos, the area is quite extensive and beautiful.

✔✔✔✔✔ **St. Moritz**: See above (Pg. 29).

✔ **Saas-Fee**: Extremely limited with only an 8 km. trail.

✔✔✔ **Verbier**: The connecting network is not exceptional. The best cross-country facilities are at the base of the Châble cable car with about 30 km. of trails. There are short 4 km. loops at the village level and up on the glacier.

✔ **Zermatt**: Cross-country is only a side pursuit, with limited trails totaling only about 25 km. There is a lighted 3 km. course.

Cross-border skiing

Skiers experience an undefinable altered state when skiing from one country to another. When crossing borders at high altitudes, there's no one checking passports (but bring it along just in case) and few customs checkpoints. You just sense that you've changed worlds. *Grüetzi* changes to *buon giorno*, lunch shifts from schnitzel to pasta, and the personalities of the border opposites are never the same.

Cross-border skiing is a unique European skiing experience. Though tales of cross-border ski adventures abound, interconnected areas along the borders are quite limited. After exploring the Alps for the past two decades I have discovered only five sections with lift-connected cross-border skiing.

By far the most extensive lift-connected area is the Portes du Soleil, straddling Switzerland and France just to the south of Lake Geneva. The Zermatt, Switzerland-Cervinia, Italy, connection beneath the towering Matterhorn is perhaps the best-known. Ischgl in Austria, connected with Samnaun in Switzerland, is unknown to Americans but packed with Austrians, Germans and Scandinavians. The small resorts of La Thuile in Italy and La Rosière in France were connected just a few years ago. If you dream of skiing over borders, pack your passport. These are the places to do it.

Portes du Soleil

This area sprawls across the French-Swiss border from Lake Geneva southward almost to Italy. Portes du Soleil is Europe's largest international ski area.

The two main Portes du Soleil ski centers are Morzine/Avoriaz in France and Champéry in Switzerland. There are also 11 smaller resorts, four on the Swiss side and seven in France, tucked into the mountain valleys in the area. Champéry is a tiny centuries-old Swiss village where, in the past three years, hotels has been renovated and upgraded and a sports complex and a new cable car has been completed.

On the French side Avoriaz is as much of an opposite as one could imagine. A skier arriving from Switzerland is dazzled by the glitz. Where Champéry is traditional, Avoriaz is a modern purpose-built resort. In Champéry you look hard for a building with more than four stories, but in Avoriaz condos tower twice as high. Nightlife on the Swiss side consists of updated oom-pah bands in smoky bars, while the French resort rocks with neon discos and simmers in dimly-lit bistros.

Wide-open, expert skiing, though, is the common denominator. All the resorts in the Portes du Soleil share the marvelous terrain. Beginners can stick close to the resorts and intermediates won't have a problem if they stay on the trails, while experts will be stretched by both the extensive off-piste skiing and the exhausting expanse.

Zermatt, Switzerland - Cervinia, Italy

This is the cross-border experience most American and British skiers have heard about. The resorts, though connected, are as different as fondue and pizza. Zermatt is the picture-perfect Alpine village overflowing with chalets, Cervinia a collection of square concrete hotels. Zermatt offers challenging skiing, which humbles most experts; Cervinia, on the other hand, makes beginners feel like pros. Zermatt works with Swiss perfection, Cervinia thrives on Italian smiles and good nature.

The cross-border trip will take a full day, including a stop for lunch. The last lifts up to the top and back to Zermatt leave at about 3:15 p.m. Lift personnel will warn you if there is impending bad weather. Heed their advice. The lifts up to the border crossing have been known to close, owing to high winds or whiteout conditions, and strand scores of skiers on the wrong side of the border. The only recourse is an expensive overnight or a four-hour bus trip over the St. Bernard pass.

Ischgl, Austria - Samnaun, Switzerland

This is a strange marriage. Both partners are small villages deep in narrow mountain valleys. Ischgl is a pulsing world-class resort, Samnaun a tiny hideaway. Ischgl harbors hundreds of hotel rooms and thousands of apartments, Samnaun's hotels can be counted on one hand. Ischgl vibrates with après-ski; Samnaun sleeps.

Ischgl is a perfect ski resort. The town is packed with accommodations ranging from excellent to budget, but with no super-luxury establishments. The skiing is high above the town and reachable by three separate gondola lifts. The wide-open skiing at the higher altitudes is shared by Switzerland and Austria. There is plenty of solid skiing to keep any enthusiast smiling from the opening of the lifts to closing time. And after the lifts shut down, Ischgl's après-ski is among the best in Europe.

The run from Austria down to Samnaun is a long intermediate trail. Samnaun is a duty-free shopping area with inexpensive whisky, perfume and cigarettes. Skiers regularly cruise back to Ischgl with backpacks bulging with contraband.

Courmayeur, Italy - Chamonix, France

This is a one-way, short-term springtime relationship. When the snows settle on the mountains surrounding Mont Blanc, the Vallée Blanche opens high above Chamonix. This is one of skiing's grand experiences and can be initiated from either Chamonix, France, or Courmayeur, Italy. A series of cable cars takes groups of border-crossing skiers up from Italy. At the top they are met by guides who lead them over the glacier and down to Chamonix. The expedition by cable car cannot be made in the opposite direction, from France to Italy. At the end of the day buses are organized to take skiers from Chamonix through the Mont Blanc tunnel back to Courmayeur.

La Thuile, Italy - La Rosière, France

These reosrts were linked about 12 years ago. La Thuile has been gaining popularity. The main lifts leave directly from a new complex of hotels. The surrounding town has remained relatively unchanged. La Rosière is still a cluster of small hotels on the French side of the little Saint Bernard pass. Both resorts are frequented respectively by Italian and French skiers with little other international influence and very quiet nightlife.

Austria

If one were to ask Americans, Canadians or Brits what they think of when they hear "Austria", chances are, they will say "skiing". Austria has marketed the concept of cozy Alpine villages and trails winding through forested mountains so well that many people imagine perpetual snow whenever they hear the name. Reality is as enchanting as the marketing images. For skiers, Austria is a wonderful mix of old-world chalet-studded villages, lift-linked ski areas, lively mountain huts, rustic wood-paneled restaurants and exceptional nightlife and après-ski.

For Americans making their first trip to Europe and finding their way into an Austrian village, there is a sense of *deja-vu*. When Americans and Canadians want to create the perfect ski resort, they send experts to study Austria. And when they build, they mimic Austria. Look at the town of Vail in Colorado, the Austrian-style condos throughout New England and the massive wooden chalet hotels constructed in Sun Valley. Though others may try to copy the Austrian style, the essence of Austria cannot be canned or crated and taken to a new mountain. It needs to steep in deep valleys and evolve over centuries in hidden villages.

As important as atmosphere, mountains, chalets and skiing may be, Austria has another secret ingredient. This is a country where sincere hospitality is deemed as important as great skiing. Austrians seem to go out of their way to make visitors feel at home. From the ski instructors to the hotel managers to the restaurant owners, they seem to take genuine pleasure in knowing that you have enjoyed yourself in their country. Their word for this feeling of warmth and congeniality, *Gemütlichkeit*, sums up what they strive for as hosts.

Theories abound as to why certain Austrian resorts are touted by veteran skiers as the most friendly and fun in the Alps, and the simplest probably strikes closest to the truth—the locals are comparatively unspoiled by success. The chances are better in Austria than in any other Alpine country that your ski instructor or Bed & Breakfast hostess either works on a farm in the summer, or did until recent years. Switzerland is more efficient; France is more sophisticated and Italy has a greater flair for food, but

Austria is down-home friendly.

After countless visits to ski resorts around the world, every contributor to this ski guide can attest that no one knows how to have fun like the Austrians. In our Après-ski chapter we outline the traditions of schnapps on the slopes, tea time after skiing and late night partying.

Although Austria is one of the skiing capitals of the world, it is very affordable; this, with the hospitality you'll encounter, will help to ensure a fond memory of your trip.

Austria's Alps

The Austrian Alps have three major chains—the Northern Limestone Alps, the High Alps and the Southern Limestone Alps. The Northern Limestone Alps have many natural valleys and are home of resorts such as Lech, St. Anton, Ischgl and Kitzbühl. The High Alps are anchored by the Oetztal resorts of Sölden and Obergurgl and stretch to Innsbruck, Zell am See and Kaprun. These High Alps have few easy passes across them. Passes like the Brenner Pass and the Grossglockner are famous for their road, tunnel and bridge engineering which allows traffic to move north and south. The Southern Limestone Alps form the border with Italy and Slovenia.

The mountain elevation in Austria is lower than that found in Switzerland, France or Western Italy. But Austria gets plenty of snow in normal years since the winters get colder the further east one travels in the Alps. However, in the early winter and spring seasons, make sure to check the snow cover before planning a major skiing vacation.

Home of the Arlberg Method

Austria's name has forever been linked with the development of modern skiing. It was in the Arlberg that a unified system of skiing was devised. Previously, skiers used a form of telemarking, but Hannes Schneider based his ski technique on the snowplow which allowed skiers to maintain control in all phases of skiing.

His methods were popularized through movies, and he set up the first organized ski race, the Arlberg-Kandahar. Later Hannes Schneider would travel to the United States, after being released from Nazi prison for banking concessions, and start the first ski school in the Mt. Washington Valley, the Eastern Slope Ski School.

Driving in Austria

The Austrian highway system has a program of highway toll stickers somewhat similar to that used in Switzerland, but more flexible. Anyone driving on the Autobahn must purchase this sticker. Drivers of automobiles can purchase the toll sticker at automobile associations before arriving in Austria or at a gas station near the border. Once inside Austria, additional stickers can be purchased for periods from one week to one year at post offices, tobacco shops and most gas stations throughout the country.

Most rental car companies have decided that they will be passing along the tolls to customers renting cars in Austria. See the rental car/Autobahn toll section page 23.

When is high season?

High season: Christmas to New Year's, February through late March.

Low season: Before Christmas, January after New Year, and from late March through April closing.

For the exact high/low season weeks outside of holiday periods, check with the individual resorts. Their dates may vary because of local school holidays.

☎ **Telephone country code for Austria is 0043.**

The Arlberg

Lech, Zürs, St. Anton, St. Christoph, Stuben

If you were to question a group of aficionados about the top Austrian ski destination, odds are they would say the Arlberg or mention one of the resorts in this region. This is, after all, where Austria's skiing took its first faltering steps in 1907 and where legendary ski hall-of-famer Hannes Schneider perfected the Arlberg Method which was brought to the U.S. in the 1930s.

Traditional in style yet modern in service and amenities, this region is what newer resorts in the U.S. try to emulate when they strive for the Austrian "look." Able to absorb thousands of guests at any one time, the towns of the Arlberg have determinedly retained their village atmospheres—"The only high-rise buildings are the churches," one local proudly told us—while at the same time providing a totally modern ski experience. And because so many British frequent the area, U.S. visitors will feel very much at home in this still very Austrian destination.

So dense are the skiing opportunities, the area has been broken down in the collective skiing consciousness into the various town-resorts that compose the region. St. Anton, St. Christoph and St. Jakob are normally discussed as a unit spread along the southern side of the Arlberg massif. Lech and Zürs hold down the west-facing side of the mountain and the small village of Stuben sits beside the road at the far western edge of the region where the Lech and St. Anton valleys go their separate ways.

Separated by miles of snow fields, peaks and passes, these towns are all linked by shuttlebuses, lifts and a single Arlberg ski pass to form a skiing wonderland for intermediate and expert skiers. Once remote—and inaccessible after heavy snow—the area is now only a two-and-a-half hour drive from Zürich Airport and less than two hours from Innsbruck.

Strictly speaking, St. Anton, St. Christoph and St. Jakob belong to the Austrian state of Tyrol, while Lech, Zürs and Stuben are part of Vorarlberg. Most skiers, however, skip such technicalities and simply call them the Arlberg slopes.

One of the allures of the region is that, while the individual resorts share the same snow, they all have a totally different flavor. Picking from them, you are sure to find your ideal.

St. Anton, the largest, is a bustling and fun resort, and could be considered the most egalitarian of the three with its wide range—from low cost to ritzy—of accommodations and dining. This historic ski town is dramatically different now that the main rail line has been moved and no longer separates the village from the slopes (the station is just outside the village, across the highway, next to the Raiffeisen Tennis Center). No more waving to the Orient Express, but also no waiting for trains to pass to get to or from the lifts. New pedestrian areas are opening up and there are now more facilities for visitors, such as a public swimming pool and activity center. With "something for everyone," the town fills up, especially on weekends. Lift lines getting up to the skiing in the morning used to be long, but new lifts have cut the waiting time dramatically. And once up on the mountain, the vastness of the slopes spreads everyone out and lift lines are minimal.

The quieter, St. Anton neighborhood of **St. Jakob**, just down the valley and comprised mainly of guest houses and restaurants, is now more accessible to skiers thanks to the new Nassereinbahn gondola.

St. Christoph, the highest Arlberg village at 5,400 feet, is a smaller, more exclusive and more expensive version of St. Anton. It's a good place to get away from it all. New high speed lifts have erased the lines prevalant just a few years ago.

Only a few miles apart at the point where the Flexen Pass ends in a snow wall in winter are **Lech** and **Zürs**. Offering a more exclusive feel (Princess Diana often stayed here), Lech is a full-fledged town with more nightlife and shopping than Zürs. On the shoulder of the hill and accessible only by cable car, one of its satellites—Oberlech—is called the "ski resort of the future" by the local tourist board because the only means of transportation are on foot, on skis or on the lifts. Small and contained, Oberlech features hotels and restaurants that are connected by a series of tunnels so the mundane deliveries of luggage and supplies are completely out of sight of the vacationer. The other, Zug, is a tiny, quaint village hidden away down a tree-lined lane and perfect for families with small children and those seeking peace after 21:00 p.m. (although it is not a ski-in, ski-out area except for experts). Zürs, only minutes up the valley, is a compact cluster of only 35 buildings, most of them luxury hotels. When celebrities go skiing in Austria, this is where they often stay.

Thanks to their location at the end of the valley and their exclusive air, Lech and Zürs have shorter lift lines and less crowded slopes than the St. Anton side of the Arlberg. From any hotel it's less than a few minutes' amble to the nearest lift and from there you can tour the four resorts until you find one that suits the moment's mood.

Stuben, a tiny and unpretentious village on the fringe of the Arlberg, is proportionately quieter, with more moderately priced hotels. Thanks to the Albona lift, which rises in two stages, the connection with St. Christoph/St. Anton is easy. Because of its altitude it can be colder than the other resorts, but Stuben has an advantage in the spring: its snow is still good when the snow in Lech and Zürs is tapering off.

The Arlberg resorts may be ranked from most to least expensive: Zürs, Lech, St. Christoph, St. Anton and Stuben.

Telephone prefixes: St. Anton: 05446; Stuben: 05582;
Lech and Zürs: 05583

Mountain layout

The available ski area is significant. More than 50 grooming vehicles prowl the slopes included in the Arlberg ski pass, creating 163 miles of piste and leaving 112 miles of deep snow. The area is served by more than 80 lifts and cable cars.

Perhaps the resort that best characterizes the Arlberg is **St. Anton** (or Stanton, as many Americans pronounce it). In mood it's an endearing mix of Alpine rusticity and the most modern elements of international ski high life.

Throughout the Arlberg you'll encounter guest houses, shops and perhaps a *Würst* stand or two named for the Valluga, the 9,220-foot rocky pinnacle—the high point in St. Anton skiing.

It is from near the Valluga summit, reached by cablecar, that one of the great intermediate skiing cruises in Europe begins. The slope from the Vallugagrat (8,692 feet) is filled with hundreds of turns as you work your way down for at least an hour to the valley floor.

Experts can take the final section of the cable car to the top of the Valluga. After a difficult climb—accompanied by a guide only—they can ski down to Zürs.

You'll find less nerve-rattling skiing further down. We recommend the massive mogul field off the Tanzboden lift, where you'll see the best skiers bouncing from bump to bump, throwing in the occasional 360-degree turn for flair. Or take the Schindlergrat triple and choose to ski the groomed Ulmerhutte or challenge yourself on the ungroomed Schindler Kar or the Mattun. The village of **St. Christoph**, which sits along the crown of the Arlberg Pass at 5,904 feet, is the other ground station for skiing this side of St. Anton.

The blue and red runs are cruises that offer great enjoyment, and there's good skiing for beginners from the base at St. Christoph. Once served only by T-bars and a tram, St. Christoph now has quad chairs taking skiers up to the Galzig area.

The other ski area on this side of St. Anton is the Kapall, a 7,629-foot summit where you'll enjoy the two blue runs to the Gampen midstation at 6,068 feet. From Gampen continue through the trees into town, or drop over the ridge into the Steissbachtal and take the last half of the Valluga run.

When the crowds are too much or the snow turns to mashed potatoes, head to St. Anton's third ski area, the Rendl (6,888 feet). It's less crowded because the single gondola that serves these slopes is a longer walk than the cable cars to the other areas. It is also served by a good shuttlebus system.

The mountain is shaded in the morning, which means it can be icy; however, by afternoon the snow is in better shape than in the rest of St. Anton, especially in the spring. The best intermediate run is from the Gampberg summit (7,895 feet) back into the village. Snowboarders will want to test their skills on the newly created half-pipe.

This area is also the scene for après-ski activities. Sun worshippers flock to Rendl Beach to catch the afternoon rays and sip "Absolut Dream," a Rendl Beach concoction made of peach schnapps and vodka.

Zürs and **Lech** can be easily skied together, but there is no real connection between St. Anton and Zürs and between Stuben and Zürs. However, as noted, guides take experienced skiers—experts with guts—from the Valluga down the Lech/Zürs side. To get back you have to depend on your car, the free shuttlebus from Lech to Alpe Rauz or the public bus from Lech to St. Anton (costs about €3 per person one way).

Either Lech or Zürs would qualify for resort status by itself, even if their lift passes didn't cover the entire Arlberg. In Lech skiing is centered on the Oberlech region. This section of the mountain easily can be reached by a cable car and two chair lifts from the center of the town. A system of 16 lifts takes skiers further up to 7,799 feet. This area will keep an intermediate busy for two days, and off-slope skiing will challenge experts. Opposite Oberlech is the Rüfikopf area, reached by a high-speed cable car. From here experts—real experts—can drop straight down the face to Lech, while intermediates can loop around or cruise down to Zürs.

Zürs is a bit tougher as far as marked trails go. All the runs from the top of the Trittkopf (7,985 feet) are rated intermediate, but most would rate a black diamond in U.S. resorts. Once again, experts can make their own trails straight into town. The Madloch side of the valley has six long intermediate runs and three long beginner runs. However, after the area is well skied, you can venture almost anywhere on this side.

One of the great runs of the area is known as the White Ring, a three-hour circuit that swings around both sides of the valley, connecting Lech, Zug, Oberlech and Zürs. Take the lifts to the 7,997-foot-high Madloch Joch and then ski the red (intermediate) Madloch run around the back into Lech. To complete the circle, take the cable car from the middle of town to Rüfikopf and ski down and across to the base of the Hexenboden lift and then to Zürs. For Zug, detour off the Madloch and then come back up on the Zugerberg lifts. From there, it's a red-rated (intermediate) cruise down into Oberlech.

Stuben, tiny with only a few lifts, is our favorite bargain village in the region. It's inexpensive, but a bit out of the way. The best run is intermediate—from the Albona Grat (7,872 feet). Stuben is connected with St. Anton/St. Christoph by the blue-rated trail from the Albona midstation to a crossover tow at Alpe Rauz. From there, take the chair lift to Pfannenkopf and work your way down into St. Anton.

Mountain rating

Intermediates run the show in the Arlberg region. St. Anton is overwhelmingly red and blue on the ski map, with plenty of challenges that merit expert skills.

Although Lech and Zürs cover all the levels, prepared runs favor the intermediates on up. Experts will never get bored thanks to the wide-open expanses of off-trail powder that are among the best in all Europe.

Real experts can find off-piste and out of bounds places that will take their breath away. There is really something for everyone here.

Ski school (2003/04 prices)

St. Anton prides itself on teaching skiing to all levels and has two ski schools, Skischule Arlberg with 300 instructors and Skischule St. Anton with 60 instructors. This is the home of the Arlberg Method, the standard for ski instruction throughout the world. The school classes form in amazing numbers each morning at the base of the Gampen. Lech and Zürs also have 300 instructors, with classes forming at the base of the Schlegelkopf lift, in Oberlech and in Zürs. Ski school prices are approximately the same throughout the region.

If you can swing it, hire a private instructor for at least a day. One contributor noted, "In less than five minutes and without having to look back at me once, my instructor pinpointed my many bad habits. We spent the rest of the day hammering them out of my system. In the process, I easily skied slopes I'd have thought twice about before. And I lost my American-bred fear of mass mogul fields after I learned the right techniques for attacking them."

Ski school prices for St. Anton/St. Christoph:

Private lessons cost €208 per day and €195 a day after three days of lessons, with €17 per each additional person.

Group lessons are €52 a day; €118 for three days.

Snowboarding lessons for three days cost €134 and a snowboard college for five days will run €186.

The **cross-country** ski school prices are the same as for Alpine lessons.

Ski school prices for Lech/Zürs are normally within a few Euros of the prices in St. Anton.

Lift tickets (2003/04 prices)

The bargain is the Arlberg pass.

High Season Rates	**Adults**	**Senior/Youth** (16-19)	**Child** (7–15)
one day	€38.50	€35	€23
three days	€106	€93	€64
six days	€179	€155	€107
seven days	€202	€174	€121
fourteen days	€329	€281	€196

Senior discounts are for men older than 65 and women older than 60. There is also approximately a 10 percent discount in middle season (January and mid April).

Accommodations

Based on high season, per person/double occupancy with half board: €€€—€125+; €€—€75–€124; €—less than €75.

St. Anton (telephone prefix 05446)

Hotel Schwarzer Adler (2244, fax 224462; €€€) Great traditional atmosphere in a place proudly doing business since 1570.

St. Antoner Hof (2910; fax 3551; €€€) Just completed renovation in 1999, making it the only five-star hotel in St. Anton. Hotel is away from the main downtown street, but close to the new location of the train station.

Hotel Post (2213; fax 2343; €€€) Hardly need to leave this beautifully comfortable hotel in the center of town, with a deck for lunch, a choice of nightlife in the basement, and a redone health spa that offers progressive steam rooms and saunas. Very friendly and thorough service with a lovely restaurant.

Sporthotel (3111; fax 311170; €€€) In the pedestrian zone. Here you can arrange a week's lodging, dance in the nightclub, and enjoy a steak in the restaurant.

Hotel Mooserkreuz (2230; fax 3306; €€–€€€) On the edge of town. Sauna and indoor swimming pool, plus at the end of the day, ski back to the hotel.

Grieshof (2331; fax 202417; €€€) Located across the street from the Mössmer. This four-star hotel boasts an indoor swimming pool and friendly service.

Montjola (2302; fax 23029; €€€) A cozy lodge with excellent dining. About a five-minute walk (uphill) from the town center. The fondue capital of the Arlberg.

Hotel Fahrner (2236-0; fax 2236-22; €€–€€€) Another uphill climb from the village center, but a lovely, family-run inn with its own hand-constructed wine cellar and a traditional Austrian atmosphere.

Kertess (tel. 2005; fax 200556; €€€) A 10-minute walk from the town center and quiet. Excellent dining and quality service. Offers a shuttle bus.

Hotel Pension Rendlhof (3100; fax 310050; €€€) This hotel has received rave reviews from readers. It is only minutes from the center of St. Anton and out of the range of the late-night singing as revelers stagger home.

Hotel Mössmer (2727; fax 272750; €) Off the pedestrian zone in an area that's quiet and close to the action. Ask for a room in the recently added wing, and pay due homage to the Mössmers' guard dog, Tino. B&B only.

Hotel Sailer (2673; 235910; €€) Affordable, homey and a local hang-out—a favorite haunt of ski instructors after a long day on the slopes. The rooms are utilitarian, but it's a quick stroll to the lifts.

Ehrenreich (2353; fax 23538; €€–€€€). Just minutes away from the lifts but away from the crowd, this quaint lodge looks over a mountain stream and the Ferienpark.

Zur Pfeffermuhle (3740; fax 37415; €€€) Among the most expensive in the neighborhood of St. Jakob, but still affordable compared to comparable hotels just a mile up the road in St. Anton proper. Offers spa facities and is child friendly.

Hotel Tirolerhof (2448; fax 2915; €€) One of the larger establishments in quiet and quaint St. Jakob offering lots of activities.

Bellamonte (3137; 313720; €) and **Haus Rosa** (3252; fax 3252; €) both small and affordable B&B options, of which the neighborhood of St. Jakob abounds.

Ski Chalets: Inghams/Bladon, Chalet World, Ski Mark Warner, First Choice. (See page 20 for phone, fax and internet addresses.)

St. Christoph (telephone prefix 05446)

Arlberg-Hospiz (2611; fax 3545; €€€) The most exclusive spot on this side of the Arlberg. The restaurant is one of Austria's best.

Maiensee (2804; fax 280456; €€€) Next to lifts with all amenities.

Lech (telephone prefix 05583)

Hotels in exclusive locations shift around in terms of which one gathers the celebrities and which one slips a bit in the gossip sheets.

The top hotel in Lech these days is the **Hotel Arlberg** (2134; fax 2134–25; €€€) which is conveniently located and oozing old elegance. This five-star hotel was where Princess Diana used to stay. The lobby recreated an old hunting lodge and log fires crackle in front of overstuffed couches and chairs.

Gasthof Post (22060; fax 2206–23; €€€) A Relais & Chateaux five-star hotel which attracts a slightly older upscale crowd, but is beautiful and cozy. Once actually the post office in Lech, this hotel still has its stuccoed-and-painted facade and is filled with antiques. It is worth a visit, if only to soak up the old-money atmosphere, to at least stop in and have a drink at the bar.

Angela (2407; fax 240715; €€€) is beautifully appointed and ideally positioned—a real ski-in/ski-out spot with plenty of solitude in Lech.

Burg Hotel (22910; fax. 229112; €€€) Top quality with sauna, whirlpool and tennis. It is only steps from the cable-car station. It is a center of aprés-ski action.

Krone (2551; fax 255281; €€€) An European Romantic Hotel with every modern amenity and with an award-winning restaurant; its sauna and pool overlook the ski slopes. It still looks much the way it did 100 years ago. The rugged chalet building is set between the church and the river.

Kristiania (2561; fax 3550; €€€) A bit out of the mainstream but nice, this hotel is owned by the 1952 Olympian Othmar Schneider.

Sonnenburg (2147; fax 2147-36; €€€) in Oberlech, is made up of twin chalets with the traditional wood/stucco facade. The terrace overlooking Lech below is a hot spot for tea-time aprés-ski.

Haldenhof (2444; fax. 2444-21; €€–€€€) A friendly, family-owned and family-run hotel—the perfect Austrian inn with delicious traditional cuisine.

Hotel Lech (22890, fax 2727; €€) and **Pension Chesa Rosa** (2289; fax 22898;

€€€) are two of the more popular guest houses.

Kristall (2422; fax 24223; €€€) is behind the church; an ideal location for beginning skiers. Friendly service.

Pension Sursilva (2970; fax 2970-22; €€€) Good value and modern facilities.

Just outside Lech, in Zug, **Gasthof Rote Wand** (3435 ; fax 343540; €€€) has a traditional atmosphere with a heavy wood interior and packed with antiques. It has an indoor pool, health club, sauna and so on.

The tiny **Gasthof Alpenblick** (2755, fax 27668; €) is a real family bargain in Zug, near the Rote Wand and the special family area.

For less expensive lodging in Lech near the lifts try **Alpenland** (2351, fax 23515; €€), **Arabell** (2181, fax 312592; €€), **Acerina** (3320, fax 337425; €€), **Bianca** (2829, fax 383515; €€), **Aurelio** (2214, fax 3456; €€), **Odo** (23580, fax 394315; €€), **Montfort** (2478, fax 247825; €€+), **Sursilva** (29700, fax 297022; €€) and **Grissemann** (2221, 22216; €€).

In Oberlech check out **Astoria** (2979, fax 297929; €–€€); **Michaela** (2617, fax 3015; €€-), **Berger** (2839, fax 29397; B&B only, €), and **Ilga** (31210, fax 312131; B&B only, €€).

Ski Chalets: Inghams, Total, Thompson, Simply Ski. (See page 20 for phone, fax and internet addresses.)

Zürs (telephone prefix 05583)

The top spot here is:

Zürserhof (2513; fax 3165; €€€) This is one of the most luxurious hotels in the Alps, in a class with the Palace in St. Moritz. This is the hotel that made the tiny village famous. It is a series of five chalets joined together and filled with the ultimate in Tyrolean luxury. Wood paneling surrounds you and oriental carpets drape the floors.

The four-star **Albona Nova** (2341; fax 234112; €€€) is tucked round the back, away from the road and right by a lift, this charming and splendid hotel has carved-wood ceilings and an intimate appeal. German-speaking critics have called it "Klein und fein." That translates to small and fine. The restaurant is fabulous.

Arlberghaus (2258; fax 225855; €€€) and the **Schweizerhaus** (2463; fax 246327; €€) are some of the less expensive (Bed & Breakfast or Half Board only).

Stuben (telephone prefix 05582)

Post Hotel (761; fax 7626; €€) A good choice for uncomplicated skiing with on-site ski rental, ski school and a bank.

Haus Erzberg (tel. 729; fax 7294; €) Small hotel (13 beds), B&B only.

Hotel Mondschein (tel. 511; fax 736; €€€) Excellent hotel in historic 1739 building. Indoor pool, friendly atmosphere.

Apartments, condominiums, flats

If you want to rent a vacation apartment, ask for the apartment listing brochure from each of the tourist offices in the Arlberg. They maintain a complete list of hundreds of apartments and chalets available in season.

In Lech, apartments can be rented with four beds for about €150 a day, high season. In St. Anton, a four-bed apartment can be rented for about €160 a day. These prices are about average.

Dining—St. Anton and St. Christoph

Here, appropriately so, most of the best restaurants are up on the mountain. Heading the list is the **Galzig Verwall-Stube** (2352501, fax 2352502) where sitting at what seems like the top of the world you can dine on lobster ravioli, baked monkfish, saltimbocca, nutty spinach leaves and finish with fresh fruit sorbets. The daily menu ranges from €30–€110. Watch your choice and you can have some of the world's best cooking in a spectacular setting for very affordable prices.

The other great dining experiences on the mountain are in St. Christoph. The **Arlberg Hospiz Ski-Club Stube** (2611, fax 3545) is a bit more luxurious than its sister restaurant the **Hospiz-Alm** (3625, fax 362510). Both establishments are owned by the same family. At the Ski-Club Stube the lunch menu is not as sumptuous as the dinner one. Try the veal filet with vegetable canneloni and have the orange pancakes with homemade toppings for desert. At the Hospiz-Alm the lederhosen-clad waitstaff sets the tone. Feast on pickled salmon terrine, then sip the lobster cream soup, move on to the lamb and finish with chocolate mousse. The fixed menus normally are €32–€60.

Down in the village of St. Anton, the best restaurant is in the only five-star hotel in the town. The St. Antonerhof's rustic **Rafflstube** (2910, fax 3551) is top of the line, but not at the top of the mountain.

A 200-year old St. Anton tradition is a meal in the old farmhouse, **Brunnenhof** (2293) with its floors strewn with oriental carpets. Enjoy game, local boiled beef, soups and salad. Main entrées are €15–€24.

The king of fondue lives at the **Hotel Montjola** (2302), ten minutes above town. Step through a painted door and enjoy any of eight different fondues in cozy, low-ceiling rooms. They also serve normal fare in monster portions. Their "Giant Wiener Schnitzle" lives up to its name.

To feel like you've been invited into a local's rustic home, choose the **Die Einkehr** (2301), were locals swear that this is the real stuff. The floors are rough-hewn boards; the walls are mellowed barnboard covered with farm implements and local game; and the fireplace flickers warmly. Try the lamb, the Tyrolean game, thick potato soup, dried mountain meats and finish off with strudel in a cream cheese sauce.

The **Alte Post** (25530) has fine local cooking served in a 17th century setting.

Museum (2475), upstairs above the Ski and Folk Museum, has three rooms where gourmet Austrian meals are served. One room is the original room of a 90-year-old mansion and a huge marble fireplace with oak paneling from the Czech Republic. Meals will cost €25–€35.

For a romantic evening head out to the **Verwall** (3249) for Tyrolean specialties by candlelight. Make reservations and call a taxi or take a horse-drawn sled and bring along some schnapps. The food is good but the experience is better. This is also a favorite stop for cross-country skiers during the day.

Other very traditional places to have Austrian fare are the **Alt St. Anton** (2432) on a sunny plateau in Nasserein by the toboggan run, or head to **Sailer** (2673) where you can fill up with the locals without breaking the bank. A new place is **Schindler** (2207) where their motto is, "Simple, yet exquisite." Locals tell me that the food here is the real traditional stuff such as salbeileber and apfelschmarrn. **The Schwarzer Adler** (2244) sets a table that brims with Austrian specialties. Prices start at €12.

Reasonably priced meals are always on the menu at the **Aquila Café** (2217), **Amalis** (221810) and **Grieswirt** (2965). The fondue, pigs knuckles and chicken wings at the **Robis Rodel-stall** (0699-10858855) are good and affordable. It is at the bottom of the lighted toboggan run and has tables around a big open fireplace. At the top of the toboggan run, go to the **Rodelalm** and have local specialties before beginning your two-km., eight-minute toboggan ride down the floodlit track.

Harlekin (3606), according to locals, has great fish.

Hazienda (2968) serves excellent steaks and seafood.

Don't leave St. Anton without a pizza from the **Pomodoro** (3333) if only to say you had one. It's cheap and friendly, and you may see your ski instructor there. But I'd spend my pizza and pasta money at **San Antonio** (3474) and squeeze in a game of bowling.

The **Funky Chicken** has the cheapest eats in town—hard to miss as you come down off the slopes. It's open to 2 a.m. and has take out. There are couches in front of the fireplace. It is a great place to people-watch over a margarita or a beer. Half a chicken sets you back less than €4.50.

For breakfast, head to **Häferl** for the best pastries and cakes in town. **Aquila** also has good pastries and coffee.

Lech and Zürs dining

In Lech, many restaurants have instituted a children's menu with a fixed price of €8 or so. For good food try the restaurants in **Hotel Montana** (2460), which has the best wine cellar in town. The **Arlberg** (2134) is highly recommended with an Austrian influenced gourmet menu. **Hotel Salome** (2306) gets good recommendations. **Hotel Krone** (2551) is a shrine of local cooking with exceptional use of local ingredients.

For nouvelle Austrian cuisine, try the **Goldener Berg** (2205), which is also known for its romantic fondue, or **Brunnenhof** (2349). The **Hotel Post** (2206) and the **Almhof Schneider** (3500) serve excellent traditional recipes. Across from the Hotel Post is **Hûs Nr. 8**, an intimate restaurant offering Austrian fare at a median price and in a cute old house with low doorways.

Restaurant Italiener (3734) has the best, inexpensive Italian in town with a fabulous anti-pasta buffet. Plus, its bar downstairs is quite a scene after 10 p.m. Relatively new to Lech is **Filomena** (2211), a modern, upscale restaurant with a salad bar everyday, regional cuisine such as wild duck and fresh fish from the Arlberg, and featuring 160 wines, only from Austria. For those with a sweet tooth, head to the **Olympia Café** at the base of the tram to Oberlech for some authentic Austrian apple strudel or "Kaiserschmarrn"—don't ask, just order it.

Fux (2992) not only has the town's hot bar, it has an excellent restaurant with heavy Asian influences. Try chicken satay, miso soup, sushi, tempura and dim sum.

Just outside Lech, in Zug (normally reached by a sleigh ride from Lech), the **Gasthof Hotel Rote Wand** (3435) offers excellent food in the best of Austrian tradition. Its specialty is an excellent fondue bourguignon with dozens of different dipping sauces, starting with soup and finishing with strudel. **Restaurant Klösterle** (3190), in a small, former monastery, is expensive but worth it with fondue specialties in a historic setting. **Gasthaus Alphorn** (2750) also has excellent meals.

For cheaper eats, try **Pizza Charly** (2339) for good Italian food and head up to **Gasthof Omesberg** (2212) for great traditional Austrian fare.

In Zürs, a meal at **Albona Nova** (2341, fax 234112) is a treat. This place has been recognized by the top critics in Europe and has a serious following. Make reservations. Try the wild duck with polenta, the goose liver ravioli, the lamb with eggplant. In between courses, clear your taste buds with cocoa sorbet. Then finish with spectacular cheeses or a soft creme brûlée.

The **Edelweiss** (2662, fax 3533) is another phenomenal dining experience. Start with a tomato mousse with carparccio, move to the roast lamb with ratatouille and risotto and finish with a tart chocolate drizzled over mangos and papayas.

You can depend on great meals in the **Zürserhof** (2516) or **Edelweiss** (26620). Also, try the **Lorünser** (2254) and **Hirlanda** (2262), for excellent meals. The **Flexenhüsle** (4143) has enjoyable fondue nights.

Mountain restaurants

On the mountain, of course, you can ski over to the Galzig or the two gourmet spots in St. Christoph. But, heck, even food lovers need to take a break from big meals and the gourmet stuff.

In that case head to **Griabli** (3673) for a fun lunch on the mountain in real Austrian style. **Gampen** (2352532) has a good self-service with a nice terrace.

In Stuben, try the **Restaurant Berghaus**, right near the base of the lift, with German specialties and pizza.

In Lech many of the Oberlech restaurants can be considered "on-mountain." And in Zürs, every restaurant is on the moutain. But otherwise, head to the **Rüfikopf Panorama Restaurant** for good eating and a great view.

Après-ski/nightlife

St. Anton and St. Christoph

In St. Anton's pedestrian zone, you'll be able to find something that suits your night tastes by simply taking a stroll. There are dozens of small bars and gasthofs. Drinking tends toward beer and schnapps.

At the **Mooserwirt**, happy hour (or tea-time) has skiers bouncing off the walls and the outside terrace. There's often live music, unless out-of-control patrons force the town fathers to take away the bar's license until things cool down. It's tough to reach on foot; partyers who can't stand on their own two skis have been known to take the tops of the picnic tables and sled back into town.

Stop by the **Krazy Kanguruh**, with its reputation as one of the region's two wildest watering holes. We can't praise it wholeheartedly: it's wild, but away from the center of town, and Bo don't know crowded till he gets there. Since you can't get there by foot, spare time on your last run down the mountain and pay your respects when the joint isn't as jammed.

Closer to town and somewhat more sedate are the hangouts at the **Alte Post Hotel** and the **Hotel Post**. On the Alte Post's outside terrace, you can sip Glühwein and watch the last of the sun's rays climb up the peaks, or you can sweat it out in the Hotel Post's two basement bars. Both feature live music, but one attracts the heavy drinking, heavy smoking, young crowd, while in the other a slightly older group disco and polka ski-kinks away.

On the right hand side of the slopes in the village of St. Anton check out the traditional and cozy **Sennhütte** with live music. I hope you don't think it is quiet and peaceful! This place can get crazy at tea-time.

The **Hotel Anton** opposite the Galzigbahn is getting pretty trendy and is a place to see and be seen.

If you are looking for a place where you can gaze longingly into your spouse's eyes, head into one of the hotel bars. They tend to be much quieter. Or head to the **Stanton Bar** where you can dance to fox-trot oldies and hit-parade music till 4 a.m.

The **Underground**, a popular British pub that's dark and loud, rocks through the late afternoon into the wee morning hours and is among the places to head if you need a fix of Guinness. Happy hour is from 4–7 p.m. You never have to leave—this place

Telephone prefixes: St. Anton: 05446; Stuben: 05582;
Lech and Zürs: 05583

has ribs, wings, steaks and fondue. This is also the hangout of the snowboarders in town.

You'll also find it at **Jacksy's**, and the **Alibi**, a small, offbeat bar with the enticing sign, "Men—No Shirt, No Service, Women—No Shirt, Free Drinks!"

Late night discos and karaoke bars abound—try your best off-slope maneuvers in the **Picadilly** or the **Hacienda.**

Après-ski/nightlife—Lech and Zürs

In Lech, après-ski begins on the slopes in Oberlech and often includes champagne as the drink of choice, especially at **Hotel Montana**. You'll find fun and friendly tea-time crowds of all ages at **Hotel Burg** and **Hotel Sonnenburg**, both located thankfully close to the tram.

Once down in Lech, choose wild and crazy at the **Tannbergerhof**—be prepared to dance in your ski boots outside at the ice bar to oompah music—or more sedate (relatively speaking) at the **s'Pfefferkörndl**, which gets going later in the evening.

After dinner, head to the jazz café and night club with the unfortunate name (in English anyway), **Fux,** right on the river. It has become quite the "cool" spot in the past year. The avant-garde wooden architecture is a real contrast to conservative Lech. It has two different bars all beating to disco and an excellent cigar bar.

A more chic after-hours address is the **Hotel Krone** where there is a disco and a good local crowd. Find disco action at the **Scotch Club** in the Hotel Arlberg as well.

The zither music played Sundays in the **Gasthof Post** is much quieter, and fun.

Younger crowds and snowboarders head to the CIA-Stube where they can whoop it up within sight of the halfpipe and a fun park.

Anywhere you go to drink, expect to pay between €4.50 and €7.70 for a drink and a coat check fee of about €1.50.

Zürs has a disco in the **Hotel Edelweiss**. The new insider spot is **Vernissage**. The **piano bar** in the Hotel Alpenhof is pleasant and **Ambiente** fills up for tea time and après-ski in the Sporthotel Zürsersee.

Child care (2003/04 prices)

Ski courses for kids from age 4 are offered, as are a ski kindergarten, and babysitting services (from age 2 1/2 upward). The ski school includes lunch with a drink and there are reductions if parents are also enrolled in the ski school. Hours are 9:00 a.m. – 16:00 p.m.

Ski school rates	St. Anton	Lech/Zürs
one day	€52	€48
three days	€118	€111
six days	€196	€160

Kindergartens, for children 2 1/2 and older, are available in all the resorts. In St. Anton you'll pay €52 a day and €196 for six days. Supervised lunch is €13 a day. Prices in Lech and Oberlech are €47 a day and €142 for six days. Lunch is €7.30 per day extra. Open from 9:00 a.m.–16:00 p.m. Babysitting on a weekly, daily or hourly basis can be arranged through the tourist office.

In Lech, hotels Austria, Goldener Berg, Rote Wand, Burghotel, Burg Vital, Almhof Schneider, Arlberg and Sonnenburg all have private kindergartens.

Other activities

In addition to downhill, there's **tobaganning, cross-country skiing, snowboarding, paragliding, walking** and **skating. Heliskiing** is available in Lech and Zürs.

On Thursday the cable car takes rodelers (tobogganers) to Gampen.

A real adventure for those from the modest U.S. is to partake of the glorious **spas** in the more luxurious hotels of the Arlberg. While the various hot tubs, steam rooms and saunas are a civilized way to end a ski day and the perfect prescription for tired muscles, Americans need to be forewarned that Europeans enjoy these in the altogether. Nobody minds if you wear a bathing suit or cover yourself modestly with a towel, but you will be the one who stands out in the crowd.

St. Anton (2380) and Lech offer **horse-drawn sleigh rides** through the forest. The price for up to five people is around €60 for about an hour. Other activities include **swimming, tennis** and **sightseeing. Shopping** in the resorts includes authentic Austrian garb, designer wear in Lech, but limited to ski wear and souvenirs elsewhere.

Getting there

You'll probably fly into Zürich, although the trip can be just as easy from Munich or Innsbruck.

Driving from Zürich, take the autobahn to St. Gallen, then to Feldkirch and the Arlberg Pass. (Tunnel toll each way is €10.) From Munich and Stuttgart, it is easiest to drive to Bregenz, then to Feldkirch and the Arlberg. From Zürich, it's a little over three hours by car, or take the train directly to St. Anton or Langen.

Lech and Zürs lie further up the Flexen Pass. Get off the train in Langen and take a bus up the hill, or get off the train in St. Anton and take a different bus.

Direct trains connect Langen with Cologne, Dortmund, Munich, Innsbruck, Salzburg, Zürich, Paris, Brussels and Calais. The Orient Express (800-237-1236) also makes a stop in St. Anton beginning in late March.

More convenient than the train is direct ski bus service from Zürich Airport to all the Arlberg resorts that runs on Fridays, Saturdays and Sundays. On Fridays, departure is at 12:30 p.m. On Saturdays, buses leave at 10:00 a.m., 12:30 p.m. and 18:30 p.m. On Sundays, two buses leave at 12:30 p.m. and 18:30 p.m. Fares are about €45 one way and €75 round trip. The bus trip takes about three hours and at times can be quicker than driving since the bus drivers know how to avoid the weekend traffic jams. Make reservations through Arlberg Express (05582-226, fax 05582-580).

There is a bus connecting the Munich airport with St. Anton. Call Tiroler Landesreiseburo at 0512-43315 or 491626, fax 0512-392854.

Tourist information

St. Anton: Tourismusverband, A-6580 St. Anton am Arlberg;
Telephone 05446-22690, fax 2532.
Internet: www.stantonamarlberg.com.
E-mail: info@stantonamarlberg.com

Stuben: Verkehrsverein, A-6762 Stuben; 05582-399, fax 3994.

Lech and Zürs: Tourist Office, A-6764 Lech; 05583-2161, fax 3155.
Internet: www.lech-zuers.at.

Zürs: Zürs Tourist Office, A-6763 Zürs; 05583-2245, fax 2982.

Telephone prefixes: St. Anton: 05446; Stuben: 05582;
Lech and Zürs: 05583

Bad Gastein

Skiing may be the number-one pastime in the Gasteiner valley, but the area's popularity as a meeting place for European vacationers keeps it lively the year round. Austrians from all parts of the country head up the valley in winter. The area is a group of four ski systems: Bad Gastein, Sportgastein, Bad Hofgastein and Dorfgastein.

If you are looking for ski-in/ski-out, this is not the place to come. You will have to do plenty of klomping around in your ski boots. This town perched on the side of the mountain was not designed for skiing. The town has set up good storage facilities to allow skiers to keep equipment near the slope, but that also limits your skiing since you always have to return to the point where you started. In addition it is also a small inconvenience to have to pay. An excellent system of shuttlebuses helps move skiers between the different resort towns.

Bad Gastein first gained fame as a thermal spa. It is still Austria's top spa and one of the best-known in Europe. The therapy is based on submersion in radon-laced water. A curious hot spring-fed pool has been carved into rock for this therapy. Another form of the treatment takes place in the nearby town of Heilstollen. Here small trains carry those seeking the cure deep into abandoned mines where different chambers with high radon content and differing temperatures above 100 degrees Fahrenheit are visited according to doctor's orders.

Because of the spas, the resort attracted the upper crust of society and a rather etiquette-conscious clientele. The formality that developed over the years, especially in the grand hotels—many of which still have private thermal pools—continues today. The winter coat of preference will probably be fur, and the lineup of shiny automobiles in front of the casino often makes it look like a Mercedes or BMW showroom. Although spa visitors still cling to protocol, the modern skiing tourist has softened the stiff rules of decorum. This is a town where you can live elegantly, complete with black tie, or casually, never changing from your ski jacket.

Mountain layout

The best skiing is from the top station on the Stubnerkogel at 7,373 feet, where an exceptional intermediate run stretches nearly seven miles. This run, the Angertal, drops 4,264 feet. From the ground there is a lift connection to the Schlossalm area above Bad Hofgastein.

There's a challenging World Cup run from the sides of the Graukogel opposite the Stubner. The lift takes you up to 6,556 feet, and the black run takes you down. (A side trail accommodates intermediates).

Also try Sport Gastein, about six miles away and easily accessible by bus. The best of the runs is from the top of the Kreuzkogel. The eight-seater Goldberg-Bahn gondola takes you to the top in 14 minutes. At the top, a choice of four different trails awaits you. The best of them is the north trail, which is left unprepared and provides great powder skiing, given the right conditions. The nearly five-mile run covers a vertical drop of almost 4,950 feet.

Snowboarders have halfpipes available in most of the Gastein areas, but they tend to congregate in Dorf Gastein with its excellent snowpark that has a bordercross course.

This is not a good resort for beginners. Movement is not convenient with the beginner slopes a bus ride away. After those easy trails, the step up in difficulty is daunting.

Mountain rating

The valley, particularly Bad Gastein, is intermediate country, with the most notable exception being the World Cup course. It is a good place to tune up one's ski legs, leaving some spring in them for partying later. Solid experts will enjoy approximately a dozen black runs, but once finished with them, they'll be ready to move on. Experts should check out an off-trail group or a guide for a morning. Both will offer little-known runs down unprepared sections of the resort, and these should provide most of the challenge.

Lift tickets (2003/04 prices)

The Amadé lift ticket cover this valley's main regions. Each town in the region offers single-day limited-lift tickets. But this lift ticket does more. It also allows skiing in a phenomenal region. The resorts are not connected, nor are they really all that close, but your lift ticket is good wherever you go in these areas.

Here are the additional regions and the towns where the lifts are included in the ski pass: Salzburger Sportwelt (Flachau-Wagrain-St. Johann/Alpendorf, Zauchensee-Flachauwinkel-Kleinarl, Radstadt-Altenmarkt, Eben, Filzmoos, Goldegg), Dachstein-Tauern-Region (Schladming-Planai, Rohrmoos-Hochwurzen, Ramsau am Dachstein, Haus im Ennstal, Pichl-Reiteralm, Forstau-Fageralm, Gröbming-Stoderzinken, Pruggern-Galsterbergalm) plus, Hochkönigs Winterreich und das Großarltal.

The lift rates are based on high, middle and low season. High season is Christmas/New Year and early February to mid March. Middle season is January after New Year through around February 1st or so. Low season is before Christmas and late March into April. Special family rates are also available.

High season	Adult	Youth (16–18)	Child (15 and younger)
One day	€31	€29	€15.50
Three days	€93.50	€86.50	€46.50
Seven days	€179	€166.50	€89.50
Fourteen days	€278.50	€269.50	€139.50

Telephone prefix: Bad Gastein, 06434;
for Bad Hofgastein, 06432; Dorfgastein. 06433

Ski school (2003/04 prices)

Six area ski schools have a total of 130 instructors. In Dorfgastein, call 06433-7538; in Bad Hofgastein, call 06432-8485; and in Bad Gastein, call 06434-2260 or 4440. Average instruction price for one hour of private lessons is €40 an hour. Group lessons cost: One day, €50; three days, €120; six days, €140. Cross-country lessons cost €29 for one day; €135 for one week.

Accommodations

Choose from a great selection of hotels in Bad Gastein and Bad Hofgastein. There is less variety in Dorfgastein nearer the entrance to the valley. Of the three, Bad Gastein probably offers the most European ski atmosphere, including a healthy helping of nightlife.

Based on high season, per person/double occupancy, with half board: €€€—more than €125+; $$—€75–€124; $—less than €75.

Arcotel Elisabethpark (25510, fax 255110 ; €€€) has plenty of amenities, but not much Austrian flavor.

Hoteldorf Grüner Baum (tel./fax 25160; €€€) was once the Archduke's hunting lodge and is set five km. outside of town and is one of the great Austrian hotels.

Hotel Weismayr (25940, fax 259414; €€€) is a centrally located, 135-bed hotel offering traditional accommodations with sturdy, old-style, European furniture, thick carpets and tapestries.

Kurhotel Salzburgerhof (6230, fax 623070; €€€) comes highly recommended by Americans and British alike.

Hotel Wildbad (37610, fax 376170 ; €€–€€€) is right in the center of town with helpful owners and spa facilities.

These hotels are all convenient to the lifts. **Hotel Mozart** (26860, fax 268662; €€), **Bärenhof** (2969; €€), **Hotel Eden** (2076; €€), and **Kur- und Sportpension Kerschbaumer** (2433, fax 243319; €€).

Chalet Wetzlgut (2065, fax 206570 ; €€) is an apartment group right under the lift. **Haus Elfi** (4662, fax 46622; €) is a B&B right at the base of the Stubnerkogelbahn.

Bad Hofgastein

Try the **Hotel Alpina** (06432-8475, fax 06432-847570; €€€), **Hotel Osterreichischer Hof** (06432-6216, fax 06432-621651; €€+) with a country manor atmosphere, and **Hotel St. Georg** (61000, fax 610061; €€€).

Good and less expensive hotels are **Kurpark Hotel** (6301; €€), **Bayrischer Hof** (86460; €€), **Hotel Austria** (6223; €€), and **Berglift** (6219, fax 85044; €).

B&Bs with excellent locations are **Pension Angerer** (tel./fax2020; €), **Gstrein** (6485, fax 648527; €), **Haus Lenk** (6740; €) and **Haus Regina** (3130, fax 3129; €).

Apartments, condominiums, flats

Most visitors stay in hotels and pensions or a few private homes in the Gastein valley; however, vacation chalets are also available. Details on chalet and apartment rentals are available through the tourist offices in any of the resorts. Write or fax to the office with the dates of your vacation and they will send you back several apartments from which to choose.

Dining

Gault Millau recommends some of Bad Gastein's top restaurants. The **Hoteldorf Grüner Baum** (25160), virtually a private village tucked in a nearby side valley, serves excellent Austrian mainstays amidst wonderful scenery. **Hotel Rader** has good fine dining.

Mozart on the Platz of the same name has good fondue. For a traditional, inexpensive Austrian meal, try the **Orania Stuben**. **The Bellevue Alm** and the restaurant in Hotel Nussdorferhof are both recommended.

The top eatery in the region by some accounts is **Römerhof** (7777) in Dorfgastein. Here try a roast with asparagus and spring onions or test the au gratin potatoes.

Après-ski/nightlife

For aprés-ski the elite choose the tables at the **Casino** in Bad Gastein or retire immediately to the bar near the playing tables. After 11 p.m. the evening grows progressively wilder at the **Ritz** in the Salzburger Hof, the **Central Park, Kir Royal** and the **Pilsquell** in Bad Gastein. **Gatz** and **Hägblom's** are packed after skiing. The **Glocknerkeller** in Bad Hofgastein is a typical Austrian pub with music and dancing each night. Other hot spots are **Francky's Kneipe** and **Sonia's**.

Child care

Child care is offered for children three years and older in Bad Gastein and Bad Hofgastein. The minimum age in Dorfgastein is four. Individual babysitting service is also offered. Get more information through the tourist office.

Other activities

The three towns have a great variety of outdoor recreation. A day trip to Salzburg with a tour down the salt mines is one of the preferred outings. Bad Gastein and Bad Hofgastein are famed thermal spring resorts. Take time to enjoy the hot springs during your visit.

For non-skiers, the view from the Schlossalm at 7,000 feet is worth the ride up from Bad Hofgastein. In Bad Gastein, visit the Nikolauskirche built in the 15th century. This church, now not in use, has an unusual star-shaped vaulted nave, several interesting murals and is built around a central pillar.

In Bad Hofgastein the Gothic church with its high vaulted ceiling is worth a visit. Dorfgastein also has an interesting parish church dating back to the 14th century.

Getting there

The best international airport connections are through Salzburg or Munich. The best way to get to the resorts is by car, driving south, along the magnificent Tauernautobahn to Bischofshofen and on to the Gastein valley. Expect about an hour's drive. Train connections from Europe are also excellent.

Tourist information

Kur- und Tourismusverband, Kaiser-Franz-Josef-Strasse 27, A-5640 Bad Gastein; 06434-253560; fax 06434-253537.
E-mail: info@badgastein.at. Internet: www.badgastein.at.
Kurverwaltung, A-5630 Bad Hofgastein; 06432-71100, fax 6432-71 1032.
Email: info@badhofgastein.com.
Verkehrsverein, A-5632 Dorfgastein; 06433-7277, fax 6433-763737.
Email: info@dorfgastein.com. Internet: www.gastein.com

Telephone prefix: Bad Gastein, 06434;
for Bad Hofgastein, 06432; Dorfgastein. 06433

Innsbruck

Innsbruck has twice hosted the Winter Olympic Games (1964 and 1976). However, Innsbruck, capital of the Austrian Tyrol, is no quaint ski village. This city of more than 130,000 residents in the valley of the emerald-green Inn River has such a collection of cultural attractions that skiing is not the dominant factor. Innsbruck just happens to be surrounded by a group of resorts with excellent skiing and it has linked its ski package offerings with two of the most famous resorts in Austria—St. Anton and Kitzbühel.

For centuries, Innsbruck has been a crossroads of civilizations. The bridge from which the city gets its name has linked the north and south of Europe since the time of the Romans, who regularly used the Brenner Pass. New rail links made Innsbruck a major junction on the east-west rail links between the Alps and central Europe. And the silver mines made this a rich and busy commercial center.

In the ancient days, this was the center of the Holy Roman Empire, which ruled over most of Europe, from Italy to the Pyrenees and to the English Channel. When you look at a city map it is easy to see where the old castle walls once stood. Colorfully restored buildings give the town center a cheerful yet medieval feel. Old inn and shop signs still hang, arcades still shelter travelers from the storms, traditional restaurants still serve patrons today as they did in Mozart's day, and merchants (all be they modern) still line the cobblestone streets.

If you stay in the city you have a longish ride to the lifts, but you can ski seven nearby areas, and can also strike out for a day to St. Anton or Kitzbühel. The shuttlebus system has been perfected over the years and makes getting to the slopes quick and easy. Innsbruck is a great place to try out a lot of Austria's skiing to get an idea of where to spend more time next season.

With a major university and lots of cultural history—castles, cathedrals, palaces and the like—Innsbruck has many sightseeing opportunities as well. It also has a great deal of beauty and charm, with the Inn River flowing through the city and good walking areas in the old city center, up and down the river banks and parks. Virtually all sightseeing is within a ten-minute walk of the city center. There is a good tram and bus system up to Igls, Hungerburgbahn and the winter hiking trails.

Those looking for the best restaurants and cafes will not be disappointed. Those looking for rollicking good all-night dancing and drinking can find it here. The city is also a good family environment, with lots of affordable restaurants, and activities for kids like the zoo, gondolas and trains going up into the mountains.

Igls, (a part of Innsbruck) a small village on the south side of the Inn Valley, is only a 20-minute bus ride (or 30-minute tram ride) from the city. Commercialism hasn't taken over. Attractive walking paths through meadows leading to nearby villages add to the relaxed charm and genuine sense of retreat. Not prohibitively expensive, it attracts a slightly older and sedate crowd. There are a few local nightspots, but this is more a place for a quiet dinner with drinks afterward than for a rocking party night of disco and barhopping.

Mountain layout

The major ski areas ringing Innsbruck are (in descending order of difficulty) Hungerburg-Seegrube, Axamer-Lizum/Mutterer Alm, Schlick 2000, Patscherköfel, Glungezer and (in a class of its own) the Stubai glacier. Altogether, nearly 130 kilometers of trails are prepared for downhill skiers.

Experts should strike out north across the Inn River to Hungerburg, which is the gateway to the great black trails of the Hafelekar. Wend your way down the mogul-studded steep black run from the 7,657-foot-high summit. It's one of the most challenging in Austria and a good test of expert status.

Of the Olympic slopes, the Axamer-Lizum is best known. The slopes of Axams, a village about six miles outside Innsbruck, start at the 5,249-foot level. Here you can find every major resort amenity short of lodging. Plans are underway to connect Mutters with Axamer-Lizum over the Birgitzköpfl and down the mountain by 2005.

Even though it's considered heresy in Axams to say, we liked three other runs better than the famous Olympic course, the Hoadl (7,677 feet). The first two, from the nearby 7,336-foot Pleisen and slightly lower Kögele, take you all the way back to the valley floor. The Kögele is the better of the two, with a great four miles of skiing. The demanding run down the Birgitzköpfl on the opposite side of the valley was the most difficult in the area. The moguls pound a skier's thighs and the steep slopes test an intermediate's courage.

Tulfes, nearly eight miles from Innsbruck, has skiing from the 8,783-foot level. For powder and off-trail skiing, we highly recommend the area around the Glungezer summit (but you have to climb half an hour to enjoy the best off-trail variations).

Igls, at 2,952 feet, is in the shadow of the Patscherköfel, the 7,372-foot summit for the men's downhill run. You can ski the same 2.4-mile course traveled by Franz Klammer to win a gold medal at the 1976 games and you have the added advantage of new snow-making equipment that will keep the entire descent white, no matter what the weather. The bobsled run is also at Igls, and visitors are allowed to try bobsledding on the course for €19 per person.

Stubaital, home of one of Europe's top summer skiing areas, guarantees Innsbruck skiable terrain throughout the ski season. This area, about an hour from downtown Innsbruck, is one of the best glacier skiing areas in the world. It offers something for every skier from beginners to experts as well as a chance to experience some of Austria's most beautiful countryside.

Mountain rating

As a twice-Olympic city, Innsbruck offers plenty for the expert. Each of the major ski areas will give the intermediate countless tests.

Beginners need have no fear. All those Austrians had to learn how to ski too, and the beginner and training lifts are usually right at the bottom of the longer chair lifts. The moment you're ready, so is the mountain.

Lift tickets (2003/04 prices)

Day tickets for the individual areas of the Innsbruck region cost €22–€32. The best bargain is the regional pass, good for a minimum of three days and includes the Stubai glacier. These are the Club Innsbruck (see Accommodations) reduced prices:

	Adult	Child (6–15)	Youth/Seniors
three days	€85	€51	€68
six days	€150	€90	€120
three of four days	€89.50	€54	€72
three of six days	€95.50	€64.50	€76.50

Buses run daily from Innsbruck to the main slopes and to the Stubai glacier. For information, call 59850. Buses also take skiers to the area's best cross-country circuits.

Ski school (2003/04 prices)

Each area has organized instruction with a total of approximately 200 instructors working in the region daily. Private and group lessons for downhill and cross-country are given. Call the Innsbruck ski school (0512-582310) for details.

4-hour private lesson	€145 (one person)	€160 (two persons)
one day group lesson	€37	
three day group lesson	€90	
five day group lesson	€120	

School courses meet on the slopes, which you can reach by shuttlebus.

Cross-country

Lusens

This area is about 45 minutes from Innsbruck in a high mountain pass, with only about 12 km. of trails, groomed in two basic loops. One loop encircles a lake (8 km.) and passes through woods, and the second (4 km.) begins at the nearby downhill ski area. Both offer beautiful high mountain scenery but no real backcountry or wilderness travel. It is also hard to lose the crowd. A couple of good inns make a handy lunch stop. Trails are well-groomed, and the lake loop can offer some thrills for advanced beginners and intermediates.

Seefeld

This cross-country paradise, with 320 km. of trails, offers lots of possibilities on beginner and intermediate runs extending into backcountry woods, deep forest and meadows; skating lanes are also available. It's generally rolling terrain, but with enough turns, dips and downhill runs to keep it interesting for most skinny-skiers. There are a few restaurants and inns along the way for rest stops and lunch. The ski bus isn't supposed to stop at Seefeld, but most drivers will, if you ask.

Trails are extremely well laid out and groomed. In complicated backcountry areas a map would be handy because many trails intersect and directions are not always well marked. Here, as elsewhere in Austria, trails tend to be overrated for difficulty, at least by American standards. An intermediate trail is usually just a little beyond beginner level, and an intermediate can easily handle one marked difficult.

Accommodations

While it may be more romantic to stay in one of the neighboring villages, the attraction of Innsbruck is that you can enjoy the benefits of a major city and one of Europe's cultural capitals.

Discounts are offered through the tourist office-sponsored Club Innsbruck plan. Rates shown here are per person based on double occupancy with half board in February. €€€—€125+; €€—€75-€124; €—€less than €75.

Europa-Tyrol (5931, fax 587800; €€€) On Südtiroler Platz across from the train station, this is the quality choice for Innsbruck. It is only a short distance from the old city and near the top attractions.

Romantik Hotel Schwazer Adler (587109, fax 561697; €€€) is not normally part of tour operator inventory, but is perfect for the discriminating upscale traveler.

Hilton Hotel (5935, fax 5935220; €€€), formerly the Hotel Holiday Inn, is Innsbruck's other top hotel. It's next to the casino and close to the ski shuttlebus stop.

Goldener Adler (571111; €€€) A four-star hotel in the city center operating since 1390 with a good Tyrolean restaurant.

Central Hotel (5920, fax 580310; €€-€€€) Another Innsbruck tradition on the Sparkassenplatz. Modernized lobby with classically Austrian rooms.

Weisses Kreuz (59479, fax 5947990; €€) Has nice single rates for comfortable rooms right in the old center. This a wonderful hotel hosting visitors since the 1400s. Known for possibly the best breakfast buffet in Innsbruck in its restaurant on the ground floor. A good deal.

Goldene Krone (586160, fax 5801896; €€) Traditional Austrian hotel in good location at the arch; rooms are a little more contemporary but hotel is also an old Innsbruck mainstay.

Weisses Rossl (583057, fax 5830575; €€) Good value in the Altstadt.

Hotel Innsbruck (59868, fax 572280; €€-€€€) A more modern hotel. Not much character or charm, but very central location and a good view of the river and mountains across the way and a back door that opens into the old town.

Hotel Grauer Bär (59240, fax 574535; €€) Newly renovated hotel across from the Jesuitenkirche with a very modern lobby and restaurant and very modern rooms.

Igls

This is a pleasant spot but for vacationers, it doesn't offer a complete package. It is just too small, spread out and isolated. If you plan to stay there check out these hotels. Bring a car. You'll need it to keep from suffering from cabin fever and to move around the village. Bus connections to downtown Innsbruck are OK. Getting elsewhere is problematical with most buses requiring a connection in downtown Innsbruck. If you want this type of Alpine atmosphere, it is best to head to nearby Seefeld where the village is concentrated and cohesive.

Sporthotel (377241, fax 378679; €€€) in the center, directly across from the bus stop. One of the top place in Igls with an outdoor terrace for drinks and lunch as well as another at night for drinks and dancing. Restaurant is upscale Austrian.

Schlosshotel (377217, fax 378679; €€€), Villersteig, has the ambiance of a retreat surrounded by woods and lawns on the edge of town, but it's a ten-minute walk (at most) from the center.

Apartments, condominiums, flats

Lodging in Innsbruck is primarily in hotels and pensions. For information on chalet and apartment rentals nearer the slopes, contact the Innsbruck tourist office.

There are more apartments in Igls. Send your requirements to the tourist office and it will send back a list of available apartments. Private rooms in Igls will end up costing, with breakfast, €20-30 per person a night.

Dining

Restaurants listed below are in the heart of the city, where you'll also find the best lodging. In the individual towns there are countless dining establishments and mountain restaurants.

Price coding (without wine) is €€€—€36+, €€—€16–35. €—€15-.

We start with the top restaurants for Austrian/Tyrolean cuisine. The top restaurants based on locals' recommendations and awards are all outside of the old center. Fax numbers are included since advanced reservations, far in advance, are recommended. **Kapeller** (Philippine-Welser-Strasse 96; 343106 fax 34310668; €€€) in the Amras section of Innsbruck serves great steak with a mustard onion crust. For dessert, try the flaming raspberries. **Schwarzer Adler** (Kaiserjägerstrasse 2; 587109 fax 561697; €€€) at the corner of Universitätsstrasse has menu wonders such as smoked halibut with red onions and potatoes and creative applestrudel. **Europa-Stüberl** (Brixnerstrasse 6; 5931 fax 587800; €€€) across from the train station offers a wonderful calf liver cooked in calvados and great plum creations for dessert. Call or fax for reservations at these three places.

The close runners up are all excellent restaurants and are oozing with Austrian atmosphere. Reservations are recommended.

Altstadtstüberl (Riesengasse 13; 582347; €€) holds a Gault Millau toque and seems to be mentioned often by locals when asked for good local meals. Go for the unusual polenta cream soup, then crayfish with vegetables in sour cream sauce. **Riese Haymon** (Haymondgasse 4; 566800; €–€€) is another Gault Millau winner where you should try the young onion soup, and the lamb carpaccio with pesto. The **Goldener Adler** (Herzog-Friedrich-Strasse 6; 571111; €–€€€) has served a whole list of luminaries engraved in marble outside the door. Try the cream soup with parsley, the roast goose and top it off with ice cream with plum sauce or enjoy bananas in Grand Marnier. Lunch menus are very affordable.

Fischerhäusl (Herrengasse 8; 583535; €€) claims to be one of the oldest. Other good Tyrolean restaurants in the old town include **Ottoburg** (Herzog-Friedrich-Strasse 1; 584338; €€) and **Weisses Rössl** (Kiebachgasse 8; 583057; €€).

Outside of the old town try **Bierwirt** (Bichlweg 2; 342143; €€) in Amras around the corner from Kapeller Restaurant. Locals swear this is the area's best regional cooking. In Igls enjoy a meal at **Batzenhäusl** (Lanserstrasse 12; 38618; €€). In Lans, not far from Igls is the award-winning **Wilder Mann** (Römerstrasse, Lans; 379696; €€–€€€) featuring exceptional Austrian meals. In nearby Völs, try **Chez Philippe** (Innsbruckerstrasse 56; 304891; €–€€€), another of the region's best restaurants.

For a special panoramic meal on Friday and Saturday, take the cable car up to Seegrube and enjoy a meal in the restaurant at the cablecar station with the lights of Innsbruck glittering far below you. Call 293375 for reservations. The cable car runs at a reduced rate for the dinner guests.

Back in town, here are some more suggestions.

Sweet Basil (Herzog-Friedrich-Strasse 31; 584996; €€) is in the arcade part of old town. Its international selection of food, including a great vegetarian selection, make for a good break from its heavier Austrian competitors. It is very popular with locals; you'll be seated next to smartly dressed Austrians chatting on their cell phones over a plate of Thai Noodles or Lemon Pepper Yellow Fin Tuna. Expect to pay about €10-20 for main dishes; their fine selection of Austrian wines begins at €20.

La Mamma Churrasco (Innrain 2; €–€€) is a bright family place right on the riverbank just outside the old city center. Enjoy pizzas and interesting pasta dishes from the Mamma side and big thick steaks from the Churrasco half.

Papa Joe's (Saillergasse 12; €–€€) serves Americanized buffalo wings, Caribbean jambalaya and Texas steaks just inside the Altstadt. It's a younger, single, sports bar spot.

You can't beat Italian restaurants for good meals at good prices. Innsbruck has plenty of them. The best in Innsbruck is **Da Peppino** (Kirschentalgasse 6; 275699; €€) only open for dinner. Try the spaghetti with baby octopus or have your fish filleted by the table and top it all off with profiteroli filled with mascapone. This is an experience—not your Mama's red sauce pasta. **Pizzeria Romantica** (Kiebachgasse 11; 586828; €) is a typical pizzeria with a bit of rustic Italian ambiance. **Solo Pasta** (Universitätsstrasse 15; €) serves more than two dozen different and very reasonable pasta dishes from lasagna to spaghetti to rigatoni. Must be good—it's packed at night. Almost next door **Il Dottore Pizza & Pasta** (Kaiserjägerstrasse 1; €) is packed as well with locals. **Al Dente** (Meranerstrasse 7; €) has very interesting creative pasta dishes with lots of variations and a good salad bar as well. **Salz & Pfeffer** (Universitätsstrasse 13; 579579; €) is a University pub and Italian place that is not only for students; it is a good relaxing atmosphere to meet others. **Panini** (Herzog-Friedrich-Strasse 17; €) is a good lunch stop, in the Altestadt, near the Goldenes Dachl. It's a step above Au Bon Pain. You'll find good pizza squares, sandwiches, soups and desserts.

Asian meals come from all corners of the continent. **Thai-Li** (Marktgraben 3; 562813; €–€€) at the Rathaus Gallery is the place to head for world-class Thai cooking—it has won a toque from Gault Millau. **Sahib** (Sillgasse 3; 571468; €) serves good Indian meals from hot and spicy curry to creamy sags. **Canton China** (Maria-Theresien-Strasse 37; €) is a good Chinese spot, with €4.50 midweek specials (Monday to Thursday, not holidays). This has attractive, upscale decor, and prices are quite reasonable. It is not at all your run-of-the-mill Chinese food. This may be the best Chinese in town. **Philippine Vegetarian** (Müllerstrasse 9; €) is an excellent vegetarian place a short walk from the center. The cooking is not at all Philippine, or even oriental. They have an interesting menu with creative dishes. The wild-rice risotto and the Greek potatoes are both excellent.

If you need a hometown fix there are the ubiquitous **McDonalds** (Maria Theresien-Strasse and Herzog-Friedrich-Strasse; €) and a **Chili's** (Boznerplatz 6; 567330; €€) with beef from the good old USA. Chili's almost always requires reservations. But even though the names are American, the prices are not, and seem to be a little high, even for Austrians. On our last trip, the family in front of us at McDonalds plopped down almost €40 for a meal for two adults and two kids. Chili's is more reasonable for what you get: Fajitas for two (with directions on how to eat them) run about €25.

Recommended: The **Hotel Grauer Bar**'s restaurant (59240, fax 574535) offers interesting and traditional cuisine.

Après-ski/nightlife

We recommend you walk through the old city for just about every version of nightlife you could desire. The view is beautiful and you'll find small pubs and bars hidden in alleys and under archways.

Check with the tourist office for a list of concerts taking place around town—tickets are also sold at the information office. You never know who's touring Europe while you're on vacation.

Innsbruck has a bit of something for everyone. Here's the lowdown:

Innsbruck's Casino, the largest in Austria, near the Holiday Inn at Salurner Strasse 15, is open for elegant gaming. Jackets are required.

The place to see and be seen is the **Europa-Bar** in the Europa Hotel. The bartender, Giuseppe, seems to know everyone by name. Another of the most popular bars in town is **Kir Royal** (Sillgasse 11) that caters to everyone with great drinks in a comfortable atmosphere.

Dom Café/Bar (Pfarrgasse 3) with a well-done antique interior is an après-ski place for a younger set that stays lively late at night. **Café Gallerie** across the cobblestone alley is also a nice spot that fills with après-skiers.

Piano Café/Bar (Herzog-Friedrich-Strasse 5) is definitely for an older (40s and older), upscale crowd, and probably the best nightspot in the center. It is relaxed and comfortable with an antique interior with paintings filling the walls. Look carefully—it's easy to miss.

Café Club Filou (Siftgasse 12) is a large Victorian bar with high ceilings and a smoking club atmosphere. Ring the bell to enter. The club has a large and spacious interior with seating in a loft over the main floor, and a quieter, more intimate bar to the side. The crowd is mixed, but leans toward the older side.

Limerick Bill's (Maria-Theresien-Strasse 9) is an Irish Pub with three upper levels and a basement. On Friday and Saturday there are bands and dance-till-you-drop evenings that can last until the wee hours of the morning.

Treibhaus tucked in a back alley behind China Restaurant, just outside the Altstadt, is Innsbruck's real bohemian hangout for all ages and types, tourists and locals alike. A spacious upstairs has a kitchen serving mediocre pizza and the basement is known for hot local jazz on most nights and Sunday mornings.

Krahvogel (Anichstrasse 12) is a very trendy "in"-bar with live music.

Prometheus (Hofgasse 2/4) is a happening place with a hip coffeehouse on the first floor and music several evenings a week in the basement.

For a spectacular place to sip coffee and drinks, try **Segafredo Sky** (on the top floor of Universitatsstrasse 15) just across the street from the Jesuitenkirche. It is nice to see the city from rooftop level. You have the mountains in one direction and the twin church towers of the Jesuitenkirche on the other.

On the ground level of the same building check out **Proseccheria Mionetto**, a sparkling wine bar, featuring the Italian version of dry champagne.

Café Brazil gets rave reviews from the 20s crowd and is packed with English-speakers. Another bar called **Jimmy's** also gets good reviews from the younger crowd.

Any guys looking for a local **Hooters** shouldn't be fooled by the place at Maria-Theresien-Strasse 10. It is pathetic. They may have imported the name, but they left the busty waitresses at the Oktoberfest. The rule is small, skinny and scowling. Hey, it's our job to check out places like this. Someone's gotta do it.

Piccolo Bar (Seilergasse 2) is rather small and cozy, with a gaudy Victorian parlor design heavy on the velvet and gilt gold. Buzz to enter. This is (probably) Innsbruck's only gay bar. It is low-key and discreet.

Austria prides itself on great cafes. Here are some of the best in Innsbruck.

Café Sacher at the entrance of the Hofburg serves coffees and rich chocolate cakes and pastries under crystal chandeliers. Try also **Cafe Mundig, Hofgarten Café,** and **Café Kröll.**

Just Outside the Center (worth a pilgrimage for pastry and coffee lovers)

Valier (Maximilianstrasse 27) won the "Golden Coffee Bean" in 1999. Critics rave about the pastries and the creams created by this cafe artist.

Gritsch (Anichstrasse 18) combines an excellent cafe with a bar and a bistro. This is a great place for a drink or snack as well. Ask for any of the following that will cure any sweet tooth—Schwarzwälder Kirsch, Apfelstrudel or Indianer mit Schlag.

Cafe Central (Central Hotel/Boznerplatz) is a true Viennese music cafe offering live piano music Sunday evenings (8–11 p.m.). It also has a meal menu with elaborate pastries and desserts. Eat amidst a semi-grand interior and enjoy a large collection of international newspapers. This is the traditional coffeehouse of Innsbruck.

Child care

Child care and ski kindergarten courses (age four and older) are available in Innsbruck's ski areas. Contact the **Schikindergarten** (582310) for details or the **Children's Day Care Centre**, Pradler Platz 6 (345282).

Other activities

Innsbruck shares with Grenoble the distinction of being a town in the Alps with more than 100,000 residents; as noted, it's a provincial capital and has a wealth of art and historical treasures. It is also on the way to the Brenner Pass, gateway to the Italian Lakes and Venice.

Innsbruck is accustomed to visitors in ski outfits, whether inside a museum or at a fine restaurant. Visitors always head for the heart of town along the Maria-Theresien-Strasse for the outstanding view of the Karwendel mountain range.

The best way to see Innsbruck is to walk through the old town. Allow about two hours. The most photographed house in the old city is Goldenes Dachl, a former royal building from the 16th century, with gold-plated copper shingles on the roof.

Visit the **Hofburg Palace** where Maria-Theresia lived and Marie Antoinette was born. At **St. Jakob's Cathedral** baroque illusion is fascinating. Look at the façade—though it looks like there are five round windows over the door, there are only three; two are painted. Plus, the ceiling of the cathedral appears to be a series of domes—all but the one over the altar are flat as a pancake. The **Hofkirche** houses the tomb of Maximilian I, comparable to the burial spots of ancient pharaohs. The massive tomb is surrounded by 28 large bronze statues of the emperor's heroes, friends and family the emperor wanted to have escort him in death—both of his wives made the list. The **Tyrolean folklore museum** gives a glimpse into the rustic small huts you see sprinkled on the mountain side. The city boasts dozens of other attractions listed by the tourist office.

The money-saving Innsbruck Card costs €21 for 24 hours or €26 for 48 hours and €31 for 72 hours. These passes are discounted by 50 percent for children ages 6–15. The card provides unlimited access to all public transportation and entrance to 21 major sightseeing attractions in and near the city. These include the Imperial Palace, the Museum of Tyrolean Folk Art, the Provincial Museum, Ambras Castle, the Alpine

Zoo, the Court Church and the multimedia displays at the Swarovski Crystal Worlds.

A good selection of classical music concerts takes place at the Concert House and the Konservatoriumsaal (music school), Museumstrasse 17a.

Cinematograph (Museumstrasse 31) is a good art cinema offering relatively contemporary and classic films in original language, not dubbed. The only cinema in Innsbruck for this and something of a rarity in Austria.

Just outside Innsbruck is a dazzling new multimedia museum dedicated to Swarovski crystals, one of Austria's most famous collectibles. **Swarovski Crystal Worlds** (05224-51080) features a spectacular array of the colorful glass, from the world's largest crystal (alas, at 300,000 carats, it is a bit large for Elizabeth Taylor's neck), collections of costumes and artifacts made with innumerous pieces of crystal and a 122-meter long wall filled with 12 tons of brilliant crystal.

Getting there

Innsbruck airport has daily jet service throughout Europe. Munich is the international airport most often used by travelers from the United States, but traffic through Innsbruck airport is increasing. Tyrolean Airways, Innsbruck's hometown airline, has scheduled service from Amsterdam, Frankfurt and Vienna, offering a perfect alternative to trains, buses, or a long drive by car.

By car from Munich, take the autobahn to the Inntal autobahn and then to Innsbruck—no more than three hours. A more scenic drive is from Munich to Garmisch-Partenkirchen (scene of the 1932 and 1936 Winter Olympic Games), and then about 70 minutes over the mountains to Innsbruck. Add at least two hours for sightseeing in Garmisch.

Shuttlebuses connect Munich Airport with Innsbruck and Seefeld with departures every Saturday from Munich at 11:30 a.m. Contact Menardi Bus at 574949, fax 571347 or Lueftner-Reisen at 589371. Bus fare is approximately €40 each way. Limousines are also available through Four Seasons Travel (584157, fax 585767) but require advance reservations. They leave Munich Airport daily every two hours. The fare is about €50 one way and €85 round trip.

Tourist information

Tourismusverband Innsbruck-Igls und Umgebung, A-6021 Innsbruck, Burggraben 3, Austria; 0512-59850, fax 0512-598507.
Internet: http://tiscover.com/innsbruck or
www.innsbruck-tourism.com
E-mail: info@innsbruck.tvb.co.at

Ischgl, Galtür and the Paznaun Valley

Ischgl (pronounced Ish-gull) is an extensive ski resort high in the Alps (4,592 feet), hard on the border with Switzerland and is almost unknown by non-Europeans. And, if you like the charm of truly being on an "European vacation," that valley is perfect.

The town itself is a small Alpine resort built on a knoll in a deep valley, easily walkable from one end to the other, thanks to elevators and short-cut tunnels. No high-rise construction seriously mars the small village effect. The ski area is far above and out of sight from the road, the base stations and the town. Eleven smaller hamlets complete the region.

Ischgl has it all—42 lifts, more than 200 km. of wide-open trails, cross-border skiing into Switzerland, off-trail areas, cross-country, small Alpine village atmosphere, inviting local cuisine, both luxury and affordable lodging options, and some of the wildest après-ski and nightlife in Austria. There is so much fun to be had in Ischgl we recommend resting up *before* you go. Be forewarned, nearly 75 percent of Ischgl's skiers are from Germany, so if you want to meet people, it helps to speak some German. But if that's not an option, you'll fit in if you just practice dancing in your ski boots.

With 90 percent of its ski area over 6,600 feet, snow is virtually assured until the beginning of May. From the slopes above Ischgl, you can cross into Switzerland and visit duty-free Samnaun.

Twenty minutes higher up the valley is Galtür, a picturesque little village of only 730 inhabitants and 20 restaurants spread out around a late-baroque church. Although connected to Ischgl by bus (and the Silvretta ski pass), it's much smaller and quieter with a correspondingly smaller ski area (40 km. of runs). It is particularly known for its cross-country and ski-touring opportunities. Since Galtür is the highest village in the Silvretta-Paznaun region, it has a long snow season (December to April).

The ski school is well-organized, with good English-speaking instructors and a popular ski kindergarten. Generation after generation has been drawn to Galtür by its quiet charms and unhurried pace. Families will find the resort caters to their needs.

Mountain layout

Ischgl's slopes are the most extensive in the valley, with neighboring See, Kappl and Galtür servicing smaller areas. Across the mountains to the south, in Switzerland, Samnaun is connected by lifts.

From Ischgl three gondola lifts rise to the main skiing area 3,280 feet above the town. The Silvrettabahn and the Fimbabahn take skiers from opposite ends of town to the Idalp area (7,582 feet). The Pardatschgratbahn goes from the eastern section of town to Pardatschgrat at 8,609 feet. A new eight-seat chair lift now brings skiers from Samnaun back to Ischgl. There should be no more bottlenecks on the Swiss side of the border. A new trail now winds between the Pardatschgrat to the middle station of the Silvretta lift.

From the Idalp sector, lifts fan out to all corners of the resort. Skiers choosing to go directly to the higher Pardatschgrat still have to pass through the Idalp area. The immediate Idalp area is a small valley in the midst of the peaks with runs and lifts radiating on all sides from its floor. It serves as the learning area, offering long, very easy swaths with excellent lift support.

From Idalp, intermediates and experts take the chair lift up to Idjoch. The Idjochbahn was the first bubble-covered eight-person lift in the world. Here, drop down into the Swiss Alp Trida section for long intermediate runs, or continue up to the Greitspitz for more challenging skiing in the Austrian section beneath the Palinkopf into the Hölltal or over another ridge to the Paznauner Taja. The slopes are so extensive, it's an adventure just finding your way around—each lift summit reveals another valley (and unbelievable vistas) and another set of runs to explore. The trail from Greitspitz into the Höllenkar, has opened a previously virgin face of the mountain.

At the end of the day, take one of the runs from the Idalp or down the Velilltal for beautiful, wide-open, intermediate cruising. Or if you want to end the day with a challenge, drop from the Pardatschgrat. If you are staying near the Silvrettabahn, you will want to head left toward the middle station, then follow the No. 1 trail into town. For those closer to the Fimba or Pardatschgratbahn stations, keep going straight down into town. Where the trail forks, ski to the right.

Determined off-trail skiers can arrange for a snowcat to take them to the Piz Val Gronda or the Heidelberger-hütte with a guide for a day of skiing across untracked snow. This area is scheduled for lift development, but it still seems to be a few years away. The Swiss must first construct an additional lift from Samnaun before the Austrian lift-builders can raise a wrench.

Over the border to Samnaun, Switzerland

Swiss Samnaun is the target of many Ischgl skiers because they are either determined to experience skiing over the border to a Swiss town, or they are hot on the trail of duty-free cigarettes, perfume or whisky. In any case, the run from the back side of the Palinkopf is relatively tame and the town itself hardly more interesting than the nearest airport duty-free store.

Duty-free here is big business. If one smokes or wants to fill up the hot toddy cabinet, Samnaun is wonderful, but once is more than enough for the run from Palinkopf. A new cable car takes skiers from the center of Samnaun-Dorf back to the slopes above Ischgl. There is normally about a half-hour wait for the tiny, slower Ravaisch cable car that, up until this season, was the only way to return.

There is another trail from Alp Trida down to Compatsch. This trail is rather difficult and often closed owing to avalanches (too much snow) or rocks (too little). If you do get down, a postbus will carry you back up to the Ravaisch cable car.

Galtür

A three-minute shuttlebus ride takes you from the village to Wirl, a collection of on-piste hotels and the gateway to the slopes. The skiing here is mellow-to-intermediate, better than Ischgl for beginners and families who want to ski together.

A quad-chair carries skiers up from the base at Wirl to Birkhahnkopf. From there, take the Ballunspitz lift to a choice of three easy expert runs or a good intermediate trail. A couple of log-cabin restaurants dot the surrounding slopes. From there you can ski down to the frozen reservoir, the Kopssee, or traverse round the back of the mountain to the Innere Kopsalpe, which offers the toughest runs. On a sunny day, this back bowl offers an advanced intermediate fun for an entire morning or afternoon.

Galtür also has night skiing on Wednesday from 19:30 p.m. to 22:30 p.m. Rates for night skiing are €10.50 for adults, €6.50 for children and €8 for seniors.

Mountain rating

Intermediates and experts will have a wonderful time in Ischgl. The area offers wide-ranging, well-prepared trails and 50 miles of off-trail challenges. Experts looking for super-steep terrain will be disappointed.

The resort is perfect for a mixed intermediate and expert group, but is not recommended for absolute beginners. English at the ski school is limited to technical ski jargon, and the nursery slopes are far above the town. Galtür, with its wide-open slopes and relaxed atmosphere, is better for younger skiers, beginners to intermediate.

Ski school (2003/04 prices)

Ischgl has the largest ski school. Both Galtür and Ischgl teach the Austrian method.

Ischgl ski school prices:

Private lessons for two hours are €108; each additional person is €15. A full day (4 hours) costs €183 with additional skiers costing €20 apiece.

Group lessons for one day cost €46, for three days are €108, and for five days cost €148.

Galtür ski school prices:

Private lessons for one hour cost €47;each additional person is €15. A full day (4 hours) is €163 with each additional skier costing €19 apiece.

Group lessons for one day are €42; two days, €71; three days, €113; five days €150; six days, €171.

Lift tickets (2003/04 prices)

All skiers except beginners should buy the Silvretta ski pass, good for all area lifts (Ischgl, Galtür, Samnaun and the entire valley), plus shuttlebus transport.

	High Season	Low Season
three days	€108	€93.50
six days	€197	€169.50
seven days	€222.50	€190.50
thirteen days	€344	€293

Individual area day tickets in Ischgl cost €38.50 in high season and €34 for low season. In Galtür prices are €28.50 for high season and €26 for low season. These are prices with the guest card for Galtür/Ischgl visitors.

Seniors older than age 60 receive about a 15 percent discount. At press time, children born after September 2, 1987 are entitled to the children's discount. Official picture identification is required for the purchase of discounted tickets for seniors and children. Children born after September 1, 1996 ski free when accompanied by an adult.

Accommodations

Based on high season, per person/double occupancy with breakfast: €€€—more than €80; €€—€50–79; €—less than €50.

We begin with lodging in Ischgl. The **Trofana Royal** (05444-601; €€€) is the top spot in town. The **Hotel Elisabeth** (05444-5411; €€€) is at the base stations of the Fimbabahn and the Pardatschgratbahn and has the perfect location, plus pool, sauna and solarium. They speak English well.

Madlein (05444-5226; €€€) Central location. Features one of the best discos in town. Pool, sauna and solarium. The **Hotel Post** (05444-5232; €€€) has been completely upgraded and features all the amenities including a swimming pool, spa, English-speaking service, a tasteful bar and more sedate après-ski, but rather wild nightlife. Staff at the **Sonne** (05444-5302; €€€) is good with English. The Sonne also has excellent après-ski.

Gasthöfe Goldener Adler (05444-5217; €€€) boasts one of the best kitchens in town, a sauna and steambath. The **Olympia** (05444-5432; €€€) near Fimba and Pardatschgrat lifts; **Yscla** (5275; €€€) near the Silvretta lift; and **Charly** (05444-5434; €€€) are convenient to everything.

The best B&B or garni in town is **Christine** (05444-5346; €€–€€€). A moderate B&B is **Sporthotel Ischgl** (05444-5351; €€)**,** formerly named Edi, though it is a bit out of the way, but a good haven for English speakers. As is the **Alpenblick** (05444-5311; €€)—ask for Martin, he also teaches skiing.

The recommended lower-priced B&Bs—**Palin** (05444-5445; €€), **Lasalt** (05444-5121; €€), and **Erna** (05444-5262; €€).

Galtür

Prices in Galtür are lower than those in Ischgl. Be sure to ask about the guest card when you arrive. It identifies you for discounts in the town for the swimming pool, and other activities. The telephone prefix is 05443. Many of the hotels have special prices for children. Also note: Galtür has dozens of excellent B&Bs—don't overlook them.

Based on high season (February), per person/double occupancy, half-board: €€€—more than €125; €€—€75–124; €—less than €75.

The best lodging here may be the **Gasthof Zum Rössle** right on the center square. It has got a fine, traditional restaurant and spa facilities (05443-8232; €€–€€€).

The **Alpenhotel Tirol** (05443-8206; €€) is another four-star. **Fluchthorn** (05443-8202; €€) Central village location. **Almhof** (05443-8253) and the **Alpenromantikhotel Wirlerhof** (05443-8231) are in the midst of the ski area in Wirl. **Zum Silbertaler** (05443-8256; €€) is a three-star near the tennis center and pool. Try **Gampelerhof** (05443-8307; €€), **Bergfried** (05443-8208; €), or **Luggl** (05443-8386; €€)

For bed & breakfasts head to: **Alpenhaus Salner** (05443-8288; €); **Dr. Köck** (05443-8226; €) or **Belvedere** (05443-8219; €), plus many more.

Apartments, condominiums, flats

The rental apartment business is well organized and bookings can be arranged through the tourist information office. When writing, provide details about when you plan to arrive, how many people will be sharing the apartment and what facilities you desire. In return you will receive a list with several choices. Make your selection and notify the individual owner, depending on the instructions you get.

Normally, linens and kitchen utensils are included in every apartment. Heat, taxes, electricity and cleaning services may be extra. Expect to pay €30 per person a night, depending on how many are sharing the apartment, where it's located and its relative position on the luxury scale.

Dining

First head to the **Trofana Royale** (05444-600; fax 05444-60090) for its five-star restaurant, which is considered one of the best in Europe, not just Ischgl or Austria. The chef here was selected as Chef of the Year in Austria in 2000. Try the deer with mountain berries and chestnut-filled ravioli. Finish up with soufflé made with Williams pear schnapps. Make reservations early.

Also recommended is the traditional kitchen of the **Goldener Adler** (05444-5217). Locals also highly recommend the **Trofana Alm** (after après-ski is over; 0544-602) for good international cooking (and pizzas as well). The **Hotel Post** restaurant (05444-5232) is elegant and sumptious, a good combination. Try the authentic-looking **Kitzloch** (05444-5618), built 15 years ago out of 300-year-old logs, for traditional food—so traditional, in fact, the spread for the bread is gramnel schmalz, which translates to "fat," but it tastes good. **Yscla** (05444-5275) has a good French and local menu. Don't ignore the on-mountain dining—join Ischgl's regulars for a long lunch break. Recommended stops include the **Alp Trida** in Switzerland for the excellent food and the **Eisbar Gampen** on the Austrian side for the fun.

In Galtür, be sure to eat once at the **Rössle** (ask for the local schnapps), **Landle** and at **Zum Silbertaler**. The **Fluchthorn** also serves hearty fare at reasonable prices.

In Samnaun, try a meal at the **Hotel Post**. It's pricey but one of the best in town.

Après-ski/nightlife

Here Ischgl shines. It has one of the best après-ski scenes from 3–7 p.m., then excellent nightlife from 10 p.m.–2 a.m.

The best après-ski spots include the **Trofana Alm** and the **Kuhstall**, just up from the Silvrettabahn and near from the Post and Goldener Adler, and the **Kitzloch** at the opposite end of town near Hotel Elisabeth and the Fimba and Pardatschgratbahn. These spots rock from about 4–7 p.m., with a disc jockey spinning music, the bar serving half-liter beers and the crowd singing and dancing in ski suits and ski boots. The **Sonne** also has a lively crowd with live bands and dancing.

The three major discos begin to crank at about 10 p.m. or 11 p.m. The **Tenne** in the basement of Hotel Trofana (go to the side door) offers the most crowded venue, with dancing and wild contests alternately competing for attention. The **Pacha** in Hotel Madlein is for a younger crowd and **Posthorndl,** in the basement of Hotel Post, has been decorated like a Gothic dungeon, complete with flickering chandeliers, marble gargoyles, and blue-lit disc jockeys. You'll find yourself wanting to shift with the crowd, depending on which club has the best entertainment. Club Madlein has a €4 cover charge.

Galtür

Almhof and **Alpenromantikhotel Wirlerhof** have lively après-ski at the bottom of the lifts. After skiing the "in" place for action is the **Weiberhimmel**. After dinner most head to the **Pyramide** in the Hotel Luggi, or to one of the other hotel bars.

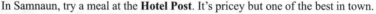

Child care (2003/04 prices)

Child care services are available. Contact the Ischgl Tourist Office (05444-52660) for assistance.

There is a guest kindergarten without ski school at Idalp. The price is €25 a day, and, €15 for a half day. Supervised lunch costs €7.

The Ischgl ski school (05444-5257 or 05444-5404) runs a children's program with lessons for kids 3–5. Costs are €40 amd €25 for a half day. Add €7 for supervised lunch.

The normal children's ski school with lessons for kids 4 and older are €40 for a full day, €100 for three days and €145 for six days. Prices do not vary much between high and low season. Add €7 for supervised lunch.

In Galtür the ski school is open for children 4 and older. It's near the Birkhahn chair lift in Wirl. Children attending ski school can get lunch and after-class supervision for an additional charge. Kindergarten for non-skiing children 3 and older runs from 9:30 a.m.–4:30 p.m. Prices per child with Galtür guest card are €8 for a half day without lunch and €20 with lunch for a full day.

The Galtür ski school has a special children's ski school for skiers 4 years and older. Lessons last four hours a day from 10:00 a.m.–12:00 p.m. and 13:30–15:30 p.m. One day costs €44; three days, €99; five days, €128; and six days, €136.

Other activities

Winter merely enhances rather than disguises the beauty of Galtür, a mountain village some 5,197 feet high. Galtür is the gateway to the Silvretta Alpine Highway, which is open in warm-weather months. If taking photographs of beautiful buildings is one of your hobbies, visit the spired parish church Maria Geburt in Galtür.

A swimming pool has opened in Galtür. Entrance fees for guests staying in Galtür are €6 for adults for three hours, €3.50 for children and €5 for seniors.

In Galtür, the Tennishalle is open from 10:00 a.m.–16:00 p.m. with charges of €16–18.50 per hour and then from 16:00 p.m.–12:00 a.m. Galtür also has Kegelbahnen, an Austrian version of bowling. You save 10 percent with a Galtür guest card.

Landeck, an Alpine crossroads near the entrance to the valley, is a regional shopping center and is distinguished by the towering Fortress Landeck.

As additional excursions, you can travel to Innsbruck and Munich.

Getting there

The nearest international airport is in Munich. From there, the easiest highway route is Garmisch, Fern Pass to Landeck or Innsbruck, and on to Ischgl. The train stops in Landeck served by regular bus service.

Tourist information

Tourismusverband, A-6561 Ischgl, Austria.
Telephone: 05444-5266-0; fax 05444-5636.
Internet: www.ischgl.com. E-mail: info@ischgl.com

Tourismusverband, A-6563 Galtür/Tirol, Austria.
Telephone: 05443-8521, fax 05443-852176.
Internet: www.galtuer.com Email: info@galtuer.com

Kitzbühel and Kirchberg

Framed by rugged mountains, Kitzbühel dates back to the ninth century, when it landed on the map as a copper mining and trading town. With storybook snow-covered scenery, it's hard to believe that skiing is relatively new here. It wasn't until 1892 that skis were first introduced. But the sport rapidly gained popularity, and two years later a large consignment of skis arrived from Norway, paving the slopes for Kitzbühel's first ski championship.

This once quaint village has been growing by leaps and bounds over the past decade. Today it is a real town with benign sprawl, well outside the old limits of the traditional village center. Among the Austrian resorts, Kitzbühel is the most commercial, glamorous and expensive. However, its lift system has not been keeping pace with changes in the rest of the region. Kitzbühel has always been known as a beautiful Alpine town as well as one of the hot spots for après-ski and excellent intermediate skiing. It lives up to its reputation but the skiing suffers from old, very old and slow lifts. On the other hand, the lift company has been spending its money on ambitious snowmaking projects that ensure snow cover throughout the season.

If possible arrive in Kitzbühel before nightfall, when the wrought-iron entranceway lamps and flickering candles in the restaurant windows lend a special charm to the streets. You'll hear the jingle of bells on a horse-drawn sleigh, and in the distance someone in a gasthaus will let out a hearty laugh that rises above the sound of a piano or zither. The exterior of Kitzbühel is old, lovely and quite romantic. The interior is modern and efficient. The atmosphere is bright, boisterous and never dull. In Kitzbühel the skiing day is long enough to tire you out, and it's followed by nightlife that can last forever. This is Austria's winter entertainment capital, with top European performers appearing throughout the season.

In January, during the famed Hahnenkamm Downhill World Cup (usually the middle weekend), Kitzbühel vibrates with action. The streets are filled even at midnight with music and laughter that ripple through the narrow alleyways. This is the perfect time (albeit the most expensive) to be in Kitzbühel.

Kitzbühel is a resort that a vacationer with plenty of pecuniary resources should consider. As at Aspen or Vail, you'll rub shoulders with the rich and famous and be treated like royalty but at about half the cost. This is a town where tour operators can save you a bundle and one that careful planning can make very affordable.

Kirchberg, a smaller town 5 km. to the west, shares the same mountain and has become a major player in the area. Everything here is within easy walking distance. Filled with a younger crowd, attracting families and more dedicated skiers, Kirchberg has some of the wildest après-ski in Austria and somewhat lower prices than its flashier neighbor. The strongest contingent of tourists in Kirchberg comes from Holland. They know how to have a good time and can define the best of wild après-skiers. If you are looking for that touch to a vacation, this is the place.

Mountain layout

If you ski well, Kitzbühel is close to unbeatable. The only hassle is the collection of old lifts that slow down the discovery of the mountain. You can spend all day on its slopes and not use the same lift or ski on the same run twice. There are more than 56 prepared runs across an amazing 150 km. of mountain. This is the site of one of the first ski safaris, where skiers travel 15 km. by lift and descend 35 km. between Kitzbühel and Pass Thurn. It's marked by round signs with an elephant on skis pointing the way. There is a short section in Jochberg where you need to take a bus. Otherwise, the entire route can be made on skis. Start early. The trip takes a full day.

The main area is a north/south ridge that is defined by a pass headed to Pass Thurn strung with the villages of Aurach and Jochberg. The valley defining the eastern side of the area finds Kirchberg and Aschau. There is more skiing on the opposite side of each valley. To the southwest there is the Kitzbühelerhorn that has become a snowboarders mountain. To the east, on the other side of Kirchberg, is the Gaisberg area.

To avoid the longest lift lines from town, drive or take the shuttlebus toward neighboring Kirchberg and take the Fleckalmbahn to the Ehrenbachhöhe above the Hahnenkamm race circuit.

Real experts can always find good skiing just off the marked trails. Some of the best spots are beyond the Pengelstein peak where the Hochsauerkase trail drops to the west and the Schwartzkogel runs to the east. Both provide off-piste possibilities at any point an expert wants to turn his or her skis. The Steinbergkogel bowl is another expert playground with an old single chair and double chair bringing skiers back to the top of the bowl. Trails like Powder Heaven and Direttissima are aptly named with the right snow. Way up the valley the Bärenbadkogel peak has plenty of expert drops where anyone with real skill can pick their own trail down the mountain.

Off the Kitzbühelerhorn, experts can take the Larchenhang then Horn Standard trails from the peak with thousands of off-piste possibilities all along the way. Gaisberg is more of a practice mountain for intermediates and beginners.

Pengelstein is an intermediate peak with short trails dropping to the west and a long trail into Kirchberg dropping to the east. The Kirchberg trail is a good morning sun route.

The best runs are a closely guarded secret. Guides are tight-lipped about where to find good powder and empty runs. For a long uninterrupted slope try the Niedere

Fleckalm, which in the morning is uncrowded and offers a very fast gondola. In the afternoon stick to the Ehrenbachhöhe, which provides a variety of terrain from intermediate to challenging.

Mountain rating

Trail skiing in Kitzbühel and Kirchberg is strictly intermediate with a few black stretches. There are enough smooth, mellow crusing runs for the beginner and lower intermediate to keep harmony in any mixed-skill group.

Experts, except those concentrating on their times down the Hahnenkamm run or the Gaisberg course above Kirchberg, should ski on something more challenging than the prepared runs. Guides can take serious skiers on off-trail expeditions from Kitzbühel or Kirchberg that will delight even the most hardened experts.

Ski school (2003/04 prices)

Group Lessons

Joining a ski group generally costs about €44 per day and is a good way to sharpen your skills if you're out of practice, and a good way to get to know the mountain.

Six ski schools compete for the Kitzbühel vacationer. Ski School Total (72011), Kitzbühler Horn (64454), Egger Hahnenkamm (63177), Ski School Aurach (65804) and Rote Teufel also known as Red Devils (62500) all charge €50–€60 for one day of lessons. Three days are €100–€120. Six days will set you back €130–€135.

Rote Teufel teaches special group and racing schools. One day of racing school is €60 and three days €120. Call Rudi Sailer (62500).

Kirchberg has three ski schools. The largest are Skischule Kirchberg (2209) and Skischule Total (3726). Prices are more or less the same, with full day lessons costing about €44, three-day lessons about €112, and five-day lessons about €120.

Private lessons

One of the best ways to discover the beauty of these mountains while improving your technique is to hire a private guide. Costs vary: most instructors for one to two people cost €150–€160 per day; €105 for a half day.

Snowboarding

The Kitzbühelerhorn has received top ratings from European snowboard magazines. Freestylers, freeriders and alpine snowboarders all have a blast. There is a permanent 450-meter-long boarder cross course with almost 300 feet of vertical and 14 obstacles for competition on Brunellenfeld. They also have an excellent 100-meter long halfpipe.

The Hahnenkamm is also a good area for snowboarders as well as the Pengelstein and beyond to Hieslegg where terrain attracts fewer skiers and remains natural for most of the morning.

The Snowboard Center at the Kitzbühler Horn (2701) rents boards. Snow Fun Centre Hochbrunn at the Hahnenkamm rents boards as well, and also offers Eagel monoskis. Rote Teufel holds special all-inclusive courses in snowboarding, starting at €60 per day. Three full days costs €150.

Kirchberg ski schools have three-day snowboarding lessons for €120 and a snowboard weekly lesson for €150.

Cross-country skiing

Cross country skiers carrying their skis can use the entire Kirchberg/ Kitzbühel bus system without charge. Overall there are 120 km. of cross-country trails in the region. There are four primary trails ranging from easy to difficult and stretching some 36 km. around Kitzbühel. But a short ride on the free ski bus gives you access to more trails in the region, with breathtaking Alpine views far removed from the frenetic pace of the downhill slopes. Kirchberg just purchased new track-setting equipment to keep its trails well groomed. The longest loop, from Kirchberg to the Brixental, is 28 km.

Lift tickets (2003/04 prices)

Kitzbühel offers a variety of lift tickets, including senior citizens' and children's discounts. All passes allow unlimited access to all 56 Kitzbühel area ski lifts, free shuttlebus service between ski areas and swimming in Kitzbühel's Aquarena (even if you're staying in Kirchberg).

High season includes Christmas and New Year weeks to mid-March. Before Christmas and late March on are low seasons.

	High Season	Low Season
one day	€34	€29.50
three days	€91	€79
six days	€160	€139
seven days	€181	€157.50

Children born after 1987 get a discount. Children born after 1997 ski free.

Accommodations

At first blush, Kitzbühel's hotels might easily be mistaken for well-kept farmhouses, with their sloping roofs and white façades. On the inside, however, they are as efficient and elegant as they are clean. We have chosen these places because they speak English and they are in the old town or very close to the Hahnenkamm gondola. Some of the smaller hotels, gasthöfe and apartments do not take credit cards. Ask before it is too late. Many will take a check.

Based on high season, per person/double occupancy with breakfast: €€€—more than €80; €€—€50–79; €—less than €50.

The **Hotel Goldener Greif** (64311, fax 65001; €€€) bills itself as an ancient Tyrolean inn dating back to 1271. However, the property was completely redesigned in 1954 and now features such modern amenities as a casino, sauna, swimming pool, solarium and Turkish steam bath.

With its sliding glass doors and wide-open lobby, the **Sporthotel Reisch** (63366, fax 63291; €€€) is by far the brightest of the Kitzbühel hotels. Also offered is a spa where trained therapists provide massages, facials, treatments and relaxation programs.

At the **Schweizerhof** (62735, fax 6273557; €€€), one of the few ski-in/ski-out inns, guests can also enjoy a full-service spa. Live après-ski entertainment is the order of the day in high season.

Another excellent ski-in/ski-out spot is the **Hotel Rasmushof** (5356 or 65252, fax 6525249; €€€) right at the finish of the Hannenkamm course. This hotel is pure quality and quiet luxury. It is about a hundred steps from the town and all the charm.

The **Hotel Zur Tenne** (64444, fax 6480356; €€€) leaves the guest with the impression of living inside a giant ark, with heavy wood walls and ceilings. Right in the middle of the town, it features some of the nicest antiques, plus a fireplace, sauna and steam rooms.

The stained-glass windows and mounted antlers in the **Tiefenbrunner Hotel** (66680, fax 6668080; €€€) tell a story of its Tyrolean heritage. Paintings and carvings lining the lobby wall narrate the history of this part of Austria.

Schloss Lebenberg (6901, fax 64405; €€€) Live like a king in a converted castle just on the outskirts of the town with all the amenities you could ask for.

Montana (62526, fax 62526155; €€€) Next to the Hahnenkamm. Pool and sauna. Great location, does not take credit cards. Bring your checkbook.

Hotel Ehrenbachhöhe (621510; €€ half board only) has rooms up on the mountain, in the midst of the Hahnenkamm area. If you are here for the skiing, this is a perfect place to be. No credit cards accepted.

Hotel Resch (62294, fax 65006; €€) The hotel has a good location near town and the lifts. Rooms vary in size but all are pretty large, however some have tables and sitting areas.

Eggerwirt (62455, fax 6243722; €€) A find with a great eatery. You'll love it.

Licht (62293, fax 62293-33; €€€) B&B but also has apartments.

These affordable B&Bs have great locations: **Haselburger** (62866, fax 6286614; €), **Rosengarten** (625280, fax 625287; €), **Hochfilzer Gästehaus** (62217, fax 05355/5864; €), **Mühlbergerhof** (62835, fax 64488; €), **Neuhaus** (tel/fax 62200; €).

These apartments are on the slopes and within a few minutes' walk of downtown: **Gisi** (62583, fax 02236/41091; €$, sleeps two to four people, breakfast included), **Maurachbauer** (tel/fax 72358; €€, sleeps up to eight people in a farmhouse), and **Johanna** (64856, fax 640547; €€, sleeps two to four people, breakfast extra).

Kitzbühel has scores of other very affordable B&Bs that are perfect for anyone traveling on a budget. Contact the tourist office for reservations and information.

Ski Chalets: Inghams. (See page 20 for phone, fax and internet addresses.)

Kirchberg

The accommodations here are not as luxurious as the five-stars in Kitzbühel nor as expensive. If traveling with your family, Kirchberg is a perfect place to stay. The clientele is also a bit younger in Kirchberg. (Note: Telephone prefix for Kirchberg is 05357.)

Hotel Alexander (05357/2222, fax 3407; €€€) the top spot in the center of Kirchberg with sauna, steam room, whirlpool, and Internet connections.

Hotel Sonnalp (05357/2741, fax 2741200; €€) has sauna and pool. It is great for families. The long walk back from town after a night out can be daunting.

Hotel Klausen (05357/2128, fax 3612; €€) is outside of town right next to the Fleckalmbahn. It is the perfect for those concentrating on skiing and not partying.

Hotel Metzgerwirt (05357/2325, fax 232549; €€) Solid four-star hotel right in the center of Kirchberg.

Hotel Cordial (05357/28420, fax 2842406; €€€) Good four-star hotel with heated outdoor pool and sauna.

Hotel Seehof (05357/2228; €) Beautifully redone rooms in a three-star hotel, great location. A real bargain.

Gasthof Kirchenwirt (05357/2852, fax 3773; €) Well-run, inexpensive gasthof right in town center with good food. What more can one ask for?

If you want to stay up on the mountain call **Alpengasthof Filzerhof** (05357/2587, fax 258752)

There are scores of B&Bs in Kirchberg with prices in the €18–€33 per night range. Contact the Kirchberg tourist office for more information and for reservations.

Ski Chalets: Crystal, Inghams/Bladon, First Choice. (See page 20 for phone, fax and internet addresses.)

Apartments, condominiums, flats

A list of apartments is available from the Kitzbühel and the Kirchberg tourist office.

A number of pensions allow visitors to rent rooms with kitchens in ski season, but as always, it's best to check with the tourist office.

Read the directory carefully and ask the property for a *Prospekt* or brochure, before deciding where to stay.

Prices per night per person for four people sharing an apartment range from farmhouse inexpensive—about €14 a night in high season—to downtown expensive, €35 a night in the same time period. Apartment prices in Kitzbühel and Kirchberg are about the same.

In most apartments in Europe you will be charged for various services. Meals, cleaning, linen and often utilities can all add up. Ask about what is and isn't included.

Dining

Prices (without wine) €€€—€36+, €€—€16–35, €—€15-.

For the best meals in the area try the following Gault Millau two-toque rated eateries. **Unterberger Stub'n** (66127; €€€) is where the very "in" people gather. This also is where the others such as ourselves wait for a reservation spot to open. **Tennerhof Restaurant** (63181; €€€) gets rave reviews for everything from main courses to avant-garde desserts. **Schwedenkapelle** (65870; €€€), actually closer to Kirchberg near the Fleckalmbahn, is exceptional and has dinner served on Saturday with musical accompaniment.

For an out of the ordinary experience try the candlelight dinner at **Restaurant Hochkitzbühel** (at the top of the Hahnenkamm Gondola; €€€). It is continental gourmet cooking with all the bells and whistles. Disappointingly, though you would expect it, there is no view of the town of Kitzbühel from the restaurant. Take time to enjoy the view on the ride up.

Finally, head to **Lois Stern** (74882; €€), just outside the old town, for creative cooking in an open kitchen where you can watch Lois cook. He is a master of cuisine tending toward Italian and also brings strong influences of Japan to his kitchen. When you have had enough meat, cheese and potatoes, this is a fascinating change.

For those of us who like quantity and traditional meals rather than dining on rarified gourmet creations, check out these spots:

The **Landhäusl** (64007; €€) serves the largest portions in the area. Make reservations! Most tables seat six to eight people, and the staff won't hesitate to seat you next to someone else—not a good idea if you want a romantic dinner for two. Worth recommending: the Wienerschnitzel and Kaiserschmarren, a pancake-style dish. Dinner for two costs about €35. Credit cards accepted.

Locals gravitate toward the **Huberbrau** (65677; €–€€), for Tyrolean specialties as well as standard Austrian fare. Eat early or late to avoid a wait. No credit cards.

Insomniacs should drop by **Zum Zinnkrug** (62613; €–€€) which is the closest thing to an all-night diner. Open all the time and recommended by every local we asked, it serves a good basic Austrian meals and spare ribs and takes credit cards.

Looking for Mexican cuisine? You're in luck; there are two restaurants that dish out tacos and cold Coronas. The most popular is **La Fonda** (73673). Service is slow, but you'll eventually get your chimichangas. Dinner for two costs about €25. Credit cards aren't taken, but there's an automatic teller machine around the corner.

In Kitzbühel, it's pizza, not schnitzel, that seems to be everywhere. Most bars serve small single-size pizzas, but they're not what you might expect—an Austrian pizza has a thinner crust and less topping than its American cousin.

Barique (Hinterstradt 19; 62658) serves an excellent selection of spaghetti dishes, as does **Il Gusto** (Obere Gänsbachgasse 5; 72790). Another recommended Italian spot is **Pizzeria Adria** (Josef Pirchl Str. 17; 65292) near the post office. Dinner for two runs around €30.

On the mountain stop in for lunch or at least a beer and schnapps at the **Seidlalm** where the World Cup races were founded and at **Sonnbergstub'n** where there is a singing chef. Coming to Kirchberg make sure not to miss **Gasthof Maierl** at the top of the Maierl lift. Try the rustic Tyrolean *Blutwurst, Grost'l mit Spiefelei or Kasespätzle mit Röstzwiebel.* Or head to **Gasthof Schroll** for *Kaiserschmarren aus der Pfanne.*

Fine dining just outside Kitzbühel is worth the taxi ride to the nearby towns of Reith and Aurach. In Reith head to **Tischlerwirt** (65416; €€) and feast on meals like deer with blackberry balsamic sauce and desserts such as cherry cake with rum. In Aurach go straight to **Giggling-Stube** (64888; €€) where you will be overjoyed with your meal. Try the creative wild game and lamb dishes.

Heading up the valley in the direction of Pass Thurn in Jochberg try **Bärnbichl-Stube** (Bärenbühelweg 35, Jochberg; 05355/5347; €€) for acclaimed Austrian meals. The Gröst'l and trout are wonderful. This is a great place to stop for lunch while on the ski safari. Also in Jochberg is **Schwarzer Adler** (05355/5215; €€)

In Kirchberg, most group arrangements are for full pension. If you want to go out on the town, one of the best restaurants is the **Pfeffermühle** (05357/2222; €–€€) attached to the Hotel Alexander, that the owner calls Austrian with a touch of Italian. It features a wood-fired pizza oven and its specialty is meat that you grill on a hot stone set in the middle of the table. It's great fun. Cost is between €14–20 depending on the cut of meat.

Geniesserrestaurant Rosengarten (05357/2527; €€), in Hotel Taxacherhof, the award-winning chef Simon Taxacher creates his versions of nouvelle Austrian cuisine and continental gourmet meals. Call for reservations. Candlelight dinner here with a lover is the perfect setup for a great dessert.

For a real traditional experience head to the **Kupferstuben** (05357/2335; €€) where you can fill up very affordably on rustic Tyrolean meals in the perfect atmosphere. Make reservations, it's packed. There is actually an Italian working at the **Nabucco** (05357/35099; €) that serves pizza and pasta. For excellent wild game, try the **Kirchenwirt** (05357/2852; €–€€).

Après-ski/nightlife

What you do in Kitzbühel after skiing is as important as the skiing itself (for some it's even more important). The nightlife should be renamed morning life, because things don't really get underway until 2:00 a.m. or so. That's when you can hear the whoops, yells, laughter and song of bar-crawling skiers as they slide down the sidewalks.

Amazingly, there are only a few bars that cater to the after-hours crowd. Jet-laggers searching for a cold brew and a warm pizza should follow the stairs in the cellar of **Prax-keller** (0664/2410600) open 10 p.m.–2 a.m., "but we really don't close until five or so," says the bartender. Watch out for the darts!

British expatriates can rely on their instincts to find the **Londoner** (71427) and **Big Ben** (71100), two almost authentic pubs. The Londoner is across from McDonald's. You'll find Big Ben if you wander along the town square in the *Fussgängerzone* (pedestrian zone). **s'Lichtl** (63924) is right on the main drag across the street from the Hotel Tenne.

Grieserl (72752) across from the parking lot beneath the Tieffenbrunner is a good meeting spot for drinks and has excellent Internet connections.

There are three discos in the town square area. **Club Take 5** at Hinterstadt 22 (74131), **Olympia** at Hinterstadt 6 (72143), and **Royal** at Hinterstadt 9 (75901) featuring the only English-speaking disc jockey. Generally, discos don't open until 9 p.m., and often close at dawn.

Gambling guests can spin the roulette wheel at Hotel Goldener Grief's **Casino Kitzbühel,** open 7 p.m. until 2 a.m. daily during the regular ski season. Visitors may try their luck at baccarat, blackjack, wheel of fortune, red dog, poker and slot machines.

Kirchberg is one of the party centers of Austria with a strong Dutch contingent of party animals. It claims perhaps the wildest après-ski bar in Europe, **The London Pub**. This bar has been copied in other towns, but none is as exciting as the original. It's dance-til-you-melt, dance-on-the-tables time from about 4 p.m.–8 p.m., when most head off to dine in their hotels. This is the wild après-ski party you've dreamed of. If you haven't tried it yet knock back a couple of "Der Flugels," a drink made with Red Bull and flavored vodka. It has a real kick and is the new drink of choice.

Later at night the party continues there or moves to the **Tiroler** that is decorated like a giant country barn. Or head to the **Fuchslöchl** for dancing. The party seems to shift locations each night, but Kirchberg is small enough to make it easy to check out the action and then head back to where everyone's hanging out.

Child care (2003/04 prices)

The Kitzbühel tourist office (62155-0 or 62272) keeps a list of licensed, multilingual babysitters. Ski schools also offer full-day lessons for ski kindergarten for kids from ages two-and-a-half to five.

Anita Halder (75063), a nurse, also watches children for an hourly charge.

In Kirchberg there is the **Krabbelstube** (4255), a kindergarten for children from infant to 6 years old, open Monday to Friday, 7:15 a.m.–6 p.m. and Saturdays from 7:15 a.m.–24:00 p.m.. Prices are €18 for a half day and €34 for a full day. Babysitting service is available through the tourist office. The ski school in Kirchberg also has special children's programs. Rates are the same as for the normal ski school, with an additional €7 for lunch. The **Children's Mini Club Total** has care for about €22 for a half day and about €36.50 for a full day.

Other activities

The Aquarena (64385) is the indoor sports area, with a **swimming pool**, **sauna**, **steamroom** and **solarium**. Admission is €6 for adults, €3.50 for children.

Tandem-Flights-Kitzbühel (67194) offers **parasailing** flights. Basic courses run from €400–€450. Clinics cost about €75 per day. Or contact Hermanns Flugschule (0664/4644661) where trial flights cost €60 and the basic course costs €455.

For **balloon trips** call Balloning Tyrol in St. Johann (05352/5666). Balloon flights cost €291 for about 2 hours.

You can go **ice skating** at Schwarzesee or at the Lebenberg rink—Adults pay €4.50; children pay €2.20.

Horse-drawn sleigh rides are available through Henntalhof at Unterbrunnweg 21, (64624) for €44 per hour, and one sleigh can seat up to five people. Rides are also offered by Eberl Hubert at Innerstaudach 58 (37242). Carriages seat up to five people and cost €44.

Kirchberg has a 4 km.-long **rodelbahn** that stays open until 10 p.m. With your ski pass the cost is about €4.50 for adults and €2.25 for children. The Gaisberg lift takes you up and you slide down. After drinks the steep trail takes on an added challenge. There is a gasthof at the top and one in the middle of the run that serve libations to lubricate the runners.

Getting there

The most common route to Kitzbühel and Kirchberg is via Munich. Innsbruck and Salzburg are also popular arrival points. Although train service is available, many prefer the 3-1/2 hour drive from Munich in a rental car. Express trains shave about an hour off your travel time and leave twice a day. Round-trip tickets are about €52 from Munich, €38 from Salzburg, and €22 from Innsbruck.

Tourist information

Kitzbühel-Reith-Aurach Tourism, A-6370 Kitzbühel, Austria; Telephone 05356/62155-0, fax 05356/62307.
Internet: www.kitzbuehel.com. E-mail: info@kitzbuehel.com.

Toursimusverband Kirchberg, Hauptstrasse 8, A-6365 Kirchberg, Austria; Telephone 05357-2309, fax 05357-3732.
Internet: www.kirchberg.at. E-mail: info@kirchberg.at.

Mayrhofen

Hintertux and Tuxertal in the upper Zillertal

Mayrhofen is one of the most beautifully situated resorts in Austria. The towering mountains seem to surround the town as you drive up the wide valley. This is not a place one would happen upon by accident and comment, "This would be nice to come back and visit." The only villages further up the mountain pass lead to dead-end glaciers. If you arrive in Mayrhofen, you probably want to be there. The locals will surely do their best to keep you in their valley.

The village, about a 15-minute walk across, could be a Hollywood set. The church steeple towers over wooden façades and balconies on whitewashed mountain houses. Konditorei display tempting pastries; the latest Tyrolean fashions—still harking back to tradition—fill dress shop windows, bakeries emit mouthwatering smells of fresh bread, dogs chase each other, restaurant candles glisten through hazy windows and hearty laughter echoes from gasthausen.

The road south to Hintertux rises steeply through narrow gaps in the mountains. After passing through ten-kilometer-long Tuxertal (connected by lifts with Mayrhofen) you'll reach the Hintertuxer Glacier— isolated at the end of the road. This glacier provides year-round skiing laced with one of Europe's most modern ski lift systems.

Five main ski regions are connected to Mayrhofen—Penken, Finkenberg, Horberg/Gerent, Rastkogel and Eggalm. They tend to keep their snow longer than most Austrian resorts because of their altitude (about 5,900 to 8,200 feet). However little of the skiable snow reaches down to the town of Mayrhofen lying at an altitude of only 2,067 feet above sea level. This is a resort where the ski runs are high above the town and skiers normally come back to town by the gondolas or by bus from one of the outlying higher-altitude villages.

English is spoken by most natives, but most visitors to Mayrhofen originate from Germany and the Netherlands, with a strong contingent of Brits and Australians and an occasional American.

In February, Austria is Mayrhofen's biggest customer, offering a steady flow of visitors on holiday. Check before making vacation plans so you don't hit a busy week.

The other villages of the Tuxertal, the next valley up the mountain road on the way to the Hintertuxer glacier, are all cute but without the amenities offered by Mayrhofen. Finkenberg hugs the steep road connecting Mayrhofen with the Tuxertal. Finkenberg is a town of up and down walking in order to get anywhere.

Of the villages in Tuxertal, Lanersbach is the largest and provides some village atmosphere. If you blink, you will miss Juns and Madseit. Hintertux is far up in the Tuxertal Valley at the base of one of the best glaciers for summer skiing. It makes no pretense of being anything but a glacier ski resort. If it had sidewalks, they would be rolled up when the lifts close. However there are good restaurants and some good bars at the base of the lifts and in the nearby town.

Mountain layout

This area has some of the most modern lifts in Austria. Considering that many feel Austria is the last bastion of T-bars, virtually all of Mayrhofen can be skied using only chair lifts, gondolas and the cable car. These lifts and the entire new mountain faces that they open change everything. The story is only beginning to be written about where the best spots to ski will be. Much of the new terrain is unexplored except by backcountry skiers.

The Ahorn sector has been relegated to beginners and lower intermediates though there can be some good skiing there. Plus, from Ahorn, skiers can drop right back into town because of good snowmaking on the lower sections. However the ski-lift company has concentrated its efforts on new lifts in the higher areas across the valley. You might call Ahorn T-bar city. There is nothing wrong with that, but some folks want chair lifts.

From Mayrhofen, you will access the main ski area by either the Penkenbahn or the Horbergbahn. Both are high-speed gondolas. Both are connected with all hotels in the town by a shuttlebus plying the route every 15 minutes during the winter.

Once at the top of the Penken those interested in the childrens' center and beginner lesson only have to step off the lift. Those looking for more challenge should head over to the Penken-Express, a six-seater high-speed lift. At the top of the Penken-Express, a snowfield of intermediate and advanced intermediate terrain opens to skiing. Beginners can swing to their left to avoid the steeper sections dropping back to the top station of the gondola. From the top of the Penken-Express, skiers can head toward Gerent by dropping down to the top of the Horbergbahn where lifts rise to serve the wide-open, off-piste, powder-filled terrain of the Gerent.

Further up the Horberg Hallow a group of lifts all meet. From here a 150-person cable car serves more wide-open skiing from an altitude of about 7,217 feet. This is expert delight country and wide open enough for intermediates to push themselves and still be able to get out of trouble.

From the top of the cable car, skiers can drop into the Tuxertal to the Rastkogel and Eggalm areas. They return to the ridge by taking the Rastkogelbahn and then another six-person high-speed chair lift. Then ski into the Hofberg/Gerent area to return to Mayrhofen. Or take the bus back down to Mayrhofen.

Hintertux and the Tuxertal

Tuxertal is made up of the Rastkogel and Eggalm areas. Both are excellent beginner and intermediate areas with plenty of off-piste for experts. Both of these areas now connect with the main Mayrhofen ski areas.

The Hintertuxer glacier opens at the end of the valley rising from 4,921 feet to top out at 10,564 feet—that's an amazing 5,443 feet of vertical. This is one of the top training areas for ski and snowboard teams from all over the world. From the ground station you can see most of the nearly 50 miles of trails above. The lift system is superb and the small mountain huts on the runs are great fun.

The best run is the trail from the Grosser Kaserer (10,700 feet) down over a great steep field of bumps to the gondola. A nice intermediate run leads from the top of the Gefrorene Wand to the Spannagel house, a cozy Alpine hut serving excellent food.

Mountain rating

This is a region that has something for everyone. Experts will delight in the Horberg/Gerent area. They have an enormous area to explore and enjoy.

Intermediates have Eggalm and Raskogel in the Tuxertal that are a blast and the Penken is a phenomenal intermediate area with super fast lifts. Intermediates can also head over to the Horberg/Gerent area where the slopes are wide open and they have plenty of room to test themselves but can get out of trouble.

Beginners have the benefit of one of the best ski schools in Austria. They have excellent learning areas at the top of the Penkenbahn and at the Penkenjoch, the top of the Finkenberger Almbahn.

For snow reports, call 62373.

Snowboarding

This is becoming a real destination for snowboarders. The resort caters to them with great snowparks and the new lift system makes the hassle of T-bars a thing of the past. Austria's top free riders come here to hang and hundreds of boarders attend summer boarding camps held on the glacier, but they stay in Mayrhofen.

The area has wide-open above-treeline snow that drops into tight trees offering plenty of challenge.

Penken has a series of snowboard jumps and a fun park. The fun park has four riding lines, backside and frontside hips, spines, rollers, tabletop jumps and a megaspine, as well as a triplekicker tabletop with a 100-foot landing area. There is also a 492-foot long halfpipe, that's almost two football fields long.

Ski school (2003/04 prices)

There are three ski schools in Mayrhofen with over 150 instructors to teach all grades of skiers. The Austrian ski method is used on all courses.

Group Lessons

Prices are uniform, and competition for the skier is tight.

Regardless of the school you select, you'll pay €49 for one day of lessons, €107 for three days. Six days will amount to €120.

Children's lessons are slightly less and include lunch. The schools are: Ski School Manfred Gager (63800), Ski School Mayrhofen Total (63939), and Peter Habeler Ski and Alpine School (62829). Most ski schools offer rentals.

Private Lessons

Mayrhofen's private lessons for one or two students cost €40 for one hour from noon–1 p.m.; €90 for two hours from 10 a.m.–noon or 1–3 p.m.; and €160 for four hours. Each additional person costs €20.

Snowboarding

Again, prices seem to vary little from school to school. Classes cost €33 a day; €80 for three days; €112 for five days. A great way to learn and save money is with friends. Some four-hour private lessons cost €150–€165 (one or two students) and €175–€215 (three or four students). Your choices: Mayrhofen Total (63939) and Peter Habeler Ski & Alpine School (62829) and Manfred Gager (63800).

Cross-country

If you left your cross-country equipment at home, don't worry. Rentals are less expensive than downhill equipment—€10 to €15 per day, depending on the store. Weekly discounts are always available.

Mayrhofen offers nine trails for a total of 20 km. All trails are rated easy, making this an ideal place to learn. Overall, cross-country opportunities are not really outstanding, though, especially for the more advanced. There can be a problem with snow cover at the low altitude. We suggest that cross-country skiers take the bus up to Tuxertal and cross-country ski on those trails. They normally have more snow cover.

Cross-country lessons generally cost the same as downhill instruction, and are usually offered privately. Your choices: Ski School Manfred Gager (63800), Ski School Mayrhofen Total (63939), and Peter Habeler Ski and Alpine School (62829).

Lift tickets (2003/04 prices)

Buying a lift ticket can be a perplexing task. Mayrhofen sells a variety of passes with a complex price structure. Want to ski exclusively at Mayrhofen, or at all 154 Ziller Valley lifts? Tickets for each individual resort are available, as well as for the regional Zillertaler-Superskipass. With the connection of Mayrhofen and Tuxertal, there is more than enough skiing for a week.

Mayrhofen/Tuxertal area lifts

half day (starting at 11 a.m.)	€28
one day	€32
two days	€60
three days	€87

Zillertaler–Superskipass

	With Glacierlift	No Glacierlift
four days	€117	€114
six days	€163	€155
seven days	€183	€175

Youths (age 14–18) get a 20% discount. Children 13 and younger get a 40% discount.

Accommodations

When considering an appropriate hotel or apartment in Mayrhofen, keep a few points in mind. First, the number of stars on a property only means you'll pay more, and not always get more. Second, price is dictated less by proximity to lifts than by which bank of the Ziller river it sits on. Cross the bridge to the west bank and you'll pay less—not just for lodging but food and drink as well. Third, for peace and quiet at night, avoid the route between Scotland Yard Pub, the Ice Bar and Nikki's. Revellers wander between the bars, then stagger and sing later in the night.

We made our selections based on whether the hotelier speaks Engish, amenities and then location, taking the above into account.

Telephone prefix: 05285

Based on high season, per person/double occupancy with breakfast: €€€—more than €80; €€—€50–79; €—less than €50.

American visitors usually prefer the **Hotel Neuhaus** (6703; €€). Guests are treated to authentic Alpine motif lobbies, with nicely furnished rooms and an indoor pool. Visitors may watch a movie, go bowling, shoot pool or get a massage in the spa.

The **Hotel Zillertaler Hof** (62265; €–€€), a quiet and modern property, also features an indoor pool. With its venerable antiques and wood carvings on display, this inn emanates style. Rates don't reflect the impressive list of amenities.

For a little extra room, try the **Hotel Neue Post** (62131; €), with its airy, tastefully decorated lobby and generous-sized rooms. One of Mayrhofen's earliest guest houses, it was recently remodeled and now includes sauna, whirlpools, solarium, extensive restaurants and dining rooms.

Hotel St. Georg (627920, fax 62792406; €€–€€€) has an indoor pool, and excellent rooms.

Apparthotel König (62235, fax 620665; €) is a good place to check out if you are traveling with four or five friends.

Prem (62218, fax 63741; €) a B&B tucked away a minute from the center.

Pension Austria (62647, fax 6264711; €) is another inexpensive cozy place about 100 yards from the town center and the Pengenbahn.

If you want to be in the middle of the après-ski action head to one of these spots.

Want lots of antiques? The **Hotel Strass** (6705; €€) prides itself in its historic furniture and decorations. But its prices are very up-to-date. Three other properties are also owned by the same family: **Sporthotel Strass, Villa/Aparthotel Strass** and **Hotel Garni Strass**. These are at the epicenter of the Ice Bar and Arena Disco.

Across the Ziller River is the **Gasthof Brücke** (62232; €), which is also a big après-ski attraction. It has a nice lobby, medium-size rooms with antique furniture and beautiful tiled floors. The Gasthof plays host to a decidedly younger crowd. Many skiers take a short stroll from here to the town's only outdoor watering hole, Nikki Shirhbar.

Hintertux has several hotels right at the base of the glacier. If you're intent on skiing and little else, they're a good choice. Contact the Tux tourist board (A-6293 Tux-Lanersbach 472; 5287-8506, fax 05287-8508) for more information.

Hotel Rindererhof (05287-501, fax 50210; €€–€€€). Excellent location right at the gondola going up to the glacier. Superb for the enthusiastic skier.

Hotel Neu Hintertux (05287-318, fax 318409; €€€). Almost as close to the lifts as the Rindererhof but more luxurious with swimming pool.

Badhotel Kirchler (05287-312; €€€). Beautiful, expensive and comfortable.

Pension Rosengarten (05287-87413, fax same; €€). A comfortable, medium-priced spot in Lanersbach.

Apartments, condominiums, flats

As elsewhere, the quality of apartments varies in Mayrhofen. Some double as hotels in peak season and offer a long list of amenities; others are simple rooms, with little else. Usually, the farther from town they are, the less you'll pay, though you'll find exceptions.

The Ziller River remains an important natural boundary—on the west bank the cost of a room drops.

Prices vary dramatically. Some properties will charge €15 in peak season for a no-frills room, while others ask for €50 per night.

A directory of apartments is available from the Mayrhofen tourist office.

Dining

Mayrhofen is not one of the dining meccas of Austria. The restaurants, though not gourmet, are excellent and many of them exude Austrian charm filled with wood paneling and lined with antlers, and the prices are not stratopheric. Note: Do not assume that Austrian restaurants take credit cards—many do not. Check before you dine or carry lots of cash. Where we know the establishment takes cards, we let you know.

Prices (without wine) €€€—€36+, €€—€16–35, €—€15-.

Wirtshaus zum Griena (62778; €€) is the most authentic Tyrolean restaurant in town. Come here for all the specialties. It is a bit out of town across the river.

If you're looking for a romantic dining spot with real Austrian cuisine, try the **Hotel Neuhaus Restaurant** (6703; €€). Be sure to make early reservations to get into one of the small Stube, a dining area with wonderful ambiance. Credit cards accepted.

Neue Post (62131; €€), next door to the Neuhaus, has a series of very cozy and romantic Stuben (small dining areas) and the cooking is almost as good as the Neuhaus.

Andrea (62601; €€) serves excellent Austrian meals as well as Italian.

Zillergrund (62377; €–€€) gets good reviews from the locals, but you will need a car or have to take a taxi. It's worth the ride.

Another good Austrian restaurant is **Karlsteg** (05286/5250; €€) but it also requires a taxi or a car.

Ländenhof (63451; €–€€) is a family-run Austrian place.

The **Grillküchl** (36126; €) is a small, cozy restaurant with only about five tables. The kitchen is open and prices certainly don't match the rich and intricate wood decor. Show up early to get a table. No credit cards.

The most controversial and garish building in town, where pronounced pastels decorate the circular edifice, is home to the **Cafe Rundum** (63737; €). It serves light meals and desserts. No credit cards. Afterwards you can move downstairs to the **Trödlkeller** for drinks.

Mamma Mia (6768; €) in the Hotel Elisabeth serves good pizza and pasta.

At the **Fleishhauerei** (literally: The Butcher Shop; €), just across the river along the Ahornstrasse, patrons may order a decent Spätzle, an Austrian pasta specialty with cheese, or any number of native meat dishes. During the evening, witness locals wagering their Euros on card games, which can be more entertaining to watch than play. No credit cards.

The **Singapore Restaurant** (63912; €) dishes out authentic hot and sour soup and flavorful main courses that will jump-start your taste buds. Credit cards welcome.

On the slopes Mayrhofen has excellent restaurants as well. Two that are good for having lunch with non-skiers are **Bergrast** (easy to get to for non-skiers) and **Gschosswandhaus** (about a ten-minute walk). Otherwise take your choice of dozens. **Vronis Skialm** is packed and noisy. **Schneekar** is hard to miss—it is a wooden pyramid. **Gschossalm** is a stopping place for schnapps on the way home and a favorite of the local ski instructors. **Sunalm** has a great sun deck when skiing in the spring. **Grillhofalm** serves fresh pizza. It's a favorite of snowboarders, right next to the fun park and snowboard jumps. Crowds gather to oooh and aaaah, and cheer and jeer about jump attempts.

Cafés are a part of life in Austria. The best in town is **Café Kostner** on the Hauptstrasse. It is in the Viennese style and gets rave reviews by the Austrian coffee and pastry critics.

Telephone prefix: 05285

Après-ski/nightlife

Most bars get hopping about an hour before the lifts close. They are packed till around 7 p.m. or 10 p.m. when everyone seems to leave to eat. Discos open around 10 p.m. and usually close at 4 a.m. on the dot.

Après-ski is wild in Austria and Mayrhofen is considered a champ at après-ski by some. **The Ice Bar** and **Nikki's Schirmbar** are the two places to be for skiers right after coming off the slopes. **The Ice Bar** claims to serve more Grolsch beer than any other bar in Europe. At **Nikki's Schirmbar**, an outdoor watering hole with loud music, expect to see skiers dancing on tables in their boots. At Nikki's, just across the river along Ahornstrasse, the fun starts around 3:30 p.m. If you're looking for a specialty drink, avoid the main bar (under the umbrella) and head to the side bar where Schnapps Shots (say that three times fast) in edible wafer shot-glasses are prepared for around €1. Don't forget the napkin!

Snowboarders congregate at **Scotland Yard** (Scotti to the locals). This is a British-style pub complete with an operating British phone booth. The selection of on-tap beers is extensive. It gets packed. Later in the evening many of the snowboarders wander down to the **Apropos Bar.**

If looking for something a bit more sedate, head to **Mo's Esscafé & Musikroom** right on the main drag, or try the **Happy End** that serves good wines.

There are two discos in town -- the **Sports Arena Disco** (6705) and **Schlüsselalm** (62232). Cover charges can vary from €1–€1.50.

Sporthotel Strass (6705) serves more reasonably priced drinks and features excellent après-ski entertainment. The crowd packs the inside and outdoor bars. It's a madhouse. After 9:30 p.m. it gets unbelievably crowded, even on weekdays.

In Hintertux, try the **Batzenkeller**, the **Almbar**, the **Nostalschi Bar** in the Hotel Berghof, or the **Papperla-Pub**.

Child care [2003/04 prices]

This is an area of resort expertise where Mayrhofen excels. Ski schools provide day care and ski instruction for children.

Approximate ski school cost without lunch is €49 for one day; for two days, €88; for three days, €107; and for six days, €120. Lunch costs €10. The ski school also takes children from age 2 for the same rates as the group lessons.

Mayrhofen's Guest Kindergarten, called **Wuppy's Kinderland,** takes children from 3 months to seven years of age. It is open Monday–Friday from 9 a.m.–5 p.m. Price for a full day of supervision is €26, and for six consecutive days, €121. Lunch costs €4 per day. The kindergarten also hires out strollers, prams, and cots for children. It has a swimming pool, nursery school facilities and other activities. Private babysitters are also available.

The Mayrhofen Tourist Office (6760) provides a babysitting referral service. They also publish a directory of services, which includes information about child care.

Other activities

Mayrhofen has an excellent indoor **swimming pool** and an **ice skating rink**. Skating is approximately €3 per hour for adults and €2.50 per hour for youths (age 16–19) and €2 for those age 15 and younger. **Tobogganing** is the extracurricular activity of choice here, perhaps because it includes heavy drinking. Sledders hitch a ride to the Tuxer Valley in a motorcoach and ascend to the top of a 6-km. run at the Höllenstein Hütte (which appropriately means the hut built on hell's stone). There, they imbibe mulled wine before zipping down the mountain. For more information, call Action Club Zillertal at 62977. Cost is €25 per person.

Snowtubing is another enjoyable alternative to skiing. Again, drinking is recommended for adults. You bounce down the slope on inner tubes. Call Action Club Zillertal at 62977. Cost is €25 per hour.

Skiers who feel a little *lebensmüde* (tired of life) can try heart-stopping **flights** over the Zillertal. About €65 will get you airborne. Three operators provide the tours.

Getting there

Mayrhofen is nestled in the Ziller valley, about 190 km. from Munich and 170 km. from Salzburg. Rail connections are available, but the most popular way of getting to Mayrhofen is by bus or car. Since the train operates on a single small track, and direct rail service is not available from either airport, passengers must switch to a train or bus at Jenbach. For more information on rail or bus connections, call the Mayrhofen train station at 62362.

Tourist information

The Mayrhofen Tourism is located at the Europahaus in Mayrhofen, Dursterstrasse 225, Postfach 21, A-6290 Mayrhofen, Austria; (05285) 6760, fax (05285) 676033.
E-mail: info@mayrhofen.at
Web site: www.mayrhofen.at or tiscover.com/mayrhofen

Oetztal

Sölden, Hochsölden, Obergurgl, Hochgurgl

If it's great skiing you want with unforgettable scenery, the Oetztal is in a class with only a handful of European ski valleys. The tall, jagged mountains are an effective barrier to severe weather, and help preserve good snow conditions during the end of the year. To the south, across a road passable only in summer, lies Italy. To the north a winding road spills out of the Oetz Valley after numerous tunnels and bridges.

With the possible exception of a few warm weeks in August and September, these mountains are always skiable. When the snow disappears in the lower elevations, vacationers ascend to the glacier and ride its eternally frozen runs.

The two main resorts in respective valleys are Sölden and Obergurgl. Hochsölden is a suburb of Sölden, huddled above the larger town, and Hochgurgl is merely a cluster of six hotels up the mountain from Obergurgl.

Sölden is stretched along the main road that traverses the valley. The road is bustling with foot and auto traffic, but gives visitors easy access to all services such as rentals, restaurants, nightlife and lifts. This energetic resort provides the on-the-go traveler with endless skiing, a snow guarantee, entertainment and culinary options. In contrast, the smaller villages of Hochsölden, Zweiselstein and Vent are quiet bedroom hamlets sporting excellent hotels and restaurants.

Obergurgl and Hochgurgl are both a 15-minute drive back into the mountains from Sölden. Obergurgl is a picture-perfect Alpine town tucked into the mountains, complete with old church steeple and picturesque hotels. Another village, Untergurgl, is even smaller and less expensive with its own rural charm, but not within walking distance of lifts; however, it is adjacent to one of the main cross-country systems.

Obergurgl is, unlike Sölden, virtually traffic-free. It has a tradition of serving British clientele. You will quickly realize you are in a true Austrian village where time-tested tradition reigns. The smaller dorf of Hochgurgl is a clutch of remote, excellent hotels clinging to the side of steep slopes.

Mountain layout

Sölden

Let's look first at the ski slopes above Sölden. They are split into three areas—the Giggijoch-Hochsölden, the Gaislachkogl and Golden Gate to the glacier. The skiing overall is wide open. Though there are trails marked on the map, with good snow, you can ski virtually anywhere, which makes Sölden a favorite of powderhounds and means plenty of skiing above the treeline. The area lends itself to various levels of intermediate with some expert off-piste runs thrown in for good measure. In fact, an adventurous expert will have no trouble keeping busy above Sölden and in the Obergurgl/Hochgurgl areas. Beginners will be limited in their choice of trails.

Access to the slopes is either by cable car at the the Giggijoch station, at the north end of Sölden, or by gondola at the Gaislachkoglbahn station, at the south end of town. The cable car ascends past Hochsölden and up to the Giggijoch Bergstation. This contemporary top station is also host to five lifts that fan out into a wide bowl. The difficulty ranges from corduroy groomed beginner to off-piste expert trails.

Great fun for a day of skiing and riding is to start at the Giggijoch area and traverse over to the Gaislachkogl summit. This intermediate to expert terrain is a wonderful adventure guaranteed to fulfill your wildest dreams about skiing and riding in the Alps. For a delicious hearty stew or to quench your thirst, stop at the Gampealm on trail 11. This Alpine hut is always hopping with fun and excitement.

The Gratlift and Stabele doublechairs, halfway up the Gaislachkogl summit, access a wonderful variety of intermediate trails and tons of off-piste riding and skiing.

The trails off of the Gaislachkogl summit are narrow and the sides of the trails drop off to nowhere, making this solid intermediate terrain. However, because the ultra-modern Gaislachkogl gondola carries both up and downhill traffic, even beginners can enjoy the views from one of the highest peaks in the Alps. On a clear day you can see the highest peak in Italy and, just a few kilometers from where you're staying, the famous site where the 5,000-year-old frozen body of Oetzi, known to some as the Iceman, was discovered several years ago.

Though the Austrians are meticulous groomers, there are ravines everywhere sporting headwalls with enough powder to make any rider or expert happy. Areas of special note are off the Langegg six-passenger lift, as well as the off-piste runs off of the Rosskirplbahn quad. Snowboarding is extremely popular in the Oetztal. A new boarders'park has been created to international standards at the Giggijoch. It includes a halfpipe, bordercross, quarterpipe high jump, rails, diamonds, half-diamonds, fried egg, fun-box spins and jumps.

Obergurgl and Hochgurgl

The skiing above Obergurgl and Hochgurgl is more extensive than Sölden, and thanks to a recently added lift, skiers can cruise down from Hochgurgl to Obergurgl, and ride back up to the Hochgurgl trails. The slopes are not particularly difficult, but more challenging than those in Sölden. Above Obergurgl, the Festkogl lift opens to a wide face with unlimited intermediate skiing. Experts can drop to the right-hand side of the lift and take the unprepared run through the Ferwaltal back to the lower lift station. This area is high (6,369 to 10,015 feet) with good, crisp snow. For a change, traverse over to the Hohe Mut area, which has a good unprepared run from the Hohe Mut Restaurant and a group of shorter lifts and runs.

Hochgurgl is reached by bus, if you aren't staying there. This town has developed into a relatively upscale community anchored by one of the best luxury Alpine hotels

Telephone prefix: Sölden, Hochsölden, Vent 05254;
Hochgurgl and Obergurgl 05256

in Europe, the Hotel Hochgurgl. Lifts peak out at 10,170 feet, where a mountain restaurant provides spectacular views. The skiing for experts is down the Königstal; for beginners in the center of the area; for intermediates under the Kirchenkarlift. Like Obergurgl, this area is perfect for continuous off-piste cruising.

Both Obergurgl and Hochgurgl have good beginner slopes.

If you want to concentrate on cross-country skiing, choose another area. Some trails exist, but not the network you'll need to ensure variety.

One last hot tip: ski on Saturday. German visitors, like clockwork, consistently and predictably use Saturday as a travel day and leave the slopes practically abandoned.

Mountain rating

With a few exceptions, particularly from the Gaislachkogl, these runs are for intermediates. Some contributors have rated every marked run some variation of intermediate.

There are enough training areas at the bottom for ski schools. The beginner has plenty of terrain, especially in the center of the Giggijoch/Hochsölden sector, to ski.

Experts looking for wild steeps in the Oetztal and diving into the off-piste will find a dream come true. In summer, when skiing is a real luxury, this is one of Europe's finest areas.

Slopes are well-marked and considerably wider than at other Austrian resorts.

The Gurgls offer wonderful above-treeline skiing where if you see it, you can ski it. There is skiing for every level of skier. Beginners have plenty of room and experts can look for wide open spaces but without much extreme challenge.

Ski school (2003/04 prices)

There are three ski schools in Sölden and Hochsölden with about 320 instructors.

Group Lessons

A day of lessons is approximately €46, €103 for three days. The weekly charge is about €150. Children's lessons are slightly less but include lunch. The schools are Sölden-HochSölden Ski School (2364), Yellow Power (tel. 2203-500) and Total Vacancia (tel. 3100).

Private Lessons

One of the best ways to tour the Oetztal is to hire a private ski guide.

Instructors are also more knowledgeable about the best off-piste skiing, which can only mean one thing— powder, powder, powder!

As elsewhere, the more people to join your private group, the less you'll end up paying. A private lesson for two people, for instance, costs about €170, but for each additional person, add around €25.

Snowboarding

Classes cost €50–52 for a day and €152–173 for six days. Private lessons (one to three people) cost €105 for two hours or €160 for four hours.

Above in the **Gurgls,** there is a ski school associated with each of the towns.

The Obergurgl Skischule (tel. 05256-6305) has about 85 instructors and is considered on of Austria's best. **Group lessons** cost €50 for a full day, €120 for three days, and €155 for five days. There is no significant reduction for children. **Private lessons** for one or two skiers are provided by half day (two hours) or full day (four hours). Expect to pay approximately €180 per day when signing up for three days of lessons and then discounts start to kick in of about €8 per day. Additional skiers will add €12 per day to the rates. Half-day rates are about €110 per two-hour session.

Obergurgl snowboard lessons cost €58 for a day, and €140 for three days of lessons. Cross-country lessons are €29 per half day for groups of at least five skiers.

The Hochgurgl Skischule (tel. 05256-6265) is much smaller with just over a dozen instructors. Its reputation is not as polished nor its courses as organized. Group lessons cost about €50 for a full day, €120 for three days, and €155 for five days.

Lift tickets [2003/04 prices]

Sölden/Hochsölden

Because the Sölden is a year-round ski area, a variety of passes and tickets are sold. The rate schedule can seem even more confusing than a lift map. High season includes the Christmas/New Year period and February through early April. Middle season is for the last three weeks of January. If you want to ski more than three days, bring a photograph for identification purposes in both the Söldens and the Gurgls. These are Solden's high-season rates; low-season rates are about 10 percent less.

	Adults	**Children (8–14)**	**Youth (15-19)**
one day	€57	€23	€28
three days	€100	€57	€70
six days	€178	€97	€125
fourteen days	€308	€148	€220

Seniors (men older than 65 and women older than 60) pay about €9 less per lift ticket than normal adults. Children younger than 8 years old ski for €1 per day.

Skiers may also buy a Rettungskarte (mountain patrol card) for about €10. If you get lost and require assistance from the patrol, or if you're injured in an accident, the card acts as insurance. Without the card, the charge is €110 or more.

The Gurgls (high season)

	Adults	**Children (8-16)**
half-day (from noon)	€30	€19
one day	€37	€24
three days	€103	€63
six days	€180	€107
fourteen days	€314	€195

Seniors older than 60 years of age are charged the same rate as children.

Cross-country skiing

There is a 16-km. loop around the Sölden region. However, 50 km. of tracks are accessible via the cross-country ski bus to Langenfeld. Rentals are available at all sport shops in the area. The daily charge for rentals is €10–25 per day, depending on the store. Weekly discounts are always available.

The Sölden-Hochsölden Ski School (2364) offers cross-country and telemark instruction for about the same prices as downhill lessons.

Obergurgl, Hochgurgl and Untergurgl have 12 k.m. of cross-country tracks near each village. Hochgurgl is pretty much for downhillers and snowboarders.

Accommodations

The prices are per person, with breakfast, based on double occupancy. €€€=more than €80; €€=€50–79; €=less than €50.

The most lavish and beautifully decorated hotel in Sölden is the

Telephone prefix: Sölden, Hochsölden, Vent 05254;
Hochgurgl and Obergurgl 05256

Central Hotel (22600, fax 2260511; €€€)—a true five-star in every sense of the word. Even its pool is a cut above anything else in Austria. With Roman architecture, tall ceilings and classic paintings, it is unlike any winter resort on earth.

One of the newer hotels in town is the **Sonnenhaus Tamara** (5040, fax 50460; €€–€€€) which offers what may be the friendliest concierge service in Sölden. The furniture is new but the antiques are real.

At the **Hotel Liebe Sonne** (22030, fax 2423; €€–€€€), modern mixes with the old. A large rock fountain, marble floors and modern art combine with minimalist furniture. Apartments are available. They have their own ski school.

Hotel Erhart (2020, fax 20205; €€–€€€) A four-star with great restaurant. Franz, the owner and generous host, features ski safari and dinner/toboggan ride to entertain guests. The ski safari starts with schnapps and then skiing. Guests are grouped by skiing ability. On Thursday nights Franz takes the guests up the mountain to a hut for dinner and a toboggan ride down. Offers both vegetarian and children's menu, beautiful wine cellar, sauna, and ski room. This newly renovated hotel is a 5-10 minute walk to the Gaislachkoglbahn Talstation.

Hotel am Hof (2241, fax 2121111; €€–€€€) This hotel has rustic post-and-beam construction, with wooden floors, fitness and massage room, sauna and steam bath, parking garage and ski room. It is off of the main road and central to town.

Hotel Sölderhof (5030, fax 50360; €€) Some rooms have showers and some have baths—if you have a preference, please request. Most rooms have a balcony. Hotel hosts weekly activites for guests from a ski safari to curling instructions and games. Sauna, whirlpool, solarium and ski room round out the amenities. The restaurant also serves the public.

Hotel Hochsölden (2229, fax 225951; €€–€€€) Halfway up the mountain, in Hochsölden. This is a ski-in/ski-out property for most of the season. There are few extras, but the location is unbeatable. They have their own ski school.

Frühstückpensions — B&Bs

Wildespitze (2341, fax 234140; €) Britta Riml runs this 20-bed guesthouse only five minutes from the Giggijoch cable car. She speaks good English. Rooms all have private bath.

Prantl Stefan (2525, fax 2525; €) is more intimate with only six rooms in a working farmhouse.

The only British-style chalet is **Gustl's Farienhausl** (2090, fax 2090-15; €) with eight beds.

Montana (5080, fax 50806; €) A B&B with apartments, sauna, tanning bed, T.V. and radio in rooms. It is at the base of the Giggijochbahn cable car. Apartment accommodates two to six people and has a living room, bedroom, T.V., and kitchen.

Arnold Andre (2269, fax 2954; €) A B&B owned and operated by World Cup ski racer Andre Arnold and his wife.

Gastehaus Larchenpark (2386, fax 2386; €) This B&B with its stained glass and crystal displays is near the Giggijoch lift. All 22 rooms have a toilet with either a shower or bath.

Obergurgl and Hochgurgl

The Special Week price is for the January package, which includes seven days half pension and six days of lifts. The last price is per person for half board based on double occupancy during the main season; high-season rates are 10–15 percent higher.

Hotel Hochgurgl (05256-6265, fax 26510; €€€+) Perhaps one of the best hotels in the Alps, by any measure. It matches elegance with the Zürserhof in Zürs and the

Palace in St. Moritz.

Hotel Edelweiss and Gurgl (05256-6223, fax 6449; €€€) Very close to the lifts.

Hotel Madeleine (05256-3540, fax 354355; €€–€€€).

Pensione Wiesental (05256-6263, fax 63583; €€) Very convenient to the lifts in the old town.

Hotel Gamper (05256-65450, fax 631760; €€) In the center of the town with an excellent kitchen. Special Week: €610–€655.

Hotel Ideal (05256-62900, fax 6302; €€) The bargain of Hochgurgl with all the amenities—sauna, fitness room, and garage.

The **Hotel Wurmkogel** and the **Hotel Laurin** in Hochgurgl are also recommended.

Dining

Sölden has over fifty different restaurants, plus the hotels offer excellent meals as part of their full- and half-board options. Dining here is strictly by the clock when not on the mountain. Lunch is served until 2 p.m., après-ski is from 4 p.m.–7 p.m. and dinner follows. Tipping at après-ski is either round up to the next Euro or pay €2–4 over the tab.

Prices (without wine) €€€—€36+; €€—16–35; €—€15-.

Restaurant Dominic (2646; €), connected to the après-ski bar Bla-Bla, provides a religious experience, with stained glass ceilings, ornate wood carvings and pew-like chairs. Bring your credit card.

The **Parkhotel** restaurant (2250; €) specializes in grilled food such as steaks and lamb chops at reasonable prices. No credit cards.

The **Stefan Restaurant** (2237; €€–€) opened in 1351 and some of the furniture appears to go back at least that far. It is as typically Austrian as you will find. Specialties are game dishes from Tyrol. No credit cards.

These next three places have great traditional Tyrolean meals. The traditionally costumed waiters at **Die Alm** (2401; €€) serve meals amidst stuffed wildlife, train tracks and churning ceiling fans. The **s'Pfandl** (3607; €€) in Ausserwald and **Grüner's Almstube** (€€) serve Ripplan, Kasspatzn, Knedlan and Gröstl.

In Hochgurgl, the **Hotel Hochgurgl** has a wonderful **Tiroler Stuben. The Hotel Ideal**, **Hotel Laurin** and the **Wurmkogl** all serve good basic cooking as well.

In Obergurgl head to the **Romantik** and **Belmonte** for Italian food. Try the **Gamper** and then the **Grüner** for good Tyrolean cooking. The **Josl** is known for its wild game. **Hubertushof** has good fondue, raclette and tyrolean specialties. The **Wiesental** also serves excellent meals in the center of town.

Après-ski/nightlife

Après-ski activities in Sölden start after 3 p.m. and last until promptly 7 p.m. when all bars empty of guests who head home to ready for dinner and nights filled with dancing, drinking, and smoking. Expect to pay a cover charge of €4.35 to get into most bars for the later night life.

On the way down the mountain make a stop at **Philipps** in Innerwald. This is a favorite outdoor bar on the Number 11 trail back into town. **Heiner's Adabei** is a good place to stop along trails 21 or 22. The **Hinterher** at the base of the Giggijoch cable car is a loud, fun, friendly bar always filled beyond capacity. **Shirmbar** outside of the Hotel Liebe Sonne is yet another outdoor bar overflowing with partyers dancing in their ski boots and singing to the cranking music.

Joker — Da ist die Hölle los (We're raising hell here) is decked out in an infernal motif, with flames, goblins and demons. Old chair lifts converted into restaurant

Telephone prefix: Sölden, Hochsölden, Vent 05254;
Hochgurgl and Obergurgl 05256

chairs are suspended from the ceiling. The early crowd is teenage and the later clients are older. They offer a selection of specialty drinks, and a climbable cliff leads to the **Bierhimml** (Beer Heaven) similarly decorated with angels and clouds. Loud music and pizza are served up. Some credit cards are accepted at both establishments.

Climb down to the **Oetzi Keller** (2234), decorated in tribute of the famous 5,000-year-old frozen body found in the nearby glacier. This is the late-night hot spot in town.

Another hot spot is the glass-enclosed **Bla-Bla Eisbar** at the Pension Dominic (2646) which opens at 3 p.m. just in time for the first après-skier. It attracts a young snowboarder crowd. **Lawine** blasts live rock'n'roll music. If you want a break from the rocking crowd, play pool if you get a table. **Nanu Pub Cafe and Bar** (2062) is a good place in the evening after dinner for ice cream specialties, coffee drinks and conversation.

Crave mixed drinks with music for ballroom dancing? The upscale **Alibi Bar** at the Central Hotel (22600) is home to the €11 margarita—not for the faint of wallet. Credit cards accepted. At **Jacob's Weinfassl** (5030) you can taste a variety of Austrian and Italian wines in a quieter atmosphere.

In Obergurgl, the **Nederhütte** rocks with accordian and guitar for aprés-ski which should lubricate you for the final run down to the hotels. A stop at the **Edelweiss Bar** at the base of the Gaisberg lift is then in order. Later head to the **Joslkeller** with country music then discover the **Hexenkuch'l** in the Hotel Jenewein, the Krumpn's Stadl at Pension Schöne Aussicht, and the **Austria Keller** in the Hotel Austria with oom-pa-pa music and mugs of beer.

In Hochgurgl the place to be seen is the either the **African Bar** in the Hotel Hochgurgl or **Toni's Almhutte** at Sporthotel Olymp.

Child care (2003/04 prices)

Sölden Region

The tourist information center in Sölden keeps a list of qualified babysitters and care providers, which is available upon request.

The ski school Sölden/Hochsölden (2364) accepts children 3 to 8 years old and is open Sunday through Friday, 10 a.m.–3 p.m. Meals are €8 per day. A full day costs €40; three days are €97; and six days are €144.

Ski School Total Vacancia for children includes child care during lunch, a terrain garden and children's racing school. The school is open 10 a.m. to 12 p.m. and 1 p.m.–3 p.m. A full day costs €40; three days are €94; and six days are €136.

Ski Kindergarten Yellow Power is open from 10 a.m. to 12 p.m. and from 1 p.m.–3 p.m. Lunch is €8 per day. A full day is €48; three days, €123; and six days, €168.

Nursery services are offered.

The Gurgls

In Obergurgl the ski school runs a special course for nonskiing children. The cost for supervised lunch in the Gurgls is €14 per day.

Children's snow day care costs the same as ski school (basically the normal adult rate). For children 3–5 yrs. old, it is open from 9:30 a.m.–12:30 p.m. and 1:30 p.m.–4:30 p.m.

Other activities

Tobogganing tops the list of extracurricular activities in Sölden. Tradition calls for lots of drinks beforehand. Call Hotel Alpenland at 2365 or Gasthof Silbertal at 2987.

At the Freizeit Arena, a hot spot on cold and snowy days, visitors can **swim**; soak in a **steambath**; bake in a **sauna**; tan in the **solarium**; work out on an **indoor tennis court** or play **volleyball, badminton** or **bowl**. For more information call 2514.

Tandem hang-gliding provides a birds-eye view of the entire mountain range. Jump off a cliff in a parachute and hang for hours on thermal currents. Call Outdoor Vacancia at 3100. One trip costs roughly €100.

Horse-drawn sleigh rides leave from the Hotel Liebe Sionne. Call 2203-0.

The **Stuibenfall,** only a short distance, is Tyrol's highest waterfall with a drop of 150 meters. The **Piburger See** is a beautiful mountain lake with phenomenal reflections on a good day.

The hamlet of **Farst** is the steepest and most daring settlement on the mountain. Viewed from below it appears that the buildings of the village are tied to the mountainside.

Getting there

Train service is not available to the Sölden area, making the bus and car the fastest way to get there. About 225 km. from Munich (3-1/2 hour drive in good conditions) and 266 km. from Salzburg. This remote Alpine region along the Italian border offers a scenic, but at times difficult to traverse, 20-minute stretch of winding roads from the Autobahn. Bus service is also available every hour from Innsbruck. Prices start at about €15, but phone the bus company at 05266-89200 before buying a ticket.

Tourist information

Tourismusverband Sölden–Oeztal Arena, A-6450 Sölden, Austria; 05254-510, fax 510520.

Tourismusverband Obergurgl-Hochgurgl, A-6456 Obergurgl, Austria; 05256-6460, fax 05256-6353.

Internet: www.obergurgl.com

E-mail: info@obergurgl.com

Tourismusverband, A-6458 Vent, Austria; tel. 05254-8193.

Internet: www.soelden.com

E-mail: info@soelden.com

Saalbach-Hinterglemm

You may have heard of Saalbach's reputation as an après-ski "Animal House," but nothing can prepare you for the reality:

You have stopped to enter the dark, woodsy Hinterhagalm tea bar on the last run down, having worked up a thirst on the nearly two-mile Asterabfahrt trail into Saalbach. By the time the first beer arrives, the waitress has to swing her tray to adjust to the unspoken rhythm of the overflow crowd, the clumping of ski boots keeping time to the beat of traditional Austrian folksongs from the live band. Even before the T-bar outside the door closes for the day, the entire chalet is transformed into a dance floor. Legs dangling over the upstairs balcony jig to the two-step. By the time you're ready to locate your skis for the final 300-yard glide into the village, the way out is blocked by a swaying mass of bodies. You have to literally get down on your hands and knees and make a crawl for it. No one seems to notice. Then, just before you make it between the last set of legs separating you from the door outside, you hit your head on something. Looking up, you see you've bumped heads with someone crawling in.

Saalbach forms the epicenter of the activity. Nestled in the narrow throat of the valley, with mountains crowding in as a backdrop for the chalet-style hotels and their carved wood balconies, the village is as quaint as any you could hope for in the Alps. The custard-yellow steeple of an old church dominates the packed rooftops, and a mountain stream rushes soothingly through the town.

The valley floor broadens considerably just a mile up the road at Hinterglemm. Here hotels are larger and the village fans out over a wider area. While it is as central to the main ski crossroads of the valley as Saalbach and has more mid- to upper-level hotels with full amenities, Hinterglemm loses some of the coziness that you find in Saalbach. While Hinterglemm has the look and feel of a resort, everything about Saalbach says that it was an Alpine village in its own right before the ski rush began.

Mountain layout

Saalbach-Hinterglemm offers one of the best interconnected lift systems in Austria. Even expert skiers determined to put as many miles under their skis as possible, would find themselves hard-pressed to cover the area from one end to the other in a single day—never mind stopping along the way to enjoy the skiing.

Lifts cover both sides of a long valley. The most central spot is Saalbach. Head up the valley for one day's ski excursion and down the next. Anyone staying in Leogang on the other side of the mountain, for instance, will find it hard to even reach the area above Hinterglemm without having to immediately turn around to catch the last lift home. (While there's excellent bus service up and down the length of the valley serving both Saalbach and Hinterglemm, Leogang actually rests in another valley.)

Experts should head directly for the Schattberg X-Press gondola. The black run directly beneath the cable car is a good example of why American expert skiers keep coming back. It has good grade, it's bumpy, it's long, and there's a single ride back up for those with enough stamina to do it again.

For another uniquely European experience, head left at the top of the Schattberg cable car down the Limberg-Jausern trail. This is the longest trail in the area and worth taking just for the sake of adventure. Vorderglemm at the bottom of this run represents the southern boundary of the area, and you can cross up to the other side of the valley on the Schönleiten cable car.

Experts who turn right at the top of Schattberg (Schattberg-East) and go up the short Westgipfel DSB III lift to Schattberg-West can enjoy a mountainside of advanced trails leading down into Hinterglemm. There's plenty of tree skiing on this broad swath of mountain, and the run all the way down is worthy indeed of an expert's interest. Rather than heading back up the two lifts to Schattberg-West, cross over to the Zwölfer and let the cable cars take you back to the summit. Ski down and continue up-valley.

The runs down to the midstation from the top of Zwölfer (6,509 feet) are nice and very bumpy, and there are lots of fine cutovers into untouched sugar for powder monkeys (snow permitting, of course). From the top cut over to the Seekar T-bar, which has advanced runs from the top and an excellent powder bowl off to the right.

The entire north side of the valley is one intermediate run after another down an open mountainside. Spend a day in the Hasenauer Köpfl and Reiterkogel area. If you head further to the left up the valley toward Spieleckkogel, you will stand about as high as you can in the valley (6,522 feet). The run all the way down to the valley floor is long and excellent with a double chair back up.

Advanced intermediates will enjoy taking the long Kohlmaisberg cable car, which begins in Saalbach near the old church. From the top, there's a long 3-km. advanced run down into Saalbach. This is one of the nicest sections of mountain in the entire area. Because of the relatively low height (5,886 feet from the top) of this area, all the runs seem to skirt or cut through beautiful forests. And at every juncture, there's the ubiquitous hut where you can enjoy a drink and a spectacular view from a balcony.

For a top-to-bottom basher, cut over to the Bergeralm chair lift, and from the top enjoy the challenging 7-km. Bergeralm-Schönleiten run (Nos. 57 and 67 on the trail map) down to the valley floor to the Schönleiten cable car. The eight-person cable cars will whisk you all the way to the top of Schonleiten, where from the restaurant you can enjoy the most spectacular view in the entire valley, and one of the truly memorable panoramas in the Alps. If you care to digest your lunch over some bumps, round the ridge toward Leogang and ski the three T-bar lifts. They're short but sweet.

Beginners should take the Bernkogelalm chair lift from Saalbach and change lifts to make it all the way to the top of Bernkogel. The run from the top to the midstation is gentle, wide and very confidence inspiring. In fact, this is where the Austrian ski instructors take their classes of first-timers. The adventurous will find manageable, broad runs down from the top of both the Kohlmaiskopf and Bründkopf lifts.

Mountain rating

There are only a few runs that are strictly for experts, but there's plenty of challenging terrain in the Ski Circus to keep excellent skiers occupied. There always seems to be a tree glade beckoning somewhere.

Intermediates have discovered nirvana. The north side of the valley is a canvas of intermediate runs for the intermediate skier to choose his or her favorite brushstroke. There is really no part of the Ski Circus that is off-limits to the intermediate with the exception of the run under the Schattberg X-Press gondola. You can enjoy all the pleasures of exploring the entire circuit without hitting a dead end.

Beginners and advanced beginners will find Saalbach-Hinterglemm much to their liking. There are plenty of broad slopes, even from the top, that lead them on a gentle curve miles down into the valley.

Ski school (2003/04 prices)

There are nine major ski schools in both Saalbach and Hinterglemm. Combined, there are over 200 instructors in the area.

Group lessons (four hours, 10 a.m.–12 p.m. and 2 p.m.–4 p.m.) are €53 for a full day, €126 for three days, and €144 for four to five days.

Children's classes are 10 a.m. to 4 p.m. A week (including lunch) costs €289.

Cross-country ski lessons are also available, and there are 10 km. of cross-country trails in the area.

Lift tickets (2003/04 prices)

Saalbach-Hinterglemm Leogang Ski Circus (high season is about December 20–January 9 and January 31–March 19). These are high season rates, the middle season rates in mid January are about 10 percent lower.

	Adults	Child (6–15)	Youth (16–18)
One day	€34.50	€17	€31
Three days	€95	€47.50	€85.50
Six days	€164	€82	€147.50

There are reduced lift prices for children 15–19, further reductions for those younger than 15 and special reductions for Family Weeks during the entire winter.

Accommodations

Based on high season, per person/double occupancy, with half board: €€€—more than €125+; €€—€75–€125; €—€75-.

Alpenhotel (6666; €€€) This is Saalbach's flagship hotel. The big red arch dominates the entrance of the village, and announces that the Alpenhotel caters to all whims—sauna, solarium, massage, exercise room, indoor swimming pool, whirlpool and so on. It also houses the most exclusive disco in Saalbach, the **Arena**.

Haider (6228; €€€) Not as fancy or as large as the Alpenhotel, the Haider is quaint in the traditional Austrian mold, with carved wood headboards on the beds and shutters. There's a sauna, solarium and a hot whirlpool, as well a hideaway lounge with fireplace. Besides an excellent restaurant serving traditional Austrian fare, there's also an informal pizzeria—always a plus for carbo-hungry skiers.

Sporthotel Ellmau (72260; €€€) and **Hotel Glemmtalerhof** (7135; €€€) in Hinterglemm are excellent and offer full amenities, such as sauna, solarium and indoor swimming pool. There's also babysitting on the premises.

The upscale **Wellness-Hotel-Kendler** (62250, fax 6335; €€€) in Saalbach, is packed with health facilities, saunas, steambaths, fitness room and spa.

Scharnagl (6284; €–€€) It's too new to rate as quaint. This pension scores high because of its location next to the old church and across the street from both the Kohlmais gondola and the Bauer's Schi-Alm, perhaps the best après-ski bar in town. The rooms are clean and airy, and the proprietress, Frau Brudermann, is always willing to help.

Another recommended pension in Saalbach is the **Berger** (7140; €). In Hinterglemm, try the **Flora** (7100; €).

Ski Chalets: Crystal, Inghams/Bladon, Neilson (see page 20 for phone, fax and internet addresses).

Apartments, condominiums, flats

Saalbach has hundreds of apartments for rent with two major agencies handling the procedure. Contact either of the two agencies or the tourist office for apartment information. Give them your arrival and departure dates and level of luxury you desire.

Dining

Austrian cooking mirrors the country and its people—hearty, simple and unpretentious. Few sights are more welcome after a full day's skiing than a generous pork filet with mushroom gravy and a heaping portion of *Spätzle*, Austria's unbeatable doughy noodles. For a sweet treat on the mountain, try *Germknödel* (a sweet doughy bread filled with jam and covered with warm vanilla sauce).

The **Hinterhagalm** (7282 or 6291) just at the top of the Turm T-bar is something of a local legend. Its 5 p.m. tea bar is one of the most notable après-ski events in the valley, yet at night this beautiful old lodge serves traditional Austrian dishes with old-world atmosphere. This restaurant was a backdrop for "The Sound of Music."

Nearly all the major hotels in both Saalbach and Hinterglemm feature good restaurants, and you'll find menus with prices conveniently posted outside. Those with man-sized appetites should try the restaurant in the **Hotel Sonne** (7202), featuring more than five different steak dinners. Highly recommended is Chateaubriand for two at the **Hotel Reiterhof** (6682). **Restaurant Kendler** (6225) is highly rated by the critics and filled with rustic atmosphere. Try the sole or the very Austrian onion roast venison and bring cash.

No ski resort is complete unless it has an informal pizzeria with good food and reasonable prices. In Saalbach the pizzeria in the **Hotel Haider** (6228) gets our vote.

No less than 40 mountain chalets serve food, and each lift seems to have one of these either at the top or bottom—or both. Two mountain huts deserve special mention—the **Wildenkarhütte** at the top of the Schönleiten gondola for its spectacular panoramic view, and the rustic **Thurner Alm** (8418; on the trail midway up the Reiteralm T-bar) for its hunting lodge flavor and ski-up bar.

We've also heard good things about **Goaßstall** (8705), a lodge in Hinterglemm at the bottom of the Reiterkogel gondola. which serves a special dinner called "Hot Goat". It's a fillet of steak served on a traditional wooden platter in the shape of a goat.

Après-ski/nightlife

Saalbach-Hinterglemm's reputation for great nightlife has more to do with the atmosphere and attitude of the area than the number of discos (officially only five). Along with the wild-and-crazy Austrians you're bound to meet, there's also a healthy contingent of Scandinavians (especially Swedes) and British.

The **Arena** disco in the Alpenhotel is the upscale nightspot. The action inside doesn't start until after 11 p.m. Expect to pay a cover (it varies depending on the entertainment) and about €8 for a mixed drink. There are two bars, a live band and plenty of overstuffed couches and tucked-away alcoves for a break from the dancing.

The disco in the Sporthotel, just up the main street from the centrally located Alpenhotel, is where the young and adventurous let their collective hair down. There's a circular balcony that overlooks the dance floor, and you need only pick out the partner of your choice from this vantage point and then leap merrily into the crowded fray.

Cross the stream just off the main street and walk uphill to the **Backstatt Stall**. The upstairs disco is on two levels, with another balcony for scoping the dance action. The atmosphere is a little more woodsy and mellower than the spots mentioned above, and it's easier to find room on the dance floor.

Après-ski has to be witnessed to be understood. Where else, except inside the **Bauers Schi-Alm** at the bottom of the Turm T-bar (across from the old church), can you see Austrians dancing the can-can to "New York, New York," stacked three on top of one another and swaying like demented totem poles? The bedlam at the **Hinterhagalm** tea bar just up the slope is a rival for honors as Après-Ski Madhouse of the Mountain.

The new **Harley Davidson and Bikers' Pub**, in the basement of the Hotel Zur Dorfschmiede, features a shiny selection of fullsize Harleys and motorcycle memorabilia, lots of leather and studs, and an owner who dishes "hog" talk with the best of them. Hokey, but a lot of fun.

Child care

There is no organized nursery. The only programs are organized through the ski school in Saalbach.

Other activities

Try an afternoon excursion by horse-drawn sleigh. Lindlingalm offers tours that include a stop for a traditional Austrian lunch (06541-7190). Sleigh rides are also offered by Taxi Schmidhofel (06541-7163) and Lengauerwirt (06541-7255).

Getting there

By train: There are direct trains to nearby Zell am See from both Munich and Salzburg. You can either take a cab the remaining 18 km. to Saalbach or wait for the regularly scheduled bus, which makes the trip to Saalbach nine times a day from the train station.

By car: The drive from the Munich airport to Saalbach takes about two and a half hours. From the Salzburg autobahn take the Siegsdorf exit, then follow signs to Lofer-Maishofen, then signs to Saalbach-Hinterglemm.

Some hotels offer parking, and you can also park in the multideck garage on the outskirts of town. Once in Saalbach you won't need a car.

Tourist information

Contact the Informationscenter, A-5753 Saalbach, Austria; (06541) 680068; fax (06541) 680069. The snow phone is 680040.
E-mail: contact@saalbach.com
Internet: www.saalbach.com

Schladming/Ramsau with Dachstein-Tauern Region

This is the area in Europe where Arnold Schwarzenegger comes to ski, but more on that later. Whether you are looking for the challenge of the fastest World Cup downhill or wide beginner and intermediate runs through thick pine forests, whether you seek the excitement of skiing on the Dachstein Glacier or the serenity of one of the most extensive cross-country areas in Austria, it's all in Schladming.

Schladming, in the center of Austria about an hour's drive from Salzburg, hosts thousands of Austrian, German, Swedish, Danish, British and Dutch tourists. Already one of the leading vacation centers for the Austrians, the region has completed an extensive series of developments that have turned the valley into a world-class resort. The local term for this area is *Sportregion Dachstein-Tauern.*

Schladming, the hub of the area, is nestled around a traditional town center, with shopping, nightlife and restaurants—all within a five-minute walk from the main lifts.

Rohrmoos, about a five-minute drive up the mountain, features more hotel rooms than Schladming, and guests can step out their door, put on their skis and set off down the mountain. But Rohrmoos is spread out and a long walk from the Schladming village.

Ramsau lies on the opposite side of the valley, with a southern exposure. It is settled on a long plateau that features some of the most interesting cross-country skiing in Austria: the 1999 Nordic World Championships were held here. Accommodations are extensive but dispersed. At the top of the Ramsau cable car (elevation 8,850 feet) you overlook the entire Taurern region mountain range and the Enns River Valley. Haus im Ennstal, a short drive along the valley from Schladming, is perhaps the most picturesque of the main villages in the region. It remains traditional, anchoring the Hauser Kaibling ski area.

The Schladming Dachstein Tauern ski pass also allows skiing in the Gasteiner Valley, Hochkönigs and Grossarltal. That brings the total available skiing and riding option in the region to 270 lifts covering 860 km. of trails. Though the lifts are not interconnected, there is a shuttlebus system that links the various resorts as well as parking at each resort.

Mountain layout

The *Amadé* ski pass opens more than 167 km. of prepared runs at the nine ski areas along the Dachstein-Tauern valley. The major areas are Planai (6,214 feet) above Schladming; Hauser Kaibling (6,610 feet) above Haus; Hochwurzen (6,069 feet) above Rohrmoos; and the Reiteralm (6,102 feet) above Pichl. Each area offers plenty of skiing for a day.

The Planai is served by an efficient gondola—waiting time in the valley is minimal even on Sundays. A new quad chair lift adds to the lift capacity in this region. T-bars open the back bowls of the Planai area; the valley face of the mountain is criss-crossed by beginner and intermediate runs. The No. 1 run, from the top of the cable car to the bottom station, is the longest on the mountain and an absolutely joyful experience. Intermediates can cruise, and beginners can handle the entire run because the steep sections (short ones) are wide, for an easy traverse.

The Hochwurzen area is reached through a series of T-bars, chair lifts and a gondola from the Reiteralm area. New high-speed lifts make the trip quick from the Planai area. For people staying in Rohrmoos or coming by shuttlebus, a gondola whisks skiers to the top or take the quad chair lift. The upper areas are intermediate and the lower ones, around Rohrmoos, a beginner's paradise.

Hauser Kaibling, rising above Haus, is normally not so crowded as Schladming. At times you'll find yourself alone on a beautiful mountain with some of the best intermediate slopes under your skis. Intermediate is the main focus of this mountain. Take the new Schischanukel to the base of the Hauser Kaibling cable car just outside town. A new gondola now adds dramatically to the uphill capacity from this village.

Reiteralm, above the towns of Pichl and Gleiming, provides a good day's worth of skiing for intermediates. Beginners have too limited an area to make the half-hour series of lifts worthwhile unless they are staying in one of the base towns.

Overall, the area uses up a week of skiing without repeating a section. Even good skiers will be hard-pressed to cover every trail in six days of all-out skiing.

Mountain rating

The area is an intermediate paradise. Beginners should center their efforts on Rohrmoos, although all sections have beginner runs. After three days of lessons, beginners can make their way all the way down each of the mountains with their instructors.

Experts should keep an eye out for good powder and test themselves high up on Hauser Kaibling or on the lower sections of the World Cup downhill runs both in Haus and Schladming. The real experts should hire a guide to take them off trail for a great day or week of skiing.

Snowboarding

A massive halfpipe drops from the Galsterbergalm at 2,700 meters of altitude, making it one of the highest in Europe. Together with the halfpipe the resort has created a massive snowpark with jumps and hits to keep riders busy for hours. Another halfpipe can be found in the middle of the Planai sector and a third at the top of the gondola at Reiteralm.

In the summer this is a good snowboard training spot with riding on the glacier. The halfpipe is open even in June, July, October and November. There is night riding in Rohrmoos on the World Cup run into the stadium.

Boarders gather at the Lärchkogel trail. This is one of the favorite spots for boarders. There are also interesting natural obstacle courses on the Fageralm and at Stoderzinken at opposite ends of the valley.

Ski school (2002/03 prices)

There is are two main ski schools. The Ski School Hochwurzen-Planai (23583, fax 613434, www.hopl.at) and Ski School Tritscher (22137, fax 611426. www.tritscher.at).

Private lessons for 2.5 hours cost €80 per person; for 4.5 hours the charge is €150 per person.

Group lessons for three days cost €105; for five days, €120.

Children's group lessons cost €40 for one day, €105 for three days and €120 for five days.

Snowboard lessons for beginners with their own equipment cost for three days €85 and for five days €120; the price including boot and board is €150 for three days and €210 for five days.

A three day freestyle snowboard course for those with their own equipment is €90 and the five day freestyle program is €125; the same courses with equipment cost €155 for three days and €215 for five days. Contact the snowboard schools at 24223, fax 22474 or check out www.snoboardschule.net or www.blue-tomato.at.

Lift tickets (2003/04 prices)

The lift tickets cover this valley's nine mountains and 86 lifts. Each town in the region offers single-day limited-lift tickets. But the nine-mountain lift ticket allows skiing and snowboarding throughout this Salburg region. The resorts are not internconnected by lifts, nor are they really all that close, but your lift ticket is good wherever you go in these areas. Here are the additional regions and the towns where the lifts are included in the ski pass: Salzburger Sportwelt (Flachau-Wagrain-St. Johann/Alpendorf, Zauchensee-Flachauwinkel-Kleinarl, Radstadt-Altenmarkt, Eben, Filzmoos, Goldegg), Dachstein-Gastein Region (Bad Gastein, Bad Hofgastein, Dorfgastein, Sportgastein), plus Hochkönigs Winterreich and the Grossarltal.

The lift rates are based on high, middle and low season. High season is Christmas/New Year to early January and early February to mid March. Middle season is January after New Year through around February 1st or so. Low season is before Christmas and late March into April. Special family rates are also available.

High season	**Adult**	**Youth (16–18)**	**Child (15 and younger)**
one day	€33.50	€31	€16.50
three days	€93.50	€86.50	€46.50
six days	€161	€148.50	€80.50
fourteen days	€278.50	€259.50	€139.50
Middle season			
one day	€31	€29	€15.50
three days	€87	€80.50	€43
six days	€149.50	€138	€75
fourteen days	€259	€241.50	€129.50

Telephone prefix: Schladming, Ramsau, Planai, 03687;
Hauser Kaibling, 03686; Reiteralm, 06454;

Accommodations

Rates are based on high season, per person/double occupancy with half board: €€€—more than €125; €€—€75–€124; €—less than €75.

Sporthotel Royer (200, fax 20094; €€) A four-star hotel in Schladming. This is a modern hotel with pool, indoor tennis and squash courts, sauna and pony rides. It is the favorite of Arnold Schwarzenegger, who grew up in a small village not far away. The hotel lounge and bar feature thick leather chairs around a fireplace. Guest rooms have plenty of closet space, CNN on the television, hair dryers and showers over the tub.

Romantik-Hotel Alte Post (22571, fax 225718; €€) In Schladming it's the oldest, most traditional hotel on the main square. It is only a three-minute walk from the Planai lift and has a new sauna area.

Hotel Zum Stadttor (24525; fax 2452550, €€) In Schladming. Whirlpool and sauna. The hotel is about a five-minute walk from the Planai lift.

Hotel Pichlmayrgut (06454-7305; €€) If you want to stay in an old Austrian estate, this fills the bill. Amenities include indoor tennis, pool, sauna and steambath. Pichl lifts and the 4 Mountain Schischaukel are a five-minute walk from the hotel.

Hotel Neue Post (22105, fax 221055; €) is smack in the middle of town.

Right across from the Planai lift station is **Gästehaus Handlos** (22633, 226333; €€). Though it is B&B only, it can't get much more convenient.

Another very convenient B&B across from the Planai lift is **Haus Barbara** (22077, fax 2207750; €). It is only a three-minute walk to the village center.

The **Kinderhotel Hauser Kaibling** (03686-23780; €€€) specializes in families with children. It is at the edge of Haus im Ennstal only two minutes from the lifts.

Alpenhotel Schütterhof (61205; €€€) is a ski-in/ski-out hotel in the Planai-Hochwurzen area. It has a new indoor swimming pool.

Gasthof Kirchenwirt/Tritscher (22435, fax 2243516; €) in the middle of town is highly recommended.

The **Schloss Moosheim** (03685-23231; €€) is a bit out of the way, but you get to sleep in a real castle. It adds to your vacation stories and has good transport to the lifts.

Gasthof Herrschaftstaverne (03686-2392; €€) is a good family spot only 200 meters from the base of the cable car. It has an indoor pool, sauna and curling alley.

For those looking to save money, try staying at **Jugend & Familiengastehaus** (24531, fax 2453188; €) where breakfast, dinner and a bunk only costs €21.80 in high season. Another money-saving tip is to stay at a pension where dozens of places have daily B&B costs between €20 and €30.

Stay near the top of the Hauser Kaibling in the **Krummholzhütte**, where you have to share a bathroom and shower, for €26–€31 a day, half pension. You get a room near the summit and about a 10-minute schuss down the mountain right out the door.

One of the best hotels in the area is **Alpengasthof Peter Rosegger** (03687-81223; €€) in Ramsau with an extremely peaceful setting. This is perfect for those planning cross-country skiing or snowshoeing.The restaurant (only for hotel guests) is considered one of the best in the area.

The Dachstein-Tauern Region has a series of lodging deals that include seven nights lodging, half pension or breakfast only, six days of lifts and pool access per person based on double occupancy during mid January.

Rates in January of 2004 are approximately €700 for a four-star hotel, €600 for a middle-class hotel, €550 for a Pension or Gasthof, €500 for a B&B, and €450 for a private room in a local's house.

Apartments, condominiums, flats

There are hundreds of units available in all shapes and sizes. Depending on the number of people in your group and the time of the year, prices per person should range from €15 a night to €30. In most cases linens and towels are extra, about €25 for the week.

Contact the tourist office and describe what you want and how much you will pay. The office has a computer system that tracks all bookings in the area.

Dining

The best restaurants in town are the **Alte Post**, **Sporthotel Royer** and the restaurant in the **Stadttor**. The place to spend the least money and still eat well is **Restaurant Tritscher**.

For great ski-slope meals on the Planai, stop in at **Onkel Willi's Hütte** (yes, Uncle Willi's Hut), only a few ski glides from the top of the main Planai lift. On the Hauser Kaibling, the **Krummholzhütte** at the top, and the **Stöcklhütte** where the three lifts meet, are good. Try **Gasthof Steger** in Haus/Ennstal.

At the base of Schladming's Planai, host of the 1982 FIS Alpine World Championships and known for its ultra-fast downhill, is a small inn called **Charly's Treff** owned by Charly Kahr, the Austrian who coached the national team at the 1960 Squaw Valley Olympics and the British women's team in the early 1970s. He also coached Olympic and World Cup champion Franz Klammer, a local hero. In his restaurant, savoring a schnapps, Charly regales visitors with stories of the skiers he has trained.

Many visit Charly's Treff to sample hearty dishes Aus Oma's Kochbuch (From Grandmother's Cookbook). The Geschnetzeltes (pork and noodles, €10) was very good and you don't leave hungry. Salzburger Käsnock (cheese and spätzle noodles) at €7 is another favorite.

Charly retired from coaching in 1985 and now spends his time overseeing his restaurant, visiting with friends like Schwarzenegger, and skiing. "I like the tree skiing and village atmosphere of Schladming," says Kahr. He also runs a ski rental shop, The Downhill Club.

The **Brand Alm,** a classic mountain hut about halfway down from the base of the Ramsau glacier cable car, is the quintessential Alpine hut. At outside tables framed by the majestic mountains, you'll see customers in lederhosen, since many people hike up from Ramsau for lunch. The Teller Erbsensuppen (split pea soup) is hearty and the Krainer sausage, served with the best sauerkraut I've ever eaten, should not be missed. You can try a Radler, a mixture of lemonade and beer that Austrians find thirst-quenching. Be sure to have your camera full of film.

Après-ski/nightlife

For wine and quiet talk, try the **Talbachschenke** in three small rooms, each built around a toasty ceramic stove. The best dancing is at the **Sonderbar** under the Hotel Rössl. Other cozy meeting places include **The Pub** and **The Beisl**, both just off the main square. The Beisl is in the passageway at 12 Main Square and is a good place to meet people. Check out **La Porta**, near the town's old gateway.

The two main discos outside town, and also the best spots for meeting European skiers, are the **Sport Alm** in Ramsau and the **Erlebniswelt** in Rohrmoos. In Haus/Ennstal, stop into the new **Pub Remise** in the old castle.

Telephone prefix: Schladming, Ramsau, Planai, 03687;
Hauser Kaibling, 03686; Reiteralm, 06454;

Child care (2002/03 prices)

There is a ski kindergarten for children (without lunch) costing €40 for a full day and €87 for three days.

Children age 4 and older can sign up for ski school, which takes children for the entire day, at the same prices as adults. Add €5 a day for lunches.

Other activities

Visit Salzburg and its neighboring **salt mines**.

The **Loden fabric factory** in Ramsau gives tours—arrange them in advance by calling 81930. The factory and outlet are only about 10 minutes from Schladming.

Some of Austria's most famous **caves** are in this region. Kappenbrullenhöhle, the Ice Cave and Mammoth Cave and are open for visits. Call 06134-362.

Horse-drawn sleigh rides are available in Ramsau/Dachstein, ice skating rinks are open in Rohrmoos and Haus/Ennstal, and there are public swimming pools in Schladming and Ramsau.

Getting there

There are good train connections from Munich and Salzburg. Both have international airports. Salzburg is a 93-km. drive from Schladming. Take the Ennstal exit.

Tourist information

The central tourist office for the region is Regionalverband Dachstein-Tauern, Kuschargasse 202, A-8970 Schladming, Austria; tel. 03687-23310, fax 23232. It handles reservation requests for any town in the area. There are also local tourist offices in Schladming, Pichl, Haus, Rohrmoos and Ramsau.

Seefeld

If you've come to get away from it all, you have found the right spot. If you had your mind set on wild skiing and late-night partying, you are in the wrong place.

Seefeld is an Austrian purpose-built resort that was developed far before modern architecture came into fashion and ski lifts made downhill skiing an end in itself. It was created more than 50 years ago. This resort was designed as a place to get away from the pressure of everyday life and work. It still is a place to relax and to refresh one's spirit.

The village has been laid out with almost no through traffic and with a town center where vacationers can meet, talk, have a coffee or drink, and enjoy events. The look is pure modern Alpine with lots of peaked roofs and wooden balconies, but without the large barns that dotted the original Alpine resorts.

Seefeld also doesn't present itself as a go-for-broke downhill ski and snowboarding resort. This is a resort where relaxation is *de rigueur* on the slopes and off of them. Enjoyment, not excitement is the aim.

This resort is the capital of cross-country skiing in Austria, and many claim that it is one of the premier spots for skinny skiing in the world. Indeed, the cross-country and biathlon Olympic competitions have been held here twice when the international winter games were headquartered in Innsbruck.

Seefeld also offers kilometer after kilometer of walking trails and plenty of additional activities for families. Between cross-country, walking, mellow slopes, swimming and dining, most visitors and their families succeed in leaving the outside world, if only for a few days.

Nearby Garmisch and Mittenwald in Germany provide additional skiing and activities. And Innsbruck is only 20 minutes away by car and about a half hour away by a spectacular train ride for plenty of cultural action, shopping and skiing if you choose. And for those with travel on their minds, the Brenner Pass crossing into Italy, with its shopping and dining, is less than an hour's drive.

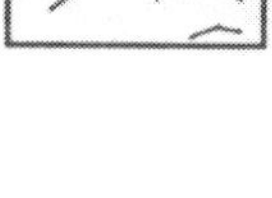

Mountain layout

There is not much exciting to say about the skiing, except that the visuals and natural beauty are spectacular. The Seefeld skiing areas are on two separate mountains.

The Gschwandtkopf is the first area and where most of the beginners start. It only has about 1,000 feet of vertical. It has a quad chair taking skiers and riders to the top from the valley station, a single chair lift rising from Reith, and then after that there are only drag lifts. If you are a hot skier or rider, a day spent here will feel like eternity. If you are a beginner or intermediate this is the place to learn.

On the other side of town is the Rosshütte/Härmelekopf area with a vertical drop of more than 2,500 feet. The old Rosshütte lift rolls skiers up the first 1,600 feet then one cable car glides to the peak of the Seefelder Joch opening long, snowmaking-covered, cruising trails that drop the full vertical of the sector. A second cable car leaves from the top of the Rosshütte rail and spans a valley reaching to the ridge just below the Härmelekopf. Most skiers wind their way along the ridge back to the base station, however intrepid experts and advanced skiers climb the last 150 feet of vertical to the top of Härmelekopf and drop down the backcountry flanks of the mountain.

The regional lift ticket includes all the lifts in Garmisch-Partenkirchen, together with the Zugspitze (see our Garmisch chapter). It also covers lifts in Mittenwald where an ancient cable car takes skiers to the tip top of the Karwendelspitz where Germany's only free-riding descent starts, dropping more than 1,400 feet of unprepared (but avalanche controlled) vertical.

Mountain rating

For beginners, this may be one of the best places in Europe to learn to ski. The English of the instructors is excellent, their sense of humor is contagious, their smiles warm and the terrain is perfect to take skiers and boarders from the first awkward snowplow turns of an initiate to the confident parallel turns of an intermediate.

Intermediates have the perfect place to start to make parallel turns. This is the place to learn to set your weight on those shaped skis and make them zip you around your turns. Most skiers would probably do better to work and practice technique on terrain such as Seefeld's rather than resorting to survival skiing down vertical that is beyond their ability.

Experts—real experts, as always, can find skiing to keep them busy. If you are into cruising or if you are planning on keeping your knees in one piece this is a great resort where you can let them rip. However, there will not be wild descents here at this place. The best is above the Härmelekopf cable car.

You might consider a trip to the nearby Zugspitze in Germany. It's included in some of the passes sold.

Snowboarding

This is a place to learn. If you are looking for places to do jumps and for terrain parks head to Rosshütte where there is a snow park and a halfpipe as well as international competitions in the Casino Arena.

Riders who really want to strut their stuff should head to Mittenwald and do the drop down the Karwendel or go play on the Zugspitze. If you stay in Seefeld, you may get restless, but there is no reason not to strike out for resorts only about 20 minutes away that are included with your lift tickets.

Cross-country

Seefeld is Europe's, maybe the world's, capital of cross-country skiing. As mentioned in the introduction, this was the site of the events for two Olympics. The Nordic Ski World Championships took place here in 1985 and a Cross-Country Skiing World Cup was held here in 1999.

The cross-country office is at the Olympia Sports Center (3060). It is open from 9:00 a.m. to 14:30 p.m. (closed for lunch from 12:30–1:30 p.m.). On Sunday, they open 45 minutes later and close 30 minutes earlier.

There is an interconnected network of 260 km. of trails that includes something for every level of skier and skater—200 km. are classic trails and 60 km. are skating trails. Take your choice of the best.

The trails are free for anyone holding a guest card (meaning that they are staying in a hotel in the village). Trails are set mechanically and groomed daily.

Ski school (2002/03 prices)

The ski school here caters to real learning. This is the perfect spot to really get the feel of carving and where to learn new tricks on your board. This is a perfect place to learn to ski.

Private lessons cost €38 for one hour; €109-€126 for a two hours; and €180 for four hours.

Group lessons are €44 for one day, €139 for five days starting on Monday.

Snowboarding lessons cost the same as downhill with an extra snowboard charge.

Cross-country lessons are the same as downhill lessons, but beginners can get a two-hour lesson for five days for €94 or for four days costing €74.

Lift tickets (2003/04 prices)

The Happy Ski Card multiday ski pass is valid in Seefeld, Neuleutasch, Mösern, Reith bei Seefeld and in the Zugspitze region (Garmisch-Zugspitze, Mittenwald, Ehrwald, Lermoos, Biberwier, Bichlbach, Berwang, Heiterwang, Grainau).

	Adults	Youth (16–17)	Child (7–15)
one day (one resort only)	€29	€26	€17.50
three days	€80	€74	€48
six days	€150	€138	€90
fourteen days	€264	€243	€158

Children age 6 and younger ski for half the normal child ticket price.

Accommodations

Rates here are based on high season, per person/double occupancy with half board: €€€—€125+; €€—€75-€124; €—less than €75.

It is hard to go wrong here in Seefeld. The most expensive in town is **Hotel Klosterbräu** (26210, fax 3885; €€€) with an indoor pool, Roman sauna and steam grotto.

The **Viktoria** (4441, fax 4443; €€€) has rooms based on different periods of history and places. Try the Tibet, New York, or the Modern Times room.

The **Larchenhof** (23830, fax 238383; €€€) combines luxury with Austrian hospitality. Food is great here, and there is entertainment organized most nights with Tyrolean nights, dancing and fashion shows.

The **Karwendelhof** (2655, fax 265544; €€-€€€) has a spectacular lobby and sits just across from the train station. It is part of Best Western reservations.

The **Waldhotel** (22070, fax 200130; €€) is directly across from the Rosshütte lift. It caters to families and is a member of the Children's Hotels of Austria.

Die Post (22010, fax 2201500; €€-€€€), the **Hiltpolt** (2253, fax 284553; €€€), and the **Diana** (2060, fax 2188; €-€€) are smack in the middle of the village.

Telephone prefix: 05212

Apartments, condominiums, flats

A list of apartments is available from the tourist office. Write ahead of time and ask for the size you require and the dates that you are planning on being at the resort. Either the tourist office or the apartment landlords will contact you with several possibilities. Make your selections and get back to them.

Prices per night per apartment are between €70–€100 for a two-room apartment during high season and €80–€150 for a three-room apartment. Local taxes of about €15 a day and a cleaning charge are added.

Dining

Seefeld is a town where the visitors enjoy a good meal. Rest assured, they can find places to dine in this village. This resort has an embarrassment of riches when it comes to fine dining. The top four restaurants are all capable of winning awards and in fact have. The first two mentioned are highly rated by Gault Millau and the next two are unique and delicious in their own way.

No. 1 on many critics' lists is the **Ritter-Oswald-Stube** in the Klosterbräu (26210). This space is filled with atmosphere and the food is delectable as well. It is packed every evening. From the starter, salmon tartar, to the dessert, mint-chocolate sorbet, your taste buds will dance. Meals here will run about €40–€50.

For elegant and wonderful regional fare dine at the **Alte Stube** (2655) in the Casino. The room was reconstructed from an old gasthaus complete with wood paneling and ceilings. It is a delight and provides the perfect setting for an elegant meal.

Finally, take time to enjoy a meal at **Kracherle Moos** (4680) where the chef creates specials in a unique setting. Two ancient farm buildings were transported here and connected to create this restaurant. It is a delight. The daily menu is €16–€20.

Dinner or lunch at the **Triendlsäge** (2580) is fun and reasonable. Take time to see the old original 1848 sawmill that has been preserved. At the **S'Alte Wirtshaus** (4824) dine in an old building dating back to the 1300s. A fun spot is the **Alten Schmiede** in the Hotel Hiltpolt.

Après-ski/nightlife

Good après-ski can be found throughout the village. Tea-time festivities take place at the **Le Dome**, the **Alt Seefeld Restaurant**, or at **Tenne** in the Kaltschmid. Stop in **Grahams Pub** for big beers. The **Siglu** serves libations and at night head back to the **Kanne** or the **Buffalo Westersaloon** or **Fun Disco Jeep**.

Child care (2002/03 prices)

The ski school (2412) operates a ski kindergarten for kids ages 3–5, from 9:30 a.m.–11:30 a.m. and noon–2 p.m.

For kids 3–5 years old, rates are: one day, €26: three days, €72; five days, €94. These rates include two hours of lessons. Supervised lunch costs €10 per day. A five-day program combining lunch and lessons costs €169.

Group lessons for kids ages 6–15 are: full day, €44; two days, €76; four days, €117; five days, €130. Lunch costs €10 per day.

Other activities

The village's Olympia indoor **swimming pool** is open daily from 9:30 a.m. to 10 p.m. Entry is €7.50 for adults. For a pool and sauna entry the price is €13. Children pay about 50 percent. There is a small increase in prices on Sunday. There are also indoor pools open to the public at Hotels

Alpenpark, Bergland and Kronenhotel.

Ice skating is available on the Olympia indoor rink for €5 for adults and €3.50 for children, 14 and younger, for a half day. **Snow rafting** is great fun. Ride a blow-up boat or a banana for €9.50. Play **tennis** at the Casino Tennis Hall for an hour for €17 or get a block of ten entries for €146.

Seefeld also has a **casino,** a German language **movie theater**, a **library, Tyrolean evenings, paragliding, tobogganing, curling, ice climbing** and **indoor golf.**

Read the Innsbruck chapter and the Garmisch chapter for most nearby activities and excursions. This region is a fascinating and historic section of the Alps.

Getting there

Munich's Airport is only two hours away by car on the autobahn. Get to the airport early when leaving—it's massive. Innsbruck is about half an hour's drive. Rail and bus travelers will find connections to Garmisch and to Innsbruck, where they can connect to any town in Europe.

Tourist information

Seefeld Information Office, A-6100 Seefeld, Tyrol, Austria.
Telephone (05212) 2313, fax (05212) 3355.
For lodging reservations call the tourist office Monday–Saturday, 8:30 a.m.–8 p.m..
Internet: www.seefeld-tirol.com.
E-mail: info@seefeld.tirol.at

Telephone prefix: 05212

SkiWelt • Ellmau, Söll, Westendorf

SkiWelt, surrounding the Hohe Salve, is Austria's largest interconnected ski area. Not only is the region the largest interconnected group of lifts in the country, it's also one of the most affordable. The wide expanse of slopes with the backdrop of the rocky Wilder Kaiser boasts more than 92 lifts, 250 km. of trails, and 160 km. of snowmaking spread above nine villages. Guests come from across Europe, but English-speakers tend to cluster in a few of the towns.

The entire ski area is perhaps the most accessible in Austria to skiers coming in from Germany. It's only 20 minutes from the Kufstein border crossing, which is about an hour from Munich.

The main villages are Going, Ellmau, Scheffau, Söll, Hopfgarten, Westendorf and Brixen im Thale. We will focus on Ellmau, Söll and Westendorf since these have the preponderance of English-speaking skiers.

Ellmau has a large group of British skiers, but more families and less party animals than Söll just down the road. In Ellmau you can find some of Austria's best dining and beautiful chalets. The small town has very convenient access to the lifts and is easy to reach from Germany or Innsbruck.

Söll has much more of the party animals with British and Swedes mixing for a great fun-time atmosphere. Westendorf also has a core of British skiers who make this their resort of choice. But all these towns share the same massive interconnected series of trails.

The village of Söll, pronounced "Sull", in the Wilder Kaiser area of Austria is a tremendous favorite with English skiers and young people.

Söll carefully cultivates its small-town image with little shops whose operators are overwhelmingly friendly and strike up a conversation in English at the first opportunity. The main street is full of visitors at almost any hour of the day or night. While traffic is heavy, pedestrians have taken priority, causing motorists to wait, sometimes impatiently, as the shoppers stroll across the roadway to browse.

It's quite clear from the heavy traffic in the local grocery stores that not everyone takes full pension. Full shopping bags mean a lot of picnic lunches and breakfasts prepared back in the room. Everywhere you encounter young couples strolling hand in hand, a change from the more elegant and expensive European resorts where the crowd is older and not always so affectionate.

Söll becomes little U.K. during the winter with a predominant number of the guests coming from the British Islands. Some vacationers who want to soak up the Austrian culture will be disappointed, however those who want to have an easy time with the language will find this village perfect.

On the other side of the Hohe Salve, in the Brixental, is the village of Westendorf. It is a small place, conveniently just up out of the reach of the main road. The town church presides over a series of chalets that provide the picture-perfect Alpine scene. The British and Australians return to this perfect setting year after year. They are joined by a strong Dutch contingent. The mix is most pleasant and the partying is not overbearing. The only major drawback is that the connection to the lifts of Ski Welt is by bus. There is no skiing into town at the end of the day.

There are plans in the works to link Brixen to Westendorf and to link Westendorf with Kirchberg on the other side of the Gampen. When that happens and these trails are linked with those of Kitzbühel and Kirchberg, this interconnected system will be even more amazing.

Mountain layout

The best skiing is concentrated in the valley headed by Söll. Up the valley are Scheffau, Ellmau and finally Going. Around the mountains in another valley are Itter, Hopfgarten, Kelchsau, Westendorf and Brixen Thale. Each has lifts, and all but Westendorf and Kelchsau are on an interconnected circuit. Free bus service is provided from Westendorf, providing skiers with a two-valley network of lifts and hundreds of trails.

Ellmau/Going access to the slopes is via a high-speed quad, a train or a double chair. Taking the high-speed lift is the best bet. At the top there are two six-seat high-speed chair lifts that fill the backside of the Hartkaiser with intermediate skiers.

One thing you will realize quickly is that this region has made a concerted effort to build fast efficient access to the mountains. What they may lack in expert terrain, them make up in speed to the slopes. There are still drag lifts, but you can ski all day, stick to the chairlifts and never need to take a T-bar.

About a 15-minute walk from Söll (connected by a frequent shuttle), an eight-passenger gondola carries skiers up the mountain. The four-passenger gondola, Itter, is usually not crowded and provides quick access to the ski area. Don't plan on taking the lift at Hopfgarten since it is old and slow. There is no need to wait at most of the other access points.

From the top of the Hohe Salve (5,670 feet) at Söll, you can appreciate the massive dimensions of the Wilder Kaiser area which the English and Austrians know from brochures as SkiWelt. Your view includes the 5,115-foot Brandstadl summit at Scheffau, the 4,820-foot Hartkaiser at Ellmau-Going and further to your right the town of Kirchberg, gateway to Kitzbühel.

On the skyline you see ski slopes as far as Pass Thurn, and the famed Grossglockner is on the distant skyline.

Good parallel skiers should do the SkiWelt tour, which begins and ends in Söll (of course you can begin and end wherever you want to). Skiers work their way up and down the ridges, visiting Itter, Hopfgarten, the outskirts of Brixen, then back up to Zinsberg, and finally back to Brandstadl and over to Hartkaiser, stopping along the way in Scheffau, Ellmau and perhaps Going.

Telephone prefix: Söll, 05333; Ellmau, Scheffau and Going, 05358
Westendorf and Brixen im Thale, 05334

The black run from the summit of Hohe Salve above Söll will challenge a good skier. It's a 4 km. trail with a vertical drop of about 2,200 feet. The best intermediate run is the Rigi along the back side and then around the Hohe Salve, all the way down to the Gasthof Kraftalm where they serve a *Jägertee* (Hunter's Tea) that will blast your ski boots off. The recipe, according to the Gasthof owner, is tea, some rum, red wine, plenty of schnapps, a goodly amount of sugar and some herbs for aroma. He adds, "Don't light a match near it while it's hot."

There is also good night skiing in Söll.

Westendorf skiers need to take a bus to the gondola in Brixen im Thale to reach the flanks of Hohe Salve. From the top of the gondola, a six-person high-speed lift makes the final ascent.

The slopes above the town are also quite good. They have a vertical drop of around 1,500 feet and the gondola links with a quad chair lift, a triple and a couple of old single chairs to open up some nice high terrain that holds snow quite well. In fact, when conditions stink in the rest of the region, Westendorf gets packed with riders and skiers.

Snowboarding

This has been rated as a good place to try snowboarding. The slopes are relatively gentle. There is a locally maintained halfpipe and a fun park at Hochsöll. The snowboard school here gets accolades for their beginning and carving programs.

Most boarders will stay on the north side of Hohe Salve. That's where the best snow stays as well as the most interesting trails. Some of the steepest terrain is around Scheffau, but other than that is all easy stuff. Pray for a big snowfall the day before you arrive.

Mountain rating

The Wilder Kaiser is intermediate country with a capital "I." You can head down any slope without hesitation and enjoy moderately challenging, well-groomed runs. A fine place to hone your skiing skills. Not recommended for the demanding skier craving black-trail thrills.

Cross-country

This is a wonderful area for cross-country. There are hundreds of km. of interconnected trails that link Söll with Scheffau, Ellmau, Going and continue on to St. Johann.

In the Brixental the trails link Westendorf with Brixen im Thale and then continue to the end of the valley and Kirchberg.

There are no trail fees and local bus transport between resorts is included in the SkiWelt guest card. Trail maps show where buses stop, restaurants and snack bars are located and where toilet facilities can be found.

Ski school (2002/03 prices)

Each town has its own ski school. Söll has three ski schools. The largest of them, Skischule Söll/Hochsöll (5454), has 150 instructors. The next is Ski School Austria (5005). Finally, there is Ski & Snowboard school Pro-Söll/Ted Kaufmann (2560184). All are noted for their English-speaking instructors, a strength in the Wilder Kaiser region.

Lessons are offered daily. Week-long lessons begin on Sundays and Mondays.

Instruction is 10 a.m. to noon and 2 to 4 p.m.

Private lessons are also offered through the ski school office for €43 per hour, with another €15 for each additional student. Beginner lessons are given directly across from the ski center on the beginner slope. Advanced skiers and experts are taken up the mountain immediately. Even beginners go up after a couple of days.

Private instructor for a day costs €165, with additional persons costing €25.

Group lessons: A full day session will cost €60, three days runs €105, five days is €115. A special half-day (two hours a day) course for intermediate skiers and above is available €67 for three days and €70 for five days.

Lift tickets (2003/04 prices)

These Ski World tickets are good for the entire interconnected area including Going, Ellmau, Scheffau, Söll, Itter, Kelchsau, Hopfgarten, Westendorf and Brixen im Thale.

Ski World	**Adults**	**Children** (age 16 and younger)
one day	€31	€18.50
three days	€87.50	€52.50
six days	€153	€92

These are high season prices.

Children age 6 and younger ski free.

Check also the special ticket which allows some variation on ski days. A choice of five out of seven ski days is €141.50 for adults and €85 for children. A choice of seven out of ten ski days is €176 for adults and €105.50 for children. A choice of ten of 14 ski days is €220.50 for adults and €132.50 for children.

Accommodations

Contact SkiWelt Wilder Kaiser-Brixental (05358-505, fax 50555; internet: www.skiwelt.at) for reservations.

Rates: Based on double occupancy with half board in February. €€€—€125+; €€—€75–€124; €€—less than €75.

Two of the best hotels in the area are in Ellmau. **Hotel Bär** (05358-2395, fax 239596; €€€) and the **Kaiserhof** (05358-2022, fax 220260; €€€) both have all the amenities including indoor pool, saunas and steam baths.

For the most part it is hard to find many hotels that will cost more than about €100 for half board during the ski season. In Westendorf, the top hotels in town don't cost more than €75 for half board during high season!

Gasthof Greil (5289; €€) a 10-minute walk from the center of town is quiet, the food both tasty and filling is served by a friendly staff.

The best hotel in town is **Postwirt** (5081; €€), a renovated, beautiful building near the local tourist office. Equally attractive and historic is **Feldwebel** (5224;€€), a 57-room hotel just down the street. **Hotel Tyrol** (5273; €€) is about halfway between the Greil and the center of town.

On the mountain we liked the **Salvenmoos** (5351; €) for skiers who want to hit the slopes immediately and don't need to go into town often.

There are over two dozen hotels in the Söll area proper. Private rooms and bed & breakfasts are numerous. The tourist office, next to the Postwirt Hotel, can arrange rooms in all price ranges (5216).

In Brixen im Thale, **Gasthof Hoferwirt** (05334-6742, fax 30094; €) is almost across the street from the gondola. **Pension Sonnhof** (05334-8532, fax 6064; €) is the chalet most imagine when heading to the Austrian Alps.

In Westendorf, head to **Hotel Schermer** (05334-6268, fax 2384; €) where you get a covered pool and covered parking. At the **Hotel Jakobwirt** (05334-6245, fax 2467; €) there is another covered pool and the place is perfect for families. The **Hotel Glockenstuhl** (05334-6175, fax 2462; €) also an indoor swimming pool, sauna and its own restaurant. There are also three youth hostels where young skiers can stay for as little as €21 a night with half board.

Ski Chalets: Crystal. (See page 20 for address, phone and fax.)

Dining

One of the best restaurants in Austria is the **Schindlhaus** (516136) in Söll. A young chef has swept in, creating exciting meals. Critics claim the wines are also priced exceptionally. The Mediterranean influences here are blended with local mountain foods.

Hotel Bär (05358-2395, fax 239596) and the **Kaiserhof** (05358-2022, fax 220260) are in the same class as Schindlhaus. At the Bär try the homemade gnocchi, the appetizer bar, the grilled specialties with a strong garlic sauce and finish off with a fine cheese. The Kaiserhof might serve salmon tartar followed by fine seafood with cream polenta. Any gourmet lover will leave pleased. Costs are in the range of €23–€50 at any of these three award-winning restaurants.

Another top restaurant in the region is **Brixner Thalhof** (05334-8468) in Brixen im Thale. This restaurant is proof positive that good simple cooking is sometimes the best. Even the most expensive meal doesn't break €25. We could eat here every night.

One of the best meals we had in Söll was in the **Hotel Greil** (05333-5289). **Stallhäusl** (05332-76342) comes highly recommended as does the **Stöcklalm** (05333-5127). **Gasthof Hochfilzer** (05333-5491) is about one-and-a-half km. out of town but is well worth the walk.

The **Stube** of the Postwirt has the most atmosphere, given the group of old timers at the big front table who puff on their pipes and argue loudly about everything from Austrian politics to the merits of retired Formula One driver Niki Lauda and current ace—and local—Gerhard Berger (both Austrian, naturally). The food is good and filling. The Stube came in second for best apple strudel in town. It was good but not quite as fine as **Cafe Mirabel**'s, up the street past the Thomson Tours office.

Après-ski/nightlife

The ski instructors and longtime visitors gather after skiing in the small bar of the **Postbierstube**. Just keep going past the Stube and you'll find the bar tucked away on the left. For laughter, some sing-along action and live entertainment, the **Pub 15**, a British place despite the name, is the place to visit. When we dropped in, the singer was American and the songs were English and American favorites. A good place to meet new friends is the **Dorfstadl** in the cellar of the Hotel Tyrol. There's a younger crowd and louder music at the **Whiskey Muhle** and **Western Saloon: Buffalo** at the Pizzeria Venezia. **Salvenstadl** rocks just across the main road from the gondola. A couple of igloos serving schnapps and hosting games of nageln, a drinking game in which the participants compete to see who can drive a nail into a tree stump with the narrow end of an hatchet first, make for merriment on the trails back to town from the gondola base.

In Westendorf, the Dutch gather at **Gerry's Bar**. The best tea-time is at **Kibo Bar** and the **Wunderbar** can be fun.

Child care (2003/04 prices)

The ski kindergarten is across the street from the ski school building. Prices are reduced for children from ages 5 to 14 who have at least one parent in the adult ski school. These are the prices for Söll. Prices in the other towns are approximately the same.

Five-day children's ski school costs €115, a three-day program will cost €105, and a full day costs €50. Meals are €11 a day.

A new Mini-Club has opened next to the gondola station for non-skiing kids ages 3-5. A full day of care (9:30 a.m. to 4:30 p.m.) including lunch will cost €40; a half day (9:30 a.m. to 1:30 p.m.) including lunch is €30.

Other activities

Söll has a well-developed recreation complex with a network of cross-country trails. The recreation center has a beautiful indoor pool with a heated outdoor extension.

Check out different activities with the tourist office. There are **toboggan runs, snowshoe tours, rustic cabin evenings, horse-drawn sleigh rides, torchlight hikes** and much more.

Both Salzburg and Innsbruck, with a wide range of museums and scenic outdoor attractions, are within an hour's drive.

In addition, it is not unusual for the visitor with a car to visit Innsbruck and then venture down the Brenner motorway for a short excursion into Italy. The same is true for a visit to Munich for those who arrive from Innsbruck or Milan.

Getting there

The main arrival airport is Munich, about 90 minutes by bus from Söll and other towns in the area. If you're driving, take the Salzburg autobahn out of Munich and then the Rosenheim cutoff (called the Inntal autobahn). You cross the border near Kufstein and take the second exit, Kufstein Sud. Söll will be marked on the autobahn exit sign. From the turnoff, it's about 15 minutes on a two-lane highway over one slight uphill grade to Söll.

Tourist Information

Ski Welt has a centralized information and reservations office at Dorf 35, A-6352 Ellmau, Austria.
Telephone 05358-505, fax 05358-50555.
Email: info@skiwelt.at   Internet: www.skiwelt.at

Tourism Söll, Postfach 21, A-6306 Söll am Wilder Kaiser, Austria.
Call 05333-5216; fax 05333-6180; Email: soell@skiwelt.com

Tourism Westendorf, Schulgasse 2, A-6363 Westendorf, Austria
Telephone 05334-6230 Email: westendorf@skiwelt.at

Telephone prefix: Söll, 05333; Ellmau, Scheffau and Going, 05358
Westendorf and Brixen im Thale, 05334

St. Johann in Tirol

St. Johann in winter is a Tyrolean resort town just far enough from the lifts to keep locals aware of the need to welcome visitors with a smile. The town is afloat in a sea of snow, lending a special atmosphere to a place that can't decide whether it is a resort village or a valley town.

Although St. Johann is only 2,297 feet above sea level, the snowfall here is certain and heavy from Christmas to March. That together with north-facing slopes pleases serious skiers. The setting is picturesque, with the familiar outline of the Kitzbüheler Horn forming part of the panorama. Kitzbühel is about 9.6 km. away.

The typical Tyrolean hotels here are large and have a deserved reputation for hospitality sometimes missing in bigger, better known resorts. At night you'll know immediately from the lower decibel levels that this is not a party town. The streets don't exactly fold up at 8 p.m., but the nightlife is quieter.

The town has an excellent shuttlebus system that links hotels and apartments with the town and the lifts.

The town has become a shopping center for the region and caters to lots of locals as well as the tourists who come to ski. The mix of visitors is fairly well balanced between British, Germans, Dutch and Swedes. It creates a real international atmosphere that adds to the vacation.

One of the year's biggest events is the Tiroler Koasalauf, an international cross-country championship staged in mid-January. It begins at the Koasa Stadium cross-country center on the edge of town. The event has its own Web site at www.koasalauf.at. St. Johann offers more than 64 km. of cross-country runs.

Mountain Layout

The trails run along the flanks of the Kitzbüheler Horn. You can reach them from neighboring Oberndorf by gondola from St. Johann.

The runs lie on the north-facing side of the Kitzbüheler Horn so they maintain their snow cover for the entire season. Snowmaking now spreads the white stuff over three wide top-to-bottom swatches of the mountain. Though the resort has spent money on snowmaking, they, like Kitzbühel, did it at the expense of lifts. It is one of the drag lift capitals of Austria.

The top station is Harschbichl at 5,577 feet. From there you have a choice of blue and red runs and one black trail.

We enjoyed the black run, which really begins from Penzing at 4,799 feet and swings down through mogul fields to the parking lot above Oberndorf. A new gondola will now serve this section of the mountain non-stop from the parking lot. As with any Austrian resort, the off-piste possibilities are endless.

For intermediates, there is the whole mountain that some say is dedicated to intermediate pleasures. Start with the run from the Eichenhof drag lift on the far side of St. Johann for a good downhill cruise and small crowds. From there you can work your way to the Jodlalm chair lift that will take you to just below the Harschbichl. From the top of the Jodlalm chair, cruise to the middle station of the gondola to reach the summit. You can follow the lines of a dozen different trails cut into the mountain.

Beginner slopes are at the bottom of the mountain.

Snowboarders have a halfpipe at Eichenhof and a snowboard jump set up about halfway up the gondola from town.

An expanded pass, Schneewinkel, opens more than 55 lifts serving 170 km. of runs through two adjacent valleys. The St. Johann pass is valid on these lifts when purchased for four days or longer. Though they claim 10 different town included in the pass, there are only five worth noting—St. Johann in Tirol, Waidring, St. Ulrich am Pillersee, and Fieberbrunn.

Again, all are drag-lift heavy and have trails for intermediates and beginners. The longest run in the other areas is in Fieberbrunn tracing a 5 km. length and dropping 2,624 feet. The most difficult trail in the area is considered Buckelpiste Reckmoos under the Reckmoos lift. Fieberbrunn opens up lots of expert off-piste possibilities, but go with a guide.

Mountain rating

St. Johann is for intermediates. The slopes are rarely challenging unless you go off-piste, and only beginners and the intermediates will find the skiing interesting enough for a week. However, with the regional ski pass advanced intermediates and experts can try a number of challenging slopes in the area, in particular those on the Steinplatte above Waidring, about 16 km. from St. Johann and the Fieberbrunn off-piste areas.

Cross-country

Well-laid-out, groomed trails extend in two opposite directions from town. The ski touring center toward one end of town provides good maps, rentals and a starting base. The trails offer pleasant rolling terrain, a taste of backcountry woods (if not all that extensive) and a plenty of traditional inns along the way for lunch, rest and refreshment. St. Johann has 75 km. of set trails basically divided equally between expert, intermediate and beginner. The adjoining trails can link 235 km. of trails stretching from Waidring to Going and Ellmau. No cross-country skier can cruise all these trails in a dedicated week.

Lift tickets (2003/04 prices)

St. Johann now has a new pass that offers lift access to the entire St. Johann/Kitzbühel/Kirchberg/Brixental region. The lifts are not currently interconnected, however buses link areas where lifts do not. A one week Kitzbüheler Alpenskipass costs €176 for adults and €97 for children.

The St. Johann pass covers 17 lifts serving 60 km. of prepared trails on the north side of the Kitzbüheler Horn. Lifts include three gondolas, a quad chair, one triple chair, two double chair, and 10 surface lifts. One day is €29; three days, €82.

Schneewinkel pass covers 170 km. of runs in St. Johann in Tirol, Oberndorf, Kirchdorf in Tirol, Erpfendorf, Fieberbrunn, St. Jakob im Haus, St. Ulrich am Pillersee, Hochfilzen, Waidring und Kössen and is good for four days or more of skiing. Four days cost €109. Six days cost €149.

These are high-season prices. There is a small discount in low season, and children pay approximately 50 percent less with those younger than six years old skiing for free.

Ski school (2003/04 prices)

St. Johann has approximately 130 instructors available for the winter season. There is the Ski School St. Johann (64777) and the Skischule Eichenhofin (61548).

Private lessons (for 1 to 2 persons) cost €90–€125 for a half day and €165–€190 for a full day.

Group lessons for one day are €52–€59; for three days, €95–€99; for five days, €115–€119; and for six days, €125–€129.

Cross-country lessons cost for three half days, €60; and for six half days, €80.

Accommodations

St. Johann has one of the best organized accommodation services in Austria. Using the St. Johann hotel-apartment list with an accompanying reservation form, available free from the tourist office, you can arrange for any type of accommodation—from simple B&B to apartment rental.

We recommend that you come in January or March when the maximum price reductions are offered. Two sport packages are outstanding. Variation A includes a Schneewinkel six-day ski pass. Variation A has a starting cost of €230 for B&B and €339 for half board. Variation B includes a Schneewinkel six-day ski pass and six days of lessons. Variation B has a starting cost of €338 for B&B and €447 with half board. The sport package price for a first-class hotel or guesthouse is about what you'd pay just for accommodations at some resorts. St. Johann hotels and guesthouses offer the mid-range all-inclusive package.

Based on high season, per person/double occupancy with breakfast: €€€—more than €80; €€—€50–79; €—less than €50.

Our favorite deluxe hotels are the **Hotel Bruckenwirt** (Kaiserstrasse 18, 62585, fax 6258514; €€) with the town center right outside your door; **Sporthotel Austria** (Winterstellerweg 3, 62507, fax 65137; €€) with a hotel swimming pool; **Hotel Crystal** (Hornweg 5, 62630, fax 6263013; €–€€) right along the ski runs; **Goldener Löwe** (Spechbacherstrasse 23, 62251, fax 62981; €–€€) the town's largest with lots of package groups; and **Hotel Dorfschmiede** (Spechbacherstrasse 24, 62323, fax 621678; €€) has a heated swimming pool and is three minutes to the lifts and the downtown.

For one of Austria's best experiences try **Hotel Gruber** (Gasteigerstrasse 18; 61461, fax 6146133; €€–€€€). It comes highly recommended for its atmosphere and service. The Gruber family does it right.

Hotel Schöne Aussicht (Berglehen 23, 62270, fax 64626; €€) with an excellent location on the slopes.

If you stay at the **Pension Aloisia** (Schwimmbadweg 8, 62419, fax 64485; €) you will have the Panoramabad right outside your door. It's almost like having a swimming pool right in your hotel for a fraction of the cost.

St. Johann has a multitude of excellent accommodations; we've never been disappointed. The tourist office can provide a full list and help with reservations. There are scores of Garni, Gasthöfe and Pensionen that have room and breakfast for less than €50 a night. That's a steal.

Apartments, condominiums, flats

Apartment rental is as easy as finding hotel or pension lodging in St. Johann. Contact the tourist office and tell them your arrival date. They will send a list of available apartments. You then contact the apartment owner directly. Apartments that sleep four range in price from €35–€70 a night.

Dining

For Austrian specialties head to one of the three following restaurants. The **Post** (62230), smack in the middle of town, oozes charm. **Hotel Bruckenwirt/Restaurant Ambiente** (62585) is the upscale place in St Johann. The restaurant is top of the line and an elegant piano lounge offers an authentic English tea service. One is expected to dress up a little for dinner in the restaurant, but things can be more casual in the lounge and bar. **Park Hotel** (62226) offers Tyrolean and Austrian specialties in a not-so-formal atmosphere. **Römerhof** (63516) has more recommended Tyrolean meals.

For the best in Italian, head to **Villa Masianco** (64630), an affordable pizzeria serving Italian meals that the locals love. This place has grown from a small pizza joint to a big restaurant over the past decade. It must be doing something right.

Pizzeria Rialto (64168). Pizza and the rest right at the station in what may have been the old station house. Pleasant and charming northern Italian/Tyrolean decor.

La Rustica (62843) serves meals from wood-fired pizza to pasta to scallopini.

Café Platzl (62380) has a very good ice cream bar and family restaurant upstairs. Lively but not too rowdy bar for the twenty-somethings downstairs. Easy to find right on the main plaza in the center of town.

Café Rainer (62235) is the best cafe in town and doubles as a family restaurant with live local (but not Tyrolean) music on the main street. It even fills up for lunch with locals who munch on treats from the impressive pastry shop attached.

Eateries with great views include **Gasthof Hochfeld** (62985) at an altitude of 3,280 feet, which also organizes sledding evenings, and **Schöne Aussicht** (62270). **Gasthof Rummlerhof** (63650) is a perfect spot for lunch or dinner if you are on the cross-country trails. For great pastries, head to the **Café-Konditorei Nill** at Kaiserstrasse 26.

Après-ski/nightlife

One of the nice things about skiing here is that the runs drop right into the town which makes starting après-ski very convenient and most people can walk back to their hotels.

Café Rainer has the best tea-time après-ski atmosphere. It kicks into full gear about 3:30 p.m. and carries on until 7 p.m. or so.

The Brewery behind the Hotel Goldener Löwe can be lots of fun.

Bunny Pub, one of the livelier places to go, and recently enlarged, is easygoing and casual, good for après-ski with a happy hour, kareoke and live music later in the night. It is filled with Brits and Aussies.

Max Pub is fairly lively. An open-air tent at the foot of the slopes. Frequented by a young crowd and music is LOUD. Also has karaoke and live music at night.

Chez Paul Bar and Café serves small meals just a short walk from the town center. Pleasant and informal, though slightly yuppified. More for a thirty-something crowd than a disco set.

Michi's in the Hotel Fischer is also a good place to meet after skiing and later.

Scala is a hopping disco/dance hall near the Café Passage, the younger hangout for those who like the music turned UP.

Child care

Ski instruction is offered for children ages 3-1/2 and older. Ski kindergarten is offered for ages 2–4 years old. For more information (64777 or 65930). Prices for instruction are the same as for adults. For details on babysitting services, call the St. Johann tourist office (63335).

Getting there

St. Johann is about 68 miles from Munich and 59 miles from Innsbruck; most visitors arrive from Munich. Take the Inntal autobahn and exit at Felbertauern/St. Johann in Tirol. Train service connects St. Johann with Innsbruck and Munich.

Other activities

In recent years St. Johann has pushed hard to expand its recreational activities. The Panoramabad complex features a 50-meter **heated pool**, **sauna**, **steamrooms**, a long **water slide** to keep kids and the kids-in-us happy, a **wading pool** and an **ice skating rink**.

Indoor tennis (63377 or 62625) is a popular activity.

Horse-drawn sleigh rides cost approximately €14 for two-and-a-half hours at the Hinterkaiser (63325). Horse drawn sleigh rides leave from St. Johanner Hof (05352/62207), Othmas Krisca (05352/62759).

There is a great lighted **toboggan/rodel run** from Hochfeld/Hirschberg down the mountain. It is open until midnight everyday, with lifts operating from 7–9:30 p.m. on Monday, Wednesday and Friday.

There are **Kegelbahns** in the Hotel Goldener Löwe (62251) and in the Tennis Kegel Center (63377). For **hot-air balloon rides** call Ballooning Tyrol (65666). They cost €290 per person. For tandem **paragliding**, try Mountain High (0664/2415561 or 5352/62101) for €98 per person.

The town itself is beautiful to look at, with one Tyrolean house after another presenting traditional Austrian scenes and motifs painted on the exterior walls.

Tourist information

Tourismusverband St. Johann, A-6380 St. Johann in Tirol, Austria; 05352-63335, fax 05352-65200.
For snow conditions call 05352-64358.
Internet: www.st.johann.tirol.at
E-mail: info@st.johann.tirol.at

Zell am See-Kaprun

Here is an Alpine combination as compatible as beer and pretzels. Yes, these two neighboring resorts fit together hand in glove, like a finely tuned dance team where both partners have learned to subtly complement each other for the best possible performance. Above the low-key village of Kaprun, the Kitzsteinhorn glacier guarantees wide-open bowl skiing the year round, while the majority of Zell am See's Schmittenhöhe slopes sweep down through the trees, more reminiscent of Colorado's Breckenridge or classic New Hampshire trails.

Together they comprise the Europa Sports Region, a land rich with winter and summer outdoor activities. In the spring, high-energy types can ski in the morning and windsurf the lake in the afternoon. Austrian and European skiers have long known the Europa Sports Region as an ideal location for skiing. The area was one of the first resorts in Austria with descents recorded as far back as 1893.

Lake Zell serves as the region's focal point. This long narrow body of water sprawls 13 kms. along a picturesque valley shadowed by the Hohentauern, Austria's highest mountain range. When the lake freezes in winter, townspeople fish through the ice, go ice-boating, or skate across Zell's surface to the village of Thumersbach on the other side.

Zell am See sits on a flat semicircular piece of land that juts into the lake, squeezed from the mountains ringing the shore. Cream-colored buildings huddle around the well-preserved 13th-century church of St. Hippolyt, and the Vogtturm (city tower) which dominate Zell's skyline, giving it the air of a medieval mountain town rather than a bustling ski village. One could wander for hours through the town's winding streets and have no trouble envisioning merchants and traders from bygone days going about their business.

Today the streets are still lined with unpretentious shops—sport stores, well-stocked markets, intriguing crafts shops. You'll also find cozy cafés, gasthauses and restaurants filled with locals and tourists alike. Zell am See, with a year-round population of almost 10,000, has honed the fine art of balancing the fantasy sought by tourists with the real needs of its citizens.

On the surface, Kaprun puts on a quieter face than does Zell am See, partly because it is much smaller in scale. But its laid-back atmosphere sets a more relaxing pace, and the village common gives it the air of a small New England college town. The Kitsteinhorn was Austria's first glacial ski area.

On the mountain, Kaprun has completed a new Alpine Center at the top of the old Gletscherbahn.

Mountain layout

There are two major areas: Zell am See's Schmittenhöhe lifts take skiers to the 6,500-foot level, while Kaprun is famed as a year-round ski area with runs on the glacier beneath the peak of the 10,506-foot Kitzsteinhorn.

To ski the Schmittenhöhe, avoid the main cable car from town and take either the Sonnenalmbahn or better still, the newly-extended Areit gondola from neighboring Schüttdorf direct to the Breiteck peak. You can also take the Zeller Bergbahn and work your way up the left side of the mountain.

The runs are good for intermediates with some expert challenges too, particularly the two runs used in the World Cup and regional downhill races. Our favorite is the trail from the Kapellenlift summit to Breiteckalm and then down a wonderful turning slope parallel to the woods. From there, it's black to the bottom. Locals call this run the Trass. Intermediate skiers may enjoy the Standard—it drops from the top to Breiteck but then breaks back to the right over the Hirschkögel trail.

Kaprun is about six miles from Zell am See and it's another three and a half miles to the base of the area's lifts. Take the two-stage cable car up to the glacier to Alpincenter. A third section of the aerial cable car continues to the top of the Kitzsteinhorn at 9,935 feet.

Kaprun's skiing is for the most part intermediate. Experts will want to tackle the final part of the run from the top of the Gletscherbahn to the Langwied midstation, run 8 from the Sonnenkarbahn, or run 2 on the left side of the glacier. While up at the peak of the Kitzsheinhorn, take your skis off and walk the 360-meter-long tunnel for a 360-degree panorama view of the Hohe Tauern National Park and the Grossglockner, a 12,460-foot-high giant of a mountain.

Finally, for the area's ultimate in off-piste expert skiing, hire a guide (contact any ski school) and leave the back side of the Kitzsteinhorn glacier and ski to the valley of Niedernsill.

Snowboarding

Competitive snowboarders should head to the Gipfelbahn area to find the "boarder cross," a gnarly race course made up of gates, bumps, gaps and a 360-degree ramp. Access the halfpipe and quarterpipes on the Kitzsteinhorn glacier via the Keeslift. Intermediate and Alpine Snowboarders will be happiest riding down the wide cruisers of the Schmittenhohe and riding the aerial lifts, rather than riding T-bars to the relatively flat terrain of the glacier. Expert boarders should hire a guide from any ski school and ride off-piste both at the Kitzsteinhorn and Schmittenhöhe. Schmittehöhe also has a half pipe at the Glocknerbahn and an area called Jumping City at the top station of Areit III that expert boarders will also enjoy.

Mountain rating

Zell am See is outstanding for intermediates; its network of trails and connecting lifts offers new challenges and different aspects to the slopes as you work your way across the area. For the beginner there are training slopes and plenty of room to take a fall or two without serious suffering. Experts will head for the glacier at Kaprun, where there are also challenging intermediate runs. The combined ski region offers 54 lifts and 130 km. (80 miles) of trails. A very efficient bus system, included with your Europa Sport Region ski pass, serves both areas.

The Kitzsteinhorn glacier is an easy intermediate area. Though there are ultra wide, gradual runs, the vast number of skiers and the altitude make it an intimidating experience for the beginner. Experts will have to search for ravines (*renne*) or gullies (*wassarkar*) to the sides of the groomed pistes for bumps and steeps filled with powder.

Lift tickets (2003/04 prices)

Tickets for the Europa Sports Region Pass:

	High Season	Low Season	Pre-Season
two days	€64	€60.50	--
three days	€94	€84.50	€89
four days	€119	€108.50	€113
five days	€143	€129	€136
six days	€164	€148	€156

Children get approximately a 50 percent discount. Daily rates at the separate sections of the Europa Sports Region are approximately €34.50. Zell am See Schmittenhöhe daily rates are also €34.50.

Shuttlebuses and local transport between Kaprun and Zell am See are free if you buy the regional ski pass.

Ski school (2003/04 prices)

Zell am See/Kaprun ski school has approximately 260 instructors. Courses range from beginner through competition racing techniques. Information is available through the ski school office in the valley station of the Sonnenalmbahn (73207).

Private lessons cost €200 for one day (four hours) or €50 per hour, €20 per additional persons.

Group lessons for a day (four hours) are €50; three days cost €120; and for four to five days run €135.

Accommodations

Zell am See (telephone prefix is 06542)

Many of Zell's hotels and pensions are near the lifts. In addition, for those who want to be closer to the Kaprun glacier, there are accommodations in Kaprun.

Thumersbach, across the lake, is separated from the best skiing but quite scenic. Check with the tourist office in Zell for further information.

Zell also offers 24-hour service to individuals who come without reservations. Visitors can use an information board similar to those used at airports: push a button next to the hotel name, and its location is illuminated on the map. You can then telephone the hotel directly and check on room availability.

The all-in one-week package is called Schnee-Okay, and is available in low and middle season. A Schnee-Okay package in a four star hotel with half board is available in January at the starting price of €588. Schnee-Okay includes seven days accommodation, a six-day regional pass, unlimited use of the ski shuttlebus and six days' admittance to swimming pools in Zell and Kaprun. Schnee-Okay also includes six days' use of the indoor ice rink in Zell, a 10 percent discount on ski rental and a €10 discount on a four or five day ski course at either the Zell am See or Kaprun ski school. At the other end of the price scale is the simple B&B starting at €308 a week.

Rates below are per person based on double occupancy with half board in February. €€€—€125+; €€—€75–€124; €—less than €75.

Lodges are plentiful in Zell am See. One of the most romantic is the **Grand Hotel** at Esplanade 4 (788; €€€) on the shores of Lake Zell. This stylish beauty was built to be enjoyed from bottom to top. Dine in its casually elegant restaurant, then head upstairs to the glass-domed Wunderbar for a nightcap.

The Hotel Salzburgerhof, Auerspergstrasse 11 (765; €€€) is Zell am See's only five-star hotel. Lodging at this large, chalet-style hotel includes a Wellness Center with a whirlpool, sauna, swimming pool, solarium, massage facilities and exceptional cuisine in its award winning restaurant.

A very nice four-star hotel is the **Hotel Neue Post**, Schlossplatz 2 (73773; €€€). Well located and handy to shops and restaurants, this family-owned condominium property features an outdoor hot tub, sauna, massage, fitness room, and television in all rooms. The lobby bar is a good place to meet friends. Friendly desk clerks will have your laundry done for a very reasonable price.

Closer to the slopes, the **Hotel Berner**, at Nikolaus-Gassner-Promenade 1 (779; €€€) sits just a block or so off the main thoroughfares, a short walk from the Zeller Bergbahn gondolas. The warm friendly personalities of the Berner family will make you feel very much at home.

Other recommended four-star hotels are: **Hotel Zum Hirschen,** Dreifaltigkeitgasse (774; €€€); **Hotel St. Georg** Schillerstrasse (768; €€€); **Hotel Metzgerwirt** Sebastian Horl Str. 11 (72520; €€€); and **Hotel Alpenblick** Alte Landstrasse (5433; €€€).

Three-star recommendations:

The Sporthotel Lebzelter, Dreifaltigkeitgasse 7 (06542/ 776; €€) is one of Zell am See's most conveniently located lodges, right in the heart of town and just a few steps away from prime shopping.

Hotel Krone Kitzsteinhornstrasse 16 (57421; €€).

An excellent two-star choice is **Gasthof Steinerwirt,** Schlossplatz 1 (72502; €).

For B&Bs or Frühstückspension try the **Alpenrose** (72570; €), the **Landhaus Buchner** (72062; €), the **Hubertus** (72427; €), or the **Klothilde** (72660; €), all of which have English-speaking employees, who are quite interested in interaction with tourists.

Kaprun (telephone prefix is 06547)

For its size, **Kaprun** boasts an array of accommodations you would expect to find at much larger resorts, and the Kaprun/Zell am See transportation system has so many pickup spots that location isn't really an issue.

Sporthotel Kaprun (8625; €€€) is one of the better full-service lodges. At the south end of town, it offers a panoramic view of the village from its north-facing side and a dazzling look at the Kitzsteinhorn from the other. Sit on the terrace in early morning and watch the sun dance off the Kitzsteinhorn's peaks. Hearty buffet breakfasts are served each morning. Lunch and dinner are also served in the hotel's spacious dining room.

One of the best four-star "downtown" hotels is the **Orgler** (8205; €€€). You'll want to tiptoe over the fine oriental rugs scattered about its light pine-paneled lobby.

Other recommended four-star hotels: **Steigenberger Kaprun,** Schlossstrasse 751 (7647, fax 7680; €€€). **Hotel Antonius,** Schlossstrasse 744, (7670, fax 76706; €€€). **The Hotel Zur Burgruine** (8306, fax 830660; €€€) is near the Kaprun fortress ruins. The hotel's cheerful dining room is excellent for dinner whether you stay here or not. **The Hotel Sonnblick** (8301, fax 830166; €€€), just off town central, is another outstanding spot if only for its wide balconies made for enjoying the views.

Other three- & two-star recommendations are: **Katharinehof** (8866; € B&B), **Alpenrose** (7240; €€ B&B), **Eschenhof** (8674; € B&B), **Alpenblick** (8477; € B&B), **Jaga-Hias** (8345; € B&B) and **Heidi**, near town center (8223; €).

Ski Chalets: Inghams/Bladon. (See page 25 for phone, fax and Internet addresses.)

Apartments, condominiums, flats

The tourist office will provide a list of available apartments and chalets in the area. In addition, you can book directly through agencies in the area. For more information, call Apartmentservice (80480). Apartments large enough to sleep four will range in price from €60–90 per night.

Dining

Schloss Prielau (72609) is acknowleged to be the top restaurant in the area. It serves internationally recognized award-winning continental cuisine. Call for reservations.

Ampere (72363) at Schmittenstr. 12, Zell am See, is a chic bistro with a horseshoe bar complete with electric generator and the main dining room upstairs. Recommended by Gault Millau. The **Landhotel Erlhof** (566370) is also highly rated by Gault Millau for gourmet cuisine.

The next restaurants all serve excellent Austrian cuisine. For the best combination of fine dining in a comfortable atmosphere (lots of wood carvings and unusual wall lights), try the **Steinerwirt** in Zell am See. It specializes in sirloin steak Vienna style (with onions and small dumplings), and the Salzburger Nockerl (a tasty soufflé) is not to be missed for dessert.

The **Guggengbichl** hut features Kasnocken (noodles, cheese and butter) baked and served in a huge skillet. Scraping out the bottom of the pan for the crusted delicacy is fun for the whole table. The inn rises above Kaprun and diners are allowed to climb 5,280 feet above and slide down to the entrance in sleds provided for the thrill. It's a good way to work up an appetite or work off the huge dinner.

Jagawirt (8737) near Kaprun is a charming inn, owned and operated by Hans and Theresia Nindl, which provides an outstanding dining experience. We enjoyed wild goat (Gamsgebraten) in mushroom sauce with black bread dumplings (Schwartzbrotknodel) and cranberries (Pieiselbeen). A venison filet (Hirschrunckenfilet) is cooked medium (Rosabebraten) with mushrooms (Steinpilen) in Burgundy sauce, €20. Nindl is an avid hunter and he takes some of the local game (venison, antelope, goat) for the restaurant. Two delicious desserts are blueberries heated with flour and eggs with vanilla ice cream (Moosbeernocking) for €6, and Mandelecken, a light almond cake floating in blueberry and kiwi sauce for €6. The inn is also a popular après-ski stop for skiers coming down from the Kitzsteinhorn glacier. African art and artifacts decorate the walls of the restaurant, attesting to the Nindls' living in Rhodesia part time. Jagawirt is only open September through May.

Limberghof, just outside Zell am See, serves rich fried pork, veal and beef steaks on wooden planks. Tropfen Amelner, about 90 proof, is a perfect *digestif*.

Dorfstadl is the locals' favorite restaurant in the region. The setting is hand-hewn post-and-beam and the food is spectacular not only in taste but in presentation. Try the garlic soup for an appetizer and apple strudel for dessert. For a main course any selection will please.

Once you have had your fill of Austrian fare, try Italian or Tex-Mex.

Delicious cordon bleu and pepper steak top the fare at **Traubenstube**. For a light meal, sample **Pizzeria Giuseppe** and **Zum Casar** (47257). **Crazy Restaurant**, located upstairs from the Crazy Daisy Pub, is a Scandinavian-owned Mexican restaurant with an inexpensive menu featuring among other items "breath killer" garlic bread.

The **Café Konditorei Mosshammer** and **Café Feinschmeck** are your best bets for a late afternoon snack, especially for mouth-watering pastries and chocolates. **Vanini** on Banhofstrasse has the best and largest variety of Austrian and other pastries.

In Kaprun, dining is good at the large hotels. Two favorites: **Sporthotel Kaprun** and **Hotel Zur Burgruine**. The **Cafe Konditorei** has wonderful pastries in Kaprun.

On the mountain, at the top of the Schmittenhöhe, **Breiteckalm** is the lunch choice. Here Peter Radcher, owner, chef, waiter, bartender and perfect Austrian host, serves a hearty traditional Austrian fare.

Gletschermühle on the glacier is a good luncheon spot with its Tyrolean fare, spectacular views, huge deck and sun chairs for rent.

Après-ski/nightlife

Come evening, intimate taverns and rollicking discos open their doors. For quieter entertainment, elegance and perfect location head for the **Wunderbar** on the top floor of the Grand Hotel overlooking Lake Zell.

The Sportstüberl, in the Hotel Lebzelter, is an après-ski bar built in the 1700s, and its bartenders wear lederhosen. It is open 4 p.m.–4 a.m. and offers an atmosphere where locals and tourists gather for a cold beer or a hot Jägertee. Here townsfolk sometimes challenge each other at *Stocknagaln*, a game where the object is to hit a thin nail imbedded in a block of wood with the sharp blade of an ax.

The **Jagawirt** is one of the most picturesque après-ski gathering spots.

Curiously, the largest (and the most lively) night haunt in the region lies on the outskirts of tiny Kaprun, not in Zell am See: **The Baum Bar** burned to the ground a few years ago, and when it was rebuilt it bounded back better than ever. A huge dance floor is usually packed by midnight. Partygoers boogie till closing time at 6 a.m.

Entertainment is harder to find in Kaprun, but it is there. The **Idefix Pub** and the **Austrian Pub** are perfect. Another good disco is the **Nindl-Dancing**. The **Vine Bar Di Vino, Roses** and **Pavillion** are recent additions to the Kaprun nightlife.

In Zell am See, one of the most popular stops for vacationing Europeans is the **Crazy Daisy Pub**, 10 Brucker Bundesstrasse, which is usually full of Brits, Dutch, Swedes and other party-hardy types. Bands play seven nights a week. Order drinks like "No Thanks I'm Fine," "Against the Wall," "Orgasm" and "Slippery Nipples." The **Pinzgauer Diele** has great après-ski 'till 7 p.m., then after 11 p.m. it's considered the top disco. It's often loud with ski movies. The **Bierstadl** features 33 different kinds of beer and is where the locals gather. **Classics** features live music, but can be a bit smoky. **Hirschenkeller** is a blues, rock and reggae bar across the street from the post office under Hotel Zum Hirschen. **Viva Club** disco heats up after 1 a.m. at 4 Kirchengasse. Après-ski can be enjoyed at the outside bar atop **Schmittenhöhe**, overlooking the church and at **Ampere** near the Zeller Bergbahn.

Child care (2003/04 prices)

Ursula Zink (56343) also sits for children from 1 year of age. Rates: one day, €36.34; three days, €87.20; six days, €138.10.

Fesienolorf Hagleituer (7187) for ages 1 year and older, Monday-Friday, 10 a.m. to 4 p.m.; €36.34 for one day, including lunch.

The children's ski school is open daily from 10 a.m. to 3 p.m. Lunch is included, and children age 4 to 10 are accepted for €120 for three days and €135 for four to five days.

In Kaprun, call 7582 or 8232 or 0664-3425317 for children's ski school information; in Zell the number is 72320 or 0664-4531417 or 0664-2530381.

Other activities

A visit to nearby **Salzburg**, made famous a generation ago by the movie *The Sound of Music* and always famous as Mozart's home, attracts hundreds of thousands of tourists each year.

The Zell skyline is distinguished by the outlines of the St. Hippolyt church and the Vogtturm (city tower). Even nonskiers will enjoy the Schmittenhöhe on a clear day when you can see at least thirty 3,000-meter (9,843-foot) or higher peaks in the region.

On Sunday evenings in Kaprun, the tourist office stages **folk entertainment** and **story telling** around a bonfire within the ruins of an old fortress. You'll enjoy the music, though the stories are in German.

At Kaprun, visit the Gothic Pfarrkirche in the middle of town and the castle ruins, even if you're not there for the storytelling and music.

The Kaprun Optimum with an indoor and outdoor **swimming pool** and **fitness center** is packed with fitness-minded Europeans and is a great place to meet other skiers. The pool is open from 11 a.m.–10 p.m. Entrance is €7.40 for adults. The pool sauna costs €12.60 per session.

Castles are in Prielau and Kaprun.

For **Alpine sightseeing flights** call 757937. Try **bowling** at Schlossstrasse (8222). For **horse-drawn sleigh rides** check out Pichlbauer (7322).

There is an illuminated **toboggan** run from Jausenstation Guggenbichl, Kaprun. There are also runs from Schaufelberg and Lechnerberg.

For **ice-skating** head to the Sports and Leisure Center (785)

For a fine selection of Austrian crafts and ceramics stop in at Hierner & Co. Stadtplatz 6, Zell am See. For souvenirs there are a plenty of choices in the village.

Getting there

Zell is about 56 miles from Salzburg, which has jet service from other European airports. The usual airport for international arrivals is Munich, about 143 miles away. Vienna is about 240 miles.

Zell has regular national and international train service and bus service to Kaprun.

By automobile from Munich, drive to Salzburg by autobahn, and head toward Bischofshofen. Rental cars are available in Salzburg or Munich.

Tourist information

Europa Sportregion Zell am See - Kaprun
A-5700 Zell am See, Austria
tel. 06542-770, fax 06542-72032.
E-mail: welcome@europasportregion.info.
Internet: www.europasportregion.info.

Kaprun Information, A-5710 Kaprun, Austria;
tel. 06547-8080, fax 06547-808080.

Les Arcs Bourg-St. Maurice

Les Arcs is not a town or village. It is a group of modern complexes high above the Savoy transportation hub of Bourg St. Maurice. It was designed expressly as a ski resort; a purpose-built collection of large sprawling hillside buildings with an unusual swooping roof design.

This resort has become part of one of the largest interconnected ski and snowboard areas in the world. Les Arcs recently linked its trail system with that of La Plagne via Plan-Peisey. The combined area will be called Paradiski and will have 420 km. of trails. The enormity is mindboggling. The joint resorts will boast 144 ski lifts: 1 funicular 4 light-weight cable cars 1 'Funitel' (twin-cable cable car), 10 sections of gondola lifts, 18 detachable chairlifts, 47 chairlifts, 28 ski lifts suitable for walkers and 25 ski lifts accessible free of charge.

A cable car, Le Vaniose Express, with 200-person cabins will span the valley from Plan-Peisey on the Les Arcs side to Les Coches on the La Plagne side. The span will be 3,000 meters and the futuristic cable car will be as much as 380 meters above the valley floor. The trip, from station to station, will take four minutes. The La Plagne (the largest individual ski are in France) trails are detailed in a separate chapter.

Les Arcs displays a remarkable unity, not only in its architecture, but also in its infrastructure and support systems. You have the sense of being inside a smoothly running machine rather than a village of competing shops, restaurants, and owners. It's not a bad feeling—just curiously different.

Many of the rooms are accessed by ramps, giving the appearance that no two rooms are on the same level. Of the three high-altitude complexes that comprise Les Arcs (each named for its altitude in meters), Arc 1600, a family-orientated area with four hotels, shops and a nursery that takes children from four months old, was the first. Rooms tend to be functional and more moderately priced, and the nightlife is minimal. Arc 1800 is the largest complex, with the biggest selection of restaurants and shops. Arc 2000 was constructed last, as the lift system expanded to reach the higher elevatios.

It offers skiing and riding for every level and easy access to the glacier. But its surrounding expert terrain has made it a famous shrine for serious skiers.

Intrawest has already begun construction on Arc 1950, Le Village. Expected to be completed in 2008, Arc 1950 intends to provide an additional 750 apartments/chalets to the area as well as numerous shops and restaurants. Arc 1950 will be an entirely pedestrian village and will be linked to Arc 2000 by a new cabriolet.

Overall, the resort is decidedly international, with a little less than half its clientele arriving from outside France. You'll have no difficulty finding someone who speaks English if you need help, nor will it be a problem striking up conversations in bars or on the lifts.

Included in the ski pass for the area (see Lift tickets) are lifts originating in the lower villages of Peisey-Nancroix, Vallandry and Villaroger. These hamlets are century-old settlements that offer a strong contrast to the stylized angular atmosphere of Les Arcs.

For visitors who want to combine a bit of local flavor with their high-tech ski adventure, a seven-minute funicular ride down the steep slope from Arc 1600 to Bourg St. Maurice offers a chance to spend a few hours in the shops, museums, and restaurants of a Savoyard town. A bustling open-air market on Saturdays offers Savoy specialties such as mountain ham, wine, and rich and creamy Reblechon and Beaufort cheeses.

Mountain layout

Les Arcs is glorious for the ski-till-you-drop-and-then-do-it-some-more crowd. Snowboarders come from all over the northern hemisphere because, as one American enthusiast was heard to say, "In France you have the right to die." This doesn't detract from France's excellent safety records, but the French are not saddled with the onerous liability problems faced by American resorts. Trails are marked but this is generally seen as a formality or as a handy guide in white-out conditions. Otherwise, ski at your own risk.

Les Arcs has three large sections and two smaller ones. The sectors are all linked. The first major area is the face above Arc 1800 and 1600, with 28 lifts servicing six expert trails, 15 intermediate runs, and 19 beginner slopes.

The second major area is a massive valley above and beyond Arcs 2000 bounded by the 10,484-foot peak and ridge formed by the Col du Grand Renard and the Arpette. The 15 lifts in this area service 10 expert, 10 intermediate, and 11 beginner trails, as well as plenty of off-piste possibilities.

Beginning Christmas 2003, the Vanoise Express, will connect Les Arcs to La Plagne and create the new Paradiski Ski Area. The 425-square-km. Paradiski area will open three glaciers and two summits, each above 3,000 meters high, to every level of skier. Skiers will have their pick of 232 pistes served by 175 ski lifts. Boarders will enjoy 2 boardercross areas, 4 snowparks and 2 halfpipes.

The connected area of Peisey-Nancroix Vallandry is part of the overall ski area, but does not have a particularly easy connection to the Arc 1600 sector. This area has one expert trail, a baker's dozen of intermediate runs, and 10 beginner runs. In cloudy or windy weather, these tree-lined slopes offer good visibility.

Finally, there is the Villaroger sector, at the end of the two long Aiguille Rouge runs. It has only three direct lifts back to the crest above Arc 2000. Another lift allows those who have skied below Arc 2000 to reach Villaroger without returning to the top of the Aiguille Rouge.

Mountain rating

This is one of the best Alpine areas, featuring something for everyone from beginner to expert. There is great intermediate skiing all across the face above Arc 1800 descending from Arpette, Col des Frettes, and Col du Grand Retard. Advanced intermediates will love the runs from the Aiguille Rouge across the glacier and down the Piste du Grand Col. Beginners and intermediates will have plenty of area at the bottom of the valley between Aiguille Rouge and Arpette. Experts face some exhilarating runs from the Aiguille Rouge across the glacier, and then can drop down the massive face above Arcs 2000.

Above Peisey-Nancroix Vallandry are relatively gentle intermediate and beginner runs. The drop along the ridge to Villaroger is for strong intermediates and experts. Experts should sign up with a guide and tackle the off-trail tours circling behind the Aiguille Grive and the Aiguille Rousse or for an itinerary off the backside of the Aiguille Rouge looping around to Villaroger.

Snowboarding

Like all major ski areas, Les Arcs has terrain for all levels of snowboarders. With a large portion of the boarding above treeline, Les Arcs has tons of open spaces for cruising, but relatively little tree boarding. If you are looking for tree boarding, though, the best place you'll find will be above Plan Peisey and Vallandry.

The never-ever boarders should head to the free bunny lifts at 1600, 1800, and 2000 (1600 lifts—TK Pierre Blanche, TS Combettes, TK Millerette; 1800 lifts—TS Chantel, TS Jardin Alpin; and 2000 lifts—TS Saint Jacques, TK La Combes 1-2, TK Rhodos). There you will find open easy terrain perfect for your first few turns.

Beginners will benefit most from the first half of the Transarc gondola and the upper sections of Plan Peisey and Vallandry, where the trails are wider than they are lower in the valley.

Intermediate riders can tackle most of the upper portions of Arc 1600 and 1800 except for L'Arpette and Col Des Frettes, which are steep and sometimes covered in moguls. Starting from Arc 2000, intermediates should stay on Plagnettes and Bosses or Bois De L'Ours and Comborciere, but should think twice when deciding whether or not to hit Grand Col, Aiguille Rouge, or Varet.

Advanced and expert boarders can walk all over the mountain, but will find the best stuff in Grand Col or off Aiguille Rouge. If you're looking for a real adventure, then go to a local ski school and ask about the awesome backcountry opportunities starting from the top of the Aiguille Rouge and Le Grand Col.

At the L'Arpette terrain park you'll find a halfpipe and some sweet tabletop jumps perfect for huge air. It's possible to buy a "snow park" lift ticket if you're planning to spend the day around the park. The ticket allows you to go on the three lifts right around the park plus a chair from 1600 and one from 1800. At Arc 2000, there is a halfpipe right at the base off of Lac des Combes, one of the free lifts at les Arcs. The halfpipe at 2000 is also lighted and can be used at night almost every day of the week. The combined Paradiski region has two boarder cross, four snowparks and two halfpipes.

Ski school (2003/04 prices)

French Ski School (ESF), **Arc Adventures**, **Virages**, and **Initial Snow** all have ski school programs in the villages.

French Ski School (ESF) has bases at Arcs 1600 (0479 07 43

09), Arcs 1800 (0479 07 40 31), and Arcs 2000 (0479 07 47 52); group and private lessons are offered to skiers and boarders of any age greater than 2 years.

Arc Aventures (International Ski School) (0479 07 41 28) is based at Arcs 1800 and offers skiers and boarders group and private lessons. They offer guides/instructors for paragliding, snowshoeing, snowmobiling, and backcountry skiing/boarding.

Virages (International Ski School) (0479 07 78 82) is based at Arcs 1800. This smaller school offers private and limited group lessons. They also offer backcountry, nearby ski area tours, heliskiing, snowshoeing, paragliding, and nighttime sled rides.

Initial Snow (0612 45 72 91) is in Bourg St. Maurice with lessons starting from Les Arcs. Group and private lessons are offered to snowboarders. Backcountry guides are available for skiers and snowboarders.

The costs for each of these schools are almost the same. Six three-hour group lessons cost €120; two-hour private lessons for 1 or 2 people cost about €65.

Lift tickets (2003/04 prices)

These lift tickets allow skiers/boarders to go anywhere in Les Arcs; tickets for specific regions of Les Arcs are available for much less. Tickets for six days or more include free access to these ski areas: L'Espace Killy, Les 3 Vallees, La Plagne on the Paradiski Area, Prolognan La Vanoise, and Les Saises; also, you have one free day at La Rosiere/La Thuile (in Italy).

	Adults	Child	Senior
Half day	€26	€19.50	€22
One day	€36.50	€27.50	€31
Four days	€125	€94	€106
Six days	€176	€132	€150
Fourteen days	€328	€242	€273

At the very beginning and end of the season, all tickets are about 40% off; other than this, there is no high or low season. Children are those younger than 14 and seniors are those 60 and older. A child younger than 7 skis free with the purchase of an adult ticket. Skiers/boarders older than 71 also ski free. Insurance per day costs adults €2.50 and children €2. There is night skiing/boarding at the base of each Arcs on Tuesdays and Thursdays (and it is free).

Accommodations

Clone architecture has created a group of hotels that are very similar, as far as location, room size, layout, and quality. They are all only a few steps away from the shops, restaurants, and the slopes. Rates are based on double occupancy during high season (Februaru) with half board:€€€—€125+; €€—€75–€125; €—less than €75. Credit cards are accepted at all these hotels.

Grand Hotel Mercure (0479 07 65 00, fax 0479 07 64 08; €€€) at Arcs 1800 is the top of the line and recommended by Michelin.

Hotel du Golf (0479 41 43 43; fax 0479 07 34 28; €€€) was the first constructed in Arcs 1800 and is still the flagship hotel. Rooms are simple, functional, clean, and comfortable, with exceptional views. It has a sauna, an extensive fitness center, and regular entertainment. Its restaurant/bar/nightclub draws guests from all over Arcs 1800.

Hotel Club Latitudes (0479 07 49 79; fax 0479 07 49 87; €€€) is only a five-minute walk from the Arc 1800 commercial center of Les Villards. The rooms are modern and sparsely decorated. It has a small fitness center. There are two theme dinners per week and one evening of entertainment.

Les Melezes Hotel Club (0479 07 50 50; fax 0479 07 36 26; €€), at Arc 2000, has 140 alike rooms. Watch out for the solo rooms sold to singles "with no supplement!" With this arrangement, you will be sharing your toilet and bath.

L'Aiguille Rouge (0479 07 57 07; fax 0479 07 39 61; €€), also in Arcs 2000, seems just as comfortable as the rest. Here the rooms are offered in packages with half-board (drinks included) and six-day lift tickets.

La Cachette (0479 07 70 50; fax 0479 07 74 01; €€) in the more family-oriented Arcs 1600. It has a fitness center and a child-care center.

Bourg-St-Maurice at the base of the funicular has an excellent collection of hotels with up to two stars at bargain prices.

Apartments, condominiums, flats

Les Arcs is oriented more toward apartments than hotels; there are thousands more apartments. An apartment is a better bargain if you're willing to do without the amenities of a hotel. Despite some horror stories about tiny French apartments, there is enough room unless you try to pack four people into one studio. There are four places you can stay in Les Arcs, including Arc 1600, 1800, 1950, 2000, and. Bourg-St. Maurice. The best way to go is with a package (includes seven nights and a six-day lift pass). Per-person prices based on two sharing a small apartment are €184 during low season in January, €199 during February, and €231 during Christmas.

Not included in these prices is the €10 booking fee (per reservation) and the daily residence tax. You can make plans by calling the Booking Service at 0479 07 68 00 (fax: 0479 07 68 99) or emailing reservations@lesarcs.com.

Dining

Here the focus is on the functional—just like the architecture. When we asked locals about the restaurants the response was usually a puzzled look and a smile, after ponderous thought.

Here are Les Arcs' best, it seems:

In **Arc 1600** try **Le Yeti - Snow Zone Café** (479 07 00 11), a restaurant and pizzeria for a sit-down or take-out meal; **Chez Maryse** (479 07 78 14) with fondue and other specialties created by the owner; and nearby **La Rive** (479 07 70 50).

In **Arc 1800:** The **Hotel du Golf** main restaurant (479 41 43 43) is the nicest restaurant in Les Arcs. The atmosphere is modern elegance and the meals cost around €38–€40 a person before considering wine.

La Marmite (479 07 44 28) is a small, cozy, friendly place with a €17–€20 menu and child's menu for €7.

L'Equipage (479 07 19 90) is a lively, more modern place that serves pizza and hamburgers under heavy beams with a picture-window view of the valley (€12–€22 menu and €7.50 child's meal).

Le Plante d'Baton (479 07 45 13), is a very traditional French looking restaurant with meals for €15–€21 and a child's meal for €7.

SOS Pizza (479 07 51 65) makes great, inexpensive pizza for takeout only. It is a hop downstairs from the tourism office. **Casa Mia** (479 070575) and **Gargantus** (479 07 44 99) also make good pizza.

In Arc 2000: Le Saint Jacques (479 07 29 45) serves fine fondue and raclette. And **El Latino Loco** (479 07 79 49) is OK. Little else can be heartily recommended.

For a special lunch on the mountain don't miss **Belliou La Fumée** (479 07 29 13) named after a Jack London story, in the valley of Arc 2000. This unique family-run restaurant was built in the 15th century by King Victor Emmanuel of Italy as a bear-hunting lodge. Omelets cooked over an open fire are served in the pan, and other regional specialties are prepared and served with care. Or after a long ski down to the bottom of the Villaroger lift, visit La Ferme, with excellent mountainside food.

La Creche (479 07 55 47), at the top of the Transarc Gondola, serves inexpensive cafeteria-style grilled food downstairs with a sit-down restaurant upstairs. The restaurant menu runs €16–€22.

Nine kilometers and one morning's snowshoe tour away (see Other Activities) sits a wonderful find: **Le Bois de Lune** (479 07 17 92) restaurant in the village of Montvenix. The dining room is in an ancient stone lodge, restored to its Old World charm. Regional cuisine is served family style. Dishes that may pass before you are duck in cider or a filet of pork in fresh blueberries. Reservations required for dinner.

Since many of the best restaurants are in far-flung places surrounding Les Arcs, visit **L'Ancolie** (479 07 93 20), reported to be a beautiful little restaurant in Peisey.

Child care (2003/04 prices)

There are excellent child care centers at three Arcs. Each center includes outings in the snow, walks, snow sports, indoor games, arts and crafts, trampolines, videos, etc. The prices for the three are similar and approximate: (remember, though, lifts are free for children younger than 7)

4 months–3 years (offered only at Arcs 1600)	
For 6 days	€170–€253
Full day	€38–€45
Half day	€23–€28
3 years–12 years	
For 6 days	€226–€329
Full day	€55
Half day	€40

Arcs 1600: **La Cachette** (0479 077050; fax 0479 077401)
Arcs 1800 **Les Pomme de Pin** (0479 041530; fax 0479 041531)
Arcs 2000 **Les Marmottons** (tel/fax: 0479 076425)

Après-ski/nightlife

In Arc 1800, the ski instructors head to **Bar Le Gabotte** (479 07 41 86) in the center of Le Charvet, as does the majority of the English-speakers when the lifts shut down. The overflow congregates in **Bar le Thuria** (479 07 40 86) across the square. Also try the small **Arc Café** (0614 73 44 56) or the **Jungle Café** (479 07 19 62) at Les Villards with its funky jungle decor and pumping beats.

In the Les Villards section of Arc 1800, the best après-ski is in **L'Ambiente** (479 07 49 51). The lounge of the Hotel Du Golf has live jazz before and after dinner in front of a flickering fire.

At Arc 1600, an older crowd (meaning over 25 or so) gathers at the chalet of **L'Arcelle** (479 07 30 50) with music after dinner. At Arc 1800, stop in at **Le J.O. Live Rock Café** (479 07 40 42) for live music and dancing starting at 10:30 every night.

There are discos in Arc 2000, 1600, and 1800, and all follow the French disco formula: drinks in the €12.50 range and opening times around midnight, closing about four in the morning. If you have insomnia, try **Le Fairway** (479 41 43 43) in the basement of Hotel du Golf in Arc 1800. For live music and dancing, make sure you take a look at the **Red Hot Saloon** (479 07 74 52) to see who is performing when. **Apokalypse** (479 07 43 77) is the place in the Arc 1800 Les Villards section. Another 1800 hot spot to check out is the **Sing Island Café** (0614 37 77 96), a 'free admission after 9:30' bar featuring billiards and karaoke. If you are staying in Arc 2000, disco **K.L.92** (479 07 34 39) normally is the place of choice for visitors of all ages. Also at Arc 2000, **El Latino Loco** (479 07 79 49) is bar/hangout open day and night.

Other activities

Arc 1600: There are 30 shops, bars, and restaurants; floodlit nighttime skiing; cross-country trails; snow park including boarder cross and halfpipe; dog sledding; snowshoeing; fitness centers; nighclub; horse-drawn sleigh rides; mountaineering; horseback riding.

Arc 1800: One hundred shops, bars, and restaurants; floodlit nighttime skiing, cross-country trails; bowling alley; ice skating rink; two squash courts; snow-shoeing; paragliding; arcade; nightclubs; fitness centers; mountaineering; horse-drawn sleigh rides; horseback riding; skidoo.

Arc 2000: Thirty shops, bars, and restaurants; lit halfpipe, open 24 hours a day; night skiing; speed skiing run; cross-country trails; ice climbing; nightclub; ice cave; ice skating rink; snowshoeing; paragliding; arcade; fitness centers; mountaineering.

Bourg-Saint-Maurice: One hundred and fifty shops, bars, and restaurants; cross country trails; snowshoeing; fitness centers; museum; horse-sleigh rides; covered swimming pool; horseback riding and more.

Also contact tourism for information about helicopter rides or reservations for snowshoeing and other guided activities. Les Arcs is home to the Speed Skiing track, built for the 1992 Olympics. For a mere €12.50, you too can test your courage by blitzing down the lower part of the one-mile slope in a timed run; €20 gets you two runs; €25 pays for three. This price includes special helmet, goggles, and skis.

Getting there

Les Arcs in directly above Bourg-St. Maurice, which is linked to Paris by TGV speed train service, Eurostar and Thaly's. The nearest major international airport is in Geneva; there are four buses a day that travel this distance. Other nearby airports are Lyon and Chambery.

By car, take the Albertville exit on the autoroute, then follow the signs to Bourg-St. Maurice. Les Arcs is a 30-minute ride by car, or a seven-minute ride on the funicular, from Bourg-St. Maurice to Arc 1600 every 20 minutes, 7:40 a.m. to 19:20 p.m.

Arc 1600 and 1800 have free outdoor parking and pay indoor parking. You can park outdoors for free 5 km. from Arc 2000 (free shuttles will run you to Arc 2000 on every hour). There is pay indoor and outdoor parking at Arc 2000.

Tourist information

There are tourism offices in all the Les Arcs villages and in Bourg-St. Maurice. They are normally open daily from 9 a.m. to 7 p.m.

Les Arcs Tourist Office (Main Office)
105 Place de la Gare, 73700 Bourg Saint Maurice

Le Charvet, Les Sapins, 73700 Arc 1800, France
Tel. : 0479 07 12 57 Fax : 0479 07 24 90
Email : lesarcs@lesarcs.com Internet: www.lesarcs.com

Central Booking Office
B.P. 58, 73706 Les Arcs Cedex, France
Tel : 0479 07 68 00 Fax : 0479 07 68 99
Email : reservation@lesarcs.com

Chamonix Mont-Blanc

Chamonix is the most famous ski town in France. It also breaks every normal European rule for a resort. None of the trails drops directly into town; instead, the ski areas are spread along a valley almost 10 miles long. Only two of the areas are interconnected. Some lift lines can be long, especially for the Grand Montet. Shuttlebuses are crowded and erratic but eventually come. The weather can change in a matter of hours from sunshine to a stormy whiteout. But what Chamonix does offer is perhaps the world's best expert and advanced skiing on spectacular mountains rising more than 12,500 feet above the valley. And Chamonix itself has a strong Alpine flair. You won't find the space-age structures that set the tone for so many of France's other resorts. The world's best expert skiing and one of the world's most picturesque settings, in the shadow of 15,767-foot Mont Blanc, creates an experience that is hard to beat.

Small-town coziness is the rule, with plenty of restaurants, narrow streets for shopping and good hotels. This atmosphere can make one forget about the logistics of getting on the trails. But remember, to fully enjoy Chamonix, you'll need a car or a bus to get to its slopes which are spread out for miles along the valley floor. There is an erratic shuttlebus service from Chamonix center to the outlying areas; some hotels provide bus service.

In Chamonix you can ski hard all day long, then sit at a café in a small square and sip a *kir*, wine or beer. The bars are crowded with an international group, and you are surrounded with other skiers who are here not for the ritz and the glitz, but for the challenge and the exhilaration of testing themselves against Europe's most spectacular slopes.

Mountain layout

From the slopes of Chamonix and on to Argentière and Le Tour, a string of lifts takes skiers up both sides of the valley. On the Mont Blanc side you ascend above outcroppings and slopes of this magnificent peak, while on the opposite side you enjoy the Mont Blanc panorama as the lifts take you to outstanding runs.

In Chamonix, most skiers choose the challenges of **Le Brévent** at 8,288 feet. The cable car rises from the town to Planpraz, where the skiing really begins. The second section of the cable car takes experts and hardy intermediates to the top of Le Brévent, and a chair lift carries the less advanced intermediates to the Les Vioz area. Try the black run from the back of Le Brévent with a buddy. If after the first few hundred feet you're not confident, you can cut to the left and take an advanced intermediate trail.

Intermediates may prefer the midstation slopes at Plan Praz, especially the chair lifts that reach 6,560 feet. In addition, work your way to the right and take the chair up to the Col Cornu's 7,488-foot level for a good intermediate run and off-trail skiing.

Ten minutes away by car is **Les Praz,** ground station for the cable car to La Flégère midstation. From here, a gondola takes you to L'Index at 7,822 feet, where the skiing is outstanding for intermediates. There are off-trail challenges to the right and the left of the upper gondola.

The intermediate run from L'Index to Les Praz base will take 30 minutes, a challenging, advanced intermediate romp. However, in high season you can wait as long as 45 minutes at the bottom to get back on the cable car. You'll want to stay on the upper mountain unless you're moving to another slope or making the last run of the day.

For our money, the best skiing in the valley is reached by driving 10 minutes up the valley to Argentière. The wait at the cable car base station at **Argentière** should not be more than a half hour, even in high season. From the midstation there are only three main lifts. But these lifts open up excellent skiing. As one instructor observes, "Why ride lifts when you can ski?" Here, you can really ski. A gondola and a chair lift offer excellent intermediate terrain and plenty of off-trail skiing for experts.

Advanced and expert skiers should head up the second stage of the cable car. You'll have to pay an additional €4.50 to take the second car—only two trips are included on a six-day Mont Blanc pass. For experts, the skiing is definitely worth the extra cost. At the top of Les Grands Montets take time to ascend the observation deck for one of the most spectacular views in the Alps. When you are ready to ski you have two basic choices—both offer 4,200 feet of vertical skiing, as good as it gets. This part of the mountain has never seen a grooming machine. You can drop down a black trail across the Argentière glacier to Croix de Lognan, or go around the other side of Les Grands Montets and ski under the cable car. There are wide-open, off-trail opportunities for any skier willing to go for it. In fact, the "trails" offer only a general direction to the midstation. The red-rated (intermediate) trail branches off from the glacier route and then drops beneath the cable car to the midstation. It is often almost as much of a challenge as the expert-rated runs.

At **Le Tour** there is a system comprised of one gondola and five other lifts at the end of the valley. This area is perfect for beginners and intermediates and families who are looking for comfortable cruising in the sun.

The most talked-about adventure in Chamonix—not necessarily the most challenging in terms of simple skiing—is the 13-mile-long glacier run from the Aiguille du Midi (12,601 feet) back into Chamonix (3,363 feet). The scenery is magnificent, and the memory of the Vallée Blanche and the Mer de Glace will remain forever.

The **Vallée Blanche** expedition could be more appropriately called ski mountaineering than simple skiing. Go prepared for changing weather and changing terrain: the weather in town may be balmy, with a howling wind at the top of the Aiguille du Midi and zero visibility. Be ready for freezing, windy weather. Pack goggles or mountaineering glasses, good gloves, a warm jacket with a hood if possible, and your ski hat.

You start by climbing—roped to your guide and with your skis tied together—down a narrow windy ridge. At the end of the ridge, you break the tether with the guide and, sheltered from the wind, step into your skis. (For this trip ski straps are recommended because snow brakes often don't work on ice.) Groups are separated from one another by several hundred meters. You may be skiing on trails for a time, then turn off for powder if your guide finds it. Sometimes the trail simply ends, which means climbing over rocks with your skis on your shoulder or balancing over a snowbridge spanning a deep crevasse.

The mountains surrounding you are all famous in the annals of climbing. The Vallée Blanche starts on the upper, smooth portion of the glacier. As it begins to break up and crevasses block the route, skiers sideslip down narrow chutes in a region called the Seracs. At the end of the Seracs and after almost two hours descending on skis, there is often a stop at the Refuge du Requin for a warm drink. From the refuge the run enters a wide-open area called the Salle à Manger (dining room).

The needlelike Aiguille de Dru, with Europe's longest climbing vertical, towers above the glacier. From this point the Mer de Glace begins its drop into the valley. As the glacier ends, another refuge, Les Mottets, offers snacks and drinks. Then it's back into the town, the entire trip having taken about four hours.

Although guides are not required, they are strongly recommended. In fact, unless you are an expert mountaineer, you'd be crazy to attempt this adventure without one. If the clouds close in, the guides bring you down by compass and you're assured of having someone to belay you when crossing over crevasses and during the initial windy climb down the ridge. As an extra precaution, each participant receives a beeper. Guides cost about €140 for one to six skiers. Add about €15 for each additional person. If traveling alone, check with the guide office in town to register for a group. With a group the cost is about €70.

What level of skier can handle the Vallée Blanche? A solid intermediate, comfortable on skis, who can sideslip easily and make quick turns can make the trip. You need to be in good enough condition to tour more than four hours at high altitudes.

An additional feature of Chamonix is the chance to travel through the Mont Blanc tunnel into Courmayeur, Italy, on the opposite side of the massif, where skiing is very good. There's often good weather here when Chamonix is clouded over.

Mountain rating

Beginners should stick to Le Tour and Le Brevent. Though experts rave about the resort, thousands learn to ski here every year. But realize that this is not a walk-to-your-lesson resort.

Intermediates choose Chamonix year after year as an ideal area to increase their skills on challenging terrain.

Experts need never worry that there may not be a bigger challenge over the mountain: here, there always is.

Chamonix can best be enjoyed by all skiers with a guide to take them to their most suitable level. Chamonix Ski Fun Tours, part of the French Ski School, has weekly packages that include a guide for small groups.

Ski school (2002/03 prices)

A total of 300 instructors offer courses in Chamonix (450 53 22 57) and Argentière (450 54 00 12).

Private lessons (one to two people) cost €33 an hour; three or four skiers cost €42. A day of private instruction is €220 during low season (12-31 January) and €237 during the rest of the season.

Group lessons for a half day (two hours) cost €21. A six-day course, consisting of daily morning and afternoon instruction (four hours a day), is about €150.

Out-of-bounds ski guides for up to six skiers can be hired for €255 (full day) and €25 for each extra person or €140 (half day) plus €25 for extra skiers.

Lift tickets (2003/04 prices)

The normal Chamonix lift ticket, called Cham'Ski, covers lifts in the immediate valley, shuttlebus service, two trips to the top of Les Grands Montets cable car if you purchase six to 12 days and four trips with a lift ticket of 12 days of longer, plus one day of skiing in Courmayeur, Italy, with passes of six days of more. These tickets are for consecutive days.

	Adults	**Children** (4-11)	**Seniors** (60+) **Juniors** (12–15)
one day	€40	€28	€34
two days	€73	€51	€62
three days	€104	€73	€88
six days	€176	€123	€150
13 days	€366	€256	€311

The Mont Blanc Skipass is valid for the entire Chamonix valley and Argentière, with Megève, St. Gervais, Combloux, Cordon, Praz-sur-Arly, Passy, St. Nicolas de Véroce, Les Houches and Vallorcine, for a total of 655 km. of trails served by 214 lifts. Four days of skiing in Courmayeur, Italy is included as well. This pass is available for six or seven days only. Six-day pass is €205 for adults; €164 for children (4–11); and €174 for seniors 60+. You also need a photo taken without sunglasses or ski hat for the Mont Blanc Skipass. Your pass must be shown at each resort for a ski pass outside the Chamonix valley. Those skiing for four days or more must purchase the Hands Free Badge which costs €3.

Accommodations

The Chamonix reservation service (which also has listings for Argentière and Les Houches) is provided by the tourist office, which you can contact at Place de L'Eglise (450 53 23 33). Nearly 90 hotels provide a range of accommodations from luxury suites to dormitory-like rooms. Because of the many restaurants and snack bars, don't hesitate to book a hotel without a half-pension plan. Rates are per person per day, based on double occupancy with half pension in February. €€€—€125+ ; €€—€75–€124; €=less than €75.

Mont Blanc (450 53 05 64; €€€) A grand old hotel that is being renovated by its owners. Most of the updated rooms are being recreated as suites, which offer roomy, upscale accommodations not found elsewhere in the town. The restaurant is considered one of the best in the region.

Auberge du Bois-Prin (450 53 33 51; €€€) A Chateau and Relais Hotel, this is best in town for quiet and coziness, but is a long walk uphill from the center of town. Rooms are decorated in dark wood and fixtures are brass and gold. The views of Mont Blanc from most rooms are spectacular, with Chamonix spread out below.

Hôtel du Jeu de Paume (450 54 03 76; €€€) Above the village of Le Lavancher, this hotel is understated, quiet luxury built in the wooden chalet style. It has an indoor/outdoor pool and well appointed rooms.

Le Prieuré (450 53 20 72; €€–€€€) This is an excellent, functional hotel with some Alpine touches. It is large, short on quaintness, and long on convenience. It also has a private shuttle to the ski areas, as well as covered parking, should you be driving.

Hôtel Savoyard (450 53 00 77; €€–€€€) This small hotel is created with a French country motif. It oozes charm and the management is very helpful. It is next to Le Brévant gondola, a steep climb from the town. Great for skiing Le Brévent.

Hôtel des Aiglons (450 55 90 93; €€–€€€) A modern hotel with a beautiful, soaring lobby and great views of Mont Blanc. It is near the popular Restaurant Impossible.

Alpina (450 53 47 77; €€) Alpina makes no attempt at Alpine or regional decor. It could just as easily be a high-rise business hotel, but the views from the rooms across the valley to Mont Blanc are spectacularly different. Its location in the center of town can't be beat, and the rooms are among the largest in town.

Sapinière Montana (450 53 07 63; €€) This hotel is only a five-minute walk from the center of town. A shuttlebus takes skiers to the different ski areas. Rooms are basic and slightly aging.

De la Croix Blanche (450 53 00 11; €€) Centrally, this property has decades-old interiors that are nonetheless well maintained and pleasant. (B&B only)

La Vallée Blanche (450 53 04 50; €€) Run by Patricia Byrne, a delightful Irish lady, this freshly renovated, small hotel is next to the river running through town and steps from Chamonix' center. Rooms feature beautiful locally-made Alpine furniture. Breakfasts are an Irish feast. Fills fast, so book early.

Ski Chalets: Simply Ski, Neilson (see page 25 for contact information).

Apartments, condominiums, flats

Chamonix has hundreds of furnished chalets and apartments offered through several agencies. Prices for a studio with sleeping arrangements for two to four: €224–€510. A two-room apartment housing six people will cost €368–€1201. The tourist office provides direct booking. Call 450 53 23 33.

Dining

Chamonix' excellent dining is augmented by the fact that it's a real town, not a resort, so prices are generally very reasonable. And it has its share of excellent, top-quality restaurants. Prices are all approximate and vary depending on beverage and meal.

Albert Ist et Milan (450 53 05 09) is Chamonix's best, where the chef mixes nouvelle cuisine with local mountain cooking. The giant dining room features expansive views of Mont Blanc. The food is praised equally by France's top critics and the locals, who are most pleased by the size of the portions. The menu is an exceptional value—about €60.

Le Matafan (450 53 05 64) in the Mont Blanc Hotel, is laid out around a large fireplace. Try the foie gras and the veal with figs. The wine cellar is one of the best in the region, with over 14,000 bottles priced from €3–€680. Gourmet menu is €60.

Auberge du Bois-Prin (450 53 33 51) is in an intimate, old home. Dinner is served by waitresses in local costume. The restaurant is noted for taking the normal and making it special. Meals cost €33–€43, with a gourmet menu at about €60.

Eden Restaurant (450 53 06 40), in Hôtel Eden, is a bit out of the center of Chamonix in the suburb of La Praz. The views of Mont Blanc and the Drus are spectacular. Specialties are fish, with trout amandine and lobster au gratin. The menu costs €23–€53.

La Cabana (450 53 23 27) next to the golf course, a few minutes' drive outside town, is a highly rated (Michelin two forks) rustic chalet with regional meat and potatoes. About €40 for a full dinner.

For a quaint evening in a picture-postcard setting, dine at **Maison Carrier** (450 53 00 03) set in a reconstructed Savoyard farm house. Meals are about €35.

Sarpé (450 53 29 31) a few km. out of town is a destination for many serious gourmands. A meal here is about €35–€40.

Restaurant L'Impossible (450 53 20 36) This eatery is built in an ancient barn and is as rustic as it gets. You'll dine around an open grill and get buzzed on peach kirs. Make reservations. This restaurant is an experience you will remember. Expect to pay around €22 for a meal.

Atmosphere (450 55 97 97) is a very jazz and blues oriented, riverbank café-esque, Michelin two-fork rated, restaurant decorated in subdued tones. Try to get a table in the sunroom overlooking the river for a most romantic spot. The evening menu will cost €22 without wine.

Calèche (450 55 94 68) is an elegant regional restaurant with the traditional mountain wood tastefully mixed with flowered fabrics and stuffed chairs. They serve everything from fondue and raclette to full dinners. A very reasonable €25 evening menu offers choices of nine appetizers, five main courses and six desserts.

Chaudron (450 53 40 34), also on Rue des Moulins, is very rustic. A heavy, stone wall lines the small restaurant. You dine under wooden beams while farm tools and a giant wagon wheel add a country flavor. Specialties are regional dishes, grilled meats and brochettes. Fixed-price menu for dinner will run about €22.

Hotel Les Lanchers (450 53 47 19) in Praz-de-Chamonix has a fine restaurant.

Boccalatte (450 53 52 14) This new restaurant serves Savoyard meals in a blond wood setting. Prices are reasonable. Fondues cost €13–€15 and the Alsace Choucroute about the same.

L'M is a brasserie serving low-ticket crêpes, galletes and meals in the middle of town. In the spring a large terrace opens, which makes snacking and nursing a long drink most enjoyable. Most selections with a drink will range between €8–€15.

Après-ski/nightlife

The immediate après-ski usually consists of having drinks in one of the bars in the center of town. Try the **Chamouny**, the **Brasserie du Rond Point** and the **Irish Coffee**. In spring the outdoor tables in the center of town fill up with skiers. **La Cabolée** attracts skiers coming down Le Brévent. For basic bars head to the **Bumble Bee** and **Mill Street**.

In Argentière, the **Office Bar** is packed with English speakers. For immersion in French head to the **Savoie** or to **Rusticana** for drinks.

Nightlife devotees have plenty of choices here besides gambling. **Arbat** has live music and is hot these days. The **Blue** is excellent, with occasional live jazz or country & Western. **Le Pèle** disco is large, loud and packed with teenagers. One of the main meeting spots for English-speakers is the **Choucas Video Bar**, which is normally packed, dark and smoky.

For the hard-partying crowd head out to **Jeckl and Hyde** which has a touch of Irish influence and is located between Hotel Des Aiglons and Restaurant Impossible. Other good spots are **Ice Rock Café** and **Cantina**. The new king of nightlife may be **Wild Wallabies Bar** where the owner whips the British and Scandinavian crowd into a drinking, singing, burping and dancing frenzy.

Child care (2003/04 prices)

The **Chamonix Ski School** (450 53 22 57) takes children 3–12 years. Lessons and lunch are included for €60 a day or for €300 for six consecutive days.

Child-care services are available at the larger hotels, and babysitting services are available for around €14 (half day) or €26 (full day). For more information, contact the tourist office.

Maison Pour Tous kindergarten on Place du Mont Blanc (450 53 12 24), takes children 18 months to 6 years. It's open 7:45 a.m. to 6:30 p.m. Monday to Friday. Rates: half day, €25; one hour, €10. Pick up kids for lunch noon–2 p.m. Reservations strongly recommended.

The Panda Club has kindergarten with ski instruction in both downtown Chamonix and in Argentière at the cable car station (450 54 04 76). The Panda Club Chamonix is on Clos du Savoy (450 55 86 12). Panda Ski at the Argentière station takes kids ages 3–12. These child care centers have games, crafts, ski lessons with videos and outdoor snow games. Older children up to age 12 can receive care and supervision for €31 for a half day, €45 for a full day, €168 for six half days, and €230 for six full days.

Getting there

Nearly everyone arrives by the autoroute or by train from Geneva. However, Chamonix—with Courmayeur on the other side of Mont Blanc—is ideal for visitors who have skied in Italy and who want to work their way up through Switzerland and France. The Mont Blanc tunnel reopened in March 2002, but we still suggest you check on its status before choosing whether to drive or take the train.

The TGV leaves Paris at around 8 a.m. and arrives in Sallanches at about 1 p.m. There is also a special train/bus combination, with the train departing from Paris just after 7 a.m., a change to bus in Annecy and arrival in Chamonix before 1 p.m.

A taxi from the Geneva airport will cost about €120, and a bus from the airport to the resort costs about €30.

Other activities

More than any other area you may visit, this one merits an aerial tour. The Mont Blanc massif and the stunning surrounding peaks are best seen from the air. Choose from four different trips ranging from €25–€95 per person. Call Air Mont Blanc at 450 58 13 31.

The swimming center has three pools, all heated, plus sauna and turkish baths. There is also an ice rink, indoor tennis, bowling and a casino.

Tourist information

Tourist Office, Place du Triangle de l'Amitié, F-74400 Chamonix, France; Telephne 450 53 00 24; fax 450 53 58 90.
Internet: www.chamonix.com
E-mail: info@chamonix.com

La Clusaz

The center of town is easy to find in La Clusaz. The church on the central square can be seen for miles around, its sturdy-looking tower is topped by a distinctive clock and graduated wedding-cake steeple reaching high above the surrounding wood-shingled rooftops. Newly restored and modernized, with excellent acoustic properties, it doubles as a concert and lecture hall for visiting dignitaries and performers. During a good winter, this town is hard to beat for intermediate family skiing.

La Clusaz has been a bustling village since the 16th century, but today, in the peak season, its 2,050 year-round inhabitants open their doors and hearts to as many as 22,000 visitors at a time. The first ski lift here was built in 1935, but La Clusaz has succeeded in keeping its lived-in, workday atmosphere. Visitors are initiated into the traditions and customs of "Les Cluses," as they call themselves, rather than the other way around. In winter on Mondays farmers turned innkeepers, and local merchants put on humorous welcome night races that end in convivial silliness on the village green (now white), a large snow play area adjacent to the skating rink and cable car and flanked by restaurants and outdoor tables. During the day it provides a safe playground and sledding slope for children.

The compactness of the village, its wraparound views of ski runs, forests and peaks, its old winding side streets and leisurely pace, make La Clusaz a winner for skiers or boarders who wish to get away from the hustle of modern life. Children are welcomed and families will find this resort easier to manage than most. Don't expect to find noisy, swinging nightlife except on weekends—here the emphasis is on lingering over dinner with family and friends, and the traditional French Alpine atmosphere makes it hard to believe that Geneva is actually a 60-minute drive away. (On weekends it becomes much easier to believe, as the city-dwellers stream in.)

Mountain Layout

La Clusaz has five different areas to ski. Visitors can ski a different section each day. Just a cablecar ride above the town, intermediate and beginner terrain allow wide open cruising. Here Beauregard Mountain rises to 5,544 feet and true to its name, offers beautiful views and cruising trails through magical forest terrain. On the right side of Beauregard Mountain (looking down the mountain) is a good expert trail. Beyond Beauregard, Massif de Manigod offers a network of 15 lifts serving mostly beginner and intermediate trails. Moving around the valley to massif de L'Etale, the runs become steeper and longer. Massif de L'Aguille has excellent advanced terrain and a long plunge through Combe du Fernuy for strong skiers.

Massif de Blame offers good bump skiing and usually has the best snow. Here skiers will find some of the best expert stuff. La Clusaz has good bump skiing as well as freestyle. There are two ways to get back from the La Balme. The return to the village is a 4 km.-long trail alongside a mountain road through the woods. A cable car runs skiers and boarders from the base of La Balme to halfway up Massif de L'Aguille.

Mountain Rating

Beginners and intermediates will have a swell time in La Clusaz. This is a wonderful place for a romantic getaway for a mixed-ability couple. Many lifts offer side-by-side beginner and intermediate trails meeting at the bottom, perfect for families or friends of different abilities. Experts who know the area or ski with a guide will find some toothy terrain with patches of difficulty especially on Massif de Balme.

Snowboarding

Las Clusaz is known as a center for freeriding and new glide.

Boarders at every ability level will find there is a part of the mountain just right for them. Try out the terrain park—with a half-pipe and a couple tabletop jumps—halfway up the Massif de L'Aguille. Take any of the Loup lifts to get to the top of the park.

Never-evers could make their first turns on the Poma lift (Champ Bleu) or the gondola (TC de La Patinoire) at the edge of town. Otherwise, take the new gondola from La Clusaz to the top of Massif de Beauregard for wide slopes. (Learning how to use Poma lifts shouldn't be more difficult than strapping yourself to your snowboard.)

Beginners could spend time at Massif de Manigod; it is easiest to get there by car or shuttle bus. Here, there are two chair lifts and an assortment of Poma lifts. With enough snow, take the scenic cat track back to town.

Intermediate boarders will enjoy cruising the slopes on Massif de Beauregard or Massif de Manigod. However, the face of Massif de L'Etale or any of the eight lifts above the town provide steeper runs. At the La Balme area the groomed trails will probably suit intermediates best.

Advanced/expert boarders can go just about anywhere and have a great time. The Aguille chair lift provides wide, fairly steep groomed and ungroomed terrain (beware, though, for at some point after every snowfall, this face turns into a mogul field). At the top of the Aguille lift, take a right and board at your own risk down the Combe de Borderan, an expansive off-piste bowl. Also, at the top of Massif de l'Etale there are some pretty steep, open terrain, along with a few off-piste trails through the trees.

For a full plate, head to La Balme (the higher elevation and lower temperatures let powder last longer here than the rest of La Clusaz). Enjoy the vast, ungroomed fields of snow and the many natural land features. Xavier, the head of snowboarding at

La Clusaz said, "La Balme is a natural terrain park!" Countless mounds and ridges provide great big air jumps with even better landings.

For expert snowboarders, there are backcountry opportunities. Above the Aguille chair lift, a 30-minute hike will lead to La Creuze, a challenging bowl that eventually funnels down to marked trails. Above the L'Etale chair lift, one can hike and reach off-piste terrain. From the top of Col de Balme chair lift, one can take a long hike over a ridge and into the Combe de Bellechat, an extremely wide valley with snow as good as at La Balme. Boarders should consult local experts before venturing into any of this terrain (in most cases, hiring a guide is the safest and smartest thing to do). Information on backcountry boarding (and guides) is available at 450 32 66 05.

Cross-Country

There is excellent cross-country in La Clusaz, with 70 km. of prepared trails, Plateau des Confins and the Plateau de Beauregard. The 52 km. on the Plateau des Confins (4 km. from town) includes circuits from 0.5 km. to 10 km. ringing a frozen lake. The 18 km. on the Plateau de Beauregard includes circuits from 1 to 4 km. long, some of which are shared with the downhillers. At both of these locations, there is parking, ski school, lockers, accommodations, restaurants, and equipment rentals. There is also a 7 km.-long trail connecting Plateau des Confins with the 30 km. of trails of Le Grand-Bornand. An all-day trail fee for adults is €6 and for children (ages 6–16) is €2.50.

Ski School (2003/04 prices)

La Clusaz French Ski School (ESF) (450 02 40 83) offers skiing and snowboarding lessons to all ages. The office is located in the village and beneath the cable car.

Private lessons: A one hour lesson for one to three people costs €31; for four to five people, €43.50. A guide for the full day costs €211.

Group lessons: Six days of lessons for adults costs €122–€135; for children younger than 12, €81–€122.

Sno Academie (0450 32 66 05) teaches exclusively snowboarders. It offers two hour private lessons starting at €55. Sno Academie also offers multi-day lessons, and snowboarding camps for beginner and advanced boarders. Sno Academie also offers lessons to handicapped people.

Lift Tickets (2003/04 prices)

La Clusaz only

	Adults	**Child** (5–15)
two days (high season)	€51	€41
three days (high season)	€75	€57.50
six days (high season)	€137.50	€99
fourteen days (high season)	€245	€172

Aravis lift ticket (La Clusaz and Le Grand-Bornand)

	Adults	**Child** (15 and younger)	**Senior** (61–75)
two days	€55	€45	€49
six days	€149	€110	€123.50
seven days	€163	€121	€135.50

Those younger than 5 and older than 75 ski/board for free. High season is December 20–January 2 and January 31–March 12. For the rest of the season, tickets for two days or more of skiing cost 10–15 % less.

Accommodations

La Clusaz has eight three-star and 11 two-star hotels. For information or reservations, call the tourist office (0450 32 65 00). All the rates listed below are based on per-person half-board, double occupancy with half board: € is €75 and less; €€ is €75–€125; €€€ is €125+. Credit cards are accepted at all these hotels.

The **Alp'Hotel** (450 02 40 06; fax 450 02 60 16; €€) offers a covered pool and sauna. It is the top-rated by Michelin.

We liked the **Beauregard** (450 32 68 00; fax 450 02 59 00; €€) at the foot of the slopes, offers a covered pool, Jacuzzi, sauna, game room, and nightly entertainment.

The **Alpen'Roc** (450 02 58 96; fax 450 02 57 49; €€), just 150m. from the slopes, is next on the list and offers a covered pool, hot tub, sauna, game room, and nightly entertainment.

Les Chalets de la Serraz (0450 02 48 29; fax 0450 02 64 12; €€) 4 km. out of town is a typical mountain chalet a bit above the town with a wonderful restaurant. It offers nightly entertainment.

Hotel Carlina (450 02 43 48; fax 450 02 63 02; €€) has great south-facing balconies and offers a covered pool, sauna, and game room.

Sapins (450 63 33 33; fax 450 63 33 34; €) is a fine place in the center of the village at prices that are hard to beat.

Les Airelles (450 02 40 51; fax 450 32 35 33; €) is in the village and has one of the better restaurants and a sauna. It is a great value.

Floralp (450 02 41 46; fax 450 02 63 94; €) is another good place only steps from the lifts with a fine restaurant.

Le Vieux Chalet (450 02 41 53; fax 450 32 33 99; €) is a small, quite rustic, cozy hotel on the edge of the slopes. It is a walk from town, but ski-in/ski-out.

The **Beaulieu** (450 02 43 48; fax 450 02 63 02; €), just on the edge of town, offers a covered pool, sauna, and game room.

La Piste Bleue Hotel and **Telepherique Hotel** are both at the top of the Beauregard cable car. They offer the best views of all the hotels in the area and are the cheapest. Half board goes for about €46. Beware, though, for there is no access if you miss the last cable car.

Apartments

In La Clusaz, there are 1500 apartments and chalets. **La Clusaz Tour** (04 50 32 38 33; fax 04 50 32 38 34) has information and package rates.

The "all-inclusive" apartment package has a starting price of €185 per skier per week during regular season and a starting price of €252 per skier per week during holiday season. Rates based on a four-person studio.

Dining

While you're in the Haute Savoie region, try some of the great local specialties. Most restaurants in La Clusaz will serve Raclette, a fun dish that includes dripping melted cheese over potatoes; Tartiflette, a dish of potatoes with tasty, creamy Reblochon cheese melted over it; Matafan, big potato fritters; Farcon, a mixture of mashed potatoes, cabbage, pears, raisons, and chestnuts; Les Diots, little pork sausages prepared in white wine; Les Atriaux, roasted pieces of pork wrapped in 'voilettes'; or La Tomme Blanche, reblochon cheese that is not yet mature.

Le Bercail (450 02 43 75) on the Massif de L'Aiguille is one of the finest dining experiences that can be found at any international ski resort. It is accessible by skis and at night by sleigh or snowcat. These unforgettable dinners, available only by reservation, include typical Savoyard dishes served in a rustic farm setting around two blazing fireplaces. The fixed menu offers plenty of options for a good deal. The Degustation Menu offers a palate-expanding meal with many, many courses.

L'Arbé (450 02 60 54) is the place to go for cheese dishes. For a great fondue or raclette you will spend around €20–€25 with wine.

Le Grenier (450 32 36 06) is a very cozy, wooden place just around the corner from the church. This restaurant specializes in the raclette dish. Customers are given huge half-wheels of Reblochon cheese that are melted by an interesting contraption. Meals can go for €16–€30.

There are plenty of other excellent restaurants in La Clusaz. **Le Symphonie** (450 32 68 00), in Hotel Beauregard, is a classic French and nouvelle restaurant. **Restaurant de Savoie; Alp Hotel Restaurant; Hotel Des Aravis Restaurant; La Caleche** (450 02 42 60) and **L'Ecuelle** (450 02 42 03) are both cozy, beautiful, old places where wood burns and regional specialties are served.

These restaurants serve tasty dishes for a little less than the rest. **La Bergerie** (450 02 63 40), offers a €7 child's meal and dinners for €12–€25. It is a small, cozy pizzeria that also serves regional specialties and Reblochon plates. **La Braise** (450 02 68 75) serves child's meals for €7.50, menu's for €12–€17 and pizza for €8-€10, and €5–€6 for tartiflette. **La Scierie** (450 63 34 68) is a well lit, open restaurant with a fireplace. It serves children's meals for less than €10 and tasty dinners for €11–€12.

If you cannot decide on a restaurant, check in at any of the inexpensive creperies or pizzerias in town. You can also save by eating a full meal at lunch, when meals generally cost less, or by picking up some bulk food at the supermarket. Sometimes, good French bread and cheese can do the job; this should cost no more than €4.

Aprés-ski/nightlife

The nightlife in La Clusaz is happening on weekends, but, shall we say, dead on some weekdays. The older, more mature crowd hangs out at **Le Salto** or **Le Pressoir**, video bars with many beer choices; they are open until about 2 a.m. **Le Caves du Pacally** is comfortable, casual, hangout; open until 2 a.m. **Bar Roc Café** is a dim, cozy place in town groovin' to '80s disco music. **Bali Bar** is a fun little bar that is usually packed with friendly people dancing to island music. **Panama Café** is a Tex-Mex bar with Cuban music.

Boarders and skiers of all ages head to either of the two disco/pub/nightclubs, both open until 5 a.m. **Club 18** blasts loud music and is great for chilling or close quarter dancing. **L'Ecluse** is also a great late-night hangout. The dance floor in this disco is not a floor but a thick sheet of glass, revealing the flowing waters of the town's river. Both of these exclusive nightclubs have cover charges of about €12.

Child care (2003/04 prices)

The two child care centers in La Clusaz are a few steps away from the church. They are both open every day in the morning 8:30 a.m. to noon and 2 to 6 p.m. For information on either, call (04 50 32 69 50). Rates for both clubs are as follows: €14.50 for a half day, €21.30 for full day, €74.10 for six half days, €110 for six full days. Lunch is available for an extra €10 per day. **Le Club des Mouflets** is right above the tourism office. It takes children from 8 months to 4 1/2 years. There are different rooms for different aged children; it offers many indoor activities such as musical games, collages and crafts. **Le Club des Champions** accepts children ages 3–6. They offer one-hour ski lessons to children ages 3–4, and two-hour lessons to children 5 and older. The other outdoor activities include snowman-making, sledding, and other snow games. Indoor activities are also offered.

Other activities

There is a **swimming complex** (04 50 02 43 01) with various open-air and covered pools, a hot tub, sauna, steam room, solarium, and fitness center; from December 20 to April 30, it is open every afternoon 13:30 p.m.-19:30 p.m. Entrance to the pools costs approximately €6.50 for adults and €5 for children; entrance to the fitness room, sauna, and steam room costs €14.

The town's **ice skating** rink is open in the morning from 10 a.m. to 12:30 p.m., and in the afternoon from 2:30 p.m.-6 p.m., and at night from 5 p.m.–11 p.m. Entrance is €3.20 and skate rentals cost €3.30. Occasionally there are **ice hockey or skating competitions** (450 02 48 45). From 5:30 p.m.–7 p.m., every Wednesday, Thursday and Friday, **ice karting** is available; €11 for a 10-minute round.

Paragliding (450 02 66 51) or (450 02 68 96) is available for €55 per person. **Snowmobiling** (450 32 35 37) costs €82 per hour for two people. There are **snowshoeing**, **heliski**, **ice-climbing**, **four-wheeling**, **husky sleigh rides**, **quad biking**, **hiking**, and **Vallée Blanche** (skiing/boarding a glacier on Mont Blanc)programs. For more information call the tourism office.

Getting there

From the Geneva airport, a daytime taxi ride costs €100 (€140 at night). The bus from Geneva to Annecy costs €9.20, and from Annecy to La Clusaz costs €6.90. The train (TGV) from Paris to Annecy takes 3-1/2 hours and costs about €76 round trip. A taxi from Annecy to La Clusaz costs about €49.

Alpine skiers and snowboarders will not need a car in La Clusaz, except to get to the one or two out of town restaurants or to Manigod, (a small complex of apartments located up the valley past Massif de Beauregard). Everything in town is within walking distance.

Tourist information

La Clusaz Tourist Office,
Place de L'Eglise, 74220 La Clusaz, France; 04 50 32 65 00,
fax 04 50 32 65 01
Internet: www.laclusaz.com; Email: infos@laclusaz.com
For ski/snowboard packages call **La Clusaz Tour** (04 50 32 38 33)

Le Grand-Bornand

Le Grand-Bornand is a pleasant little resort set in a rambling valley. It is an intermediate area great for family getaways. It has two centers; one is the old town Le Grand-Bornand at 3,250 feet (1000 meters) and the other is what the tourist board refers to as the second floor of the resort, Chinaillon, set at 4,225 feet (1,300 meters). The village of Le Grand-Bornand functions like any European resort, but instead of being clustered around a central point, it is set along a skirting road that eventually winds up the Vallée du Bouchet. A farmer's market is still held every Wednesday morning in the town center, defined by the church.

Access to the skiing/boarding from the village is a bit convoluted, but once aboard one of the two gondolas, everything falls into place. We recommend that visitors choosing to stay in Le Grand-Bornand try to select one of the hotels or B&Bs near the lifts. It will make life much more convenient.

Chinaillon, 6 km. from Le Grand-Bornand village, is more a modern collection of hotels and restaurants than a traditional village. It has the best access to the downhill slopes and slightly better nightlife than the village does.

Mountain Layout

Le Grand-Bornand is split into four sections. These sections are not as large nor as defined as those of La Clusaz. The bulk of the skiable terrain is pastureland in the summer so excellent skiing is possible even when snow depths seem low. There are no large rocks to cover.

La Joyère area is directly above Le Grand-Bornand village facing southwest and garnering maximum sunshine. The skiing here is mellow and perfect for families and beginners. There is a special beginner ski pass for this area.

Chinaillon has a north and northwest exposure with trails for all levels of skiers. This is also where much of the snowmaking has been focused and where the snowboarding facilities have been located.

Lachat is the top of the resort at 6,825 feet (2,100 meters). From this point strong intermediates and experts will find plenty of challenge. The Noire du Lachat is considered one of France's most difficult runs when it is open.

Maroly is the section with the surest snow and the best views. It is an intermediate playground with long cruising trails and plenty of snowmaking.

Snowboarding

Snowboarders will not have a hard time getting around Le Grand Bornand. There are only a couple long, flat cat tracks and they should be bearable for even beginner boarders. There is good range of difficulty in the runs here, and it is not a pain to access the more difficult ones. However, in shabby conditions, there are very few options for advanced and expert boarders.

The snow park consists of seven or so well maintained flat tops alongside a boardercross course, with a fairly steep 150-foot halfpipe at the bottom. The halfpipe is not maintained in the springtime. It is in the Vallee du Maroly area. Boarders can reach it by taking the Chouly Poma lift or the Terres Rouge chairlift.

First-timer snowboarders should start out in the area at the top of the Rosay gondola or off the quad chair, Les Gettiers. Here, the runs are wide and flat. Be careful not to take the Lachat chairlift; the easiest way down will probably be via the same chairlift you ride up in.

Beginner and lower intermediate boarders can venture almost anywhere at Le Grand Bornand. There are wide runs in the Vallee du Maroly area. The three chairlifts that meet at La Floria (1800 m) lead to more challenging terrain. There still may not be an easy enough way down Le Lachat for beginners.

Intermediate and advanced riders will enjoy the steeper, ungroomed terrain on La Floria. On these runs there are many turnoffs that lead to ungroomed snow fields. From the top of the Maroly Poma lift, boarders can reach a vast area of ungroomed terrain with many fun land features. Plenty of ungroomed terrain can be reached from the top of the Lachat chairlift, but sometimes these runs may be covered in moguls. Also, snow permitting, there is some good tree boarding on the Tete des Annes, a region that is a little hard to reach.

Experts should stick to the two peaks, La Floria and Le Lachat. The marked runs are mostly ungroomed, and are comprised of more steep terrain than the map is able to show. Also, there are many opportunities to drop into off-piste bowls or chutes; just beware of cliffs. The bottoms of these steep runs merge into the intermediate runs that the lower lifts serve; in order to get back to the steep stuff, boarders must take these flatter, more crowded runs.

Mountain Rating

Beginners and intermediates will have a swell time in either La Clusaz or Le Grand-Bornand. These are wonderful places for a romantic getaway for a mixed-ability couple. Many lifts offer side-by-side beginner and intermediate trails meeting at the bottom, perfect for families or friends of differing abilities.

Experts who know the area or who ski with a guide will find some toothy terrain with patches of difficulty especially on Massif de Balme at La Clusaz or dropping from Le Lachat at Le Grand-Bornand.

Cross-country

The 58 km. of scenic cross-country trails in the Grand-Bornand area follow paths through clusters of winter farms and century old chapels. With varied trails in the Valley du Bouchet and Chinaillon, cross-country skiers of all abilities will have plenty of terrain to tackle. In Chinaillon circuits range from 2 to 12 km. and in the Valley du Bouchet circuits range from 3 to 20 km. in length. A 7 km. trail links the Valley du Bouchet with 45 km. of trails at Plateau des Confins.

Ski school (2003/04 prices)

Le Grand-Bornand French Ski School (ESF) is in the village (0450 02 79 10) at the tourist office, and at Chinaillon (0450 27 01 83) under the chairlift La Floria.

Private: An hour lesson for one or two is €30; for three to four people, €40. A guide for a full day is €251 (high season) and €204 (low season).

Group: Six adult half-day lessons cost €94 (high season) and €89 (low season). Six half-day lessons for children younger than 13 cost €89 (high season) and €83 (low season).

International Starski (04 50 27 04 69) specializes in snowboarding lessons. Six two-hour lessons cost €96. For one to two people, private one-hour lessons cost €31, two-hour lessons cost €56.

The cross-country ski school in Grand-Bornand (450 02 78 17 fax: 450 02 36 02) offers six half-day group lessons for €89 (high and low season). Five full-day group lessons cost €120 (high and low season).

Lift Tickets (2003/04 prices)

Aravis lift ticket (La Clusaz and Le Grand-Bornand)

	Adults	**Child (14 and younger)**	**Senior (61 and older)**
two days	€55/53.50	€45.50	€49
six days	€149/128	€110	€123.50
seven days	€163/140	€121	€135.50

Le Grand-Bornand only

	Adults	**Child (14 and younger)**	**Senior (61 and older)**
half-day	€19	€15.70	€16.50
one day	€24.40	€19.50	€20
six days	€117.30/105.50	€96.90/87.20	€110.90/99.80

Accommodations

Le Grand-Bornand has three three-star hotels and 11 two-star hotels. For information or reservations, call the tourist office (04 50 02 78 00). Rates listed are based on per-person half-board, double occupancy: €—€75 and less; €€—€75–€125; €€€—€125+. Credit cards are accepted at all these hotels.

Le Roc Des Tours (450 27 00 11; €€) is a three-star with ski-in/ski-out access and a spectacular swimming pool, Jacuzzi and sauna.

Best Western Chalet Les Saytels (04 50 02 20 16; €€) Near the church, Chalet Les Saytels offers a bar, restaurant, satellite TV, a sauna, Jacuzzi, and billiards.

Les Cîmes (450 27 00 38; €) Relatively near the slopes at Chinaillon, Les Cîmes is a three-star hotel. It is small and cozy with lots of blond wood furnishings and only 10 rooms.

Le Vermont (450 02 36 22; €) is a chalet-style two-star hotel with a Jacuzzi, sauna and swimming pool, close to the two main gondolas in the village.

In Chinaillon, check out **Les Flocons** (450 27 00 89; €), a two-star right on the slopes where you will have to walk across the snow to reach your room.

Les Glaieuls (450 02 20 23; €), known for its good food, is the closest you will get to the gondolas in the village.

Apartments, condominiums, flats

In Le Grand-Bornand there are 500 chalet apartments. Contact Le Grand-Bornand tourist office by phone or e-mail. For two people, expect to pay at least €366 in high season and €160 in low season. For 3–5 people, it will cost at least €430 in high season and €185 in low season. For 6 or more people, it will be at least €540 in high season and €245 in low season. (These are per-person rates.)

Dining

Le Traîneau d'Angeline (450 63 27 64) is an interesting place to eat, as it blends modern art with the antique French style, and then adds techno music to the background. Daily menu costs €17–€20.

Aux Deux Guides (450 02 23 65) is like stepping back in time into a dark stone-wall castle. Daily menu is €15.10–€17.50.

L'Auberge du Pré Vieux (450 02 23 66) has excellent meals in a wonderful woodsy atmosphere. The daily menu is €23–€25; child's menu is €7.

At **Au Bon Vieux Temps** (450 02 32 38) you can watch your dish cook over an open fire. The atmosphere in this cozy farm house is friendly and active. Daily menu is €15.20–€19.80.

Apres-ski/nightlife

The nightlife in La Clusaz is happening on weekends, but, shall we say, dead on some weekdays. The older, more mature crowd hangs out at **Le Saltu** or **Le Pressoir**, video bars with many beer choices; they are open until about 2 a.m. **Le Caves du Pacally** is comfortable, casual, hangout; open until 2 a.m. **Bar Roc Café** is a dim, cozy place in town groovin' to 80s disco music. **Bali Bar** is a fun little bar that is usually packed with friendly people dancing to island music. **Panama Café** is a new age bar and hangout for a slightly younger crowd. Here the techno/pop music plays until 5 a.m.

Boarders and skiers of all ages head to either of the two disco/pub/nightclubs, both open until 5 a.m. **Club 18** blasts loud music and is great for chilling or close quarter dancing. **L'Eccluse** is also a great late-night hangout. The dance floor in this disco is not a floor but a thick sheet of glass, revealing the flowing waters of the town's river. Both of these exclusive nightclubs have cover charges of about €12.

Child Care (2003/04 prices)

Garderie **Les P'tits Maringouins** has been moved from the tourist office to its own building in Le Grand Bornand village. It also has a separate location in Le Chinaillon. In the village, they accept children 3 months to 5 years old, and in Le Chinaillon they accept children 8 months to 5 years old. Both the garderie in the village and in Le Chinaillon are open from 9 a.m. until 5:30 p.m.

A half-day without meal costs €20. A full day with meal costs €32. Six half-days without meal costs €100. Six full-days with meal costs €160.

Other activities

There is a **swimming complex** (04 50 02 43 01) with various open air and covered pools, a whirlpool tub, sauna, steam room, solarium, and fitness center; from December 23 to April 29, it is open every afternoon 1:30-6:30 p.m. Entrance to the pools costs adults €5.80 and children €5.08;

entrance to the fitness room, sauna, and steam room costs €11.50.

The town's **ice skating rink** is open in the morning from 10 a.m. to 12:30 p.m., and in the afternoon from 2-6 p.m., and at night from 9-11 p.m. Entrance is €3.20 and skate rentals cost €2.90. Occasionally there are ice hockey or skating competitions (450 02 48 45). From 5–6 p.m., every evening, **ice-bumper-cars** are available; €9.15 for a 10-minute round.

Paragliding (450 02 40 83) or (450 02 66 82; www.h3d.com/pgvaux) is available for €53.50 per person. Snowmobiling (450 32 35 37) costs €72 per hour for two people. There are **snowshoeing, heliski, ice-climbing, 4-wheeling, husky sleigh rides, quad biking, horse-drawn carriage, hiking**, and Vallee Blanche (skiing/boarding a glacier on Mont Blanc) programs. For more information call the tourism office.

Getting there

From Geneva airport, a daytime taxi ride costs €88 (€137 at night). The bus to Annecy costs about €9.50. The train (TGV) from Paris to Annecy takes 3 hours and costs about €91.50 round trip. From there Le Grand-Bornand is reached by bus or taxi (a taxi from Annecy is about €45.70).

Tourist Information

Office de Tourisme Le Grand-Bornand
74450 Le Grand-Bornand
tel. 0450 02 78 00; fax. 0450 02 78 01
Internet: www.legrandbornand.com
E-mail: infos@legrandbornand.com
In Chinaillon tel. 450 09 60 09

Flaine

Flaine is an all-or-nothing proposition: either you take to this purpose-built, concrete and steel, French resort in the Haute Savoie, or you search deeper into the Alps for quaint chalets and sleighs as backdrop to your downhill adventures. You may or may not like Flaine's exterior appearance, but its skiing, which is overwhelmingly intermediate, is bountiful and good. And this is a car-free resort which makes it great for families.

Let's face it: to anyone expecting an Alpine village, Flaine is an odd sight. The rectangular flat-topped buildings, reputedly designed by Marcel Breuer, clinging to the slopes of this narrow valley, appear to have all been poured from the same grey cement in an effort to spare time and expense. However, in terms of practicality, they seem to serve the purpose: cars are unnecessary, and housing and services are clustered to provide maximum convenience for skiers. There is also a cluster of Scandinavian-style chalets, Le Hameau de Flaine, only a kilometer from the base area and served by a regular, free shuttlebus.

Everything here is designed with winter sports in mind, and at 5,183 feet (almost a mile high), snow is practically guaranteed from December to May. When the blue piste of la Cascade is open, Flaine is connected by a system of lifts to the more traditional lower-altitude towns of Les Carroz, Morillon and Samoens, and by bus to Sixt. Together they form a wide-ranging ski circus of 78 lifts and more than a hundred marked trails totalling 257 km. of downhill adventure. Marked runs are predominantly intermediate and upper intermediate, but adventurous experts will find numerous possibilities just off-piste.

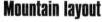

Mountain layout

First, all but beginners should take the cable car to the top of Les Grandes Platières to drink in the magnificent views of Mont Blanc and the jagged-toothed range running north (to your left) from the Aguille du Midi. Here on the treeless top of the world you can get a feel for the distances and a variety of terrain spreading out in three directions. Behind you, down the cable car route, are a black run and several alternate intermediate routes running directly back into Flaine or connecting with the chair and surface lifts in this section.

To your right is the Lindars section, reached by another cable system from Flaine, "The Eggs," and a chair to the top.

To your left stretches another whole system of lifts and trails, served by a new eight-seat chair. The trails drop down, on the near side to the gentle beginner area near Flaine center, on the far side to the Gers expert terrain, and further left to the long, winding trails down to Samoens, Morillon or Les Carroz. Each of these villages is at the bottom of its own system of trails and lifts, so plan one or two all-day excursions on this side when you have time to explore, stop for lunch and still wend your way back to Flaine before the lifts close.

Les Carroz, Morillon, and the valley town, Samoens, are Flaine's supporting cast, but their attraction lies in their more traditional Alpine accommodations.

Of the runs above these towns, we liked the blue-rated trail from Cupoire summit (6,166 feet) to the chair near the parking lot in Morillon. With easy turns, a few moguls, and trees for orientation, it's a fine cruise. The runs on this side are almost invariably intermediate. One exception to try is the black trail from Plateau des Saix summit to the Grand Massif Express (formerly the Vercland lift station.)

Mountain rating

Beginners will find great training slopes and excellent ski instruction.

Intermediates are in the majority here, and the slopes are laid out with that in mind. Les Grandes Platières is an intermediate's mountain, offering at least 15 different red-rated variations.

Experts will find plenty of challenges, particularly if they enjoy off-trail skiing.

Ski school (2003/04)

Flaine excels in ski instruction. There are two schools here: the French Ski School (450 90 81 00) and the International Ski School (450 90 84 41). Prices between the two are about the same.

Private lessons cost €32 per hour for one or two skiers; €64 for two hours for one to four skiers, and €79 for two hours for five to six.

Group lessons: The ESF guarantees a limit of not more than 10 people. Group lesson prices for six half days of instruction are €87 (adults); €83 (children age 4–12, a.m. and p.m.); €73 (children age 6–12, a.m. only).

An extended ski school with four hours a day for six days costs €118 for adults, €99 for children (age 4–12).

Snowboard lessons will cost €118 for six days of three-hour lessons for adults or €95 for children (age 12+).

Lift tickets (2003/04 prices)

These prices are for the entire Grand Massif area. A half day costs €28; a full day, €32; two days, €63.50; four days, €121; six days, €160; seven days, €183; 13 days, €334.

Juniors (12–15) ski for half day €22.50; one day, €25.50; two days, €50; four days, €96; six days, €128; seven days, €144; 13 days, €268.

Children (5–11) pay half day, €20.50; a full day, €23.50; two days, €47; four days, €89; six days, €117; seven days, €136; 13 days, €250.

Seniors (60+) pay half day, €23.50; a full day, €27; two days, €54; four days, €103; six days, €136; seven days, €155; 13 days, €283.

Kids younger than age 5 ski free.

Accommodations

Flaine primarily offers apartment accommodations, although you can also choose from the hotels listed below near the Forum Square. Most of the hotels have been taken over by tour operators except the Chalet La Cascade.

Rates: high season, half-board for one based on double occupancy €€€—€125+, €€—€75–€124, €—less than €75.

Hotel Totem (450 53 88 88; fax: 450 53 88 77; €€) is run by Crystal Holidays.

Hotel Club Le Flaine (1 45 77 52 62; fax: 4 92 12 62 20; €€) and **Hotel Aujon** (450 90 80 10; fax: 450 90 88 21; €€) are both run by Mer Montagne Vacances.

Chalet La Cascade (phone/fax: 450 90 87 66; €).

Le Hameau de Flaine is a village of Scandinavian chalets. Weekly rates are from €622 for a two-room apartment that sleeps four (or six in a squeeze) during January low season to €1,303 during the high season. A four-room chalet, for eight to 10, costs €1,318 during January low season and €2,167 during high season.

Apartments, condominiums, flats

Apartment complexes in Flaine have been built on three levels. Above the Forum on the hillside are the units of Flaine Forêt. These are the better apartments, many privately owned. Apartment buildings are also clustered around the main Forum square and there are more below the Forum level at Front de Neige. The most convenient are those in the Forum area.

The least expensive studio apartment on the Forum level in middle season (first two weeks of February) costs about €250 a week, and in high season (end of February and holidays) about €600.

For rental bookings there are four agencies: Maeva (450 90 87 99); Agence Renand (450 90 81 40); Agence Home International (450 90 82 93); Agence Astrid (450 90 86 41).

Dining

Choice of where to eat is limited because most guests are on full-pension plans with tour operators and apartment guests cook in their own kitchens.

Dine in a rustic chalet atmosphere in the restaurant **Les Chalets du Michet** (450 90 80 08) which serves good food in a converted cow shed, or try **La Perdrix Noire** (450 90 81 81) for excellent basic French food. At **Chez Daniel** (450 90 81 87) try raclette or fondue, or sizzling your meat on hot rocks. The restaurant in the **Aujon Hotel** (450 90 80 10) serves local Savoyard specialties. Reservations suggested. Pizza can be found at **Chez la Jeanne** or **La Pizzeria** (450 90 84 56).

On the mountains lunchtime offerings are pretty much standardized; you pay less on the Samoëns-Morillon side. Halfway down the Morillon side, **L'Beu** (450 90 17 89) serves simple, good regional specialties.

Après-ski/nightlife

Plan on staying in Flaine, because the road down the mountain can become treacherous, particularly after the sun goes down. Hotel bars are good meeting spots. Try the very British (and nice) **White Grouse Pub** or strike out for **Le Skifun** if you are looking for more disco action. **Les Cimes** has karaoke twice a week.

Child care (2003/04 prices)

A ski kindergarten for kids age 3–12, the Green Mouse Club, is conducted Sunday to Friday from 9 a.m. until 5 p.m. The fee for six days is €167 without lunch or €216 with lunch. Full-day ski kindergarten for those 6 months to 3 years runs €24.40 or half day for €12.

The Rabbit Club ski school is another children's program, which costs €215 for six days with lunch (€166 without lunch).

Other activities

There is an ice-driving school (450 90 82 59) with one- to three-day lessons. Helicopter rides (450 90 80 01), a climbing wall (450 90 80 74), paragliding (450 90 81 00, 450 90 01 80 or 450 03 33 46) and a cinema are available. The swimming pool (450 90 84 99) is open three mornings a week and every afternoon. Entry is €5 for adults for six swims and €4.40 for children for six swims.

Getting there

Geneva airport, about 45 miles away by the Geneva-Chamonix autoroute, is the closest. Take the Cluses exit.

There are three shuttles to Flaine daily from the Geneva airport or the downtown Geneva bus station. Tickets are €39.40 one way and €67.05 round trip.

You can also take the train to Cluses and then a Transport Alpbus (450 03 70 09) to Flaine. The bus costs €10.

Tourist information

Office du Tourisme Flaine, F-74300 Flaine, France
Telephone 450 90 80 01, fax 450 90 86 26.
Internet: www.flaine.com
E-mail: welcome@flaine.com

La Plagne

This is the largest single ski resort in Europe, if you base such a superlative on the number of lifts and lift capacity. Other ski regions may be larger, but they are formed by combining several independent resorts such as the Trois Vallées, the Dolomites or the Portes du Soleil.

That said, as large as it is, it wanted to be bigger. La Plagne recently linked its trail system with that of Les Arcs via Plan-Peisey. The combined area will be called Paradiski and will have 420 km. of trails. The enormity is mindboggling. The joint resorts will boast 144 ski lifts: 1 funicular 4 light-weight cable cars 1 'Funitel' (twin-cable cable car), 10 sections of gondola lifts, 18 detachable chairlifts, 47 chairlifts, 28 ski lifts suitable for walkers and 25 ski lifts accessible free of charge.

A cable car, Le Vaniose Express, with 200-person cabins will span the valley from Plan-Peisey on the Les Arcs side to Les Coches on the La Plagne side. The span will be 3,000 meters and the futuristic cable car will be as much as 380 meters above the valley floor. The trip, from station to station, will take four minutes. The Les Arcs trails are detailed in a separate chapter.

La Plagne claims a vertical of 6,500 feet. The lower 1,700 feet of that is through trees and along winding roads. Still, when the snow is good a skier can start out from Roche de Mio at 8,775 feet and drop to Montchavin at 4,062 feet, which means more than 4,700 feet of working vertical. Another vertical drop across the western face of Bellecote down to Les Bauches provides almost 4,000 feet of nonstop vertical that will challenge any skier.

Even in the modest upper ranges of the resort, the working vertical is about 2,500 feet. Since it is one of the highest resorts on the continent, La Plagne can't be beat for certainty of snow; there will be snow here, up on the glacier, even in the middle of August.

La Plagne revolves around apartment life. It offers about 47,000 beds in small apartments, and only about 1,500 beds in the eleven hotels in the region. The purpose-built sections of La Plagne consist of the six high-altitude modern clusters, connected by a creative series of public conveyances called telemetro, telebus, and telecabine, and traditional shuttlebuses. Each complex has apartments, with stores and ski shops all interconnected by tunnels and walkways. These underground passages, while extremely practical in snow country, give several of the areas an oddly urban feel, reminiscent of a subway shopping mall. Four lower villages are also connected to the lift system.

Plagne Centre at 6,463 feet is the original, constructed 30 years ago as one of France's first built-for-skiing villages. What the buildings lack in charm they make up for in convenience—two hotels, dozens of restaurants, scores of shops, a cinema and apartments are all connected by underground passages with 20 lifts fanning out from the just outside its doors.

Plagne Villages at 6,726 feet is a cluster of small apartment houses and Alpine-style buildings with wooden features and peaked roofs. There are no hotels, only apartments and shops.

Plagne 1800 is a consistently designed neo-Savoyard mountain village with wooden chalets and peaked roofs. This grouping contains squash courts.

Aime La Plagne, also sometimes called Aime 2000, is a newer purpose-built complex above Plagne Centre. Many consider it the most convenient, with many of the best apartments in the resort. There are a cinema and a good collection of shops and restaurants. A cable car connects Aime La Plagne with Plagne Centre.

Plagne Bellecote is a group of massive, interconnected, high-rise buildings over an underground shopping mall. There are no hotels in this group, but it has La Plagne's only heated outdoor swimming pool and is the starting point of the gondola to the glacier at 8,858 feet.

Belle Plagne is the newest of La Plagne's centers, built in the Savoyard chalet style. An underground garage system allows one to reach each of the chalet groups. A multilevel shopping arcade with covered walkways provides a touch of Alpine charm. There is also a fitness center.

Villages that are part of the complex have ski schools and ski kindergartens for children plus ski rentals.

Plagne Montalbert at 4,429 feet with a couple of two-star hotels, a selection of apartments and eleven restaurants has its own lift system that connects with the rest of the La Plagne region.

Montchavin and Les Coches are at 4,101 feet and 4,757, feet respectively. Les Coches is the new station of the Vanoise Express that will link to Les Arcs. These villages have separate lift system tickets which may be purchased separately as well as a two-star hotel, some chalets and apartments and 14 restaurants.

Champagny-en-Vanoise at the top of a valley separating La Plagne from the Trois Vallées area is a picturesque town clinging to the mountain walls. A cable car takes skiers up to giant snowfields that connect with Plagne Centre, Plagne Bellecote and Belle Plagne. During the past two years, new lifts have made the connections between Champagny and Belle Plagne very easy. Skiers staying in Champagny-en-Vanoise can ski into town down two challenging intermediate trails with plenty of off-piste possibilities.

Mountain layout

There are 132 trails, including nine black and 37 red, covering 220 km. of ski area with 108 ski lifts, eight of which are gondolas, and one that connects Bellecote and Belle Plagne with the glaciers.

Beginning Christmas 2003, The Vanoise Express, will connect La Plagne to Les

Arcs and create the new Paradiski Ski Area. The 420 square-km. Paradiski area will open three glaciers and two summits, each above 3,000 meters high, to every level of skier. Skiers will have their pick of 232 pistes served by 144 ski lifts. Boarders will enjoy 2 boardercross courses, 4 snowparks and 2 halfpipes.

The remainder of the lift network comprises 34 chair lifts and 64 surface lifts.

What you see, you can ski. Just take off and explore different sections of the resort on different days. No intermediate will get into any trouble here if they stick to the upper slopes and stay off the glacier. This is one of the best intermediate resorts in the world. The distances here are extreme. Be sure to plan your day before finding yourself on the wrong side of the resort when lifts start to close.

Adventurous skiers can find plenty of challenge along the fringes of the resort. Experts will want to drop behind the ridge above Aime La Plagne basically following the Morbleu and Les Etroits trails looping around to the Les Coqs lift and then challenge the Les Coqs and the Emile Alais trails.

Another expert adventure is to take the Bellecote cable car from the peak of Roche di Mio to the Glacier of Bellecote at 10,662 feet. This spectacular ride takes skiers down 500 feet before rising almost 1,640 feet. From the glacier, advanced skiers in tip-top shape can follow the lazy Bellecote or Le Rochu runs down more than 2,000 feet of vertical to the Chalet de Bellecote lift. Skiers with guides will take the Traversé lift and set off across the face of Bellecote and drop towards Les Bauches some 1,200 meters (3,900 feet) of vertical below. It is a daunting ski afternoon or morning. The restaurant at Les Bauches certainly seems welcoming after that descent. From here lifts reconnect skiers with the network.

A similarly challenging descent can be made from the Bellecote Glacier to Champagny-le-Haut along the Cul du Nant with a guide. A shuttlebus takes skiers back to the cable car at Champagny-en-Vanoise.

Experts can drop alongside the bobsled run for some good skiing through trees and across pastures down toward Plagne Montalbert. Snow is fine during most of the season, but in the spring ask about coverage.

The combined Les Arc/La Plagne Paradiski region will have two boarder cross courses, four snowparks and two halfpipes

Mountain rating

La Plagne is an intermediate and beginner mountain, at least as far as the prepared trails go in the Bellecote, Belle Plagne, Grand Rochette, Montchavin, Les Coches, Plagne Montalbert and Champagny sectors.

Intermediates will think they have died and gone to skier heaven. The rolling mountains offer acceptable steeps where intermediates can play, and mellow, off-trail areas for developing deep-snow skills. The Champagny section is pretty tame but the run into the town and return ride makes a great outing.

Beginners and lower intermediates are in one of the best European resorts for learning to ski. Here beginners can have the experience of taking a lift to the highest point, with all the thrill of the spectacular views, and still be able to get back down the mountain safely.

Advanced skiers will find challenging skiing on the back of the Biolley sector. There are plenty of spots for creative experts to go off trail and find more than enough to keep them busy for a week. Any expert will be challenged by the runs down the glacier. The more skill you have, the further off the basic trails you can venture. With good snow this glacier area is fantastic for even the best skiers.

Cross-country

The resort also has 90 km. of excellent cross-country trails. The cross country trails can be found running all along the base of the Alpine ski area from Les Coches to Plan Bois to Les Frasses to Plagne Bellecote to Plagne Centre to Le Fornelet to Plagne Montalbert and Longefoy.

On the Champagny-en-Vanoise side of the range, extensive cross-country skiing is available at Chapagny le Haut with trails going into the Parc National de la Vanoise Laisonnay.

Ski school (2002/03 prices)

The La Plagne ski schools has 550 instructors available throughout the various village complexes. Prices vary depending on which program and village you select for lessons.

Private lessons are available for full days, 9:15 a.m. to 4:45 p.m., for €214. Hourly lessons are about €31 on Sundays. Private lessons are limited to five or fewer.

Group lessons: Six full days cost about €160; six half days cost from €94. *Nouvelle glisse* courses which alternate between skiing, monoskiing, telemarking and snowboarding as well as competition courses are available.

Lift tickets (2003/04 prices)

The La Plagne region have a lift ticket system that is made up of four sectors. Lift passes may be purchased for only the villages of Montchavin/Les Coches, Plagne Montalbert or Champagny. The La Plagne overall pass prices are below. They have some limitations; however, together with an inter-resort shuttle pass will allow skiers to go virtually anywhere in the area.

	Adults	**Children** (ages 6-13)	**Seniors** (ages 60+)
Full day	€37	€27.40	€31.50
Six days	€176	€131	€150
Fourteen days	€338	€254	€287

Lift tickets bought for six days or more permit one day a week skiing in Val d'Isère, Tignes, Les Trois Vallées or Les Arcs.

There is a separate pass for Paradiski.

	Adults	**Children** (ages 6-13)	**Seniors** (ages 60+)
Full day	€30	€23	€26
Six days	€220	€165	€187

Accommodations

Rates here are daily rates for half-board based on double occupancy in February, unless otherwise indicated: €€€—€125+; €€—€57–€124; €—less than €75.

Hotel Eldorador (479 09 12 09; fax 479 09 29 52; €–€€) Overall the atmosphere in Belle Plagne makes the Eldorador's location desirable, but what one gains in atmosphere one loses in choice of restaurants and shops. If you are a single and someone tells you that there will be no supplement, beware. "Half rooms" for singles with no supplement mean you share a shower and toilet with another unfortunate half-roomer.

Hotel Les Alpes in Aime (479 09 70 24; €) This small hotel only has 14 rooms.

The new **Chalet/Hotel Les Montagnettes** (479 55 12 00; fax 479 55 12 19; €€) in Belle Plagne has some wonderful apartments with more space than the older apartments in Plagne Centre. This is an upscale choice in the region.

In the villages there are two-star hotels. **Hotel l'Ancolie** (479 55 05 00; fax 479 55 04 42; €–€€) in Champagny has a great location right at the base of the cable car. **Les Glières** (479 55 05 52; fax 479 55 04 84; €-€€) is also in Champagny. **Hotel Bellecote** (479 07 83 30; fax 479 07 80 63; €) in Montchavin has rooms by the week. **Hotel l'Aigle Rouge** (479 55 51 05; fax 479 55 51 14; €) in Plagne Montalbertis a good value. Children normally get a 30 to 50 percent discount in most hotels.

Ski Chalets: Crystal, Simply Ski, Thompson, Neilson (see page 25 for phone, fax and Internet addresses).

Apartments, condominiums, flats

Apartments are by far the most popular form of accommodation in La Plagne. There are more than 20 times the number of apartment beds than hotel beds. Accommodations range from tiny 17-square-meter rooms to spacious. Two can make it without any trouble in a normal two-person French apartment, but will be much more comfortable if they can afford to rent a place advertised for four. In Belle Plagne, a studio or one-bedroom apartment with plenty of room for two will run €255–€300 a week in January. There are also bargain weekly rates starting from only €210 per person, including ski lifts, lessons and equipment rental discounts (if more people share) in January. Such rates are hard to beat. For information call 479 09 79 79.

Dining

Most of the restaurants listed below are in Plagne Center. Since Plagne Center is connected with both Aime La Plagne and Plagne Villages by cable car and telebus, it serves as a center for these three complexes. The restaurants here prove that even in modern surroundings small, cozy eating spots can be created with all the atmosphere and charm one might expect to find in a traditional town bistro. Although La Plagne is considered an economical resort by French standards, meals can still cost a bundle. Top restaurants here will run about €32–€35 for a full meal, excluding wine. The moderate restaurant meals run about €18–€25, including wine, and the inexpensive ones will have a fixed-price menu at about €15 without wine. For those looking for less expensive meals, try one of the crêperies or a pizzeria where a meal can end up costing as little as €10, with a beer.

Plagne Center

Le Bec Fin (479 09 10 86) offers excellent French cooking for a fixed-price menu of €10–€25. The decor is best by candlelight. English is spoken.

Le Chaudron (479 09 23 33), in the open field in the middle of Plagne Center, presents excellent grilled specialties cooked over an open fire in the middle of the dining room. Expect your meal to cost €20–€30.

Le Refuge (479 09 00 13) is the oldest in the resort. Photographs of bobsled champions cover the walls in the very local, very French bar out front. In the dining room each table is centered under a telescoping copper hood, which vents smoke while guests barbecue their own steaks at the table. Expect to spend about €10–€25.

Follow the Rue de la Gaité to discover three moderate to inexpensive restaurants: **L'Estaminet** (479 09 12 69) serves Alsatian specialties in huge portions; **La Metairie** (479 09 11 08) has Savoyard specialties on wooden tables with a fixed-priced menu of €13; and **Le Bistroquet** (479 09 22 11) has lace curtains, and red tablecloths.

Walk to the end of the hall and pick up—would you believe—a pizza to go at **Pizzeria Domino**.

Aime La Plagne

Here, our favorite is **l'Arlequin** (479 09 05 29). After winding down a circular staircase you will have the chance to sample pizza if you insist, but with a difference. They make a pizza *quattro formaggio* with four French cheeses; its owners also have created a smoked salmon pizza. One unique creation you've probably never tasted—*tagliatelli foie gras*. Try the normal raclette and fondue or the special *rouergat*, a duck fondue where the duck is cooked in liver oil. Or order the "royal stone," a superheated rock upon which you grill mixed meat and foie gras. For the atmosphere, unique food and good service you'll end up spending €25–€35 and leave stuffed.

La Soupe aux Schuss (479 09 06 44) is a tiny place with space for less than 30 diners. The atmosphere is pure French country, with wooden tables, lace tablecloths, wine in baskets, and pine cupboards. The food is excellent but on the expensive side—expect to walk out spending at least €22 without wine.

Au Bon Vleux Temps (479 09 20 57) on the slopes above Aime 2000 in a charming old chalet, offers specialties from €12 for lunch, or dinner with reservations starting at about €15.

Belle Plagne

The most popular restaurant is **Le Matafan** (479 09 09 19), which is normally packed. Tables fan out around an open fire, country cupboards stand against the wall and lace curtains drape the windows. A series of eleven different luncheon plates are offered, including mountain ham, paté and cheese for €10, or an omelet with bacon, salad and fries for €11. Dinner portions are mountain-sized.

La Cloche serves up good food in a less formal atmosphere. **K2**, which offers a meal plan for the Résidence Carene, has a €14 menu for good regional specialties.

Head to **The Cheyenne Café** for a taste of Tex/Mex at affordable prices.

Plagne 1800

La Mine (479 09 07 75) is perhaps the best gourmet-type restaurant, with the average meal in the €32 range before you add in wine. The elegant dining room with open fireplace and beamed ceiling accompany the upscale meals and price. **Loup Garou** (479 09 20 17) also offers tasty dinners. Be careful not to confuse the Loup Garou with Loup Blanc which doesn't offer dishes quite as tasty.

Plagne Bellecote

La Ferme (479 09 29 32) has good local food with fish specialties.

On the slopes

There are 21 different mountain restaurants, not including the restaurants in the complexes themselves, which offer excellent midday dining. Included are **Vega, La Galerne** and **Le Chaudron** in Plagne Center. Most of the mountain restaurants are self-service. **Le Biollet**, above Aime La Plagne, gets the most sun. For sitdown meals, try **Le Val Sante** at the far left edge of the resort area and be ready to ski home slowly, stuffed with lots of great food. **L'Arpette,** just above Belle Plagne and recognizable by the motorbike hanging from the rafters, serves up good mountain food. **La Bergerie** above Plagne Bellecote has a rustic atmosphere and pricey mid-mountain dining. **La Grande Rochette**, at the top of the gondola from Plagne Center, offers spectacular views at lunch and dinners on Thursday.

Après-ski/nightlife

The Showtime Cafe in Plagne Bellecote has live music some nights and karaoke on others.

The King Cafe in Plagne Center is a coffee house offering concerts and a gathering place for the young crowd.

Child care (2002/03 prices)

Each complex in La Plagne has a nursery for children age 2 to 6. These facilities offer indoor activities, as well as outdoor snowgarden play depending on the age of the child.

Nursery Marie-Christine in Plagne Center (479 09 11 81) takes children older than 2 years for €32 a day, without meals, or €18 for a half day.

Belle Plagne nursery (479 09 06 68) accepts children eighteen months to 6 years.

Children eighteen months to three years old are welcomed at the nursery where they can enjoy themselves with drawing, games and toys, singing and videos and snowplay. One half day is €22; one day without meal is €32; one day with meal is €39; six half days are €110; six days without meals are €139; six days with meals are €214.

Children age 3-6 years old have a ski kindergarten called Club Piou Piou. One half day is €33 EUR; six days without meals are €165; six days with meals are €243.

For older children (13 and younger), the ski school has special programs designed for young skiers. Never-evers can take a course that includes lifts and for six days for €305. Six normal lessons will cost €205 for full days, six half days cost €155.

Other activities

The **heated pool** in Plagne Bellecote is open from 3:30 p.m. to 7 p.m. The ice rinks, in Plagne Bellecote, Aime la Plagne and Les Coches are open from 2:30 p.m. to 7 p.m.; on Wednesdays and Fridays they're open to 11:30 p.m.

Rent squash courts in Plagne 1800 at Maeva reception.

In 1989, La Plagne constructed an Olympic bobsled run for the 1992 games, making it the official bobsled capital of the Alps. Visitors may arrange a hair-raising, 80-kilometer per hour plunge down the 19 curves of the track in a special (safe) sled when the track is not being used for competition.

There are English-speaking doctors in the Plagne Centre medical center. It is open 8:30 a.m.–7 p.m.

Getting there

Local transport: Plagne Centre to Aime La Plagne is served by a telemetro 8 a.m.–1 a.m. Plagne Center and Plagne Village has a telebus from 8 a.m.–1 a.m. Plagne Center and Plagne 1800/Bellecote are connected by shuttlebus on the hour and half hour, 8:30 a.m.–12:30 a.m. Bellecote–Belle Plagne cable car links Belle Plagne from 8 a.m. –1 a.m. Bellecote–Plagne 1800–Plagne Center are connected by a shuttlebus at quarter past and quarter to the hour, 8:45 a.m.–12:45 a.m.

Telebus is approximately €3 for two trips. The Telemetro and shuttlebus are free.

Taxi: Christian Bouzon (479 09 03 41); or Taxi Silvestre (479 09 70 58).

condominiums, hotels, restaurants, shops and cafés are all truly ski-in/ski-out.

Jean Vuarnet, the sunglass king, returned to France with a gold medal from the 1960 Olympics at Squaw Valley and persuaded a big real estate agency to invest in the altitudinous Avoriaz 1800. The original structures of 1966 have now grown to a cluster of 42 modern condos, a Club Med, two hotels and 30 restaurants.

Avoriaz's Children's Village, managed by Olympic-medalist Annie Famose and a staff of 120 instructors, is acclaimed for teaching youngsters 3 to 16 to ski.

Avoriaz 1800 is at the center of the Les Portes Du Soleil wheel, the main link between France and Switzerland. The question becomes, "Do you just go there to ski, for a meal, for a drink and a look around," or "Do you stay?" In the old days, getting there meant climbing into a cable car and then taking a reindeer-drawn sled to your room. Today, there are a number of choices. A road climbs up from Morzine, 14 km. and a half-hour drive away, for those with cars. For those without, a gondola and two ski lifts reach from the heart of Morzine up to the Avoriaz hub, a 25 minute trip on skis. You can also take a free bus from Morzine to the cable car base; the cable car runs every 15 minutes and continues well into the evening, for those who want to explore one town or the other. Finally, those planning an extended stay in Avoriaz may choose to arrive by bus from Geneva and avoid the parking fees and hassle of having a car here. You won't need it.

Mountain layout

Morzine-Avoriaz is perhaps the best base from which to explore the Portes du Soleil area. The question is, where to begin. As well as easy access to the Les Crosets/Champoussin sector via the Swiss Wall, Avoriaz has easy access to Plaine Dranse which has perhaps the most enjoyable and varied skiing of the region. The slopes directly above Avoriaz will challenge skiers of every level. Another plus: Avoriaz has been aggressively replacing older lifts with high-speed quads and six-seated lifts, making lines rare here. In 2001 a new chair lift was built to connect Avoriaz with Lindarets, eliminating one of the last bottlenecks in the area.

You can easily spend a couple of days just on the Morzine/Les Gets slopes, which offer a nice mix of terrain and are especially popular with families. Beginners go to Le Pleney, which is a one-stop ascent by tram or cable car. Nyon has a nice mix of black, red and blue descents, and Chamossière has outstanding views, good long black runs and some fine cruising through the Col de Joux Plane. Le Ranfolly has four side-by-side red runs while La Rosta is ideal for parties of different abilities. Mt. Chéry, reached by a ground connection from the Les Gets base, is best for advanced skiers.

Some of the most enjoyable challenging skiing of the entire Portes du Soleil is best accessed from Morzine and Avoriaz: Pointe de Nyon, Chamossière, and Col du Fornet in France and, in Switzerland, Planachaux, Grand Paradis, and Champéry are all classic higher altitude alpine peaks, each with difficult decents. There are many places in the Portes du Soleil where a simple 15 minute hike can get you expert couloirs and powdery bowls. If you are looking for the most expert terrain in these mountains, plan to go with a an avalanche-savvy guide, however. Otherwise, try The Wall of Death between Avoriaz and Switzerland. Appropriately named for it's difficulty, negotiating this descent can be exciting. It can be skied by an intermediate when the snow cover is good, because there are broad segments for traverses and turns, and fearful skiers can take the chair lift down. The Swiss Wall at the top of Chavanette in Switzerland is another difficult decent. Be sure your knees are up to it, though, because this run is one of the longest mogul fields in the area. Be forewarned that the lifts on the Swiss side have not been updated as have their French counterparts. When skiing from one side to the other, allow plenty of time to return: It's a long, expensive cab ride back if you get stuck.

In Morzine there is night skiing and riding at the Pléney from 5 p.m.–10 p.m. It is free for anyone with a lift ticket.

Snowboarding

Morzine/Avoriaz has everything a boarder could want: few drag lifts, quality snow parks, endless off-piste opportunities, and well groomed trails for all caliber riders. Les Portes du Soleil also devotes five or six runs every year to boarder cross courses.

The Portes du Soleil stations are well connected; there are few cat tracks and no tough traverses, and you will never have to take your board off to hike. As a boarder, you can go all over the area without having to worry about time spent "getting there" because wherever you go, you will be riding good slopes the whole way. If you are looking for some good tree riding, hit the open forests under the Prolays, Brocheaux, and Lindarets lifts in Avoriaz, or, when there is enough snow, much of the lower runs in Champery in Switzerland. For back country riding, hire a guide to take you down into La Vallee de la Manche, the valley between the Avoriaz 1800 and the Morzine mountain masses. After a little hike from the top of Pointe de Nyon or from Col du Fornet, above Avoriaz 1800, the descent is remote and fresh tracks are easy to find. Either way, the beginning of the run is one big powder field, and the end is bouncing through open forests. Don't go without prior preparations for a ride back waiting for you at the bottom of the run.

Mountain Rating

The sheer size of Les Portes du Soleil allows for anyone to find his or her niche at the areas. A good mixed bag of skiing opportunities awaits, and most trails can be enjoyed by an intermediate. With wide, above-treeline slopes and trails that descend to the village through the forest, this region lets you enjoy the full experience of skiing. Morzine is a very good place for beginners, relaxed and wide-open. The variety of lifts and terrain makes sometimes less than challenging runs interesting.

Avoriaz has some of the best beginner facilities in the Portes du Soleil region. For experts, Avoriaz has what locals call *sauvage* or wide-open, all-terrain, all-condition descents. For intermediates, you'll never have to ski the same run twice. (See Mountain Rating in the Swiss Portes du Soleil chapter.)

Ski school (2003/04 prices)

Ecole de Ski Francais (ESF): In Morzine (450 79 13 13, fax 450 79 17 70, www.esf-morzine.com) there are 140 instructors who teach one quarter of Morzine's visitors. The office and meeting place is at the bottom of the Teleski du Pleney. In Avoriaz, you can sign up for lessons in the Place du Telepherique, or in the Tourist Office or in the Cap-Neige building near Fonaines Blanches. The meeting place is either at the Place du Telepherique (at the bottom of the Plateau chairlift) or on the Plateau, near the Plateau chair lift and the Dromonts ski lift.

Ski passes are not included in the lesson prices and the prices do not vary much between Morzine and Avoriaz.

Group lessons: Half days 9:30 a.m.–noon or 2:30 p.m.–5 p.m., cost €21–€25 for adults and children; six half days are €87–€97; six full days cost €125–€140.

Private lessons: one hour, €31 for one or two skiers, €41 for three to five skiers.

Snowboarding lessons cost €103 for six half days, €27 for one half day.

Freeriding lessons cost €120 for three hours of guided touring across the Portes du Soleil region for one to five people.

Cross-country lessons with pass is €150.20 for five 2-and-a-half hour lessons; €82 for six mornings (pass not included).

Ecole de Ski & Snowboard International (E2SA) in Morzine is slightly more expensive than ESF, as lessons are taught in smaller groups (maximum of 8 people). The office is a few doors down from ESF and the meeting points vary according to the kind of lesson.

Freeride lessons: (ski or snowboard) €40 for 3 hours or €130 for 5 days of 3 hours.

Snowshoeing: €18 for a 3 hour excursion.

They offer good **guides** for the Valee Blanche and other off piste trips in France and Switzerland, and also have half and full days of **Heli Skiing. The Ecole de Ski Internationale** in Avoriaz offers similiar trips starting at €230 for one to four skiers or boarders.

Lift tickets (2003/04 prices)

	Portes du Soleil		**Morzine/Les Gets**		**Avoriaz**	
	Adult	**Child**	**Adult**	**Child**	**Adult**	**Child**
1 day	€35	€24	€25.50	€19	€30	€20
2 days	€69	€46	€46.80	€34	€59	€39
3 days	€98	€66	€69.20	€52		
4 days	€124	€83	€89.40	€67.10		
5 days	€149	€100	€109.90	€81.60		
6 days	€171	€115	€128	€96		

For €15.70, Snowboarders can get a lift pass that gives them access to a few chairlifts around the snowparks above Avoriaz.

The age for children is 5–15 years old inclusive. Children younger than 5 ski free.

The lift ticket system in the Portes de Soleil is a hands-free pass that you can keep in a pocket. Simply pass by a scanner that picks up data from a computer chip on the ticket and ride. This system makes it easy to add time or regions to your ski pass electronically at any ticket office.

Accommodations

Rates: half-board for one based on double occupancy with half board. €€€—€125+; €€—€75-€124; €—less than €75.

Our recommended hotels in Morzine with star rating noted by ***s:

Les Airelles*** (450 74 71 21; fax 450 79 17 49; €€€) is modern, well-designed, and centrally located, with a big swimming pool, a toilet and phone in each of its 55 rooms. It has a big swimming pool and a fitness room.

Le Champs Fleuris*** (450 79 14 44; 450 79 27 75; €€€) has an indoor pool, tennis, a sauna and a fitness room.

Le Dahu*** (450 75 92 92; 450 75 92 50; €€€) has similar amenities to Le Champs Fleuris for just a bit less per night.

Le Tremplin*** (450 79 12 31, fax 450 75 95 70; €€€) has a friendly atmosphere and a pleasant sitting area and bar. It has a Jacuzzi and a fitness room and is located next to the slopes.

La Bergerie*** (450 79 13 69, fax 450 75 95 71; €€) is a residence hotel without a restaurant, but has rooms with kitchenettes as well as telephone, television, a parking garage, sauna and an outdoor swimming pool.

Just outside downtown, **Chalet Philibert***** (450 79 25 18; €€) has 18 rooms, including three suites, all with television, safe, radio, hairdryer and telephone. It also has a pool, sauna, Jacuzzi, fitness room and an excellent dining room.

Le Carlina ** (450 79 01 03; fax 450 75 94 11; €–€€) is near the center of town and the lifts.

Le Sporting** (04 50 79 15 03fax 450 79 11 25 €) is also near the center of town and has a pool, sauna, and fitness room.

Similar but just outside of town is **Le Petit Cheval Blanc** ** (450 79 13 89). Enjoy a nice swim in the pool after coming in from the slopes. Here, your day will start out right with an included breakfast that just hits the spot.

Bel 'Alpe** (04 50 79 05 50; fax 450 79 22 76; €), **Hermine Blanche**** (450 75 76 55; fax 450 74 72 47; €), and **Les Côtes**** (450 79 09 96; fax 450 75 97 38; €) are all inexpensive and excellent places to stay.

Also in Morzine is **Le Mas De La Coutettaz, the "Farmhouse"** (450 79 08 26; fax 450 79 18 53; €€), an 18th-century manor house, the oldest building in the valley, has six spacious rooms. English tea is served in the afternoon, and at night guests sit around an expansive table for a family-style four-course dinner with wine.

In nearby Les Gets (part of the Portes du Soleil region) try **Hotel Labrador** (450 75 80 00; fax 450 79 87 03; €€) with an indoor pool and great views. **Nogano** (450 79 71 46; fax 450 79 71 48; €€)is a great bargain. **Alpages** (450 75 80 88; fax 04 50 79 76 98; €€)has one of the best affordable restaurants. And **Bellevue** (450 75 80 95; fax 450 79 81 81; €€) is the best bargain of all for a simple hotel.

There is a great **youth hostel** in Morzine, equipped with 76 beds, car & cycle parking, luggage storage, credit card acceptance, a bar, and a pool; it is located just outside of the center of town and very close to the lifts. A reservation is strongly recomended during December, February and Easter.

Avoriaz:

This is primarily a resort of condos. The two hotels do not take groups. High seasons, when rooms are toughest to get and prices are highest, are Christmas, Easter and February.

Hotel les Dromonts*** (450 74 08 11, fax 450 74 02 79; €€–€€€) which was entirely renovated in 2001 has 31 rooms.

Hotel de la Falaise (450 74 26 00, fax 450 74 26 20; €€–€€€) has 29 rooms with accommodations for one to four per room/suite.

Ski Chalets: Crystal, Crystal, Thomas Cook/Neilson. (See page 20 for phone, fax and Internet addresses.)

Apartments, condominiums, flats

This is what Avoriaz 1800 is all about. The tourist board will send you a list of rental agencies who will make arrangements.

Approximate prices (for one week) with contact agency:

Immobiliere Des Hauts-Forts (450 74 16 08; fax 450 74 06 33; online reservations at www.avoriaz-holidays.com): studio for four, €343–€817; two-room for five, €439–€985. Ski Chalets for eight to fourteen people are also available for €1737–€5480 per week.

Pierre et Vacances (450 74 35 35; fax 450 74 01 82): studio for four, €395–€1040; two-room for four to five, €515–€1350.

Immobiliere des Dromonts (450 74 00 03; fax 450 74 05 94; email agence.dromonts@wanadoo.fr): studio for 4 persons €350–€790; two-rooms for four to five persons is €450–€1100. Chalets are also available from €2600–€3800.

Maeva (450 74 28 00; fax 450 74 11 49): studio for four, €320–€1075; two-room for four to five, €370–€1,180.

In Morzine, contact Morzine reservation at 450 79 11 57, fax 450 74 73 18, email reservation@morzine.com.

Dining

In Morzine, head to **La Grange** (450 75 96 40), where Chef Fabrice Broux, who trained with celebrated chef Paul Bocuse, prepares gourmet and Savoyarde specialties and serves them in an intimate setting that's both elegant and rustic. Fixed-price menus range from €30–€50, the latter Broux's Surprise Menu of six dishes based on the availability of fresh products at the market place.

At **La Chamade's,** owner, Thierry Thorens, also trained with Bocuse. Most folks order the pizzas, but don't ignore the other items on the menu.

More typical of the regional and traditional food, with raclette and fondue, is **L'Etale**, where a meal will run €15–€20. There is a disco downstairs.

Restaurant **Le Clin D'Oeil** (450 79 03 10) is a good choice for traditional regional foods as well as pizza. It's tucked away in Le Bourg section of Morzine, next to the post office. A three-course menu is €15–€25.

Les Sapins (450 75 90 56) with a spectacular view of Lake Montriond is known for its home cooking. Roger Muffat, father of the owner, prepares everything himself including the dried meat and ham. A five-course meal is €18–€30.

Nearby Les Gets has good affordable meals at the **Alpages Hotel** (450 75 80 88) and **Hotel Regina** (450 75 80 44) where daily menus start at less than €15.

Avoriaz 1800 has a good collection of restaurants, but book in advance. The three-star **Christophe Leroy Restaurant** in Hotel Dromonts charges about €50 for a meal; **Crepy** runs €20–€25. **La Reserve** serves good fish or cheese dishes for about €35. **Le Petit Vatel** specializes in trout; **Bistro** prepares mountain specialties that with a bottle of wine will cost about €22. For late-night fare try **Shooters**.

Since Avoriaz is on the mountain, its restaurants qualify as mountain restaurants. However the tiny village of Les Lindarets, on the other side of the ridge, has a wonderful collection of small restaurants. They are all good but **Les Marmottes, Pomme de Pin**, **Crémaillère** and **La Terrasse** stand out.

On the slopes of Super Morzine, **Les Cretes de Zorre** (450 79 24 73) serves hearty and inexpensive regional food such as Beignet de Pomme de Terre (potato fritters) and occasionally Croute du Valais (fried bread pieces soaked with melted cheese and wine accompanied by green salad and roasted ham). No one leaves without a "squirt" of Pschit (pear brandy) right out of a squirt bottle. Parties of 10 or more may book the cabin for an evening.

For a true alpine atmosphere and a grand view of Mont Blanc, lunch at **Le Belvedere** (450 79 81 52) at the top of the Mont Chéry gondola in Les Gets. Menu is about €12. For a taste of Switzerland, enjoy a lunch of croute at **Chez Gaby**, in Champousson, overlooking the Dents du Midi.

Après-ski/nightlife

Generally low-keyed and relaxed, Morzine is no jet-set town crammed with sports cars. It is, however, good for pleasant wandering and window shopping, with several opportunities to stop for a hot chocolate or beer. **Opéra**

Rock disco attracts locals and young people. **Dixie Bar** is a nicely decorated piano bar near the church. **Le Café Chaud** attracts young swingers. **Boudha Café** and **Le Crépuscule** are also a good time.

If you do go for a stroll in Morzine, watch out for cars on the narrow, winding streets of the upper part of town. This area lends itself to a pedestrian village, but no such luck yet.

Avoriaz has plenty of action: **The Place**, **Le Choucas** and **Shooters** are fun, and **Festival** begins filling up after midnight.

Child care (2003/04 prices)

In **Morzine**, kindergarten l'Outa (450 79 26 00) welcomes children and infants from 3 months old to 6 years old without ski lessons. The chalet is in the center of the resort, near the slopes and ski school. There is a playroom for indoor activities, a nursery and a very large yard where instructors give first lessons to the youngest. Parents can bring a meal or take advantage of the special menu. L'Outa pricing is €17.50 for a half day, €95 for six half days, €31 for a full day, and €166 for six full days. Meals are €5.50 each.

Club des Piou Piou (450 79 13 13) welcomes children ages 3–12 with ski lessons. Costs are €67 for a full day including lunch, €308 for six full days with meals. Half days cost €31 without meal; six half days cost €205 with lunch and €123 without lunch. Instructors speak English.

Avoriaz 1800 child care takes care of children and teaches them to ski. The Children's Village (450 74 04 46), in the center of Avoriaz, is open 9 a.m.–5:30 p.m. and accepts youngsters 3–16. Children not taking lessons can play in the snow playground. Half days are €20; full days, €36 (€30 without lunch); six half days, €95; six days, €180 (€160 without lunch). The Snowboard Village is for children 6–16. Rates are €20 for a half day, €39 for a full day (€35 without lunch); €98 for six half-days, €190 (€168 without lunch) for six full days.

The town also has a nursery, Les Pétits Loups (450 74 26 96; fax 450 74 24 29), for children 3 months to 5. It's open Sunday–Friday, 9 a.m.–6 p.m. Rates are €20 for a half day up to four hours, and €35 for a full day. Six consecutive days cost €175 and six consecutive half days cost €100. Lunch costs an additional €5.50 per day.

Other activities

The arena complex at Morzine offers **curling, skating, ice hockey, horse-drawn carriage tours**, **skidoo**, **dogsleigh rides**, **helicopter tours**, **mountain biking on the snow**, **table tennis**, a **weight room**, **dancing and gymnastics**. Painting exhibits, **figure skating**, **ice dancing**, **hockey** games and **movies** are also scheduled. For information in Morzine, call 04 50 74 72 72.

Fruitiere de Morzine is a frommagerie or **cheese-making** facility that is open to the public Wednesdays and Thursdays at 9 a.m. to watch cheesemaker Nicolas Baud make Abondance, Reblochan, Tomme, and other cheeses, which are sold in the shop upstairs.

At the turn of the century, more than 200 men worked in Morzine's **slate mines**, today only four men still do. Miner Franc Buet explains the process and demonstrates slate-cutting tools on Fridays at 11 a.m. The one-hour long program, conducted primarily in French but with some English explanation. The mine is on the Route Des Ardosieres, the road to the Avoriaz cable car, just past the rotary with the turn-off to Avoriaz resort. Just look for the fish sign; while you're here, you can also **catch your dinner.**

At Avoriaz, all in a small radius and easy to find, there are **para-sailing**, **ultra-lights**, **squash** courts, a **fitness center** with exercise machines, weights, squash courts, sauna and whirlpool tubs, **skating** rink, a **cinema** and **bowling** alley.

The tourist office also publishes a regular schedule of movies. A multi-activities card, available for €16 per person/week or €12 with a six-day Portes du Soleil ski pass, provides unlimited entrance to the ice-skating rink, including skates, the fitness center, squash and the Turkish bath. A weekly entertainment program is also offered. It may include balloon sculptures, skate-dance parties and children's programs; most are free.

Getting there

The nearest airport is in Geneva. From the airport a bus runs daily. The tourist office at the airport has the schedules.

Avoriaz and Morzine can be reached by a train/bus combination. Trains from Paris and Geneva arrive several times a day, and a bus makes the 40-km. climb.

Driving, take the Geneva-Mont Blanc autoroute and take exit 18, Morzine/Avoriaz. Morzine is 60 km. from Geneva and Avoriaz only 15 km. further.

Open-air parking in Avoriaz costs about €40 for a week; covered parking for a week is about €76. Transfers, available 24 hours a day from the parking lots in the town center, cost €5–€13 for one to four people; luggage costs an extra €2.

Parking in the Morzine lot at the bottom of the cable car is free. Avoriaz is a 20-minute drive from Morzine. Cable cars leave every 15 minutes, 7 a.m.-9 p.m.; on Friday and Saturday it closes at 1 a.m. Those with lift passes ride free 9 a.m.-5 p.m.; otherwise the charge is €5.50.

Tourist information

Morzine Tourism Office
Place de la Crusaz, 74110 Morzine-Avoriaz, France; 450 74 72 72; fax 450 79 03 48
Internet: www.morzine-avoriaz.com
E-mail: touristoffice@morzine-avoriaz.com

Avoriaz Tourism Office
Place Centrale, 74110 Avoriaz, France; 450 74 02 11; fax 450 74 24 29
Email: info@avoriaz.com

Tignes

The group of towns on the Tignes side of Espace Killy is a very good built-for-skiing resort. The series of modern villages string from 5,000 to 6,900 feet, with the main village, Tignes le Lac at 6,825 feet. Les Brevieres, Lavachet, and Les Boisses, and Val Claret are the four other villages at the base of one of Europe's largest Glaciers, La Grande Motte. The villages, which are really clusters of apartment buildings with shop arcades and restaurants on the first floors, were built in the 1950s after the old town of Tignes was flooded by the construction of the Chevril dam. With door-to-slopes skiing in mind, the layout of the buildings and lift-systems gives skiers 24 different lifts that leave from within the five towns.

The average visitor to Tignes stays in one of over 15,000 apartment beds as there are only a mere 1,500 beds in the 19 hotels. Reservations are required, especially during the February French school holidays. To avoid the busiest times in any French resort, make sure to plan around the kids.

At a glance, it is hard to appreciate how big this area really is. Tignes is connected seamlessly with Val d'Isere, one of Europe's most famous resorts, to create Espace Killy. The combined network features 300 kilometers of runs linked by 102 lifts. Continuous drops of over 5,000 feet is one reason Tignes attracts so many skiers.

Tignes is very proud of the Grand Motte glacier. In 1993 the resort constructed an underground funicular that reduced the ride from the village of Val Claret to the glacier from 20 minutes to a only six. The funicular operates in all weather conditions, year-round, with a capacity of over 3,000 skiers per hour.

The runs at Tignes are primarily geared towards intermediate cruisers, while the off piste terrain ranges from classic difficult couloirs to peaceful rolling snowfields. There is enough physical space that you could not cover even half the resort trails in a three-day stay. Au contraire, if you are into tricks and jumps, you could easily spend all day at the two-and-a-half-kilometer long snow park. An efficient shuttle bus system allows you to end your day in any of the towns and make it quickly home.

The resort is quite international, with plenty of British skiers and riders. From ski school to take-out pizza, you probably won't have trouble communicating. The après-ski tends to be a little cliquish, as the bars often end up uniligual.

An important thing to know is the bus schedule. Free shuttle buses run around and between the different towns every ten minutes from 8 a.m. to 8 p.m., every half-hour from 8 p.m. to midnight, and every hour from midnight to 8 a.m.

Parking is taken rather seriously in Tignes. Any cars left on the streets are consistently and diligently towed. Since legal parking is only available in the lots and indoor garages, the bus system is usually your best way to get around.

Mountain layout

The ski area can be broken into five main sectors. If La Grande Motte is directly in front of you, La Tovière/Lavachet is on your left and the Palet/Aiguille Percée/Palafour areas rise on your right. A few lifts rise from the villages of Les Brévières and Les Boisses, 1,640 feet lower.

The skiing in La Tovière/Lavachet area is a steep 1,950-foot vertical drop back into town. There are some great off-trail runs over the back side of Lavachet into Val d'Isère, or around the cliffs back into Tignes.

At Le Grande Motte, skiing on the glacier is wide open and relatively mellow—this sector offers the only lower intermediate terrain. The run under the cable car is a good intermediate test of stamina, and experts can go off the trail over the Rochers de la Grande Balme into the Palet sector. Many skiers come to Tignes and never leave this section of the mountain since there is so much variety. On the expert slopes there is often avalanche danger, so check with guides.

The Palet/Aiguille Percée offers relatively mellow terrain under the Col du Palet, with relatively tough intermediate runs down from the Aiguille Percée. Experts have a wide swath of off-trail possibilities, as well as itineraries over the Col du Palet, or over the back side of Aiguille Percée down Vallon de la Sache to Les Brévières.

Night skiing is also available in Le Lac, Le Lavachet, and Val Claret. Your lift ticket for the day takes care of the costs.

Mountain rating

It's easy to see why the area has been rated as tops in every category. Just the expanse of snow is mind-boggling. With a vertical drop of more than a mile and a third, coupled with 30,000 acres of terrain, there is something for everyone. Beginners and intermediates can cruise all over the upper reaches.

Experts can push themselves on extensive off-trail and powder skiing. It is best, at least for a day, to take a guide along who will show you the best places to test your skills. Before skiing off-piste, check with the ski school for the latest information on snow conditions.

Snowboarding

Intermediate to expert snowboarders will be more than satisfied with Tignes. With the majority of runs above tree level, the trails in Tignes are wide and bordered by easily accessible off-piste terrain. For those who buy the Espace Killy lift ticket, the backside of Col de Fresse in the Val d'Isère section supplies a natural off-piste terrain park. For serious shredders craving some of the best backcountry in the Alps, there are ample treks and traverses leading to intense chutes and powder fields well worth hiking for. Of course, Avalanche Victim Locators are required for any serious off-piste excursions. Evolution 2 Ski and Snowboard School provides the best guides for backcountry; a half day is €45 and four half days are €160. Unfortunately, Tignes is not the best resort for never-ever or beginner boarders. They officially list only one green run in the entire Tignes area, compared with a total of twenty greens in Espace Killy.

The snowpark itself, the largest in the world, is a reason to go to Tignes. Covering 1,600 vertical feet, the 2.5 km long park sports a quarter- and half-pipe, a boarder-cross course, and a plethora of table-tops for skiers and boarders alike. The best riders in Europe come to Tignes to compete and practice.

During the summer and early winter before the park above Tignes le Lac is built, head up to the La Grande Motte, where another half-pipe and more tabletops are kept in shape all year 'round.

Ski school (2002/03 prices)

The French Ski School in Tignes has 220 instructors for any level of skier. English is spoken by many of the instructors, so mention that you'll need an English-speaking instructor when signing up.

Private lessons: A lesson (three skiers maximum) for two hours are €81, three hours are €116, and a full day €250. The services of a certified guide for powder and off-piste for a group cost €250 per full day.

Group lessons: Three-hour courses are given mornings or afternoons. Five days of half-day lessons are €107 for adults and €100 for children age 4–8. Five days of full-day lessons costs €158 for adults and €149 for children.

A full-day off-piste class for good skiers from 8:30 a.m. to 18:00 p.m. costs €55. This class might traverse between Tignes, La Plagne and Les Arcs.

The ski school has four offices:

In Tignes le Lac, call 479 06 30 28; in Val Claret, call 479 06 31 28; in Lavachet, call 479 40 08 84; and in Rond Point des Pistes call 479 06 56 08.

There are five other ski/snowboard schools at the resort. **Evolution 2** with offices in Le Lac, 479 06 43 78; Val Claret, 479 40 09 04; and Lavachet, 479 06 35 76. In Le Lac, **Tetra** 479 41 97 07 and **Kebra Surfing** 479 06 43 37. In Val Claret, **333 Ski and Snowboard**, 479 06 02 88 and **The Snocool** 479 40 08 58.

Lift tickets (2003/04 prices)

The prices below are for **Tignes only**, which includes 47 lifts serving 65 runs. There's a 1,900 meter drop and 150 km. of runs.

	Adult	Children (5-12)	Senior (60-74)
Half day	€23	€17.50	€20
One day	€31.50	€24	€27
Six days	€146	€109.50	€124.50
Seven days	€164	€123	€139.50

A special halfpipe-only pass costs €7.50 per day

Tignes has a limited local pass for snowboarders and freeskiers, called **Snowspace**, that includes 20 lifts in the southern part of the ski area including the famous snow park complete with jumps, a halfpipe, and a freestyle zone. Lifts for this area cost €19.50 for a half day and €27.50 for a full day.

The prices below are for **l'Espace Killy** that includes 97 lifts serving 129 runs in the interconnected Tignes/Val d'Isère area with more than 300 km. of runs.

	Adults	Children (5-12)	Seniors (60-74)
one day	€38	€28.50	€32.50
three days	€97.50	€75	€83
six days	€181	€136	€154

Note: Insurance is not required but strongly recommended. The fee covers the cost of rescuing you and taking you down off the slopes. The cost is €2.50 per day per person for adults and €2 per day per person for children and seniors.

For tickets valid for more than two days a photo is needed. The ticket is valid for one day of your stay on La Plagne and Les Arcs ski lifts. Six-to-21-day tickets are also good for a day at Trois Vallées and a day at Valmorel.

Children younger than 5 ski free, and there are five free ski lifts available to skiers of all ages. Limited night skiing is available for free during the French school system's Christmas and February breaks.

Accommodations

A special low-season-only program has been organized by the tourist office and hoteliers. Low season normally runs from the end of September to Christmas week, for most of January except New Year, and late April and May. Check with the office for exact dates. Tignes is very affordable.

Hotels are rated by price. These designations are based on daily high-season (but non-holiday) cost per person based on double occupancy with half board. €€€—€125+; €€—€75-€124; €—less than €75.

Val Claret

Oftentimes hotels boast "on the slopes" when really they should say "a tough 5-minute outdoor adventure to get to the nearest lift." Well, have no fear, for at Tignes the worst that could happen is that the ski runs might creep under your door. Both Val Claret and Le Lac are navigated by pedestrians, skiers, and snowboarders alike.

Ski D'Or (479 06 51 60; fax 479 06 45 49; €€€), in Val Claret, is the classiest four-star hotel in the Tignes/Val d'Isère area. Room 23 is the honeymoon suite; ask whether it's available, if you like. Each of the rooms is tastefully and uniquely decorated, and the restaurant is excellent.

La Vanoise (479 06 31 90, fax 0479 06 37 06; €€) is another great option; less pricy, but regarded highly. It offers a package of 7 nights half-board and a 6-day ski pass for €534-782.

Hotel Diva €€ (0479 06 70 00; fax 0479 06 71 00) is the third option up in Val Claret. It's slightly more expensive than La Vanoise, but has amenities such as a fitness room, sauna, and a child care center (18 months to 11 years old).

In Tignes Le Lac

In Le Lac you can choose from 10 different hotels, ranging in ritziness from the youth hostel (**Auberge de Jeunesse Les Clarines** (04 79 41 01 93) is located in Les Boisse) to the four-star suites in the Village Montana.

The **Suites du Montana** (0479 400144, fax 0479 400403; €€-€€€) is the largest and most accommodating complex in all of Tignes. It has everything a four star hotel can offer, including an extensive spa/fitness center, a great restaurant, and a few cozy spots to hang out in its large, beautiful lobby.

You can choose a three star: **L'Aiguille Percèe** (0479 06 52 22, fax 0479 06 35 69; €); **Alpaka Lounge** (0479 06 45 30, fax 0479 06 58 09; €€); **Les Campanules** (0479 063436, fax 0479 06 35 78; €€); **Le Lèvanna** (0479 06 32 94, fax 0479 06 33 18; €€); **Le Refuge** (0479 06 36 64, fax 0479 06 33 78; €) or two stars: **L'Arbina** (0479 06 34 78, fax 0479 06 32 99; €); **Gentiana** (0479 06 52 46; fax 0479 06 35 61; €€); **Le Paquis** (0479 06 37 33, fax 0479 06 36 59; €€).

For rock-bottom prices, stay in the village of Les Brévières, the **Relais du Lac** (479 06 40 03; €) is quiet and out of the way, but a gondola takes you to the Tignes' lift system. Another bargain spot is **Les Seracs** (479 06 03 61, fax 479 06 17 90; €).

Ski Chalets: Crystal, Thomas Cook/Neilson (see page 20 for phone, fax and Internet addresses).

Apartments, condominiums, flats

When you learn that Tignes has only 1,200 beds in hotels but almost 15,000 in apartments, you realize the importance of the rental system. The tourist office acts as a clearinghouse, providing a listing of rental apartments.

A typical sample of apartment rates from AB Immobilier, per week per apartment, is provided below. The centrally located units are only about 100 meters from the lifts. The easiest means to finding an apartment that is a good fit for you is to communicate with the tourism office.

	high season	**mid season**
studio: two persons	€556	€367
2BR four persons	€944	€560
3BR six persons	€1235	€745

In many cases, linen is not included, but can be rented from the apartment owners or agencies. The normal linen fee is €15 a week per person.

Most agencies and individual owners offer apartments in a similar price range. Note the differences between high and mid seasons—even in high season lodging costs will only be about €33 a day per person, based on four people sharing a two-bedroom apartment. Cable TV is available, with CNN, Sky Channel and the BBC.

Dining

There are more than 70 restaurants spread through the resort. Visitors can find everything from gourmet and bistro French to fine Italian and pizza to Tex/Mex to Japanese.

Val Claret

The restaurant in the **Hotel Ski d'Or** (479 06 51 60) serves exception gourmet meals and is relatively expensive. The restaurant **Le Caveau** (479 06 52 32) is also excellent and considered by many as the best in town. There is a Japanese restaurant, **Myako** (479 06 34 79). For Savoyard decor and food try **Grattalu** (479 06 30 78) or **Brasserie du Petit Savoyard** (479 06 36 23). For crêpes try **La Datcha** (04 79 06 35 39). For good pizzas head to **Pizzeria 2000** (04 79 06 38 49) or **Roma** (04 79 06 36 25). For Tex-Mex (well a French version) head to **Daffy's Cafe** (04 79 06 38 75).

Tignes le Lac

Try **L'Eterlou** (479 06 33 53) or **Le Bistro** ()for typical Savoyard cooking. **Carlings** is very English, in the Hotel Alpaka (479 06 32 58) or test the restaurant **Escale Blanche** (479 06 45 50).

Le Lac Le Rosset/Les Almes.

If you are looking for big and busy, **L'Escale Blanche** (04 79 06 45 50) should be your journeys end. Right off the Aeroski gondola, regional specialties are ski in ski out during the day. Just less than 50 meters away, you'll find **L'Arbina** (04 79 06 46 83) restaurant on the second floor of the Arbina hotel. Here you'll find plenty of fish dishes and a daily menu for €23.50. Or, warm yourself by the fireplace at another hotel restaurant, **La Montagne** (04 79 06 31 30). Don't leave without having a crepe or a gallette. For a different kind of experience, head to **Le Clin d'Oeil** (04 79 06 59 10). This small cozy joint sits only 26 people, and charges €30 for the fixed menu. Don't fret however. This popular food is worth every penny if you are able to reserve ahead of time. The larger **Le Paquis** (04 79 06 37 33) works other threads with its spacious view over town. The €21 fixed menu is enjoyed peacefully overlooking the slopes. **Les Chanterelles** (479 40 01 44) in Village Montana is excellent and **La Chaumiere** in the same hotel has reasonable meals.

Le Lavachet

Dining in this area is more sparse than the other divisions of the towns, but it does host the **Le Brasero** (04 79 06 30 60), a good place for a variety of meat dishes. They also offer a €22 buffet regional Savoyard specialties on Tuesday evenings. The alternative is **Le Grenier** (04 79 06 37 79), a straight up typical Savoyard Restaurant. Standard regional specialties start from €13.80.

On the slopes

Head to **Le Panoramic** (04.79.06.60.11) at the foot of the glacier wth spectacular panoramic views. The snack bar is overpriced but the view is worth the pause. The gastronomic restaurant is excellent with a Savoyard evening meal on Thursdays.

Le Bollin is on the slopes but only a short walk from Val Claret. Bring your credit cards without a limit. The dining is as they say in France, tres cher!

Savouna at base of the Col de Palet lift is easy to reach and recommended.

Après-ski/nightlife

If your vacation resolutions include paying as much respect to the nightlife as the skiing, stay at Val Claret (or be sure to at least visit). The hottest spots are right in the center of town, around the corner from the Office de Tourisme. Val Claret is much more compact that Tignes Le Lac, so finding each hub shouldn't be very hard. Get jiggy at the **Crowded House** with a variety of good dance music, a social atmosphere, and occasional theme nights. **L'@robaze Café** (0479 06 49 94) kicks it off at 4 p.m. with hot chocolate and warm wine and keeps its bar open until 1:30 a.m. You can use the internet here at €8 per hour, shoot pool, or dress up for theme night (two nights a week). **Daffy's Café/Tex Mex** (0479 06 38 75), decked out with Mexican/Western decorations, is great for the boisterous (or hungry!). It serves snacks and drinks from 4 p.m. to 1:30 a.m. You should at least swing through **Grizzly's Bar** (0479 06 34 17). If the light, warm atmosphere, comfy seats, or vast fire place entice you, stay for a while. The **Mover Café** (0479 06 32 64), where the young and British seem to gather, sports a layout just right for groups of party people.

At the foot of the Tufs chair lift, you can choose from 3 beers on tap at the **Fish Tank** (0479 06 46 60), which tends to be mostly an après-ski destination (don't miss happy hour everyday from 4 p.m. to 6 p.m.). It boasts a couple of large screen TVs that show sporting events from 8:30 am to 1 a.m., and offers mixed drinks and snacks too. Drop into the **Roadhouse Café** (0479 06 35 91) for some pool, some drinks and occasionally some live music.

If you are staying at Tignes le Lac, you'll find almost all the action at Le Bec Rouge, on rue de la Poste. **Le Café de la Poste** (0479 06 36 10) is a spacious bar/nightclub with fun employees and a billiard table. You may find live music entertaining and a dance floor that should be hoppin' until the early morning. This is one of the places the seasonals like to party. Stacked right on top, **La Grotte du Yeti** (0479 40 07 36) invites those 18 and older to hang out in a wide open, rustic, wooden après-ski/bar. The atmosphere attracts young people from a variety of European countries. Across the street you'll find the **Powder Café** (0479 40 07 36), a small internet café/snack-bar, alongside **Le Bar American** (0479 06 37 80), a quiet, well-lit, pizzeria/café/bar that serves crepes and pizzas.

Nestled within the huge clump of that defines Bec Rouge, the **Embuscade Café**

(0479 06 59 51) usually hosts an older crowd; it is a dim bar with a high ceiling for conversation or billiards. On the east side of the clump (within which there is a fairly extensive gallery of shops and restaurants), there is another hub of nightlife. **Le Bowling** (04 79 06 39 95) consists of a simple little bar alongside 10 bowling lanes, which are open from noon to 2 a.m., seven days a week. A few steps away, beside the video arcade (also open from noon to 2 a.m.) you'll find **Jack's Club** (0479 06 54 84), a typical pub/bar and disco open from 9 p.m. to 4 a.m. **Pub Marilyn** (0479 06 55 20) shows freeride videos all day long for hearty après-skiers and then through the night as the in-house DJ lays down the tunes.

When the bars close, if you're still energized, head to the discos that don't even begin to crank until around midnight. **Sub Zero** pumps euro-dance music and regularly hosts celebrity DJs. It's a big place with plenty of space to either sit down or dance dance dance. **Le Blue Girl** (0479 06 51 53) plays music just as loud and hosts excellent DJs.

Harri's Bar, in Le Lavachet, is a stop in from the cold. With a warm fireplace and warm people, this joint is always a good stop after a long day of skiing. Live bands entertain the international crowd three nights a week. People in Le Lavachet not looking to bus to the other towns tend to gravitate towards Harri's.

Also in La Lavachet is **Le Petit Pub**, a small apres ski sports bar where a good game is always showing. Head to **TC's Bar** (0479 06 46 46) for their 4 to 6 p.m. happy hour, or for snacks anytime. Check out www.TCSBAR.com for more info on special events and on theme nights.

The bus system runs into the night, but the stops change to pick people up in front of the discos.

Child care

Les Marmottons, in Tignes le Lac (479 06 51 67) and Val Claret (479 06 37 12), accepts kids 2 1/2–10 years old for one week, a day or a half day. Those older than 4 years old are taught to ski.

The ski school children's program (479 06 30 28 or 479 06 31 28) accepts those age 4 to 6. Packages cost €107 for six days of three-hour lessons or €170 for six full-day lessons.

Five half days of snowboarding lessons for kids 8 and older costs €86.

Another children's course, **Stage Mini Champion,** teaches children technical skills and racing techniques. It includes videos, free skiing and powder techniques. The five-day program costs €166 and the six-day program is €196.

Other activities

In addition to skiing that's available 365 days of the year, Tignes has several interesting activities for those who want to spice up a weeklong visit or for nonskiers. In March and April, if the conditions are right, Evolution 2 Ski and Adventure School leads s**cuba diving tours under the ice** of the small lake in Tignes Le Lac.

Tignes also lays claim to another unique activity. The **Aquatonic fitness center** spa is one of two of its kind in France. A complex jet massaging system in connected pools provides hydromassage as you take a lap through the different sections of the pool. The facility also hosts the most extensive **weight room** in the resort and offers strengthening and workout classes in the pool. Many Olympic athletes use the facility after races and competitions. Tignes hosts many different high caliber competitions that vary from year to year.

At the Hotel Village Montana there is a three-star (04 79 40 05 12) and a four-star (04 79 00 21 01) **spa**. The four-star was renovated and opened new in January 2003. Both offer full services, from massages and steam rooms to Jacuzzis and tanning rooms. The three star spa has an outdoor heated pool (€20 for adults, €15 for kids) open every day from 10 a.m. to 8 p.m., but it closes at 7 p.m. for kids younger than 15.

Hang-gliding lessons are offered for €69 a flight. The **bowling** alley in Tignes le Lac is the highest in Europe. It has ten lanes and games are €7.60. Kids can **ice skate** on the lake for €4.30 from 2 p.m.–8 p.m. A day of ice climbing costs €110.

The **Lac du Tignes Espace Forme** (479 40 04 40) has wieghts, saunas, Jacuzzis, steam baths, four squash courts, indoor golf simulation, a climbing wall, an all purpose gym space, and two indoor tennis courts. It also has a media center with Internet connections and computers available for working or writing home.

Getting there

The closest international airports are Lyons (150 miles from the resort) and Geneva (about 86 miles). A smaller airport that offers some flights is Chambéry. A daily bus to Tignes from Geneva airport (00 41 900 57 15 00 for reservations) and weekend service from Lyons airport operate in winter.

TGV trains now run directly from Paris to Bourg-St. Maurice in 4-1/2 hours. A bus connection gets you to Tignes. A joint rail/bus ticket is available at the railway station or from travel agents.

If you drive, the best route from Geneva is autoroute A41 to Annecy and then N90 to Albertville. From there, follow signs to Bourg-St. Maurice and on to Tignes. From Lyons, take autoroute A43 to Albertville, then follow the signs to Moutiers, Bourg-St. Maurice, and on to Tignes.

Tourist information

Office du Tourisme, BP 51, 73321 Tignes Cedex, France
Telephone 479 40 04 40; fax 479 40 03 15.
For hotel and apartment booking, call 479 40 03 03; address is the same as above.
Internet: www.tignes.net
E-mail: information@tignes.net

Les Trois Vallées

Courchevel, Méribel, Les Menuires, Val Thorens

All skiers dream of virtually endless slopes and trails at any resort where they plan to vacation. The Trois Vallées is about as close as anyone can come to that dream of a chance to wake up each morning and choose a different village to explore, mountain to schuss, or scenic vista to capture. If it is the call of an endless ski safari that you hear, then the epicenter of that siren song is France's Trois Vallées region.

The four main villages comprising Les Trois Vallées, all purpose-built for skiing, are Courchevel, Méribel, Les Menuires and Val Thorens. Newly-built La Tania near Courchevel and the traditional town of St. Martin de Belleville near Les Menuires are also important parts of this region.

On paper the area is overwhelming; in person it is mind-expanding. Two hundred ski lifts on a single pass, 600 km. of ski runs, 130 km. of cross-country trails, 1,500 snow cannons, 360 ski patrollers, 1,200 lift attendants.

Even with all the lifts providing access to virtually every point in the valley, the region is so vast that intrepid skiers can head off into the hinterlands and ski for thousands of vertical feet without ever seeing a lift, and in some cases without seeing another skier. If you are someone who feels comforted by lifts within sight, you will have your fill. If you are the type of skier or snowboarder who wants to feel you are alone in the winter wilderness, the Trois Vallées has plenty to offer.

Skiing just doesn't get any better served than that found in this region. When you gaze at the mountains from any valley, what you can see you can ski—and it is most likely lift-served to some degree. Mountain restaurants are plentiful and the food is as good as anyone imagines when they conjure up French cooking. Make sure to test the tasty local specialties such as tartiflette, fondue and raclette.

Another way to look at the expanse of this region is to take a look at how many of the largest ski resorts in the United States can fit into the Trois Vallées region. The late *Snow Country* magazine concluded that the six largest ski areas in the United States could fit inside Les Trois Vallées. That means that Killington, Vail, Heavenly, Steamboat, Squaw Valley and Park City could all fit inside the space covered by Les Trois Vallées with almost 10,000 acres left over. So you can throw in Jackson Hole, Taos, Sun Valley, Keystone, Crested Butte, Alta, Solitude, Cranmore and Stowe and still have room. The expanse is breathtaking. The scenery is spectacular. And the overall skiing is unmatched.

We deal with each resort separately, since each one is large enough to be treated as a separate resort. Courchevel starts on page 194, Méribel starts on page 198, Les Menuires is found on page 203 and Val Thorens is described starting on page 207.

Lift tickets (2003/04 prices)

Each area offers three lift-ticket combinations: one covers only the lifts in the resort area, the second covers lifts in the individual valley; and a third is a full Trois Vallées lift ticket.

Skiers who are staying for a week or more will want to purchase the Trois Vallées combination ticket. This combination ticket gives unlimited access to all the lifts and runs in the region. It also entitles holders to a day in another Olympic resort—Val d'Isère, Tignes, La Plagne, Les Arcs, Peisey Vallandry, Pralognan la Vanoise and Les Saisies. Photo identification is required for passes of three days or more.

Prices for Les Trois Vallées combination pass are:

	Adults	Children (age 5–10)	Seniors (age 60-72)
one day	€40	€30	€34
three days	€116	€87	€99
six days	€198	€149	€158
seven days	€218	€163	€174
13 days	€356	€265	€282

Children younger than age 5 and seniors older than age 72 ski free.

Carte Neige Ski Insurance, that will pay for evacuation from the mountain and immediate medical care should you get injured skiing or riding, can be purchased for €2.50 a day for adults and for €2 a day for children younger than age 13.

Parents skiing with children receive a 20% discount on passes for 6 days or more with the family pass. The Three Valleys Family Ski Pass costs €635 for two parents and two children younger than age 18 to ski for six days. Each added child costs €149.

Getting there

The closest airports are Geneva (149 km.), Lyon (180 km.) and Chambéry (110 km.). A welcome desk is operated by the region at the Geneva Airport. This season regular air service will connect Courchevel with Geneva three times a day, four days a week.

Buses and trains leave daily from the Geneva airport. The cost is about €62 one-way or €105.50 round-trip. Call Société Touriscar (04 50 43 60 02). Weekend bus service connects the region with Lyon for about €86 round-trip on Satobusalps (04 37 25 52 55). The Chambéry bus with Transavoie Transport (04 79 35 21 74) costs €70.13 round trip.

Rail reaches Moutiers, 37 km. away (a 40-minute drive). Buses and taxis are available from the station. Buses cost approximately €15 and taxis run about €75.

If driving, follow the signs to Chambéry and Albertville, then take the four-lane road to Moutiers and up to the Les Trois Vallées.

For those piloting a private plane or helicopter, Courchevel and Méribel have small mountain airports as well as heliports with charter service.

Once at the resorts, shuttlebuses move you efficiently within each valley, but moving between valleys is inconvenient and expensive. For example, a taxi from Courchevel to Val Thorens is more than €140 or a time-consuming bus via Moutiers would cost about €25. Plan on skiing between resorts and don't get stuck in Val Thorens when the lifts close if you need to be in Courchevel to spend the night. It will be expensive.

Tourist information

Courchevel Office du Tourisme, La Croisette, B.P. 37, 73122 Courchevel, France;
Telephone 04 79 08 00 29; fax 04 79 08 15 63.
Internet: www.courchevel.com E-mail: info@courchevel.com
Telephone reservations 04 79 08 14 44; fax 04 79 08 33 59.
E-mail reservations: reservation@courchevel.com

Méribel Office du Tourisme, 73550 Méribel, France;
Telephone 04 79 08 60 01; fax 04 79 00 59 61.
Internet: www.meribel.net; E-mail: info@meribel.net
Telephone reservations: 04 79 00 50 00; fax 04 79 00 31 10.
E-mail reservations: info@meribel-reservations.com

Les Menuires Office du Tourisme, 73440 Les Menuires, France;
Telephone 04 79 00 73 00; fax 04 79 00 75 06.
For reservations only, call 04 79 00 79 79; fax 04 79 00 60 92.
Internet: www.lesmenuires.com.
E-mail: lesmenuires@lesmenuires.com.

Saint Martin de Belleville Office du Tourisme
73440 Saint Martin De Belleville, France;
Telephone: 04 79 00 20 00; fax 04 79 08 91 71.
Internet: www.st-martin-belleville.com
E-mail: stmartin@st-martin-belleville.com

Val Thorens Office du Tourisme, 73440 Val Thorens, France;
Telephone; 04 79 00 08 08; fax 04 79 00 00 04.
Internet: www.valthorens.com. E-mail: valtho@valthorens.com
Reservations are handled by Val Thorens Reservations;
Telephone 04 79 00 01 06; fax 04 79 00 06 49.
Internet: www.valthorens.com. E-mail: reserver@valthorens.com

La Tania Office du Tourisme, 73125 La Tania, France;
Telephone 04 79 08 40 40; fax 04 79 08 45 71
Internet: www.latania.com
E-mail: info@latania.com

Brides les Bains Office du Tourisme,
BP 73572 Brides les Bains Cedex
Telephone: 09 79 55 20 69 Fax 09 79 55 20 90 Internet
www.brides-les-bains.com Email tourism@brides-les-bains.com.

COURCHEVEL

This is perhaps the most cosmopolitan of the four villages. It was France's first real jet-set resort, created to cater to the upper crust and become the darling of those in the upper-crust French Riviera group who didn't flock to Megève.

Courchevel itself is really a series of smaller villages whose names reflect their heights in meters—Courchevel 1850, Courchevel 1650, Courchevel 1550 and so on. Courchevel 1300, also called Le Praz, is the quaintest, but its lower altitude may mean a sacrifice of snow for charm. There is another village, Saint-Bon on a fifth level (but with no lifts). Courchevel l850 is the highest and priciest, but it's also where most trails run right outside your hotel or apartment door. It is where the best restaurants are found and where the nightlife continues until the sky begins to lighten with coming day. Built for ski-in/ski-out, Courchevel 1850 really works. Its lift system covers both sides of the valley. The world's largest cable car, heading up to La Saulire (8,885 feet), connects Courchevel to the rest of the Les Trois Vallées area.

La Tania is a small separate new resort set at the base of the ridge separating Courchevel and Méribel. It has its own relatively quiet nightlife. From La Tania it is about a half-hour bus ride to either of the larger resorts straddling the ridge.

Mountain layout

The skiing above the various levels of Courchevel varies widely. Experts will enjoy all of the chutes dropping down from La Saulire, around the left side of the telepherique and the ones that shoot down under the Suisses chairlift. On the other side of the valley at Chanrossa and Roc Merlet (2734 meters) experts to intermediates will find this whole area to their liking. Beginners will enjoy the wide-open pasture below the Saulire cable car base station. A truly gorgeous run through the trees can be had by starting at the Col de la Loze, and skiing down to Le Praz or to the newly developed resort of La Tania. The series of runs ending at La Tania offer wonderful, uncrowded cruises that will bring smiles to all skiers' faces.

Mountain rating

Something for everyone. This vast region has some of the better intermediate cruising terrain of the entire area. Beginner terrain is next to accommodations. Experts and advanced skiers will have a grand time at the higher reaches of the resort

Ski school (2002/03 prices)

Courchevel has hundreds of instructors who speak English. You can find 350 of the instructors at the Courchevel 1850 ski school, 80 at the 1650 ski school and and another 120 at Courchevel 1550.

Courchevel 1850 (04 79 08 07 72) private lessons are €52–€58 for 90-minute lessonl €230–€280 for a full day. Group lessons cost €38 full day; €158 for four days; and €210 for six days. Snowboard lessons are €193-231 for six days.

Discovery off-piste courses cost €308 for six days.

Other Courchevel ski schools are E.S.F. 1650 (04 79 08 26 08); E.S.F. 1550 (04 79 08 21 07); Ski Academy (04 79 08 11 99) and The British School (04 79 08 27 87).

Accommodations

These resorts have every type of lodging from luxury chalets to dormitories. Accommodations in the Courchevel villages all fall in the same price range, except for Courchevel 1850, which is slightly higher.

Even though its prices are higher than the other resorts, Courchevel 1850 still offers somewhat reasonably priced accommodations in luxury surroundings, but you must be very careful to make arrangements for low season. The tourist office will send a complete list of hotels with information about White Week (discount/off-season) periods, and details of making reservations.

Prices are per person based on double occupancy during February with half board. €€€—€125+; €€—€75–€124; € is less than €75.

Bellecote (479 08 10 19; €€€) This hotel is more Alpine, cozier and exclusive than the Byblos, described below. Its wealthy guests have had their fortunes for some time and are not interested in letting the world know their every activity. Much of the furniture was imported from the Himalayas; that which is in the lobby is leather and very soft. Heated pool and a well-equipped exercise room.

Le Byblos (479 00 98 00; €€€) The mountain version of the world-famous Byblos in St. Tropez, this was conceived as an all-encompassing hotel. The soaring wooden archways, the heavy wooden columns in the bar, the secluded pool and the luxury rooms cater to hedonism at its best. Here you rub shoulders with the winter jet-set elite.

Hotel Trois Vallées (479 08 00 12; €€€) This, for our money, the best of the four-star properties in Courchevel. The hotel itself is delightful with excellent light pine decor. Its designers paid special attention to the bathrooms, which are at the leading edge of design, featuring giant tubs—some marble, others black, brass fittings and every amenity. The hotel is only steps away from the finest restaurants, as well as the wildest nightlife.

Au Rond-Point du Pistes (479 08 04 33; €€) This hotel is right in the middle of the action and is one of the relative bargains among three-stars.

Caravelle (479 08 02 42; €€) Boxy and square with modern rooms, but with all the amenities right on the slopes.

Chabichou (479 08 00 55; €€€) Flowery on the outside with modern woodsy rooms on the inside. Cute but not cheap.

Crystal (479 08 28 22; €€–€€€) This hotel is great for children with some of the best slopeside accommodations. It is a short walk to the downtown area.

Hotel Mercure Coralia (479 08 11 23; €€€) This hotel out of the center of the "commercial" district in what is called the residential area but, right on the slopes. The views are lovely, the location is right on the lake. The rooms very businesslike.

Les Ducs de Savoie (479 08 03 00; €€) This is the best of the three-star lot with spacious rooms, a great swimming pool and lots of wood. The hotel is right on the slopes and within easy reach of the gondola. But, at night you'll have to walk 10 minutes to get back to the hotel or take a cab.

Courcheneige (479 08 02 59; €€) A good two-star find, with 86 rooms, sauna, Jacuzzi and terrace on the slopes.

L'Aiglon (479 08 02 66; €) This recently renovated hotel is perhaps the best two-star property in town, with exceptional rooms for comparatively low rates. Its location near the slopes is excellent, with only a short five-minute walk into town. People who stay keep coming back.

In "1650" head to **Hotel du Golf** (479 00 92 92; €) that offers great value, good rooms and great views right on the slopes.

Also in "1650" is **Le Portetta** (479 08 01 47; €) which is a bit less expensive than the Hotel du Golf, not as traditional but just as convenient.

Ancolies (479 08 27 66; €) is a good example of how prices drop dramatically when you head to "1550." Rooms are about half of the costs of "1850." Rooms are beautiful and the hotel is a great value.

Le Flocons (479 08 02 70; €) is another traditional hotel with a great reputation.

Les Peupliers (479 08 41 47; €) down in the village of Le Praz across from the Praz an La Forêt lifts has a wonderful following. Great value.

If you drop down to Saint-Bon there is an excellent nine-room hotel, **Allobroges** (479 08 10 15; €). With good snow you can ski back to the hotel at the end of the day. A shuttle connects you to the lift system in only a few minutes.

Ski Chalets: Crystal, Inghams/Bladon, Thompson, Thomas Cook/Neilson (go to page 25 for phone, fax and Internet addresses).

Apartments, condominiums, flats

Apartments are the French choice for accommodation. In fact, apartment beds outnumber hotel beds by at least 5 to 1. What you get is the ability to schedule off-slope life at your own pace and a good way to avoid the high hotel prices. In most of January, two-room apartment rates in "Residences" in Courchevel 1850 at Belledonne and Chalets du Forum are about €780–€950 a week. In "1650" the rates for varying luxury with a more out-of-the-way location range from €500 to €900. In "1550" Domaines du Soleil has high season rentals for €680 to €1,050.

There are ten rental agents for apartments in Courchevel. The tourist office will send more information and a registration card, and will help make reservations.

Dining

Get ready for sticker shock in restaurants, both downtown and on the slopes. Make sure to check out a few places before settling in for dinner or lunch. For bargains try pizza spots, then Tex-Mex restaurants and raclette/fondue places.

This is considered to have the best food of any French mountain resort. The **Chabichou** (479 08 00 55) maintains a friendly rivalry with the **Le Bateau Ivre** (4 7908 36 88) for the top restaurant in town. Both rate two Michelin stars and both will end up costing about €60–€90 per person. A meal in **La Bergerie** (479 08 24 70) shouldn't be missed. Come with plenty of money.

Le Bistro du Praz (479 08 41 33) in Courchevel 1300, serves some of the best local specialties in the area. The French country atmosphere eatery adds a special flavor to the experience.

For the more reasonable restaurants, try **La Saulire** (479 08 07 52) with good local specialties and an owner who likes Americans thanks to years of living in Canada. Expect to pay €35–€55 per person for dinner. **Le Fromagerie** (479 08 27 47) has the best fondue in town and Michelin agrees, giving it a fork.

La Mangeoire looks almost Western with cowhides, wagon wheels and lanterns. The food is simple but the crowds in the evening are great. Expect to pay €23–€30. **l'Arbe** (479 08 26 03) is where the locals eat. It seems to be crowded from lunch time on, first with the lunch crowd and then with the après-skiers, then with the dinner folk. Another good spot for pizza is **La Smalto** (479 08 31 29).

The following were all enthusiastically recommended by locals. **La Chapelle** (479 08 19 48) is a small place where they say you'll swear your grandma was cooking (hope that's a pleasant memory). **La Cendrée** (479 08 29 38) serves Italian meals and has one of the best Italian wine cellars in the region.

For traditional Savoyard meals try one of these restaurants. **Le Génépi** (479 08 08 63); **Le Mazot** (479 08 41 72) for raclette, fondue and tartiflette; **L'Alpage** (479 08 24 87); **Le Carnozet** (479 08 41 47); and **La Montagne** (479 08 09 85) for meals cooked in the original mountain style.

For great atmosphere head to **La Bergerie** (previously mentioned) or **Les Allobroges** (479 08 10 15) in a wine vault.

On the slopes stop in at the **Chalet de Pierres** (479 08 18 61) if you want to see and be seen. Bring your credit cards—the menu and wine will run about €30–€40 for lunch!

Child care (2002/03 prices)

The tourist office, your hotel or apartment manager can put you in touch with qualified private baby sitters who provide child care services at any time of the day or night. Each resort also offers child care programs. Here's a resort-by-resort rundown.

Courchevel has six ski schools for children. Children's lessons are offered by the E.S.F. 1850, E.S.F. 1650, E.S.F. 1550, Ski Academy and the British Ski School.

The children's program for those ages 3–12 costs €33 for a morning, €47 for a full day, or €219 for six days. Lifts are included in these prices. Lunch costs an additional €14–€18.

Two nursery programs for children from age 2 are available in Courchevel 1850 at Le Village des Enfants (479 08 08 47) and Courchevel 1650 at Les Pitchounets (479 08 33 69). Both are open from 9 a.m. to 5 p.m. Prices will be about €18 for a morning, and aproximately €44 for a day with lunch or €29–€31 for a day without lunch.

Other activities

Courchevel has a bowling alley, hotel indoor swimming pools, saunas, squash courts and an Olympic-size skating rink, hang-gliding, ski jumping, paragliding, deltagliding and mountain flying courses.

Tourist information

Courchevel Office du Tourisme, La Croisette, B.P. 37, 73122 Courchevel, France
Telephone 04 79 08 00 29; fax 04 79 08 15 63.
Internet: www.courchevel.com.
E-mail: info@courchevel.com
For reservations:
Telephone 04 79 08 14 44; fax 04 79 08 33 59.
E-mail: reservation@courchevel.com

MÉRIBEL

Méribel has been developed into a first-rate ski resort but has taken pains to retain a semblance of the traditional mountain architecture of the French Alps. From a skier's point of view, the resort has two sections. There is Méribel that basically stretches from La Chaudanne, at 4,757 feet elevation with traditional village atmosphere with a major lift center and the tourist office, to the Altiport—a small area on the mountain with runway and lot for pilots who have their own small planes at 5,577 feet. (Pilots must have special training to use the altiport.) About four km. up the valley is Méribel-Mottaret, a smaller village with a larger lift hub, and more ski-in/ski out accommodation. These villages are set in the central valley of Les Trois Vallées. There are 57 lifts in the valley, 18 of them that start in the village and link up with another 150 lifts in Les Trois Vallées.

Old Méribel center, called La Chaudanne, was founded by the British; it still retains many of its British trappings, and English is spoken almost everywhere. Above this original center rises the rest of Méribel with 750 vertical feet of the hotels and chalets built up the side of the valley toward Courchevel with excellent ski slope access. It is about a 10-minute ride from the Altiport and Rond Point des Pistes down to the tourist office.

Half as old and still growing, Méribel-Mottaret is higher up in the same valley. It has more direct lift access to Les Menuires, Courchevel and Val Thorens via the Cote Brune chair lift. Méribel-La Chaudanne is about a 10-minute ride from Méribel-Mottaret. They are linked by a free bus.

The lift to La Saulire provides the best access to the Courchevel valley and the lifts to either Roc des Trois Marches (8,868 feet) or Mont de la Challe (8,448 feet) provide the best connections to Val Thorens and Menuires.

Mountain layout

The skiing on both sides of the Allues valley, home to Méribel and Méribel-Mottaret, ranges from easy to hair-raising difficult. Though a trail map won't provide black run thrills, runs marked as intermediate here would be considered black-diamond runs at most American resorts.

One of the key advantages to this area is most in evidence in this section of the Trois Vallées: bottom-to-top cable cars that not only take you to long, undisturbed cruises, but also can get you across the valley very quickly. Experts and advanced intermediates shouldn't miss the very worthy runs and wide-open off-piste opportunities down both sides of Mont Vallon.

Mow down Mont Vallon in the morning after the sun has had a bit of a chance to soften the snow, then for gut-sucking action, mogul-busters should try the short drop under the third stage of the Plattieres lift. Advanced beginners and intermediates will find the run below the final two sections of the Plattieres lift both gentle and extended. Off-piste possibilities for intermediates abound in the area between Roc de Fer, site of the women's Olympic downhill, and Méribel (for those interested in dropping into the Vallées des Belleville from the top of Roc de Fer more intermediate skiing awaits).

The snowfields stretching beneath Saulire are wonderful with varying pitches that will delight both lower intermediates and experts. The chutes directly beneath the gondola, reached only by a scramble, and the wide couloir to the left of the ascending gondola make for expert runs that will be the subject of conversations for years.

The skiing above the various levels of Courchevel varies widely. Experts will enjoy all of the chutes dropping down from La Saulire, around the left side of the telepherique and the ones that shoot down under the Suisses chairlift. On the other side of the valley at Chanrossa and Roc Merlet (8,969 feet) experts to intermediates will find this whole area to their liking. Beginners will enjoy the wide-open pasture below the Saulire cable car base station. A truly gorgeous run through the trees can be had by starting at the Col de la Loze, and skiing down to Le Praz or to the newly developed resort of La Tania. The series of runs ending at La Tania offer wonderful, uncrowded cruises that will bring smiles to all skiers' faces.

The sector near the Altiport is an intermediate delight. More and more families have been skiing there and recently, Méribel installed a new high-speed eight-seat chair lift to move skiers. There is plenty of lift capacity in that section now.

Off Piste: In the Méribel valley the best off-piste skiing is in sectors between Mont de la Chambre and Les Plattieres as well as from the top of Mont Vallon. Watch out, however, for the national wildlife refuge surrounding Mont Vallon. Skiing is now prohibited here and skiers have been given merciless fines since enforcement began in July 1990. Another off-piste gem is free skiing from Roc de Fer along the ridge then dropping down to Le Raffort or Les Allues. The slopes as far as Le Raffort normally have adequate snow. For Les Allues, check on snow conditions.

Mountain rating

This valley, as in all other valleys of this region, has something for everyone. No beginner will go wanting for good practice slopes. No intermediate will long for more cruisers. No expert will feel like there is just not enough. It doesn't get better than this.

Snowboarding

There are two snowparks in this valley. One is in Méribel and the other in Mottaret. In Mottaret the total area of the snowpark is 15 acres. It is 5,000 feet long and the vertical drop is almost 1,000 feet. There is also a halfpipe, a babypipe, two quarterpipes and tables, spines and a boardercross course.

In Meribel the Arpasson snowpark is 4,000 feet long with a vertical drop of 660 feet. There is a competition halfpipe, another beginner halfpipe and a 3.3 km. boardercross course with whoops, tables and obstacles.

Ski school (2003/04 prices)

Méribel has three ski schools. **The French Ski School** (479 08 60 31) is exceptional with children and lessons from private to group and cross-country to powder skiing. Group lesson costs are €39 for a full day lesson or €170 for five days. Morning private lessons cost €134–€140 for one to four skiers. A full day private instructor will cost €280–€295. Snowboarding lessons for five half days costs €113.80–€124.90.

Children pay €33 for a full day lesson or €137.90 for five days.

Magic in Motion (479 08 53 36) features multilingual lessons with private instructors speaking English, French, Spanish and Czech.

The ski school forms groups that ski all day Monday through Friday. Cost for the five half days is about €130–€160. It is highly recommended. You will be put into a group with similar skiers to get the most from your experience.

Special lessons for powder skiing, snowboarding, mono-skiing, ski ballet and freestyle skiing are available. There are also racing clinics and a ski kindergarten. A special accompanied ski adventure through Les Trois Vallées and another tour through the 12 valleys of the Tarentaise—including the resorts of Val Thorens, La Plagne, Les Arcs, Val d'Isère and Tignes—are also offered.

Accommodations

Méribel has every type of lodging from luxury chalets to dormitories. The tourist office will send a complete list of hotels with information about White Week periods (discounted, off-season), and special packages for both hotels and apartments. Call Méribel Réservations at 479 00 50 00; fax 479 00 31 19 or e-mail: reservations@meribel.net.

Prices are per person based on double occupancy during February with half board. €€€—€125+; €€—€75–€124; € is less than €75.

Le Grand Coeur (479 08 60 03; fax 479 08 58 38; €€€) This hotel is filled with fine antiques, paintings and furnishings. There is normally a list of returning clientele, so make reservations early. The lounge, built around a large stone fireplace and the dining room has sweeping views.

Allodis (479 00 56 00; fax 479 00 59 28; €€€) This beautifully decorated hotel features a combination of modern color and design, with traditional classical architecture featuring arches and columns. Perfectly located for skiing, it is not close to town.

Mont Vallon (479 00 44 00; fax 479 00 46 93; €€€) In Méribel-Mottaret, this is a real luxury hotel with rustic lodge-like flavor. You have everything here: pool, exercise room, Jacuzzi, sauna, squash courts and spectacular rooms. Walk out the door and onto the lifts, but take a shuttlebus or taxi to the center of town.

Hotel de l'Altiport (479 00 52 32); fax 479 08 57 54; €€€) This hotel is at the top of the resort. Access to the slopes is perfect. The exterior exudes Alpine charm and the interior has classic touches.

Alpen Ruitor (479 00 48 48; fax 479 00 48 31; €€) Beautiful lobby and modern rooms with a new emphasis on the hotel meals and a larger dining room. Ask for a room with a view of the valley rather than the parking lot.

Marie Blanche (479 08 65 55; fax 479 08 57 07; €€) A small intimate hotel in a residential district only steps from the slopes and a stairway from the center of town.

Adray Telebar (479 08 60 26; fax 479 08 53 85; €€) This hidden treasure has a mountain-lodge feel. The 26 country-style rooms are all unique, the owners charming and the food out of this world. Visit for the food even if you're not staying here.

l'Hotel du Moulin (479 00 52 23; fax 479 00 58 23; €€) A one-star hotel on the outskirts of Méribel with seven rooms in an old flour mill. You'll have to take the bus to the slopes, but it's the best bargain you'll find.

Hotel La Tarentaise (479 00 42 43; fax 479 00 46 99; €€) In Méribel-Mottaret, right on the slopes with a big British clientele. Enjoy great barbeque on the terrace. Bland rooms but great location.

Les Arolles (479 00 40 40; fax 479 00 45 50; €+) Also in Méribel-Mottaret on the slopes, this hotel also has a large group of British skiers, especially families. Basic modern rooms, nice pool and on-slope location.

Hotels l'Eterlou/Le Tremplin/La Chaudanne (479 08 61 76; fax 479 08 57 75; €€) A complex of hotels and condos smack in the middle of the Méribel-La Chaudanne section and steps from the lifts. Rooms are decorated in warm wood, the restaurants are very good, all amenities are shared between the properties.

le Yéti (479 00 51 15; fax 479 00 51 73; €€) This great value hotel is highly recommended. It has small rooms which has been expanded in the past years. Near the previous two hotels—steps from skiing and a shuttlebus ride from the center of town.

l'Orée du Bois (479 00 50 30; fax 479 08 57 52; €) This hotel provides good value; it is on the slopes but is far out of the center of town for nightlife and restaurants.

Le Merilys (479 08 69 00; fax 479 08 68 99; €) This is a cozy B&B with an Alpine flavor at the upper reaches of the resort near the Altiport. Great slope access, but a long walk to nightlife and the downtown shopping. There is a public shuttle service however.

Croix Jean-Claude (479 08 61 05; fax 479 00 32 72; €) in the small village of Les Allues has very comfortable traditional rooms. Great restaurant. Reach the slopes by gondola or bus.

Ski Chalets: Crystal, Inghams/Bladon, Simply Ski, Thompson and Thomas Cook/ Neilson (see page 25 for phone, fax and Internet addresses).

Apartments, condominiums, flats

Apartments are the French choice for accommodation. In fact, apartment beds outnumber hotel beds by at least 5 to 1. What you get is the ability to schedule off-slope life at your own pace and it is one way to avoid the high hotel prices. The descriptions in the brochures are based on maximum skiers per apartment. We have found that for the American/British market, more room is expected. Ask about the number of bedrooms carefully.

According to one realtor, apartment prices for a week's rental in Méribel-Mottaret during most of January start from €380 for a studio for two to €775 for a three-room place that will hold six. In February the prices jump to €460 and €950 respectively.

The tourist office will send more information and a registration card, and will help make reservations.

Dining

Meribel has excellent restaurants. Our routine is to eat on the slopes for about €10 to €15 for a great lunch and then cook in the apartment for dinners. However there is no shortage of places to dine like a king.

Le Grand Coeur (479 08 60 03) has a view over the chalets of the town. The experience is hard to beat, with excellent fish as well as local specialties. Expect to spend €40 per person.

Make the effort to dine at the **Hotel Allodis** (479 00 56 00). The restaurant, especially during lunch, is wonderful. The evening dining room offers meals in an architectural harmony of modern and classic lines. Expect to pay €40 per person.

Chez Kiki (479 08 66 68) is the Méribel version of Courchevel's original Bergerie. The rustic atmosphere is cozier downstairs near the fireplace. For an adventure during the meal find the Alice in Wonderland door in the basement. Meal costs about €40 apiece.

La Cave is a traditional fromagerie where cheese and wine is kept at the perfect temperature in the basement. Head here for the best fondue and raclette in the valley.

In Les Allues try **Restaurant La Croix Jean-Claude** (479 08 61 05) Excellent meats, mushrooms and vegetables. Great dinners and lunches. Reservations required. In the same village try **La Chemina** (479 01 12 70).

For more economical dining try Moroccan food in **Marrakech** in the new Aspen Park Hotel (479 00 51 77). For pizza and the least wallet damage try **Scott's**.

On the mountain, a good affordable fixed-price menu is served at **Les Choucas** just below the middle station of the Burgin Saulire gondola. If you are staying in Méribel, a nice stop on the way home is the **Bar Rhododendrons**.

In Méribel-Mottaret try **La Baleine** where you can have a wonderful duck fondue for two for only €20. The reasonable prices attract the locals.

Après-ski/nightlife

Méribel-Centre now has a Trois Vallées version of the famous and successful **Dick's Tea Bar** from Val d'Isère. That spot promises to be hoppin' just like in Val d'Isère. It will be staying open until 4 a.m. Another late night spot is the **Le Loft**. Try **The Pub** or **Scott's**—they seem to be filled often, or try **Le Post**, **Le Refuge** and **La Taverne**, all a few steps from one another. Méribel-Mottaret has **La Rastro** for dancing and in Méribel-1600 head to the **El Poncho**.

Child care (2003/04 prices)

The tourist office, your hotel or apartment manager can put you in touch with qualified private baby sitters who provide child care services at any time of the day or night.

Méribel has a highly respected child care program. **Le Club Saturnins** accepts children between 1-1/2 and 3 years. It is associated with the ski school and ski lessons are offered to children ready to ski (479 08 66 90). Le Saturnins costs €19–€21 for a half day; €36 for a full day. A five-day week costs €159. Supervised lunch costs €18.40 a day or €88.30 for a five-day week from noon to 2 p.m.

Also associated with the ski school, the **Jardin des P'tis Loups** accepts children ages 3–5 for child care and has a ski playground to encourage beginners. Les P'tits Loups costs €19–€21 for a half day; €36 for a full day. A five-day week costs €159. Supervised lunch costs €22.10 a day or €96.70 for a five-day week.

Other activities

Méribel facilities include an **indoor swimming pool, bowling alleys** and an **Olympic ice skating rink**. The rink has public skating daily and two nights a week. Figure skating lessons are available. Entrance fees: Adult €4.60. Skate hire: €3.10.

An olympic-sized swimming pool is open daily and two nights per week. There is free entrance for children younger than 5; adults pay €4.30; children pay €3.40.

A **climbing wall** is available in the Olympic Center open from 9 a.m. to 9 p.m. Excellent walking trails criss-cross the entire valley. Discovery tours of the valley on skimobiles are organized daily. Paragliding with instructors is offered by three organizations. You can even find a six-lane bowling alley in the Olympic Center. Mountain flying lessons are offered as well as air sightseeing flights. Call the Aéro-Club at 479 08 61 33.

The tourist office has all phone numbers and contacts.

Tourist information

Méribel Office du Tourisme, 73550 Méribel, France;
Telephone 479 08 60 01; fax 479 00 59 61.
Internet: www.meribel.net; E-mail: info@meribel.net
For reservations:
Telephone 04 79 00 50 00; fax 04 79 00 31 10.
E-mail: info@meribel-reservations.com

LES MENUIRES

From a distance Les Menuires' original buildings look like a misplaced spaceship resting on the snow. This isn't a judgment of good or bad, the resort works wonderfully and has been making dramatic strides in blending into the environment and adding an Alpine feel to the area.

New construction has been created with wood and peaked roofs. Giant pines were planted at the entrance to the area to improve the first impression and covered wooden arcades now connect the buildings adding a natural feel to the compound. Inside there is Savoyard decor with plenty of wood and farm influences. The original center still serves as the resort focus and is a convenient meeting place for ski schools and children's programs.

The village has been created to keep cars out of the way. It offers one of the best family spots in the Trois Vallées. Les Menuires has also quietly assembled 11 two- and three-star hotels. The base of Les Menuires unfolds onto the crescent boardwalk of the central La Croisette shopping mall. The newer satellite section of Reberty-Les Bruyeres has concentrated on smaller buildings built in community clusters.

In Les Menuires you will find skiers traveling with families and those looking for the steeps. The skiing is wide open on the west-facing slope, with lifts running up toward Val Thorens. An abundance of beginner and intermediate runs pass picturesque shepherd huts on the way down the valley toward the traditional village of St. Martin de Belleville. The east-facing side of the valley offers more challenging skiing from Pointe de la Masse (9,213 feet), which can be reached rapidly by riding a combination of two high-speed lifts. In the afternoon the area is deserted as skiers follow the sun. The off-trail skiing from here and nearby Cîme de Caron is exceptional, especially in spring when skiers can drop over the backside of these mountains with certified guides.

The lifts taking skiers to the Roc des Trois Marches and to Mont de la Chambre provide the best connections to Méribel and the rest of Les Trois Vallées.

The village of St. Martin de Belleville with its Baroque churches and pastoral aura, 8 km. down-valley from Les Menuires, offers pension accommodations and plenty of apartments. It is now connected with the entire Trois Vallées area with convenient lifts.

Mountain layout

Les Menuires area has excellent expert and intermediate skiing from the top of La Masse. These runs are often less crowded here. On the other side of the valley above both Les Menuires and Val Thorens, the runs are generally intermediate, rather wide-open cruisers with an expert run named after Marielle Goitschel, the Olympic darling of the valley. One of our absolute favorite runs for intermediates is the mogul-studded connector path leading down to Méribel from Mont de la Chambre above Les Menuires.

Off Piste: Always-present avalanche danger makes skiing with a guide very advisable and with a friend a common-sense requirement. Experts who want to explore the path less traveled should head for the Val Thorens/Les Menuires valley. Besides the aforementioned fourth valley, there is also excellent off-piste skiing above the Pointe de Thorens. At this point, be prepared to shed your skis and hike up to the glacier du Bouchet or in the other direction toward either the Glacier de Gébroulaz or to the Aguille de Péclet.

One of the most popular sections of the mountain rising from La Croisette to Mont de la Chambre will be served by two new high-speed chair lifts moving 4000 skiers per hour. There were rarely any lines, however this will ensure that skiers will not be forced to wait for these lifts that connect over to Méribel.

The summits of La Masse and Cîme de Caron, also in the Val Thorens/Les Menuires valley, are the richest sources of off-piste skiing in the entire Three Valleys circuit. From the top of both there are long off-piste trails down by Lac (lake) du Lou. Take particular notice of the ski hut at the peak of La Masse—a steep initial descent from this hut intimidates most and conceals desolate, expert terrain leading more directly toward Lac du Lou than the itinerary routes. From the top of La Masse there is more serene off-piste skiing to be found by heading down to La Gratte via either the Les Encombres route or the Le Chatelard route. Advance arrangements for a taxi or a car to pick you up and bring you the short distance to the St. Martin de Belleville lift should be made.

Mountain rating

C'est magnifique! This area is so vast and varied that no skier should have trouble finding the perfect slope for his or her ability. The basic rules here are that intermediates can stick to the slopes dropping from the Meribel ridge down to Les Menuires. Experts and advanced skiers will want to head to the other side of the valley to drop down from La Masse.

Expert skiing is everywhere however. What you can see, you can ski. No expert will go wanting. In the Val Thorens/Les Menuires valley. Here, on the Cîme de Caron and descending from Pointe de la Masse, experts can find the best steeps, the best powder, and the smallest crowds

Ski school (2003/04 prices)

All of the area's resorts have excellent instructors and offer skiing, cross-country and snowboarding lessons. There are 120 English-speaking instructors in the Les Menuires ski school (04 79 00 61 43).

Private lessons are €36 per hour for one to two persons; €52.50 per hour for three to five skiers.

For skiers looking for a guide, the ski school forms groups that ski all day Monday through Friday. This is highly recommended. You will be put into a group with similar skiers.

Special lessons for powder skiing, snowboarding, mono-skiing, ski ballet and freestyle skiing are available. There are also racing clinics and a ski kindergarten. A special accompanied ski adventure through Les Trois Vallées and another tour through the 12 valleys of the Tarentaise—including the resorts of Val Thorens, La Plagne, Les Arcs, Val d'Isère and Tignes—are also offered.

A snowboard school provides morning lessons for experienced boarders. It costs €126.50 and afternoon lessons for beginners cost €97.50.

Accommodations

These resorts have every type of lodging from luxury chalets to dormitories. The tourist office will send a complete list of hotels with information about White Week periods, and details of making reservations.

Prices are per person based on double occupancy during February with half board. €€€—€125+; €€—€75–€124; € is less than €75.

Hotel l'Ours Blanc (479 00 61 66; fax 479 00 63 67; €–€€) is run by a young English lady and her French husband who does the gourmet cooking. The interior woodwork was finished by the father and child care is free for guests.

Hotel Les Bruyeres (479 00 75 10; fax 479 00 70 70; €€) Great location. Rooms are modern with great views but no Alpine charm. Located in the Bruyeres area next to the new 12-person gondola.

Hotel Le Menuire (479 00 60 33: fax 479 00 60 00; €) This is a small, clean hotel on the road entering the complex. It is a good upscale hotel and is close to the lifts.

Chalet 2000 (479 00 60 57; fax 479 00 22 25; €) in the Reberty section right next to the Club Med has a wonderful terrace. Good slope location.

Le Pelvoux (479 00 61 09; fax 479 00 28 80; €) is right in the center of the modern village. Again don't expect tradition. You get great location with small rooms.

Pierre Blanche (479 01 37 37; fax 479 00 69 60; €) has 68 rooms in the Crêt Voland area above Le Croisette, the main modern village. This area is non-Savoyard and very modern, but with good location.

Hotel Carla (479 00 73 73; fax 479 00 73 76; €) This is a two-star hotel in La Croisette just beneath the main modern center.

St. Martin de Belleville

In the village of St. Martin de Belleville the **Hotel Saint Martin** (479 00 88 00; fax 479 00 88 39; €–€€) is a perfect spot, in chalet style and only steps from the lifts.

The **Alp-Hotel** (479 08 92 82; fax 479 08 94 61; €) near the Hotel Saint Martin. It connects with the Trois Vallées system and offers a nest of traditional architecture.

Also in St. Martin de Belleville try **l'Edelweiss** (479 08 96 67; fax 04 79 08 90 40; €) for simple accommodation and good food but a bit of a walk to the lifts.

In **La Bouitte** (479 08 96 77; fax 479 08 96 03), you can sleep like a king in a two-person room for €950–€1,050 per week.

All-in-one weekly packages in St. Martin de Belleville including lifts and half-board cost €545–€705 in three-star hotels during January and the first week of April.

Ski Chalets: Neilson (see page 20 for contact information.)

Apartments, condominiums, flats

Apartments are the French choice for accommodation. In fact, apartment beds out-number hotel beds by at least 5 to 1. What you get is the ability to schedule off-slope life at your own pace and an excellent way to avoid the high hotel prices.

During all-in-one package periods in Les Menuires, for example, a two-bedroom apartment that will sleep four people for a week in January costs €197–€420. For four-person apartment in February high season, expect to pay €615–€791. Rates vary based on the luxury and location of the apartment. Individuals sharing flats during the package periods will pay approximately €231 per person for a week with Three Valleys skipass.

Gorgeous apartments that will sleep six to eight in the Reberty Montagnettes village, as well as the brand new Les Alpages de Reberty or Les Chalets du Soleil, cost approximately €1,350–€1,970 in most of January and spike up to €1,720–€2,395 for the holidays.

The tourist office will send more information and a registration card, and will help make reservations.

Dining

With the emphasis on apartment living, one would expect only mediocre meals, but Les Menuires is a pleasant surprise. **La Bouitte** (479 08 96 77) in St. Marcel is probably the best restaurant in the valley with a one-star Michelin rating. The **Hotel Saint Martin** restaurant is also excellent. The **Etoile des Neiges** (479 08 90 40) next to the church is highly rated by Michelin.

Next on the list and the best in Les Menuires, according to locals, is the restaurant of the **Hotel L'Ours Blanc** (479 00 61 66) with excellent gourmet cooking.

La Marmite du Géant (479 00 74 75) serves great food in a modern, rustic setting near the skating rink. **La Mousse** (479 00 69 06) has the best fish in the valley.

Just above La Croisette and reached by a short walk is the **L' Etoile** (04 79 00 75 58) with tables around a giant fireplace. It has one of the region's best chefs.

Try **Chalet des Neiges** (479 00 60 55), where you'll get simple good food for €12–€15. In the evenings the restaurant sponsors fondue dinners, and a guide takes skiers down to the lower village with torches.

Les Roches Blanches (479 00 60 22) on La Masse is a rustic chalet serving a menu of the day, pizza and spaghetti.

Après-ski/nightlife

Les Menuires has two small discos, packed with the very young, tucked into the basement of the massive apartment buildings. The best is **Leeberty** in Les Bruyeres.

Child care (2003/04 prices)

The tourist office, your hotel or apartment manager can put you in touch with qualified private babysitters who provide child care services at any time of the day or night.

The **Schtroumpfs' Village** is divided into three sections: 3 months to 2 1/2 years, 2-1/2 to 3 years, and 3 to 6 years. Introduction to skiing is provided for children age 3–6; different programs are offered to each group. Reservations are suggested (479 00 63 79). A second kindergarten, called **Les Piou-Piou**, in the Les Bruyères area takes children 2 1/2–6 years (479 00 69 50).

The ski school also runs special programs for kids 4 years and older. The lessons are coordinated with the Schtroumpfs' Village to allow children to spend the time after and before lessons at the child care facility.

Rates for the kindergarten in Les Menuires are €29 for a full day; €120 for six half-days; and €180 for six full days.

Other activities

There are two **heated outdoor pools** open daily from 2:30–7:30 p.m., one in les Bruyères and one in la Croisette. The **outdoor skating rink** in Bruyères is open from 4 p.m.–8 p.m. Call 479 00 69 98. The resort also has two fully equipped **fitness centers**, Espace Tonic and Chalet du Capricorne. There are 28 km. of **cross-country trails** surrounding the resort as well.

For **parasailing** call Adrénaline Sports (479 00 62 49). **Snowshoeing** and **ice climbing** as well as extreme skiing are organized by the ski school. Call 479 00 61 43.

Tourist information

Les Menuires Office du Tourisme, 73440 Les Menuires, France;
Telephone 479 00 73 00; fax 479 00 75 06.
For reservations only, call 479 00 79 79; fax 479 00 60 92.
Internet: www.lesmenuires.com.
E-mail: lesmenuires@lesmenuires.com

Saint Martin de Belleville Office du Tourisme, 73440 Saint Martin de Belleville, France; Telephone 479 00 20 00; fax 479 08 91 71.
Internet: www.st-martin-belleville.com

VAL THORENS

None of the Trois Vallées villages is more attuned to the single-minded pursuit of winter sport than Val Thorens. From the moment you park your car in indoor parking near this cluster of high-rise apartments and hotels, you can feel the hum of sport activity. At 7,546 feet, Val Thorens is designed for the young and restless, or at least for the young-at-heart and active. Its altitude is the highest of any European resort. Besides some of the best year-round skiing offered anywhere, there's a huge indoor sports complex where you can play tennis on one of three courts, work out in the gym, or try your hand at squash. The sports complex and the Aqua Club will be renovated for the 2003/04 season.

Outside, the crowd is one teeming mass of rainbow-colored movement: snowmobilers, skiers, snowboarders, parasailors, and monoskiers riding high-speed lifts and winding through the apartment and hotel complexes. The real claim to fame is the atmosphere of sport, sure snow and the lofty location of this fun town.

The neon signs, bright splashy ads and general carnival atmosphere of Val Thorens makes it feel like a video arcade. In some Alpine resorts they play acoustic oom-pah, but here it's bass-heavy "Techno Euro-Rock" blaring from speakers. After a slight decompression period, however, the look feels in sync with the area's character: fun-loving, sporting, and slightly outrageous. If you're looking to have a drink of wine and a laugh with the locals, then you'll fit right in. If you want to be waited on and pampered by lift attendants and polite locals alike, better to book St. Moritz.

Mountain layout

Even with the high altitude of Val Thorens, one of the biggest capital improvements has been the continued installation of snowmaking. Though this resort gets plenty of snow, the strong sun during the spring makes snowmaking on the southern-facing slopes desirable. It is one more example of the region trying to make the skiing experience as good as possible.

As the highest resort in the Alps, Val Thorens, is wide-open, bowl-type skiing above the tree line. The Péclet cable car takes skiers up to the Péclet glacier, offering year-round skiing for intermediates and above. While most of the skiing in the bowl-shaped area above Val Thorens is intermediate and advanced, experts can find plenty of challenges.

The cable car ride to the top of Cîme de Caron, the highest point in the three valleys, is spectacular if you are lucky enough to be blessed with clear weather and limited winds. The view is worth the trip, the rocks on top make a perfect picnic spot and the runs seem endless. From here you can take a black run straight down, or a slightly easier advanced intermediate. True experts will want to ski over the ridge to the little-used fourth valley and then take the Rosael quad chair that will bring you back. There are some newly developed trails in this valley with a new chair lift just added. When skiing Val Thorens be ready for changeable weather. At this altitude the winds can pick up in an instant and clouds can move in quickly. Dress for winter conditions, even if the skies are clear and the sun strong when you leave the base area for Cime Caron.

Off Piste: see the Les Menuires section on page 203.

New for 2003/04: The Funitel Bouquetin is a new lift which has been specifically designed to transport skiers between Val Thorens the rest of Les Trois Vallées even in bad weather conditions.

Mountain rating

No one will have any problem finding the perfect skiing for their level. Beginners will be able to stick close to the village. Intermediates will have the run of all the slopes surrounding the town. Advanced and expert skiers will have off-piste opportunities and plenty of steeps to challenge them.

Ski school (2002/03 prices)

All of the area's resorts have excellent instructors who teach Alpine skiing, cross-country and snowboarding. There are more than 140 in Val Thorens. Val Thorens has five different ski schools. The French Ski School or E.S. F. (479 00 02 86), Pro-Neige (479 01 07 00), Ski Cool (479 00 04 92), and Ski School International (479 00 01 96).

At the French Ski School, **private lessons** start at €33 per hour. Private guides cost €230–€252 for a full day for five skiers.

Group lessons cost €123 for six mornings, €96 for six afternoons, and €159 for six full days with meals.

Children's lessons cost €120 for six mornings, €85 for six afternoons, and €236 for six full days with meals.

Snowboarding lessons cost €126 for six mornings or €105 six afternoon lessons.

For skiers looking for a guide, the ski school forms groups that ski all day Monday through Friday. The cost for the full week group is about €260. This is highly recommended.

Accommodations

Val Thorens has a sporty feel. This is not luxury hotel territory, however there are several excellent hotels that have virtually every ammenity. Prices are per person based on double occupancy during February with half board. €€€—€125+; €€—€75–€124; € is less than €75.

Fitz Roy (479 00 04 78, fax 479 00 06 11; €€€) The luxury hotel in town. Meals are a quantum leap above those of the Val Thorens.

Le Val Thorens (479 00 04 33, fax 479 00 09 40; €€) For American tastes this is perhaps the best hotel in town. The breakfast is not the usual croissant and coffee but a full buffet complete with eggs. Walk out your door and onto the slopes.

Hotel Bel Horizon (479 00 04 77; fax 479 00 06 08; €€) Right on the edge of the complex with south-facing rooms, this hotel offers good-sized rooms but a very French atmosphere, limited English speaking help and excellent food.

Le Sherpa (479 00 00 70, fax 479 00 08 03; €€) It is family-run and offers excellent value for money, with excellent food. It has 14 new luxury rooms.

Les Trois Vallées (479 00 01 86, fax 479 00 04 08; €€) In the center of action with a good bar and good service.

Novotel (479 00 04 04, fax 479 00 05 93; €€€) The resort's biggest with 104 rooms complete with most ammenities but no pool.

Le Portillo (479 00 00 88; fax 479 00 05 65; €€) has 15 rooms and every one is different. It just was raised from a two-star to a three-star property.

La Marmotte (479 00 00 07; fax 479 00 00 14; €) Sparsely furnished, very basic.

Les Montagnettes du Soleil (479 00 20 51; fax 479 00 24 39; €€) only has suites for up to four. It is an apartment with hotel services. For foursomes, it's a big bargain.

Ski Chalets: Crystal, Thompson, Thomas Cook/Neilson (go to page 20 for phone, fax and Internet addresses).

Apartments, condominiums, flats

Apartments are the French choice for accommodation. In fact, apartment beds outnumber hotel beds by at least 5 to 1. What you get is the ability to schedule off-slope life at your own pace and a way to avoid the high hotel prices.

Val Thorens has a bevy of "residences" that are basically apartments with hotel services. You have a restaurant and beds will be made up upon arrival but there is no housekeeping or room service.

The **Village Montana** (479 00 21 01), one of the most luxurious, costs about €700 a week for a two bedroom with living room and kitchen from mid-January to mid-February. The **Chalet Altitude** (479 00 85 00) with similar amenities is around €950 for about the same space during the same timeframe.

Less expensive locations are the **Balcons de Val Thorens** (479 00 90 70) and **Pierre et Vacances** (479 09 30 30).

The tourist office will send more information and a registration card, and will help make reservations. Make sure to impress on them that you are Americans or British and want a larger apartment. If you are four people and you pay for an apartment for five, it is probably worth the extra money. Nothing is worse than being stuck in a room about the size of one found on a cruise ship when you have all your ski equipment.

Dining

In Val Thorens, lovers of fine French food should head for the **Fitz Roy Hotel** (479 00 04 78). The atmosphere is romantic, the surroundings plush, and the price steep. The other top restaurant is **Bergerie** (479 00 77 18) with meals rated by Michelin as worthy of two forks ranging from €37–€46.

After those two spots the next on the restaurant list in descending order are **Le Bellevillois** (479 00 04 33), **Auberge du Sherpa** (479 00 00 70), and **La Grange de Pierette** in the Portillo Hotel.

Le Vieux Chalet (479 00 07 93) has wonderful typical upscale Savoyard specialties. For more local blue-collar specialties, try the **Galoubet** (479 00 00 48). **La Fondue** (479 00 04 33) has cheese fondue and raclette. **Bloopers** (479 00 05 75) has its fans as well. **El Gringo** waiters decked in cowboy gear serve the highest altitude Tex-Mex dinners in Europe with killer margaritas. The best pizza—and for that matter the best deal—in town is at **Pizzeria Gianni/Scapin**.

Après-ski/nightlife

The nightlife in Val Thorens used to be limited, but now you can choose from three discos which don't start until after midnight and keep on throbbing until 4 a.m., or you can drink in one of ten pubs. Those hot to trot head for **Beach Mountain** nightclub, which has a €15 cover (one drink included). Prepare yourself for outrageous prices, by U.S. standards, if you plan on drinking much. **Bar Malaysia** just outside the tourist office is a surprise. Don't let the small entranceway fool you: the bar itself is underground, and very classy. The live music tends toward the avant-garde, and there are pool tables (€5–€11 per drink, no cover). **The Ski Rock Cafe**, **Gringo's**, the **Frog and Roast Beef**, and the **Viking** all have lively action.

Child care (2003/04 prices)

The tourist office, your hotel or apartment manager can put you in touch with qualified private baby sitters who provide child care services at any time of the day or night.

Val Thorens has two Mini Clubs associated with the ski school (479 00 02 86 and 479 00 02 38). These Mini-Club kindergartens accept children ages 3 months to 6 years. Ask about discounts for three or more children from the same family. Children age 3 months to 18 months cost €27 for six half days without meals. Children age 18 months to 4 years cost €121 for six half days without meals.

Beginners lessons for ages 4 and younger are €240 for six full days with meals and €86 for six half-days without meals.

Other activities

Facilities include an indoor swimming pool, whirlpool baths, saunas, squash courts, six indoor tennis courts, a gymnasium and an outdoor skating rink. Hang-gliding and aerobics are offered.

Val Thorens also has Europe's highest toboggan run set in a natural 6-km.-long valley with a vertical drop of more than 2,200 feet. It is in the Tête Ronde sector at the foot of the Péclet glacier. The run is reached by the Funitel.

Tourist information

Val Thorens Office du Tourisme, 73440 Val Thorens, France;
Telephone: 479 00 08 08; fax 479 00 00 04.
Internet: www.valthorens.com. E-mail: valtho@valthorens.com
Reservations are handled by Val Thorens Reservations;
Telephone: 479 00 01 06; fax 479 00 06 49.
Internet: www.valthorens.com. E-mail: reserver@valthorens.com

Val d'Isère

Val d'Isère has long been one of the true European meccas of skiing. Although the professional ski world knew Val d'Isère, the average skier began to hear more about it after native Jean-Claude Killy won his Olympic gold in 1968. The town was also home to three other Olympic champions who won a total of nine gold medals.

The town lies at 6,012 feet and the ski area rises to 11,336 feet, with working verticals of more than 3,250 feet in all sectors of the resort. Skiers looking for the best on- and off-trail runs in the world need look no further.

Unlike many French purpose-built resorts, Val d'Isère is actually a town. Unfortunately, when it was initially being developed, architects opted for functionally square, flat-topped hotels. Recently, though, new buildings have been constructed in the Savoyard Alpine chalet style, and many of the unprepossessing buildings have been dressed up with facades to create more of a mountain atmosphere.

The ski area is linked with Tignes, creating "l'Espace Killy," with 186 miles of marked runs for every level of skier, tried-and-true off-piste itineraries for serious experts and 104 lifts, including an underground lift with an uphill capacity of more than 3,000 skiers per hour.

Mountain layout

An area as enormous as Val d'Isère/Tignes is virtually impossible to describe in words. Even the trail map, on a relatively small scale, gives no feel for the immensity of the area. Your first clue will be when you exit from the Funival or Bellevarde cable car and look out over the seemingly endless fields of snow.

The Val d'Isère share of l'Espace Killy is divided into four sectors corresponding with the three main ridges dropping into the town and the glacier area.

Le Fornet sector is reached by Le Fornet cable car, which rises the first 1,246 feet. From the top of the cable car, skiers can drop back down into the town on a steep and narrow expert run directly under the cables, or loop to their right around an advanced beginner trail. There are also two choices of lifts further up the mountain. The gondola leaving from the cable car building reaches the Col d'Isèran area, which provides access to skiing on the Glacier de Pissaillas or allows skiers to take the connecting lift to the Solaise sector. The very long Signal drag lift will take you to just under the Signal peak, at 10,633 feet. From there you can take a tough intermediate trail back to the cable car or drop into the off-trail Le Vallon powder fields which then drop more than 3,000 feet back to the base of the Fornet cable car.

The Solaise sector is also reached by cable car from the village center. This area is a wide-open beginner and intermediate paradise. About 1,500 vertical feet wait for open slope cruising. Off-piste itineraries from the Solaise will keep any expert happy.

The Bellevarde sector has the best access, with four methods of getting to the top of Rocher de Bellevarde and two additional lifts serving intermediate and beginner runs from La Daille. The Funival, a high-speed subway, rises from La Daille through the rock to the top of Rocher de Bellevarde. A new cable car, l'Olympique, carries skiers up the La Face side to the top of Bellevarde. Beginners have a series of runs at higher altitudes and a choice between two long runs with more than a 2,900-foot vertical back to La Daille. Intermediates have their choice of two more challenging drops back to La Daille. Intermediates can drop down La Face or into the valley back to the town. There are also excellent off-piste routes from the top of the Bellevarde sector. Take Le Kern around the front of the cliff and drop through powder back to town, or take the drag lift to the side of the Charvet rock cluster and ski around the backside of the formation entering the valley, eventually returning to town, or drop down to La Daille off-piste.

Mountain rating

There is something for everyone; the upper reaches are excellent for any skier level. Experts can test themselves on the steeps that sail into town, as well as extensive off-trail and powder-skiing pockets. It's a good idea to take a guide along, at least for a day, to find the best places to test your limits. Also, if you plan to ski off-trail, check with the ski school before you leave for the latest information on snow conditions.

Snowboarding

Most snowboarders, based on economics and terrain, tend to spend time at Tignes rather than Val d'Isère. However, the drops into the town will thrill any rider. The main problem is the series of flats that sprinkle the upper reaches of the resort that mean walking or hopping along. There is a snowboard park at the top of the La Daille serviced by the Mont Blanc chair lift.

Ski school (2002/03 prices)

The Val d'Isère French Ski School boasts Jean-Claude Killy as its technical adviser. Its ski instructors are among the most qualified in the world: three former world champions and many members of the national ski team serve on the staff. In total, there are 300 instructors including 19 mountain guides who can teach any level of skier, from the basic beginner to the Olympic caliber racer. English is spoken by many of the instructors. (If required, ask for an English-speaking instructor.)

French Ski School (ESF) offices are in the Village Center (479 06 02 34) and in La Daille shopping center (479 06 09 99).

Private lessons: A lesson lasting an hour costs €34. One-and-a-half hours will cost €50. Private lessons are limited to five students. Instructors or guides can be hired during high season for the full day from 9:30 a.m. to 5 p.m. for €257 for up to four people and €280 for five to seven. Morning lessons from 9:30 a.m. to 12:30 p.m. cost €153; afternoon lessons, 2 p.m. to 5 p.m., are €140.

Group lessons: Courses cost €190 for six full days of lessons, which run from

9:30 a.m. to 12:30 p.m. and from 2:30 p.m. to 5 p.m.; a full day is €38; and a morning lesson is €25.

A Top Ski class that takes place every morning from 9 a.m.–1 p.m. allows you to ski in a group with an instructor on most of the off-trail itineraries. There are also powder skiing lessons for a six-day course and day trips to La Plagne, Les Arcs and La Rosière/La Thuile for expeditions.

There are several other ski schools and guide organizations in Val d'Isère. Instructors are bilingual, speaking English and French. Sign up with the English section of **Snow Fun**, the largest non-EFS school, at the Solaise Gallery (479 06 19 79). **Altimanya Ski School** specializes in moguls, **Alpine Experience** focuses on off-piste powder instruction, **Surf Rider Club** is a snowboard school and **Top Ski** has instruction in extreme skiing.

Heliskiing is offered. The helicopter drops you into Italy for backcountry skiing. Call 479 06 04 53 for prices.

Lift tickets (2003/04 prices)

These prices are for the entire l'Espace Killy, including the Val d'Isère/Tignes area pass.

	Adults	**Children (5-12)**	**Seniors (60-69)**
one day	€38	€28.50	€32.50
three days	€97.50	€73	€83
six days	€181	€136	€154

Insurance adds about €2.50 per day for adults and €2 per day for children.

Children younger than 5 ski free. A photo is needed for all tickets two days or more. The ticket is valid for one day of your stay on La Plagne and Les Arcs ski lifts. Six- to 21-day tickets are also good for a day at Trois Vallées and a day at Valmorel.

All lift tickets are offered with insurance for an additional charge varying based on the length of your lift ticket and the age of the person buying the ticket.

The lift company will refund part of your lift ticket price if extreme weather forces closure of the lifts when you have a three- to 15-day lift ticket. Apply to the ticket office for the prorated refund.

Accommodations

The tourist office and the hoteliers have organized special weekly discount programs organized for low and shoulder season periods. Costs for the program are based on the hotel category and the package being offered. Packages include seven nights accommodation with bath or shower, seven-day lift ticket and pool pass. For instance, during mid January, a four-star hotel package will be €198 per person each day for half board; a three-star package is €105 per person each day for half board; a two-star will cost €82 per person each day for half board and the one-star hotel package is only €58 per person each day for half board.

The central reservations system, run by Val Hotel, can make arrangements in any of these hotels unless noted otherwise. They will also provide more information on the packages. Contact: Val Hotel, BP 73, 73153 Val d'Isère Cedex, France; (479 06 18 90).

The hotels listed here have all been visited by *Ski Europe* journalists. Rates are based on double occupancy during February with half board. €€€—€125+; €€—€75–€124; €—less than €75.

Hotel Grand Paradis (479 06 11 73; €€€+) This three-star hotel has one of the best locations in the resort—just across the street from the lifts—plus, underground parking. The lobby is decorated in elegant dark wood with Tiffany lamps and mirrors.

Hotel Latitudes (479 06 18 88; €€€+) This is a recent four-star built in the village center. The lobby and bar step up several levels. Rooms are very businesslike, with-little of the Alpine charm the exterior of the hotel promises.

Hotel Christiania (479 06 08 25; €€€) Chalet-style, four-star hotel two minutes from the lifts and full of atmosphere. The suites available on the top floor are among the best in the resort, with beautiful bathrooms and antique country furniture.

Hotel Mercure (479 06 12 93; €€) A three-star modern hotel in the center of the village that would be the perfect business hotel—clean, convenient and efficient.

Hotel Savoyarde (479 06 01 55; €€€) This is our favorite hotel in Val d'Isère. This three-star is chalet-style and has a cozy sauna and an excellent restaurant. Its best feature is being in the center of town, only steps away from the lifts.

The Kandahar (479 06 02 39; €€) This is a relatively new three-star lodge built over the Taverne d'Alsace.

Hotel Samovar (479 06 13 51; €€–€€€) Another three-star oozing with charm, this hotel is out of the town center at the base of the Funival. Its restaurant is consistently rated as one of the best in town by locals, but its best section remains reserved for hotel guests or outsiders who often wait two weeks for reservations. The rooms are weathered but comfortable. The owner says he wants to create the atmosphere of a chalet rather than a hotel. Ask for room 10—an Old World, old wood masterpiece. Breakfast is sumptuous.

Hotel Sorbiers (479 06 23 77; €€€) This is a beautiful three-star hotel built in modern chalet style. The interiors are rich with golden wood and rooms are cozy. The hotel offers only B&B arrangements.

Hotel Altitude (479 06 12 55; €€) This hotel has one of the coziest restaurants of any hotel in the village. The rooms have been recently renovated.

Chamois d'Or (479 06 00 44; €€) This two-star hotel is filled with old Alpine charm. The restaurant has a giant fireplace. Rooms vary in size, but all have ample space. The hotel is only steps away from the cable cars up to the Solaise and the Bellevarde. If you want atmosphere, this is the place.

For a quiet change of pace outside of the town try **Le Chalet du Lac** (479 06 25 47; €–€€), a new hotel alongside the lake a few kilometers outside of La Daille. This hotel offers, for those with a car, a position between Tignes and Val d'Isère.

Hotel Barnes de l'Ours (475 00 06 02; €€€) is a four-star luxury hotel at the bottom of La Face.

Ski Chalets: Crystal, Inghams/Bladon, Total, Thompson (see page 20 for phone, fax and Internet addresses).

Apartments, condominiums, flats

The tourist office acts as an information clearinghouse. It maintains an extensive list of individuals and agencies who will rent apartments in the resort.

Aparthotels combine apartments with hotel service. The most elegant of these new establishments are the **Les Domaines du Soleil** which has a swimming pool. Two similar new aparthotels are **Jardin Alpin** and **Eureka Val**. The **Alpina Lodge** also offers similar arrangements. Apartment prices are about €280–€570 for a studio in mid January, and €510–€1,100 for a two-room apartment during the same period. In February and early March the rates jump to €450–€1,030 for a studio sleeping two to four, and €940–€1,720 for a two-room unit which will sleep five to six. In many cases, linen is not included but can be rented for the week from the apartment owners or agencies.

For apartment accommodation in the region contact **Val Location** (479 06 06 60, fax 479 41 45 59).

Dining

Surprisingly, Val d'Isère has no nationally recognized restaurants. The smaller places that have traditionally offered the top meals are being pressed by the hotel dining rooms, which offer excellent meals at reasonable prices.

Le Grande Ourse (479 06 00 19) still reigns as the top restaurant in Val d'Isère after decades in that position. The interior is the most beautiful of any restaurant in the region. It's almost worth the price just to eat in such surroundings. Meals here are as gourmet as they get in Val d'Isère. Expect to pay €35–€50 for meal with wine.

Hotel Savoyarde Restaurant (479 06 01 55) is consistently mentioned as the second-best eatery. The dining room has a beautiful wooden ceiling, a warm Savoyard atmosphere, and a menu that will allow you to walk out for €30–€40, including wine.

The Hotel Bellier Restaurant (479 06 03 77) serves excellent fare. Menu prices are about €25 with wine. The dining room is an elegant and cozy Alpine spot. Reservations are recommended unless you're a hotel guest.

All three of the following restaurants are within a stone's throw of one another in the La Daille ski area, serving good meals in some of the resort's most rustic settings.

The Samovar (479 06 13 51) in La Daille serves wholesome meals. The real atmosphere is upstairs, where the hotel guests eat as well as those lucky enough to have reserved one of the two tables allotted to outsiders.

La Vieille Maison (479 06 11 76) also in La Daille serves Savoyard specialties with the atmosphere of a flickering fire, whitewashed walls and flagstone floors.

These restaurants serve up less costly meals:

Restaurant La Corniche (479 06 02 05) tucked between the stone buildings of the old village, is a new spot with an atmospheric dining room. Stone walls alternate with wood—this is how a modern Alpine restaurant should look. Expect to spend €20.

Restaurant Le Kern (479 06 06 06) is in a small two-star hotel and has genuine old Alpine charm. Meals are excellent and reasonable. Prices will be about €20.

Taverne d'Alsace (479 06 02 39) serves up German-Alsatian cuisine, including a potent onion cake, in a very cozy bar setting.

Restaurant Bellevue, across the street from the tourist office, is a good, inexpensive restaurant where you can get away for less than €17–€20.

For pizza, try **Perdrix Blanche**. Cheese fondue (€12), fondue bourgogne (€20) and raclette (€12), are best sampled in **La Raclette** in Hotel Avancher (479 06 02 00) and **Restaurant Arolay** in Le Fornet (479 06 11 68).

On the slopes, try **La Folie Douce** and **La Fruitière** at La Daille midstation and **Bellevarde** at the top of the funival. Also try **Cabaret des Neiges** at the midstation at Solaise; **La Datcha** at Solaise; **Les Tufs** at the base of La Daille; **La Taniere** at the midstation of La Face.

Locals will promote their favorites—ask for recommendations.

Après-ski/nightlife

Val d'Isère has some of the best nightlife in France for Americans and British.

For après-ski head to **Moris Pub**, or **Dick's Tea Bar**. Check out the various happy hours 4–7 p.m.

For nightlife, **Dick's Tea Bar** is the main English-language hangout. Dick's Tea Bar also has good immediate après-ski with happy hour, videos and then jazz, before the disco scene cranks in. New bars in town are the **Café Face** in the Christiania Hotel and **St. Hubert Pub** under the St. Hubert Hotel. Avoid these places if you are searching for a quiet spot to talk. For real French discos, try **Club 21, Aventure** in the Sofitel and **Blue Night** in the basement of the Hotel Latitudes. For Scandinavian bars, try **Petit Danois** or **Victors.**

Perdrix Blanche is normally packed with a young crowd after skiing and **Taverne d'Alsace** offers a very rustic bar and quieter après-ski for a slightly older crowd.

Child care (2002/03 prices)

There are many alternatives for child care in Val d'Isère. The hotels and the tourist office can put you in touch with private babysitting services (479 06 06 60).

Le Petit Poucet (479 06 13 97) is for children between ages 3 to 10. Approximate costs are €42 a day and €240 for six days. They open from 9 a.m. until 5:30 p.m. and Le Petit Poucet offers bus service that picks up the children.

Another facility is the **French Ski School**, which has an extensive children's program for kids ages 4–13 (479 41 99 82). **The Jardin des Neiges** takes those age 4 and 5 for lessons at a rate of €32 for three hours. The Village des Enfants takes kids age 3–13. Rates for morning or afternoon without meal is €23; a full day with meal is €45; six days with meals €230; one hour is €8; supervised lunch is €18.

Other activities

The town offers good, but limited activities for non-skiers. There is a covered, heated **swimming pool** open from 3 p.m. to 8 p.m., with a daily entrance fee of €4.80 for adults and €3 for children (free to holders of seven- to 15-day ski passes). Cards for 10 entries are available.

Paragliding courses are offered for approximately €230 per day, including equipment and insurance. Flight with an instructor costs approximately €55. Contact G.R. Sports: 479 06 11 37.

Viking Snowmobile offers night **snowmobile** rides on the Tovière plateau. Rides cost €46 per hour. Contact Viking Snowmobiles at 479 06 05 27.

Snowshoeing walks and lessons are organized by Pascal Bertres (613 85 64 77) for €18 per person.

Getting there

The closest airports are in Lyons and Geneva. Geneva is about 112 miles and Lyons is 137 miles from the resort. Rail transport via TGV is quick and easy from Paris to Bourg-St. Maurice, where a bus takes you to the resort.

Driving from Geneva, take A41 to Annecy; then N90 to Albertville, where you follow the signs to Bourg-St. Maurice and on to Val d'Isère. From Lyons, take autoroute A43 to Albertville and on to Val d'Isère. Direct bus service leaves from Geneva airport three or four times a day, and there is weekend service from Lyon Airport to Val d'Isère.

Tourist information

For information, contact Office du Tourisme, BP 228,
73155 Val d'Isère, France; tel. 479 06 06 60; fax 479 06 04 56.
For hotel accommodations, contact Val Hôtel, BP 73,
73150 Val d'Isère, France; tel. 479 06 18 90; fax 479 06 11 88.
Internet: www.val-disere.com
E-mail: info@val-disere.com

Garmisch-Partenkirchen Germany

The Olympic city Garmisch-Partenkirchen, at the base of the Zugspitze, the country's highest mountain (9,721 feet), is Germany's best and most famous ski resort. Here, Germany hosted the Winter Olympic Games in 1936. Those games were the impetus to link the two villages into one. The villagers were less than enthusiastic so Hitler gave them an alternative that was much less pleasant, so unification was quickly approved. Even though these two towns are officially unified, they unofficially still compete with each other. There are two of everything: two fire stations, two schools and so on. Only the Olympic venues are shared, but to this date the Partenkirchen side handles all the arrangements for the ski jumping competitions and keeps the proceeds. The town of Garmisch takes care of the World Cup downhill races and those riches. Even though Garmisch-Partenkirchen strives to keep from being termed a city, it has a population of 28,000, and has many benefits of city life such as concerts, shows and great shopping.

Partenkirchen is cute, cozy, with narrow streets and a center filled with painted houses. Unfortunately the town has a couple of square highrises interrupting the Old-World harmony. Garmisch seems more organized with a grid of streets lined with new concrete buildings intermingled with Alpine chalets and more organized, upscale shopping streets. The Munich/Innsbruck highway abruptly divides the two sections of the city—there is no easy transition from one to the other.

Garmisch-Partenkirchen's location, less than an hour's drive from Munich and about an hour and a half from the new Munich airport, makes it a natural tourist attraction. The city government has just purchased the Zugspitzbahn which gives them control over all lifts. New alliances have been created with former competitors just over the border in Austria—Lermoos and Seefeld—to make an international series of ski areas which can be skied with one lift ticket.

The Garmisch-Partenkirchen lifts and slopes are not located right in the town. For the most part a car will make a vacation a bit easier, especially if you plan to take advantage of any of the Austrian resorts included in the area passes.

Hotels distribute a Visitor's Card to overnight guests that allows free use of the buses, free accident insurance, free entrance to town, free access to many venues and discounts on others. Visitors will have to ask for the best bus routes to reach the lifts. Once the system is figured out it works smoothly and on time. Some hotels also issue a special visitor card for weeklong guests which includes entrance to the museums, a horse-drawn-sleigh ride, iceskating, an introduction to snowboarding, telemark, or skating courses and more.

Lermoos and Seefeld are the two largest Austrian villages linked with Garmisch by a common lift ticket. Both are about a half-hour drive away, but both offer an Alpine village setting rather than the hustle of a little city. These may be considered for those planning a vacation with young children.

Mountain layout

Garmisch offers nearly 75 miles of runs, but the rugged Alpine landscape prevents any sort of continuous ski circuit between the seven different slopes. You ski in one of two large areas. One is on the high slopes of the Zugspitze plateau. You can get to the top by cable car from Lake Eibsee above Garmisch or from the Zugspitze cog train; the cable car is more scenic, the train more direct. Skiing here is at its best in early November and December, and in spring—April and May—when other resorts are closing. Best of the trails is the two-mile run from the Schneefernerkopf at 9,427 feet.

Garmisch hosted the Winter Olympics in 1936, and its facilities are well maintained. The World Cup runs on the Kreuzeck and the neighboring Hausberg provide several difficult turns, but overall it's perfect terrain for intermediates.

Our favorite runs are from the Osterfelderkopf. From here you can make the only real skiing circuit in Garmisch, linking up with lifts from the Hausberg below.

For Zugspitze fans there is a new double chair to the glacier at 9,186 feet. A tunnel from the cog railway eliminates walking and climbing, and allows direct access to the slopes. During the past years, the resort has established many new and more difficult trails on the Zugspitze. According to locals, the plateau is now great for all levels of skiers rather than only intermediates and beginners.

For another ski adventure and often shorter lift lines, take the border highway past Grainau into Austria. On the other side of the Zugspitze, less than a 30-minute drive away, you can try the slopes of Ehrwald: when Garmisch's weather is bad, the sun will sometimes be shining here. Neighboring Lermoos and Biberwier, in Austria, are popular with local skiers.

Lermoos has a great skiers' mountain. A gondola, then a high-speed quad take skiers up to a surprising wonderland perfect for intermediates. A section of the mountain called "the gumdrops" is dotted with small mounds of snow that form over bushes and provide a playground for snowboarders and kids of all ages. A day here is a must for anyone in the area.

In the other direction, at Mittenwald, the Damkar run from the 7,822-foot Karwendel summit is challenging and the mountain panorama is superb.

Mountain rating

Garmisch is intermediate country but with new trails is becoming a good spot for advanced and expert skiers. The challenging parts of red runs might be considered

Telephone prefix for Garmisch-Partenkirchen: 08821
Telephone prefix for Germany: 0049

black in other areas, the Zugspitze has added advanced terrain and the difficult World Cup sections on the Kreuzeck and Hausberg provide upper-level skiers with a test.

The advanced beginner and intermediate will find it the place to be. Beginners could not come to a better place for outstanding ski instruction.

In nearby Austria, Lermoos has great intermediate trails and is a snowboarder heaven. Seefeld has mellower trails but offers a larger Austrian village atmosphere.

Garmisch has excellent cross-country trails. There are 45 km. of maintained trails in the area. Nearby Seefeld in Austria is considered by many to be the premier cross-country area in Europe. It was twice the site of Olympic competitions. Lermoos, Ehrwald and Biberwier also are connected with a 60 km. tracked cross-country network and linked with another 40 km. of trails in the surrounding region.

Ski school (2003/04)

Garmisch's ski school program includes off-trail touring instruction, snowboarding and an outstanding climbing school. Eight schools offer instruction in the area. Rates for the various schools are all within a few Euros of each other.

Private lessons for one hour are €35.

Group lessons for one day cost €30 (three hours); for three days, €80; for five days, €100.

All the following ski schools have good reputations, but their locations may play a role in your choice. The schools also offer cross-country instruction and most have snowboarding equipment for lessons for every level and age.

Skischule Sprenzel (1496) near Hausberg.

Skischule Garmisch-Partenkirchen (76260) At the Hausberg slope.

Skischule Wörndle (58300) At the Hausberg cable car station.

Olympia Skischule (4600) Near the Osterfelder.

Skilanglaufschule (1516) Cross-country school at the Olympic stadium.

Bergsteigerschule Zugspitze (58999) Mountain climbing and ski touring instruction with skins and ice climbing.

Lift tickets (2003/04 prices)

An all-inclusive lift ticket for Garmisch-Partenkirchen lifts and several of the surrounding towns called the Happy Ski Card, is available. It is good for transport on all 101 lifts in the Zugspitze region, including the Zugspitze itself.

	Adults	**Youth** (16/17)	**Children** (5–15)
three days	€80	€74	€48
six days	€150	€138	€90
thirteen days	€252	€232	€151

The Happy Ski Card includes skiing at the following resorts—Garmisch-Partenkirchen, Seefeld, Reith, Mittenwald, Ehrwald, Lermoos, Biberwier, Bichlbach, Berwang and Heiterwang.

A day ticket for Garmisch-Partenkirchen (excluding the Zugspitze) is €28 for adults, €22 for those ages 16 and 17, €18 for kids from age 5–15. The Zugspitzbahn ride to the top of Germany costs €35 for adults, €25 for youths, €21 for children.

A day ticket for the Eckbauer area (E Tageskarte) costs about €16. A day ticket the Wank area (W Tageskarte) costs €16 for adults; €11 for those ages 16 and 17; €9.50 for children age 5–15. The Wank area is designated for hiking and walking only.

To ski the Zugspitze, you need the Z Tageskarte, which costs €33 daily.

Accommodations

Fortunately, the lift-ticket confusion is not carried over into accommodations. You can quickly find a place to stay, anywhere from a farmhouse or an ultra-luxurious hotel.

The tourist office offers a series of inclusive one-week vacation plans that combine hotel, lifts and local transportation. Prices range from about €300 for a room in a private home without private bath, to €664 for lodging in a luxury hotel.

Hotel Sonnenbichel (7020; fax 702131) and the **Dorint** (7060; fax 706618) are considered by many to be the best in town. But these international hotels are are out of town and lose much of the Bavarian flavor of a vacation in Garmisch.

I recommend that skiers try to take advantage of the wonderful hotels in the middle of the towns. These places are full of atmosphere and will provide a vacation you'll remember for a long time.

Posthotel Ludwigstr. 49, Partenkirchen (93630; fax 9363222)
Partenkirchner Hof Bahnhofstr. 15, Partenkirchen (58025; fax 73401)
Clausings Posthotel Marienplatz 12, Garmisch (7090: fax 709205)
Garmischer Hof Chamonixstr. 10, Garmisch (9110; fax 51440)
Hotel Staudacherhof Höllentalstr. 48, Garmisch (9290; fax 929333)

Other excellent lodging with easy USA reservations is available at **Best Western Hotel Obermühle** (7040; fax 704112) €67–€95 per person per night with breakfast. It has one of the resort's best restaurants.

Aschenbrenner (58029; fax 4805) €40–€60, B&B only.

Hotel Hilleprandt (943040; fax 745448) €37–€47, quiet, family-run hotel within walking distance of the Hausberg ski school. Lower priced rooms begin at approximately €180 a week. A good choice for the budget plan.

Haus Hohe Tannen (54647) is run by a great family. They have wonderful rooms from €26–€34 and speak excellent English.

Haus Schell (95750; fax 957540) €23–€46, is a B&B that is very close to the station. None of the rooms have baths so guests share one down the hall.

Apartments

The popularity of apartments has increased in Garmisch in recent years. The Garmisch tourist office provides an accommodations booklet, which not only lists available apartments but also includes pictures of some of them. Of those we saw the most interesting were the apartments in the Husar section with furnished apartments for two to six people. Prices start at €30 a day and range up to more than €120 a day. Once again, check to make sure you are near to buses for transport to the slopes and within easy walking distance of the town for nightlife and dining.

Dining

All visitors here should have their fill of the Bavarian experience. Garmisch is full of great old Bavarian restaurants where lederhosen is part of the uniforms; beer runs freely and *schweinhaxen mit knodln* is the meal of choice. Here is a rundown on the best of the middle-of-the-road Bavarian spots. The first two restaurants have live Bavarian music and dancing.

Fraundorfer, Ludwigstr. 24, Partenkirchen (2176 or 9270). Closed Tuesday.
Werdenfelser Hof, Ludwigstr. 58, Partenkirchen (3621). Closed Monday.
Braüstüberl, Fürstenstr. 23, Garmisch (2312).
Zum Schatten, Sonnenbergstr. 10, Partenkirchen (2432). Closed Wednesday.

Telephone prefix for Garmisch-Partenkirchen: 08821
Telephone prefix for Germany: 0049

Zum Rassen, Ludwigstr. 45, Partenkirchen (2089). Closed Monday.

Drei Mohren, Ludwigstr. 65, Partenkirchen (9130).

For slightly more upscale and expensive Bavarian restaurants try **Husar** at Fürstenstr. 25 (1713) and **Clausings Posthotel** (7090) at Marienplatz 12 in Garmisch, the **Post Hotel Partenkirchen** (93630) or the **Reindl Grill Restaurant** (58025) in the Partenkirchnerhof in Partenkirchen on Ludwigstrasse.

You can eat less expensively, surrounded by an international group at the **Chapeau Claque** bistro, Mohrenplatz 10, (71300) for a French flavor. **Grand-Café**, Klammstr. 14, (79699) serves cuisine with an Asian flare and has vegetarian menus and a quaint bar. **Café Max**, Griesstr. 10, (2535) cooks excellent German meals as well as international dishes. **Mukkefuck Bistro**, Zugspitzstr. 3, (73440) serves wonderful salads, sandwiches on bagettes and good pasta. **Kurpark-Pavillion**, Am Kurpark 2, (3179) serves excellent German fare in a modern setting on the top shopping street.

Italian food is a mainstay in Germany and Garmisch has good spots to enjoy it. **La Baita**, Zugspitzstr. 16, (78777) has good pizzas and pastas. **Colosseo**, Klammstr. 7, (52809) upstairs above the Spar Supermarket, has excellent Italian meals. **Da Elia**, Sonnenstr. 3, (73740) serves creative Italian and French bistro foods. **Da Roberto**, Griesstr. 12, (2829) is a cozy Italian restaurant where you get great value. **Bruno's Pizza Flizza**, (1209) has affordable food mixed with great music during the Friday night jam sessions, plus they deliver to the hotels. The **Rose'n Crown** at Zugspitzstr. 70 (51282) has a British pub flavor with good pub grub. **Cerveceria** on Von-Brug-Str. 18 (912668) serves tapas, Argentinian steaks and fancy cocktails.

Another **Hotel Post** (08825-211) in Wallgau, about 12 miles from Garmisch is worth the trip for the meals amidst traditional Alpine decor.

Après-ski/nightlife

Garmisch-Partenkirchen rocks when it comes to après-ski. Naturally you are in Bavaria, home of great beer and of knee slapping oom-pah-pah fun. For a basic Bavarian floor show try dinner at **Fraundorfer** in Partenkirchen (2176), or head to **Werdenfelser Hof** (3621), both on Ludwigstrasse in Partenkirchen.

Somewhat elegant après-ski can be found in the big hotels such as the Partenkirchner Hof at **Enoteca - Michel's Weinbar** (58025) and **Tenne**, the **Post-Taverna** (51067) in the Posthotel Partenkirchen, the **Mühlradl** (7040) in the Obermühle Hotel or **Post-Hörndl** (709126) in Clausing's Posthotel.

Otherwise, après-ski means a trip to the **Irish Pub** at the corner of the Hauptstrasse and Bahnhofstrasse (78798) with a great international crowd and plenty of suds and singing. For a late-night spot to party with a good bar crowd and live music, duck into the **Zirbelstub'n** at Promenade 2 (71671).

Late night disco action pulses at **Exit** (4710) at Chamonixstr. 1a and **Evergreen** (55098) at Klammstr. 47 by the swimming pool.

Child care (2003/04 prices)

Larger hotels provide day care services. In addition, check with the tourist office for a listing of babysitters in the area.

Ski kindergarten and ski courses for youths are available. For the kindergarten call 797851 and for the ski school call 4600 or 58300.

Ski school for children 4 and older costs €30 for three hours of lessons. Five days of lessons (three hours a day) costs €95.

Children's lunch with these programs costs €3.10 per day.

Other activities

The resort has an excellent **swimming pool**, the Alpspitz-Wellenbad (753313), with a wave machine, diving platforms up to 15 feet, kids pool, baby pool, solariums, saunas and hot tubs. The pool is open from 9 a.m. to 9 p.m. on weekdays and closes at 7 p.m. on weekends. Entrance is included for one day with your visitor's card then it will cost around €3.60 (more on Sunday) for three hours or €4.60 for an unlimited admission. Kids pay €2.10 (€2.30 on Sunday) for three hours or €2.80 (€3 on Sunday) for unlimited stays. There are reductions for 10-day tickets and families. Saunas cost €5.20 alone or €7.20 when combined with swimming.

The ice stadium offers **ice skating** during the season. Two hours of skating costs €2.6 and rentals cost €3. Call 753291 for information.

Within an hour's drive are world-famous attractions. Chief among them is **Munich**, the Bavarian capital. Above all, visit the **Deutsches Museum**, the German technical museum that rivals the Smithsonian. Central Munich, around the Marienplatz, should be included on any tour. Best view of the city is from the 1,000-foot television tower on the Olympic grounds.

Garmisch-Partenkirchen also has an excellent English-language **movie theater** that shows first-run films. Kinocenter Garmisch & Aspen-Theater im Lamm is on Marienplatz. Call 2470 for the current movie schedule. Normal entrance charges are €7.70, but many hotels and bars offer discount coupons and Mondays and Tuesdays have discounted shows.

Oberammergau, site of the famed Passion Play, is about a half-hour away by bus or car. Visit dozens of **woodcarving shops** displaying the work of artisans, many of them trained in Oberammergau's woodcarving school.

Along the road to Oberammergau, take a trip up the Graswang valley to Schloss **Linderhof**, the ornate palace built by Ludwig II, the Mad King of Bavaria. Also consider a full-day trip to **Neuschwanstein**, the most famous of Ludwig's castles (near Füssen) and to Berchtesgaden.

Getting there

Munich's Airport II is only an hour and a half away by car on the autobahn. Get there early if you are departing from this airport—it's massive. Innsbruck is about an hour's drive. Rail travelers will find connections to Garmisch from Munich excellent.

Tourist information

Tourist Information, Richard-Strauss-Platz 2, D-82467 Garmisch-Partenkirchen, Germany; (08821-700; fax 180755).
E-Mail: tourist-info@garmisch-partenkirchen.de
Internet: www.garmisch-partenkirchen.de

Telephone prefix for Garmisch-Partenkirchen: 08821
Telephone prefix for Germany: 0049

Italy

Italy, geographically, has more of the Alps than any other country. Mont Blanc, the highest mountain in Europe, straddles the French-Italian border, and the Matterhorn is right on the Swiss-Italian border.

Italy also has the entire Dolomite range, which many consider the world's most spectacular mountains. Italian ski areas here are world class, and the skiing is augmented by the Italian love of life and matchless cuisine and wines. If the weather changes, there is always a beautiful city such as Milan, Turin, Verona or Venice just a few hours away from the slopes.

This border region of Italy has distinct influences from both the French and the Germans. The cooking in the northwest has distinct French overtones and the wines of Piemonte are more like beefy French reds than the lighter Italian wines. In the far northeast, the Italian and German languages share the limelight—both are spoken with ease. The cuisine is a pleasant mixture of German and Italian taste as well. Here, the locals work with German efficiency and live life with Italian enthusiasm.

This is a land where the people go out to enjoy life as much as they can in the mountains. No one seems to take skiing seriously, even the Italian Olympic and World Cup champions. Relax. Enjoy long, long lunches. Or, if you aren't into massive midday meals, use the time to ski—the slopes empty between 1 and 3 p.m. Once you get into the Italian swing of skiing, you will have the time of your life. Remember, you can always squeeze that next run in tomorrow, or next year for that matter.

When are the seasons?

Some Italian resorts have adopted a rather complicated series of mini-seasons. Basically, the high and low seasons remain, but are sometimes separated by in-between seasons. If you follow these season breakouts for planning you will not go too far wrong:

High season: Christmas and New Year holidays, and all of February and March to mid-April.

Low season: January after New Year holidays.

Pre-season: 6 December to Christmas.

Cervinia

Walt Disney's film "Three Men on the Mountain," about the dangerous climb of the Matterhorn, had an image of grandeur that characterizes the best of the Alps. It, along with many works in all media, added to the mystique of the Matterhorn and Zermatt, but there is another side to the mountain—the Italian side. Cervinia, Zermatt's Italian opposite number, is the prototype purpose-built resort in Europe.

Despite being ravaged by architects and developers in infancy, Cervinia manages to delight skiers year after year. The wide-open slopes, the reliable snow and the chance to ski Zermatt on the cheap bring Germans, British and Americans who zip across the slopes during the week until the weekend hordes from Milan and Turin arrive for their days in the snow.

One other important point to note—the dramatic improvement of lifts from the village to Testa Grigia. Once some of the worst lifts in Europe, the old cable cars have been replaced by sleek six- and twelve-person gondolas and a 140-person cable car.

Mountain Layout

To the Italians the Matterhorn is *Il Cervino*, and the village at the base of the Italian side of the mountain is called Cervinia. Cervinia has hotel and lift prices about 30 percent lower. Its lift system has been connected with Val Tournenche, a nearby village, to provide more than 100 km. of prepared ski runs with an extensive lift system. The longest run covers more than 20 km.—from Plateau Rosa to Val Tournenche—with a vertical drop of nearly 5,000 feet.

Skiing here is wide open and virtually all intermediate. The descent to Zermatt starts from Plateau Rosa. Special lift tickets for use on the Swiss side should be purchased before you go up the mountain; otherwise, expect to pay double for the lifts back up the Swiss side. The Zermatt side has much steeper terrain and narrower trails. An expert can have a field day on the Swiss side, while the beginner and intermediate can find enough easy runs to make the trip enjoyable.

In Cervinia experts can drop from Plateau Rosa, or try out the lifts above the Cristallo Hotel. Cervinia is paradise for beginner and lower intermediate skiers—the gentle, wide-open snow fields above Plan Maison build confidence.

Snowboarders are allowed everywhere, and there's also a snowpark in the Plan Maison area which has jumps, a halfpipe, slalom runs and a few boarder-cross runs.

Mountain rating

The Cervinia/Valtournenche slopes support beginner and intermediate skills. Wide open and excellent for practice, they offer a number of challenging steeps.

Expert skiers can enjoy several great days of cruising the wide slopes, but may also become bored. However, should a group of experts invest in the services of a ski instructor, they'll find the most challenging slopes Cervinia has to offer. Experts will also have a great time on the Zermatt side, and this is part of the allure of Cervinia as a resort: it lets you take advantage of the savings made possible by staying in Italy and skiing the wilder-and-woolier Swiss side.

Ski school (2003/04 prices)

There are three excellent ski schools in Cervinia – Scuola Di Sci Del Brueil (phone/fax 0166-940960); Scuola Di Sci Del Cervino (0166-949034, fax 0166-949885); and Scuola Di Sci Nuova Cielo Alto (0166-948451, fax 0166-949990). Make arrangements at any hotel reception desk, or visit one of the schools. Ask for an English-speaking instructor.

The main ski school, and most convenient for most, is the Scuola di Sci del Cervino. Its prices follow.

Private lessons cost approximately €30 an hour for one; €36 for two persons; €41 an hour for three, and €46 for four.

Group lessons (three hours a day of instruction with about five to nine skiers per group). One day, €40; three days, €100; six days, €155.

Lessons are available for cross-country, racing (six-day course), off-piste skiing and summer skiing. Groups require a minimum of five participants.

Lift tickets (2003/04 prices)

Prices are for the Cervinia/Valtournenche area only covering 31 lifts:

one day	€30	six days	€163
three days	€87	seven days	€181

The supplement added to the Cervinia ski pass to ski in Zermatt costs €21.

A **combination Cervinia/Zermatt ski pass** is available for all lifts in Zermatt and Cervinia or limited for only the Matterhorn lifts and Cervinia lifts.

six days (all lifts)	€198
seven days (all lifts)	€218

Our recommendation is to stick with the Cervinia pass and then purchase the supplement whenever you want to head to Switzerland unless you are here for a week.

Accommodations

All rates are based on high season double occupancy, with half board. €€€—€125+; €€—€75–€125; €—€74-.

Hermitage (0166-948998, fax 0166-949032; €€€+) This beautiful hotel is the best choice in Cervinia. Everyone who stays here loves it.

Bucaneve (0166-949119, fax 0166-948308; €€€+) Center-of-town location with a woodsy elegance. In the evening a piano player entertains.

Punta Maquignaz (0166-949145, fax 0166-948055; €€) This hotel has a spectacular lobby with a massive stone archway and unfinished wide wood floors. Elegant touches of wood are everywhere except in the rooms which are quite modern.

Europa (0166-948660, fax 0166-949650; €€) In the center of town, just a few minutes' walk from the lifts. Clean and modern with parking.

Breithorn (0166-949042, fax 0166-948363; €) Furnished in knotty pine, this hotel is about 200 yards from the lifts and has one of the better restaurants in town.

Excelsior Planet (0166-949426, fax 0166-948827; €€) This hotel is modern and convenient to the slopes. It has a tiny swimming pool as well as steamroom and sauna.

Fosson (0166-949125, fax 0166-949720; €€) This family-run hotel also has a small steamroom, sauna and fitness room.

Mignon (0166-949344, fax 0166-949687; €€–€€€) Very small and cozy, just minutes from the lifts. The casual family atmosphere is hard to beat.

Lyskamm (0166-949074; fax 0166-948692; €–€€) This small hotel is as close as one can get to the base of the Cretaz lift, one of the two main access lifts.

Fürggen (0166-948928, fax 0166-948929; €–€€) Bed & Breakfast only. On the slopes above the town, this is the place you want if you want to ski out your front door; however, slope access makes it a bit inconvenient to the town.

Perruquet (0166-949043; fax 0166-940014; €) Bed & Breakfast only. In town center; clean and roomy.

Apartments

Cervina's stock of apartments is somewhat limited but often offer bargains. The rental agencies in town are Il Cervino, tel/fax 0166-949510; La Maison de Vacances, tel/fax 0166-948267; Nuova San Grato, 0166-949442, fax 0166-949644; and Valtour Casa, 0166-949242, fax 0166-949732.

Dining

One of Cervinia's best restaurant is the **Hotel Hermitage** (0166-948998). It is head and shoulders above the rest of the pack when it comes to fine cuisine. But let's face it, most of us would rather have a good typical meal in a traditional setting in the mountains. Here Cervinia has plenty to offer.

Maison de Saussure (0166-948259) gets rave reviews from the critics and even locals have to make advanced reservations to get a seat for a cozy traditional mountain meal. It only seats about 30 people, so, call before you get here.

After asking locals, several restaurants seemed to be mentioned time and again. We'll start with three which are on the slopes but reachable with a van or jeep if you call ahead—**Baita Cretaz** (0166-949914), **Les Clochards** (0166-948273) and **La Bricole** (0166-948274. **La Nicchia** (0166-949842) serves good local specialties along with a larger menu in a much more modern and elegant atmosphere.

Try *bagna cauda*, vegetables covered with an anchovy sauce; *tomino*, a delicate riccota, normally covered with parsley or peppers; *bresaola*, smoked ham from the mountain regions; *lardo d'Arnaz*, a fatty bacon that has been cured in a secret mountain concoction.

We were also told that **Le Blason - Da Mario** (0166-940039) and Hotel Maquignaz's **Ymeletrob Restaurant** (0166-949145) serve excellent meals. Just off the slopes next to the Cielo Alto chairlift, **Casse Croute** (0166-948783) provides good basic fare either for a slopeside lunch or a dinner later in the evening.

Many of the hotels such as **Hotel Fosson**, **Mignon**, **Breithorn**, **Bucaneve**, and **Excelsior Planet** are open to the public and have excellent kitchens.

Other recommended inexpensive eateries are **Grivola** (0166-948287), **Matterhorn** (0166-948518), **Pavia** (0166-949010) and **Copa Pan** (0166.949140). These were recommended by plenty of tourists and several British tour guides for good cheap fare and lots of it.

On the slopes, everyone seems to agree that **Etoile** (0335-7069685) is the place to have lunch. They serve a full meal in a rustic mountain atmosphere.

Après-ski/nightlife

Cervinia does not have a lot to choose from; however, there is growing English-speaking clientele at the few spots in town.

The town has two discos—**The Etoile,** which attracts an older group, and the **Garage**.

The four most popular bars are the **Yeti** and the **Dragon Pub,** just across from the slopes, and **Pub Grivola** and the **Ymeletrob Bar,** across the street from each other. You'll find plenty of English-speakers, be they from the England, Scotland, Wales, Ireland, Sweden or the Netherlands. All bars have good happy hours and all are within five minutes' walk of each other.

For a more elegant and quiet après-ski try the **Samovar Tea Room** for drinks, tea and pastries. Head to **Le Bistrot de L'Abbé**, a rustic winebar only a few steps away in the Hotel Meynet. Or try a drink in **the Lyskamm Bar**.

Child care

Babysitting services and special ski classes for children are available. Contact your hotel for more information.

Getting there

You can drive here easily from either Geneva or Milan airport. From Geneva come through the Mont Blanc tunnel (when it is open). The resort can also be reached from Geneva via the Great St. Bernard Tunnel. From Milan and Turin, take the autostrada; the Cervinia exit is only 27 km. from the resort.

Buses make the trip between Aosta and Milan three times a day with a change in Chatillon. It is not a simple trip.

Other activities

An Olympic-size pool in the Club Med is open to the public. Cervinia has an ice-skating rink and bowling alleys. Day trips can easily be made to Geneva, Lausanne, Milan or Turin.

The ski trip over the Alps to Zermatt is a must-do side trip.

Heliskiing and Ski-Doos are available. Call 0166.949267.

On January 30 and 31 every year, the Feast of Sant'Orso, one of the largest craft fairs in Italy, takes place in Aosta. Fantastic wood carvings and other crafts can be purchased at great savings.

During *Carnevale* the town of Ivrea is one of the wildest places in Italy. Costumed residents and a "Battle of the Oranges," in which a castle defended by bad guys is besieged by good guys hurling more than a ton of oranges, makes for pre-Lenten fun.

Tourist information

In Cervinia: Via J.A. Carrel, 11021 Cervinia, Italy. 0166.949136; fax 0166.949731.
In Valtournenche: Via Roma, 11028 Valtournenche, Italy. 0166.92029; fax 0166.92430.
E-mail:breuil-cervina@montecervino.it
or valtournenche@montecervino.it
Internet: www.montcervino.it

Courmayeur

At the Italian end of the Mont Blanc tunnel, Courmayeur enjoys a phenomenal resort location. Mont Blanc, the highest mountain in Europe, guarantees snow; the Alps here are among the most spectacular in the range; and Courmayeur lies at the junction of Switzerland, France and Italy. If a skier tires of skiing the Courmayeur slopes, Cervinia and La Thuile in Italy are within striking distance; Chamonix in France and Verbier in Switzerland can also be reached for a full day of skiing.

Courmayeur is a small picturesque Italian village with the ski area across the valley. The village provides a cozy atmosphere with a warren of narrow cobblestone streets, small bars and fabulous restaurants. For skiing, the slopes are reached by cable cars stretching across the valley, and the short return to town is by bus. During the past three years the resort has invested heavily in snowmaking to ensure good snow conditions on the Val Veny side of the resort. But, its star quality is found in the restaurants, where Italians seem to spend far more time than on the slopes.

Mountain layout

The major ski area is on the opposite side of the valley from Mont Blanc, with half centered around the Plan Checrouit and the other half dropping down to the Val Veny. The Plan Checrouit is a transfer point for the cable cars from the town to the lifts servicing the major ski areas. This ski area is split by a ridge. One side offers a northeast exposure and the other a northwest exposure. After stepping off the cable car there is about a 100-yard walk to the three main lifts that take skiers to the upper slopes. Most skiers will want to head directly to the gondola and go to Col Checrouit. From there another smaller cable car heads to the Cresta Youla. The skiing from Cresta Youla at almost 8,700 feet is excellent, but the wait for the cable car can take more than half an hour even on relatively good days.

The highest lift arrives at Cresta Arp at 8,954 feet. However, the skiing from that point is for experts only, and only with the assistance of guides. The highest skiable point for the run-of-the-mill skier is the Cresta Youla. From here you can ski a good, tough, intermediate trail that ends up at the base of the cable car. Skiers can then either drop down a long cruising run to the base of the Plan de la Gabba chair lift at about 6,800 feet, or drop down narrower steeper terrain and several cat tracks to Zerotta at about 5,000 feet. Either run will allow you to ski greater vertical than 90 percent of the resorts in North America.

Much of the skiing on the Val Veny side of the ridge is through trees. The drops off the ridge line are relatively steep. Unfortunately, skiers will have to return to town via this cable car or by a short bus ride from the base of the Val Veny lifts. It's a hassle.

Off-piste adventures include skiing around the back of the Cresta d'Arp and dropping down a wide open bowl then winding through the Val Veny; or skiers can traverse from Cresta d'Arp to Dolonne or Pré-St-Didier. Or those with a guide and return transportation can strike out down to La Balme and end up near La Thuile.

Otherwise expect to have a bland intermediate and beginner playground. Real beginners will be a bit cramped with limited facilities at Plan Checrouit. They may be happier at one of the other baby slopes in Val Veny or below at Dolonne.

The second major skiing area at Courmayeur is Mont Blanc itself. Here a cable car carries skiers in three stages to almost 11,000 feet where they can ski back down toward Courmayeur, over the mountain to Chamonix or take some time skiing on the glacier accompanied by a guide.

Mountain rating

If you are an absolute beginner this is probably a mountain you should avoid. Although there are some beginner areas, the terrain is steep enough to take the fun out of skiing if you are over your head. For the intermediate this is heaven. There are plenty of semi-steeps to make the intermediate feel like an expert and enough moguls to keep his head from swelling. The expert can find some challenging slopes off-piste. The ski instructors can take experts down slopes that will keep them coming back for more. Even the marked trails are good enough for a good day of cruising.

Lift tickets (2003/04 prices)

These are the regular season prices for the Courmayeur Mont Blanc pass. There is approximately a 10% discount for skiing in early or late season. Also passes valid for three days or more can be used to ski either in the Aosta Valley, Flaine or Chamonix. Call the tourist office for more information.

	Adults	**Seniors (65 and older)/ children (9–12)**	**Children (8 and younger)**
one day	€34	**	**
three days	€93.50	€70	€46.75
six days	€175	€131	€87.50
fourteen days	€330	€248	€185

Ski school (2002/03 prices)

The ski school of Mont Blanc has over 100 instructors. Many speak English—be sure to ask for one who does. Lessons are given every day. These are high-season prices.

Private lessons for one or two costs about €31 per hour and €5.50 for each additional person. A ski instructor for an entire day costs €197–€234.50 and €25 per additional person.

Group ski lessons (three hours a day of instruction with up to 10 skiers per group). Six days cost €137.

Group snowboard lessons (Monday to Friday from 1:30 p.m.–4:30 p.m.) cost €141.

Lessons are also available for cross-country, ski competition (six-day course), and off-piste skiing.

The ski school is on Strada Regionale, up the hill from the Chécrouit cable car.

Accommodations

The recommended hotels and apartments in Courmayeur are all close to the town center. €€€—€125+; €€—€75–€125; €—€74-.

If you are looking for the most luxurious, head to **Hotel Pavilion** (0165.846120, fax 0165.846122; €€€) one of the best in Courmayeur, with indoor pool, sauna, garage and TV. Only 100 yards to the lifts and ski school. **Hotel Gran Baita** (0165.844040, fax 0165.844805; €€€) has a heated pool. The **Royal and Golf** (0165.831611, fax 0165.842093; €€€) in the middle of town also has a heated swimming pool.

These hotels show up in tour operator brochures and are excellent. **Hotel Les Jumeaux** (0165.846796, fax 0165.844122; €€€) is a first-category hotel, brand new and closest to the lifts with sauna, TV and exercise room. **Hotel Palace Bron** (0165.846742, fax 0165.844015;€€€), **Hotel Cresta et Duc** (0165.842585, fax 0165.842591; €€), **Hotel Cristallo** (0165.846666, fax 0165.846327; €€), and **Hotel Lo Scoiattalo** (0165.846721, fax 0165.843785; €€) are all good. **Hotel Walser** (0165.844824; €€) is a good place for kids, but about a 10-minute uphill walk to the Via Roma après-ski and nightlife.

For B&Bs, try the **Bouton d'Or** (0165.846729; €€), **Croux** (0165.846735; €€) or **Vittoria** (0165.841494; €).

Apartments, condominiums, flats

This is a relatively new development for Courmayeur. There is one very basic group of apartments in town—**Bon Souvenir** (0165.8428800; fax 0165.841390).

In Pre-St. Didier, **Residence Universo** (0165.87066; fax 0165.87087) features several types of rooms, including a studio for two or three people and two-room apartments for up to five. All are equipped with TV and complete kitchen equipment. A free shuttlebus takes guests to the lifts. **Chécrouit** (0165.844477; fax 0165.844995) and **Etoile des Neiges** (0165.831800; fax 0165.831873) form a simple group of condos in the same town. In La Thuile head to **Planibel** (0165.884541; fax 0165.884535). This large apartment grouping sits at the base of its own ski area that connects to France.

Dining

This is a town dedicated to eating. On the slopes you can't go wrong at any one of 59 different restaurants. Even the self-service at Plan Checrouit is good, filling and cheap. The **Christiania** (0165.843572, fax 0165.846381) serves incredibly reasonable pizzas and pastas as well as full meals. The owner, originally from the island of Elba, prides himself on fish dishes. However they are only cooked to order—call ahead. **Maison Vieille** (337230979) has a wood-fired oven. **Chateau Branlant** (0165.846584, fax 0165.846363) is worth the dining experience if only for its tasty desserts. Dropping down into the Val Veny try to find **La Grolla** (0165.869095, fax 0165.869783) at Peindeint for a great (and expensive) meal. Or head to the base of the Zerotta lift and grab a bite at the **Petit Mont Blanc** (0165.869066).

Most of the hotel restaurants are good. If you want to get out and explore the local restaurants, follow the old rule: if it is crowded with locals, then it must be the place.

Try **Cadran Solaire**, a diner's delight, on the main street (tel./fax 0165.844609). **La Palud** (tel./fax 0165.89169) serves excellent fresh fish and **Pierre Alexis 1877** (tel./fax 0165.843517) on Via Marconi also has fine dining. Or try the very reasonable **Mont Fréty** (0165.841786, fax 0165.845095) at 21 Strada Regionale. One of the best spots in the middle of town for traditional Valdostana cuisine is the small and quaint **Leone Rosso** (0165.846726, fax 0165.847747). **Le Coquelicot** (0165.846789, fax 0165.845500) has a French owner and therefore French fare. **Pizzeria Tunnel** has great pizzas and is normally packed.

For a change of pace turn down the narrow alley, Via dei Giardini, skip a few steps from the American Bar and step into **Pan Per Focaccia**. Try a piece of focaccia created by Tony Saccardo. He is a kick and his focaccia is excellent as well.

Outside of town **La Maison de Filippo** (0165.889797, fax 0165.889705) in Entrèves, where for a fixed price (about €30) you are served some 40 courses. The stream of food seems never to end, with servings of antipasti, pasta, sausages, contorni, salads, various meats, and baskets of nuts and breads. It used to be exceptional, but has grown far too much over the past decade. Also in Entrèves is the top-rated Michelin restaurant, **La Brenva** (0165.869780, fax 0165.869726) that gets two forks and a reasonable menu accolade.

Chalet Proment Da Floriano (0165.897006, fax 0165.897900), known locally as simply Da Floriano, is an out-of-the-way, romantic and traditional spot next to the cross-country area La Val Ferret. The owner prides himself on his local specialties of *boudin*—blood sausage with beets, fontina cheese, marinated smoked pork and excellent wines. Across from Da Floriano is the **Miravalle** (0165.869777, fax 0165.869729) which receives rave reviews from many local chefs. It has a selection of more than 120 local wines. Val Ferret also has **La Clotze** (0165.869720, fax 0165.869785) restaurant that has been awarded two Michelin forks.

The local red wines are excellent. Try *Donnaz*—a strong heavy dry wine; and *Enfer d'Arvier*—lighter and fruitier. A good grappa or *genepy* finishes off the meal in Val d'Aosta style.

Après-ski/nightlife

Here Courmayeur shines. Après-ski is a long, drawn-out affair with several elegant bars. Start with the **Bar Roma** on the main street. Here in an old-world atmosphere enjoy mixed drinks, wine and beer with substantial snacks (put out from about 6:30 to 8:30 p.m.). A bit down the Via Roma is the **Café della Posta** that is just as full of old-world charm but with the addition of a massive fireplace surrounded by couches in the back room behind the bar. A newer spot, but just as crowded, is the **Cadran Solaire**, a wine bar in a cozy wine cellar atmosphere. The **American Bar** and the **Red Lion** face each other and are more traditional bars. In the American Bar push through the crowd at the bar and you will discover a hidden room with comfortable seats and a fireplace. Above the American Bar a new tapas bar, **Le Privé,** is run by Papo, a local, and Marta, from Barcelona. It is a cozier version of the **Café della Posta** with top-shelf drinks and tapas. Just beyond the church and under the Museo Alpino is the **Bar des Guides**—one half is *bierkeller-esque* with long tables and the other half has couches around a crackling fire.

The most popular discos are **The Jimmy Night Cafe**, **Poppy's Pub**, **Planet Disco Bar** and the bar in **I Maquis**.

Child care (2002/03 prices)

Hours for the children's program are 9 a.m.–6 p.m. and children as young as nine months are accepted. The hourly rate is €8; a half day costs €21; and a full day is €26. Lunch is extra. Call 0165.844036 for information.

The Ski School Monte Bianco runs the Kinderheim Runsby at the top of the cable car in Plan Checroui for ages six months and older. The children's ski school cost for one day is €34, for six consecutive days €130. Call 0165.842477 for more information.

At the sports center in the Plan des Lizzes area, the Baby Club Courmayeur offers a combination of day care, lunch and ski school for five days costing €232 and for six days at €259 (high-season prices). Call 349.7741417 or 348.7623811.

Other activities

Geneva, Milan and Turin offer excellent sightseeing and museums. The Val d'Aosta is spectacular in itself and features one of the best collections of castles in Italy, as well as excellent Roman ruins in Aosta, the capital city.

On January 30-31, the Feast of St. Orso is held in Aosta. It is one of the largest crafts fairs in Italy, with fantastic wood carvings and other handicrafts.

During *Carnevale*, the town of Ivrea is one of the wildest places to be in Italy. The residents are decked out in costumes reminiscent of "Star Wars." They participate in the Battle of the Oranges, which features a castle defended by the bad guys being assaulted by the good guys who hurl over a ton of oranges during the siege.

A sports center (0165.844096) is open from 10 a.m. to midnight daily with **tennis** and **squash courts**, **ice skating**, **fitness club**, **curling**, **indoor golf** and a **climbing wall**.

Other activities in Courmayeur include **snowbiking**, **dogsledding**, **paragliding**, **snowshoeing**, **heliskiing** and **heliboarding**.

The valley also boasts a **casino** in St. Vincent. Milan, in addition to its sights, features La Scala, the largest opera house in Italy and one of the greatest opera companies in the world.

Getting there

The closest airports are Geneva and Milan. Both are within a two-hour drive. Train and bus services connect Milan and Turin with Courmayeur. Car rentals are available at both airports.

Tourist information

For any additional information, contact: Tourist Office (Azienda Informazione e Accoglienza Turistica Monte Bianco) Piazzale Monte Bianco #13, 11013 Courmayeur, Italy; 0165.842060; fax 0165.842072;
Email: aiat.montebianco@psw.it.

Cortina d'Ampezzo

Since hosting the 1956 Winter Olympics, Cortina's wide, sunny valley in the eastern Dolomites has been one of the world's top ritzy ski resorts, attracting celebrities of all types.

The town's picturesque square is framed by two massive mountain ridges: to the east lies the connected area formed by Cristallo (9,613 feet) and Faloria (7,690 feet); to the west, Tofana (9,317 feet) and Pocol and Socrepes (7,487 feet) form another connected area, accessible from the town. Further to the west, approaching the Falzarego Pass (6,906 feet), the areas of Cinque Torri (8,438 feet) and Lagazuoi (9,009 feet) beckon the adventurous skier.

These areas are loosely connected by a system of inexpensive buses and taxis.

Mountain layout

Cortina has what amounts to eight semiconnected ski areas. All eight areas are connected by ski bus. However, the Faloria and Cristallo as well as the Cinque Torre and Passo Giau areas are also interconnected by lifts. The main Cortina area Pocol-Tofana rises to the west of the town to Tofane at its highest point stretching to Pocol on the far left as you look up the mountains. This is the best area for intermediates and those graduating from beginner. Eighteen lifts that include three spectacular cable cars lace the area providing excellent capacity with few lines. The entire area between Duca d'Aosta and Pocol is excellent for any intermediate and most beginners. The higher area just under Tofane is more difficult and the connecting run down from Tofane to Duca d'Aosta is a tough expert run that can be made by most intermediates with plenty of traversing.

Faloria and Cristallo are linked at the Tre Croci pass. Skiers either take the bus to Tre Croci and then ski from there or they can ride from town to Faloria on the cable car. Many skiers come here and ski the Cristallo area in the morning. During the midwinter it gets earlier sun. Then for lunch they head up to Faloria from Tre Croci. The best restaurant there for an elegant lunch is Capanna Tondi or skiers can drop down to the lower self-service at Faloria. After lunch, ski Faloria's handful of intermediate trails through the trees. Take the long run back into Cortina or glide down on the cable car at the end of the day.

The Falzarego, Cinque Torri, and Passo Giau are about a 15 km. drive out of downtown Cortina. They will take care of plenty of skiing for a day. Cinque Torri has a new quad chair that opens up a good skiing bowl as well as two or three good trails to the base area. From the top of the quad chair at Cinque Torri a snowcat pulls skiers to the small rifugio which sits at the top of the Averau. *(Rifugi*—or rifugio, singular—are mountain huts found on the slopes, where skiers can find shelter and taste a few good typical dishes. Some of them are real mountain restaurants, but most of them still have the feeling of cozy mountain retreats. Rifugi are very popular places for après-ski, and some even provide lodging.) Skiers can drop down open slopes from the Averau (off the trail map) and take a double chairlift back to the top of Cinque Torri.

Just up the road from the Cinque Torri base area is the incredibly spectacular Falzarego-Lagazuoi cable car. This lift takes skiers to the top of a cliff where solid intermediate trails lead back to the parking lot, or where skiers can ski down toward the Val Badia. The run off the back of the Lagazuoi, dropping in the direction of Armentarola, is basically a beginner/intermediate rolling trail but the views must be seen to be believed. Plus, the first highlight of this run is a stop for lunch (plan for it) at the Rifugio Scotoni halfway down the run. This rifugio is known for its excellent grilled meats. You can also order simple pastas, soups and raclette then enjoy them on the deck if the weather permits. After lunch continue down toward Armentarola. You'll pass the Capanna Alpina, but don't stop there. Keep going for the second big adventure on this run—being pulled by horses along the runout to Armentarola. This is more fun than a ride at Disneyland. About two dozen skiers hold onto a long rope trailing behind a team of two or three horses, then the horses begin to pull the skiers along the trail. Many might be expecting the trip to be slow and uneventful; the team drivers have a different idea. They whip the horses into a run with this snake of skiers whooping and screaming behind them. This is an experience that is hard to find anywhere else in the skiing world. In the USA no area would do this for fear of being sued. From the base at Armentarola taxis wait to take skiers back to the Falzarego pass. There will be a charge for the taxi back up the pass of about €3.50 in a full taxi.

Whatever your choice, there is plenty of skiing.

Mountain rating

This area is an intermediate and advanced paradise. With the exception of a few slopes, it is probably a bit too challenging for most beginners, and it will push most intermediates.

The intermediate will find Tofana, Faloria and Cinque Torri enjoyable areas. Beginners should stick to the Pocol-Socrepes area and the lower lifts on Cristallo, as well as several at Faloria. Experts will enjoy shooting down the Lagazuoi. The cable car ride to the peak is a thrill in itself. Other good expert areas are the Tofana and the upper lift of the Cristallo section. The off-trail skiing is exhilarating, although it should be done with a good guide or instructor along to get the most out of your day.

Ski school (2003/04 prices)

Cortina has three main ski schools and there are courses for all skill levels. The ski school "Cortina" is at Piazza San Francesco, 2 (0436-2911 or 0436-3495), Scuola di Sci Azzurra at Ria de Zelo, 8 (0436-2694) and Ski School Cristallo-Cortina, (0436.870073). Ask for an instructor who speaks English.

Low season for lessons is early December, the January after the New Year holiday and late March. Prices are competitive. The prices that follow are current at both schools within a couple of Euros.

Private lessons cost €41 per hour in high season and €36 per hour in low season.

Group lessons are organized for six day classes. Lessons (9:30 a.m.–noon) cost €385 in high season and about €300 in low season. Six consecutive days of full day lessons cost €575–615 in high season and about €425 in low season.

Lift tickets (2003/04 prices)

Local area lift tickets can be purchased. However, the difference in price between these tickets and the Super Ski Dolomite pass is small (about 10 percent). The prices listed below are for the Super Ski Dolomite lift pass.

	Low Season	**High Season**
one day	€32	€37
two days	€63	€72
three days	€91	€103
six days	€160	€182
seven days	€170	€193
fourteen days	€292	€315

Note: Children and seniors get 11 to 30 percent discounts. Make sure you have proper identification and be sure to ask for the discount. Ski passes for eight days or more will require a photograph. Long lines are the norm for obtaining these passes on Saturday—it's quicker on Sunday afternoon and Monday morning.

Cortina-only passes cost €30 in low season and €34 in high season.

Accommodations

Cortina is a mature resort. The quality of room size and furnishings can be uneven: when checking in, check the room before accepting it. If you have a reservation, ask to see several rooms to choose from.

The hotels listed below are centrally located, offer good value, and have been visited by a *Ski Europe* representative. Based on half-board during high season per person based on double occupancy: €€€—€125+; €€—€75–€124; €—€74-.

Hotel Miramonti (0436-4201; fax 0436-867019; €€€) The most luxurious and elegant hotel in Cortina, a bit out of the center of the town. This hotel is a massive Old-World hotel left over from the days of understated elegance (not that understated). They have a beautiful pool, full fitness room and more lobbies than I could count. One can get lost in this place. The main drawback to the Miramonti is its distance from town. One of the joys of Cortina is having time to enjoy the beautiful town and its stores, restaurants and bars. Some tour groups offer rooms here for excellent rates, but for my money I'd stay in town.

Hotel Ancora (0436-3261; fax 0436-3265; €€€–€€) Our favorite hotel in Cortina is directly on the central square. This place now provides a cozy haven for those who demand pampered luxury. Normal clients are served half-pension meals in a beautiful arched dining room, but for those looking for true gourmet meals, the intimate **Petit Fleur** restaurant in the basement is hard to beat. Every motif of this beautiful hotel reflects its Alpine heritage from the intricate massive wooden ceiling that hangs overhead in the entranceway and the radiating ceramic stove to the pale blue paintings on the rooms' ceilings and the arched canopy of the Café Vienesse. This hotel is also one of the mainstays of the art scene in the region. You will probably have the opportunity to see an exhibition by one of Italy's top artists. According to top art organizers, Hotel Ancora supports the arts more than any other spot in Cortina. Staying at the Ancora is an experience you will savor long after your vacation. Make sure to meet the proprietress, Signora Flavia, who speaks good English and will make sure your stay is memorable.

Hotel Cortina (4221; fax 860760; €€–€€€) The lobby is big and plain, a step above a big cafeteria, but the location, smack in the middle of town, is hard to beat. Reports from tourists staying there indicated rooms were nothing special and ranged from sizeable to closets. The food reports for the half pension meals are mediocre.

Parc Hotel Vitoria (3246; fax 4734; €€€–€€), at the southern end of the walking street (Corso Italia), is a bit long in the tooth and could use some tender loving care, but the public areas, especially the wooden barrel-vaulted lobby filled with antiques is a joy. On the night we checked out this spot the music was playing and the clients were dancing up a storm. It can't be all bad.

Europa (3221; fax 868204; €€€–€€) Good basic hotel in the center of town.

Hotel de la Poste (4271; fax 868435; €€€) In the middle of town with great food.

San Marco (866941; fax 866940; €€) An absolutely beautiful hotel that was recently restored with fantastic woodwork. Don't let the inexpensive price fool you.

Hotel Aquila (2618; fax 867315; €€) Still family-run, is great value for money.

Hotel Italia (5646; fax: 5757; €) This two-star serves hugh portions of well-prepared food and it is right across the street from the Faloria cable car.

Hotel Impero (4246; fax 4248; €) B & B only; some rooms have kitchenettes.

Apartments, condominiums, flats

There are beds for 18,000 visitors and a special rental apartment list. Prices for rooms are €13 to €20 per person in low season, €20 to €28 per person in high season. For more information, contact the tourist office.

Dining

If you get a chance, don't miss a lunch high above Cortina at **Capanna Tondi** on Monte Faloria (0436-5775). They serve excellent full-service meals in a chalet setting at 7,677 feet with wide views of the town and surrounding mountains. Call for reservations, especially on weekends. The same family has been running this refuge for more than half a century. The current proprietess, Signora Rosie, is a striking blond bundle of energy who ensures every detail is handled perfectly. The dining room is built with wrought iron and wood brought from Austria, then carried up the mountain on mule back and assembled before anyone dreamed of a cable car lift. A full meal here with wine, starter, main course and dessert will run about €30–€35. The view is priceless.

Just below the Tondi is another less intimate, more modern mountain restaurant with self service as well as regular service. It is frequented by tour groups since it is right at the top of the Faloria lift from Cortina.

Another excellent mountain lunch accessible by virtually every skier is the **Rifugio Scotoni** on the Lagazuoi-Armentarola trail. Head there for excellent grilled meats, raclette and local specialties.

The following restaurants, recommended by several local residents, have excellent food. Expect to pay around €13–€15 in a pizzeria and up to €60 in the top restaurant, including house wine.

Tivoli, Lacedel 34; (0436-866400). Overlooking Cortina, and rated as one of the best in town with prizewinning, home-made *tortelli di patate*. Try the deer and other mountain specialties. This is the only Michelin-star restaurant in town. Call before coming to the resort for reservations. Closed Monday.

El Toulá, Ronco 123; (0436-3339). A once-upon-a-time hayloft converted to cozy restaurant boasts three Michelin forks (not quite a star). It is considered one of the most chi-chi restaurants in town. Hence, it is expensive, very expensive—this restaurant will push the €60 price if the meal has starter, first and second course and dessert with wine. Closed Monday.

The Petite Fleur (0436-3261) in the basement of Hotel Ancora has wonderful gourmet local Cortina fare (Cucina Ampezzana) in a small elegant room.

Lago Ghedina has a great setting on the lake and good food but you need a car to get there.

Da Beppe Sello (0436-3236) One of the best. Must have a car or take a taxi and it is expensive. Another two-fork Michelin spot.

Baita Fraina; Fraina, 1; (0436-3634). Hard to get to but very worth it. Michelin gives this place two forks. Closed Monday.

Lago Scin; At Lago Scin; (0436-2391) is another Michelin recommended restaurant with two forks. Closed Wednesday.

Siesta has simple homemade food (cucina casalinga) with medium prices.

Mezcal. Here you find Mexican food in the center of town at affordable prices where the food is served with Latin spirit. They dance on the tables until the wee hours.

Ristorante Amadeus, Verocai 73; (0436-867450) serves affordable meals with a fixed-price menu of €25 including house wine on Thursday and Friday evenings.

Ra Stua, Via Grohmann 2; (0436-868341). Great ambiance but mixed reviews for the food. Closed Wednesday.

El Zoco, Cadamai, 18; (0436-860041) gets good reviews. Closed Monday.

For pizza try **Croda Caffé,** Corso Italia, 163 (0436-866589, closed Tuesday); or **Cinque Torre,** Via Stazione, 3 (0436-866301 closed Thursday) **Da Pino** (very elegant pizzeria with prices pushing the levels one expects to pay for pizza).

Après-ski/nightlife

For all its jet-set reputation, Cortina is relatively quiet at night after the *passeggiata* (Italians, dressed to the hilt in furs and the latest styles) stroll to see and be seen.

An old wine bar, the **Enoteca**, is normally packed with merrymakers. Recently the Enoteca expanded with a new room where you can buy wine by the bottle together with cold cuts and cheese. The best part is still the narrow original bar room. Another later-night meeting point is the **Hyppo American Bar,** which fills up nightly with foreigners and ski school instructors. For elegant and quiet après-ski, head to **Terrezza Viennese**, attached to the Hotel Ancora. Here they serve rich Austrian pastries and coffee with a background of soft piano music. In the evening they offer crepes flambé. The Hotel Savoia has the **Ballads Piano Bar**. **Bar Arnika** (102 Corso Italia—down a passageway between 85 and 106) serves scores of pure Scotch Whisky Malts until around midnight. It is a good place for a restrained evening.

Hacker-Pschorr Hause, a Bavarian-style beer place, serves liters of beer for around €3.50 and has live electric oom-pah-pah music from about 10 p.m. onward. This spot fills up early. Closed Mondays.

Discos don't really start up until midnight. The disco at the Europa hotel, **VIP Club**, seems to be the main action place. **Metro Club** gets a pretty good group of Americans and Brits on tour groups. The **Limbo** and the **Bilbo Club** are discos that mainly cater to a young crowd earlier in the evening and an older group later on. These discos are erratic regarding clientele—it really depends on hitting them on the right night.

Child care

Child care in Cortina is not a school affair. There are scores of private babysitters and services available through the hotels or private homes where skiers stay. Child-care services are relatively inexpensive, and children seem to get more than their share of affection from the Italians who take care of them. The ski school also runs a children's ski course for those old enough to begin skiing.

Getting there

We suggest going by car. The nearest airport is Venice, about a two-hour drive. The closest train station is in Calalzo, with a regular bus service to Cortina. Trains from Innsbruck and Munich arrive at Dobbiaco, a 50-minute bus ride from Cortina. A daily bus service also connects Cortina with Venice and takes about four hours. Check with your travel agent, because there are some packages that include meeting incoming skiers at Milan and Venice airports, and busing them directly to Cortina.

Other activities

Regular tours to Venice and other towns are scheduled most days. There is also excellent ice skating, bobsledding, horseback riding in the snow, curling championships, World Cup ski races, ice hockey, indoor tennis, and more. The tourist office publishes a list of activities, and the local paper, *Il Notiziario di Cortina*, provides daily activity summaries in Italian.

Tourist information

The main office is located on Piazzetta S. Francesco 8, 32043 Cortina d'Ampezzo, Italy. A second, smaller information office is on Piazza Roma. Call 0436-3231 or 0436-2711; fax 0436-3235.

Madonna di Campiglio

One of the jewels of the Brenta Dolomites in Trentino is Madonna di Campiglio. This resort has become Italy's largest resort in terms of beds, runs and lifts.

The town has grown significantly. Whereas downtown Madonna was once where the hotels were concentrated, growth has given Madonna thousands of new rooms in the Palu section and above in the Campo Carlo Magno. These new hotels, especially those in the far reaches of Palu, are a bit of a walk from the lifts which remain centered around the original village. The hotels at Campo Carlo Magno have good lift service but are separated from downtown's shopping and nightlife.

The Brenta massif is typified by wild limestone rock formations and multicolored rocks that are as stark and beautiful during the winter as they are in the summer. These mountains, just like those in the sister Dolomites across the Adige River, have to be seen to be believed. They are truly castles and fortifications built by God. The Val di Genova is one of the most beautiful in the region and is only minutes from Madonna di Campiglio. When the road is open, a trip up to the 300-foot-high Nardis waterfalls is worth the effort.

The Campo Carlo Magno gets its name from a reported visit from Charlemagne while he was Holy Roman Emperor. Today it is part of the extended lift ticket area. The Great Rock (*Pietra Grande*) is impressive.

Mountain layout

One of the best parts of skiing here is that the majority of the folk come for nature and relaxation rather than for all-out skiing. Another plus—the town has aggressively built new lifts. This translates into very few places where skiers will have to wait at lifts. In fact, even when the town seems packed, the slopes can seem deserted with a few slow-lift exceptions.

This is also one of the best-groomed group of trails in Italy. Here the clientele demands pool-table smooth slopes that help them look beautiful when they slip down the trails. During our last visit, we were lucky enough to have about eight inches of snow in the early morning. This allowed us to have the resort almost to ourselves until the afternoon when most of the powder was skied off.

The skiing areas surround the town. For lift purposes it can be divided into four areas: 5 Laghi, Pradalago, Grosté and Spinale. Pradalago and Grosté are the easiest. Spinale and 5 Laghi have more challenging terrain. Little at Madonna will scare away any competent intermediate.

The most development over the past few years has been in the Pradalago region of the resort where wide cruising trails predominate. This sector is now served by a gondola from town and a new quad lift rising from Fortini, near Campo Carlo Magno.

As always, one way to approach a resort is to follow the sun. This means starting your day taking the 5 Laghi cablecar (if the resort is crowded this cablecar can be a bottleneck—it only carries 465 skiers an hour) or take the Miramonte chairlift (also slow). Once up the mountain, a handful of intermediate and decent expert runs are served by a high-speed quad. They will provide a good start to the day and you will find any early morning sun. This area has about 1,600 feet of working vertical with great pitch. A looping intermediate run called Trampolino will take you over to the Pradalago section.

Pradalago has some good upper intermediate and advanced ungroomed terrain dropping down the the mountainside facing 5 Laghi. On the other side of the ridge a series of lifts yo-yos skiers to the connection point with Folgarida. A drop down the Pradalago Diretta then Zeledria brings skiers to the base of the Fortini chair or the new quad chair lift that brings them back to the top of the Pradalago section.

From Fortini, skiers and boarders can also head to the other side of the valley by taking the Grosté gondola that rises about 2,500 feet in two stages to the top of the Passo Grosté. Here, high above treeline, the mountaintop visuals are spectacular and skiing is easy. Six lifts keep skiers above treeline on the wide-open slopes. Snowboarders will enjoy the Ursus Snow Park in the Grosté Area. It has a halfpipe, quarterpipe and a boardercross area for boarders of all levels.

The drop into the village from this area is very flat along the Poza Vecia trail. To avoid lots of pushing, take the Boch chair lift then drop down the Nube D'Oro trail and then Fortini or Spinale Diretta to get back to town. The Spinale runs that are linked to Grosté by the Boch chair lift offer more challenge than Grosté. The expert Spinale Direttissima trail is the toughest in the area.

Most of the original village hotels are at the base of the slopes, making them convenient both for lunch breaks and quitting time.

Madonna di Campiglio is linked with two other smaller ski areas, Folgarida and Marilleva. The Folgarida and Marilleva areas add another 24 lifts and 60 km. of prepared slopes to the overall region..

The highest lift-accessible point is Groste at 8,235 feet.

Cross-country skiers will find this region enjoyable, if not convenient. Pinzolo is only about 20 minutes away, and the Campo Carlo Magno boasts one of the world's best expert cross-country courses with about 15 km. of prepared trails.

Madonna has most of its slopes covered with snowmaking.

Mountain rating

The area is good for beginners and intermediates. There is a lot of mountain perfectly suited for learning from top to bottom and intermediates will feel like experts with some challenge. Overall, let's call this ego-boosting terrain for everyone. While the 3 Tre, Amazzonia and Spinale runs will give experts some good exercise, the area deserves an overall rating of Mellow. Experts ski off trail (but the lift system doesn't really support off-trail skiing—you'll end up climbing a lot) or go ski mountaineering, but there really isn't enough expert or advanced skiing to make a trip worthwhile.

Ski school

Private lessons (per hour) are for one person, €36; for two, €44; for three skiers €54.

Check with your hotel for recommendations of the best English-speaking instructors. There are a total of 150 instructors.

Group lessons are two hours each day for six days for €120 for groups sizes up to eight persons maximum.

Children's lessons are given three hours each day for six days. Maximum of ten per group. Cost: €160.

Lift tickets (2003/04 prices)

The Madonna high-season lift pass prices follow. Low-season prices are approximately 10 percent less.

	Adults	Children/Seniors
one day	€33	€29
three days	€91	€72.50
six days	€157	€125
seven days	€170	€136.50

Note: Tickets longer than seven days require a photo. Children are those born after November 30, 1995 or those shorter than 150 cm. Seniors are those born before Nov. 30, 1938. High season is Christmas/New Year and about February 8–April 7.

The Super Skirama Pass includes skiing in Folgarida and Marilleva. It costs (high season/low season) €35/€32 a day, €177/€157 for six days, and €190/€168 for seven days. A tour pass is also available allowing limited use of Folgarida and Marilleva plus Pinzolo lifts for several days as well.

Accommodations

Madonna's hotels are for the most part modern. There probably is not a bad hotel in the bunch. Even the least aesthetic provide good-sized rooms and good food. This resort does not have the overflowing complement of restaurants that seem to be found in many resorts. Hence, taking half pension is a good idea and will save money.

Hotels listed here were visited by a *Ski Europe* representative. All rates are based on seven days, double occupancy, with half-board. €€€ indicates luxury hotel with low-season prices more than €600. €€ notes hotels with mid-season prices from €350 to €599. € indicated hotels and pensions with mid-season prices starting from less than €349. Mid-season is normally around January 25 to February 8 and the March 7 to March 21. High season is about 20 percent more expensive.

Only the first three hotels have swimming pools.

Relais Club Des Alpes (0465-440000; fax 0465-440186) €€€ Traditionally, the best hotel, built around the former hunting lodge of the Austrian emperors. But the size is large and the staff is limited, so those demanding perfect service may be less than satisfied. The 5 Laghi and Pradalago lifts are only a couple of minutes walk away.

Spinale Club Hotel (0465-441116; fax 0465-442189) €€€ This hotel is pushing Des Alpes in terms of tip-top service. It is smaller and more intimate than its competition. A ski lift takes skiers to the top of the Spinale area just out the back door.

Hotel C. Magno (0465-441010; fax 0465-440550) €€ This is out of the center of town, but provides luxury only a short walk from the lift system.

Hotel Golf (0465-441003; fax 0465-440294) €€€ Elegant hotel outside of the village center in Campo Carlo Magno, but with good access to the lifts.

The following hotels are in the original village center with the best lift access to 5 Laghi:

Majestic (0465-441080; fax 0465-443171) €€ A small intimate hotel, across from the 5 Laghi lift. The hotel is owned by a family that returned from living in the USA.

Savoia Palace Hotel (0465-441004; fax0465-440549) €€€ One of the originals in the town still providing good service in the right location.

Hotel Cristallo (0465-441132; fax 0465-440687) €€€ Overlooking the football-field sized ice-skating rink, only about two minutes from the 5 Laghi lift.

Hotel Milano (0465-441210; fax 0465-440631) €€ Very plain, nothing fancy, simple food, but a great location.

These hotels are in the original village center with the best access to the Pradalago gondola: **Bertelli** (0465-441013; fax 0465-440564; €€€); **Alpina** (0465-441075; fax 0465-443465; €€); **Ariston** (0465-441070; fax 0465-441103; €€); **Hotel Laura** (0465441246; fax 0465-441576; €€€) our favorite during our first visit a decade ago—now only better; **Bellavista** (0465-441034; fax 0465-440868; €€); **La Baita** (0465-441066; fax 0465-440750; €€); **Miramonti** (0465-441021; fax 440410; €€€)

The following hotels are in the original village center with the best lift access to the Spinale gondola: **Oberosler** (0465-441136; fax 0465-443220; €€€) where the lift is in its back yard and the old downtown is only two minutes away with the outdoor skating rink stretched out below the front. **Cerana** (0465-440552; fax 0465-440587; €€€), just a few yards uphill from the Spinale lift, is close to everything. **Grifone** (0465-442002; fax 0465-440540; €€€) with a light pine motif, is across the street from the Garni Palu.

Recommended bed & breakfasts: **Garni Palu** (0465-441695; fax 0465-443183; €€) is a cozy, warm and beautiful B&B about a five-minute walk to the nearest lift (Spinale). **St. Hubertus** (0465-441144; fax 0465-440056; €) is cozy, clean and right across from 5 Laghi lift. **La Montanara** (0465-441105; fax 0465-441105; €) is equidistant from the 5 Laghi (downhill) and Pradalago lifts (uphill). **Cristiania** (0465-441470; fax 0465-443310; €), **Arnica** (0465-442227; fax 0465-440377; €) and **Dello Sportivo** (0465-441101; fax 0465-440800; €) are all near the Pradalago gondola.

Alternative Lodging: Madonna also has a series of mountain refuges where skiers who want a head start can stay on the slopes. The largest is **Rifugio Graffer** (0465-441358) where seven days of half board in a bunk bed is less than €300—discounts apply for mountain club members from any club such as AMC. For instance, half pension for a day is approximately €45 or €40 for mountain club members. (If you come during the summer, the prices are about 15 percent less.)

One refuge which is treated as a hotel is **Dosson** (441507) which is very small with a week of half pension for about €300. The other refuge with beds is **Viviano Pradalago** (0465-441200).

Ski Chalets: Crystal (see page 20 for addresses, phone and fax).

Apartments, condominiums, flats

Apartments rent from Sunday to Sunday.

Residence Roch (0465-503900; fax 0465-503902) has apartments for three, four or five people. In low season, expect to pay approximately €200 a week per person; in high season, €300. The price includes daily maid service (except kitchen cleanup). Garage space rents for about €30. Both sauna and solarium are available.

Residence Perla (0465-446010; fax 0465-440879) is the most luxurious but at the far end of town.

Torre del Brenta (0465-441078; fax 0465-441078) is the newest construction right next to the Pradalago gondola.

The tourist board can provide additional listings of apartments in the town. There are five other flat rental agents in Madonna with two additional sets of apartments in Campo Carlo Magno. As always make your selection based on location.

Dining

Madonna di Campiglio isn't up to par with resorts such as Courmayeur and Cortina when it comes to on-mountain dining. The refugi serve good risotto and meat you can grill on hot rocks, but they don't have a gourmet flair. You can, however, have a very good meal at Malga Montagnoli with full service.

With that said, one of the best experiences at this resort is taking a snowcat ride for a dinner up on the mountain at **Malga Montagnoli** (0465-443355), **Boch** (0465-440465), **Malga Ritorto** (0465-442470) or **Cascina Zeledria** (0465-440303). The latter may serve the best food, but all are excellent and great fun.

Down in the town recommended restaurants are:

Da Alfiero (0465-440117) gets the nod as top dog in town from Michelin and has average prices of about €45. **Artini** (0465-440122) once was the top dog, but still holds a Michelin one-fork rating where you can expect to pay €40. Another of the top spots to try is **Al Sottobosco** (0465-440737) about a km. out of town where meals will set you back about €40. **Locanda degli Artisti** (0465-442980) has wonderful ambiance and affordable food with a fixed price menu for less than €15. Both **Belvedere** (0465-440396) and **Pappagallo** (0465-442717) also have good food. A very plain place but a good value for meals is **Ristorante al Sarca** (0465-440287) where the fixed-price menu is €15. **Lanterna d'Oro** (0465-442104) serves good basic local cooking. Two good pizzerias are **Le Roi** (0465-443075) and **Antoco Focolare** (0465-441686).

Après-ski/nightlife

This town is very Italian in terms of après-ski—eccentric and very late. It all starts with the scene at **Bar Suisse, La Cantina del Suisse** or **Franz Josef's Stube**. If you are in Campo Carlo Magno, head to **La Stalla**.

There are only three discos in the area. Crowds are mixed from the young to a more middle-aged clientele. The **Des Alpes** has a pricey disco, as well as a very cozy piano bar where you can nurse a drink for as long as you want. Evening cabarets are presented in the restored Hapsburg ballroom. The **Zangola** (which translates to butter churn) with male strippers and dancing babes all in a restored cow-bar atmosphere is legendary in Italy, but you need a car to get there.

Child care

There are children's ski classes. The ski school office has details. The nursery recently closed. Contact the tourist office for babysitter information or check with your hotel about child-care facilities.

Other activities

For **ice skating** call 0465-440503. Entrance is about €5 or €10 with rentals. They have lessons and discounts for Madonna hotel guests.

Once you are in Madonna, it is not an easy task to get out of the region—the drive to the autostrada is torturous at best. But if you insist on breaking away, you can get to Venice in about three-and-one-half hours. Verona, with its giant

Roman amphitheater and Romeo and Juliet balcony, is about two hours away. Vicenza with the wonderful Paladian villas is also about three hours away.

During the drive to Madonna, enjoy the multitude of castles that dot the Trentino countryside. The town of Trento has the Castello del Buon Consiglia (Castle of Good Counsel) that used to be home to prince-bishops. Today it is the Privincial Art Museum. The Cathedral towers over a cobbled square and the Via Belenzani is lined with Venetian-styled palaces.

During Carnevale just before Lent, Madonna di Campiglio hosts many costume balls and special events.

Getting there

By car: Madonna di Campiglio is two hours north of Verona. The closest airports are in Milan, Verona and Venice. All have rental car services. From Verona take the Trento exit and follow the signs for Madonna di Campiglio. From Milan take the Brescia exit and follow the signs for Lago Idro, Tione, and Campiglio.

The southern route from Trento or from Rovereto to Riva and then up to Madonna Via Pinzolo is the most visually dramatic. Another road leaves the autostrada just north of Trento at San Michele and goes north toward Cles through the Valle di Non and crosses one of the deepest gorges in Italy.

The Passo di Mendola to Bolzano is torturous at best.

By bus: A shuttle bus connects Madonna with the main airports in Verona and Milan once every Sunday. Round trip from Verona is €40. Round trip from Milan is €45. For booking and information call 0465-442000 or fax 0465-440404 or check with your hotel.

By train: Go to Trento and transfer to a bus (about 50 yards from the Trento station), which runs on a regular schedule.

Tourist information

The tourist information office, or *Azienda di Promozione Turistica*, in Madonna di Campiglio is located in the center of the resort in the Centro Rainalter. Its staff is well organized with information. Reservations at local hotels can be made through Campiglio Holiday Travel Agency (SNC), 1 Via Porta, Caderzone (TN), Italy; 0465-806053, fax 0465-806382.

Tourist Office, Centro Rainalter, 38084 Madonna di Campiglio (TN), Italy; 0465-442000, fax 0465-440404.
E-mail: info@campiglio.net
Internet: www.campiglio.net

Val Gardena

While a trip through the spectacular Italian Dolomite mountain range is worthwhile in itself, when combined with the experience of skiing one of the largest interconnected lift systems in the world, a vacation in the Dolomites rates as tops. The natural panoramas found in the Dolomites around virtually every bend in the roads and ski trails are hard to properly describe. And Val Gardena, with some of the best prices in Europe, is hard to beat.

The Ladin culture is centered in the five main Dolomite valleys, in eastern Switzerland and in Italy's far northeast. Val Gardena is a stronghold of the culture, and its residents speak Ladin, a Latin derivative, as their first language. They also speak German and Italian.

The people of this region have a Germanic passion for detail and hard work, so everything works perfectly; and they also have the Italian love of life, so they play as hard as anyone in the world enjoying great music and food. The cooking is a wonderful marriage of Italian creativity with pastas and wines and German meat and potatoes.

The Gardena valley has three main villages. The first and largest, coming from Bolzano, is Ortisei. The second is S. Cristina, and the third, just at the start of the Gardena Pass and Sella Pass is Selva Gardena. S. Cristina is spread out along the highway and does not have much of a town center in which to congregate after skiing, so book your accommodations in Ortisei or Selva Gardena if après-ski is a priority. Selva Gardena, smaller and closer to the other Dolomite slopes, has improved in terms of nightlife over the last few years. It's rumored to now have more après-ski than Ortisei which is further away from the interconnected ski areas. The atmosphere in the entire valley is more German than Italian, with a beer-hall flavor.

Whichever resort you choose you will have a great vacation and you will have the opportunity to move easily between the towns on the two-euro shuttle service which links Ortisei, Selva Gardena and S. Cristina.

Mountain layout

The interconnected Dolomite Superski lift system, with 464 lifts, reaches more than 1,180 km. of prepared slopes, and hundreds of kilometers of off-piste skiing through rocky crags and spectacular mountain scenery. Seceda, directly above Ortisei, is the highest elevation on the lift system in the Gardena region at 7,740 feet.

Perhaps the biggest draw for the region, besides the panoramic views, is the Sella Ronda, a 23-km. section of interconnected runs, allowing you to ski around the Sella mountain group. This full-day expedition involves visiting eight different ski areas. The runs are well marked and the Sella Ronda can be skied either clockwise or counterclockwise. Any reasonably competent skier can complete the basic circuit. Better skiers will find many opportunities for adventurous detours.

The major requirement for doing the entire Sella Ronda in one day is stamina. Intermediates should allow about 5-1/2 to 6-1/2 hours of skiing time, starting early enough to get back over the last passes before the lifts close from 4 p.m.–5 p.m. If you are planning to do the Sella Ronda, the best day according to locals is Saturday, when most vacationers are either leaving or arriving.

Cross-country skiers will find a paradise up on the Alpe di Siusi, one of Europe's highest Alpine meadows with an altitude ranging from 6,500 to 7,150 feet.

Mountain rating

Judged solely on the extensiveness of its skiing opportunities, this area might be considered one of the best. However, expert skiers will have to go off-piste for real excitement. While there are some hair-raising runs above Selva Gardena and S. Cristina, experts in search of off-trail action should hire the services of a good guide. Try the Langkofel or the Passo Pordoi at your own risk. If you decide to go without a guide, be sure to check in with the ski school for a word about your proposed route, snow conditions and avalanche warnings.

The intermediate and the beginner will find ample suitable terrain—when skiers tire of one area, they can just head over to another for variety. The Alpe di Siusi above Ortisei is a beginner's paradise.

Ski school (2003/04 prices)

The three ski schools, Ortisei Ski School (0471-796153), Ski and Snowboard School S. Cristina (0471-792045) and Ski School Selva Gardena (0471-795156), bring the number of instructors in the valley to almost 300. Prices are relatively uniform throughout the valley. These prices are average. Make sure to ask for an English-language instructor.

Private lessons (per hour) €29–€33.

Group lessons are €130–€160 for five full days.

Children's Ski School (4–12 years) for a full day including lunch is €30, and five full days with lunch costs €170.

Lift tickets (2003/04 prices)

Local area lift tickets can be purchased. However, the difference in price between these tickets and the Dolomite Super Ski pass is small (about 10 percent). The prices listed below are for the Dolomite Super Ski lift pass. Children younger than 8 ski free. High season is Christmas/New Year and February to mid-March. Low season is most of January and late March into April.

	Low Season	High Season
one day	€32	€37
three days	€91	€103
six days	€160	€182
fourteen days	€292	€332

Note: Children, age 16 and younger, and seniors, age 60 and older, get 20 percent discounts. Ski passes for eight days or more require a photograph. Long lines are the norm for obtaining these passes on Saturday—it's quicker on Sunday afternoon and Monday morning.

Accommodations

The following hotels and pensions come recommended by locals who have also traveled extensively in the United States. They are listed in descending order of luxury.

All rates are per-person based on double occupancy with half-board. €€€ indicates luxury hotel with high-season prices more than €125. €€ notes hotels with most high-season prices from €75–€124. € indicates hotels and pensions with high-season prices less than €75 per person for half-board.

In Ortisei: Head to **Adler** (0471-796203; €€€) one of the best, in the center of town; **Genziana-Enzian** (0471-796246; €€€); **Grien** (0471-796340; €€+); **Hell** (0471-796785; €€); **Cavallino Bianco** (0471-796392; €–€€), right in the middle of town; **La Perla** (0471-796421; €€), our favorite in the area—beautiful and a bit out of town, but there's bus service to the lifts and a pool; **Gardena** (0471-796315; €€); **Villa Luise** (0471-796498; €€) with 13 rooms, out-of-the-way with panoramic views; **Cosmea** (0471-796464; €); and **Stua Catores** (0471-796682; €), recently renovated and a bit out of the way, but with a very local flavor.

Far above Ortisei in the tiny dorf (village) of Bulla the 10-room **Uhrerhof-Deur** (0471-797335; €€) provides a quiet and affordable retreat with wonderful views above the town and a great kitchen open only to guests. **Sporthotel Platz** (0471-796982; €) is a great bargain also in Bulla with great views. This is a perfect spot for cross-country skiers and walkers.

In Selva Gardena: The best are **Hotel Tyrol** (0471-7741000; €€€), **Genziana** (0471-795187; €€€) with a great restaurant, or **Alpenroyal Sporthotel** (0471-795178, €€€). The next level is **Gran Baita** (0471-795210; €€) and **Chalet Portillo** (0471-795205; €€€). Then head to **Mignon** (0471-795092; €€) or **Laurin** (0471-795105; €€). The least expensive, but still Michelin-rated is the quiet **Pozzamanigoni** (0741-794138; €) is somewhat out of the way. All of these hotels are excellent—it just depends on the level of service you demand. For an inexpensive B&B try the **Eden** and **Somont**.

In S. Cristina: Try the **Diamant** (0471-796780; €€€), **Interski** (0471-793460; €€), **Sporthotel Maciaconi** (0471-793500; €€), or **Villa Martha** (0471-792088; €).

Ski Chalets: Inghams and Thompson (see page 20 for contacts).

Apartments, condominiums, flats

The tourist office has an extensive listing of vacation apartments that can be rented for a minimum of one week.

General descriptions included in its brochure indicate TV, garage, balcony, etc. The apartments all have fully furnished kitchens, but not all provide bedding, which may entail a small, extra cost. Weekly prices start with two beds from €200; four beds from €250; and six beds from €350.

Private rooms: A great chance to save money. Rooms rented in private homes include breakfast. Once again, the prices vary depending on the room. The price ranges for a room with bath (per person, per day) are: Low season €16–€20; High season €18–€30.

Dining

For an authentic Ladin meal, head off to the **Stua Catores** on Sacunstrasse 47 in Ortisei. The food is hearty and the atmosphere rustic and unpretentious. Don't be afraid to ask among the restaurant patrons for someone who speaks English and can help you with the menu selection. Another typical Ladin restaurant is **Stua Zirm** on Str. Stafan 123.

Some of our suggestions are *crafuncins*, a type of ravioli; *panicia*, a barley soup with a type of bacon; *jufa*, a puréed version of polenta; *patac cun craut*, potatoes and sauerkraut; *anes enzucredes*, pancakes with anise and sugar; *ribl da furmenton*, a buckwheat pancake; *bales da furmenton*, a buckwheat dumpling; and *crafons* for desert.

Other recommended Ortisei restaurants:

Concordia Romstr. 41, Ortisei (0471-796276) for ravioli in truffle sauce and game. This restaurant gets two forks from Michelin and is noted for affordable meals.

Waldrand Furdenanstr. 9, Ortisei (0471-796385) for game. Make reservations.

Hotel Adler Stuben Reziastr., Ortisei (0471-796203) is still serving traditional meals in an authentic 1600s Tyrolean restaurant.

Hotel Gardena Vidalongstr., Ortisei (0471-796315).

Mar Dolomit Str. Promeneda 2, Ortisei (0471-797352) has local and traditional Italian specialties with an open wood-fired pizza oven.

Mesavia (0471-796299) and **Vedl Mulin** (0471-796089) have an excellent mix of Germanic and Italian food and are reasonable.

In Selva Gardena try:

Hotel Tyrol Str. Poez 12 (0471-774100) has won prizes for its local fare.

Armins Grillstube Str. Mëisules 161 (0471-795347) has great lamb.

Des Alpes Stuben Str. Mëisules 157 (0471-795184) is somewhat upscale and has chateaubriand and fondues.

Gérard Str. Plan de Gralba 37 (0471-795274) has a Michelin fork and is noted for very affordable menus. The views of the Sassolungo are inspiring.

For fondue and cheese dishes try **Gardenia, Dorfer** or **Olympia**.

Sal Fëur (0471-794276) at Str. Puez 6 for pizza.

Bargain meals can be found at the self-service **Dopolavoro FF.SS** in Selva at 46 Plan (0471-795165).

In S. Cristina head to:

Uridl Str. Chamun 43 (0471-793215) for wine, soup, venison and pumpkin ravioli.

Plaza Str Cisles 5 (0471-793463) serves Tyrolean dishes and fine fresh trout.

For pizza try **Bruno**, **Da Peppi** and **Pizza Beppe**.

On the Sella Ronda try lunch at the **Sellajoch** right at the Sella pass.

Après-ski/nightlife

There is a collection of good bars with some local music, and several small discos crank up late at night. In Ortisei try the **L'Igloo** next to the ski school for immediate après-ski. **Purger's Pub** and **Siglu Bar in the Hotel Adler** often have an early crowd as well. Later head to the **Old England Pub, Mauriz** and **Cianél.**

In S. Cristina try **Crazy Pub,** which starts cranking about when the lifts close.

The Selva crowds can head to their version of the **Igloo**, to **Laurinkeller**, **Luislkeller** and the **Speckkeller**. Later bars are **La Bula** and **La Stua**.Yeti's **Umbrella Bar** is also popular. Dance at **Dali**, **Heustadl** and the **Savoy Tanzkeller**.

Child care

The ski schools accept children from the age of 4 and offer a course that runs 9:30 a.m.–4 p.m. with midday supervision. Prices are slightly lower than those for adults. Register at the ski school.

A ski kindergarten is available both for children who want to ski and for those who are not interested in skiing.

Getting there

The closest airports are in Verona (about a three-hour drive), Milan (about a four-hour drive), Munich (about a three- to four-hour drive), Bolzano (about one-hour drive), Innsbruck (about two-hours drive). Major rental car companies have offices at the airports.

Trains come to Bolzano and Bressanone, connected to Val Gardena by about 10 buses daily. A taxi to Val Gardena from Bolzano costs a maximum of about €130.

Other activities

Val Gardena is a woodcarving capital with thousands of artisans. Browse through the stores for carvings of everything from figurines to bowls and utensils.

The music society schedules concerts in the winter.

Horse-drawn sleigh rides glide on the Alpe di Siusi, Monte Pona and Vallunga.

There is a swimming pool, a new public sauna and steam bath in Ortisei. Covered tennis courts and ice skating are found in Ortisei and Selva Gardena.

The tourist office or your hotel will provide a free schedule of events, including folk nights, band concerts, film evenings, ice hockey games and toboggan races.

Tourist information

Ortisei/St. Ulrich
Tourist Office, Reziastr. 1, 39046 Ortisei
Telephone 0471-796328, fax 0471-796749.

S. Cristina
Tourist Office, Chemunstr. 9, 39047 S. Cristina
Telephone 0471- 793046, fax 0471-793198.

Selva Gardena
Tourist Information Office, Mëisules 213, 39048 Selva Gardena
Telephone 0471-795122, fax 0471-794245.
Internet: www.valgardena.it
E-mail: info@valgardena.it

Switzerland

For many, Switzerland *is* the Alps—Switzerland *is* skiing in Europe. Of course, only part of the Alps is in Switzerland and Europe has other places to ski, but as the heart of the Alps and the home of Alpine skiing, Switzerland deserves all its superlatives. Its skiing is excellent, its resorts efficient, its tourist offices well organized, its lift systems well run and its hotels exceptional.

When is high season?

High Season: Christmas and New Year holidays and all of February through mid-April.

Low Season: January after New Year and late April.

Pre-season: December 6 to Christmas holidays

Swiss currency

All of the countries covered in this book, other than Switzerland, have switched their currency to euros. Switzerland still uses its own currency, the Swiss Franc (CHF). Prices throughout this book, even in the Swiss chapters, are listed in euros to help you make comparisons while you are planning your trip. However, be aware that the preferred method of payment in Switzerland is in Swiss Francs (CHF). According to Swiss friends of ours, Swiss ski resorts will accept euros if that's all you have for a cash payment, but the exchange rate may be well in the ski resort's favor.

Switzerland's romantic mountain railways

The visitor whose timetable is not completely filled with skiing adventures can take a scenic ride on one of the most advanced mountain railway systems in the world. The regional Swiss railroad lines and the postbus have organized three spectacular Alpine routes.

The Glacier Express: Perhaps the most famous of the Swiss rail trips, this is advertised as the world's slowest train. Indeed the trip, some 90 miles as the crow flies, lasts seven and a half hours—spanning more than 291 bridges and burrowing through 91 tunnels—on its way from St. Moritz in Switzerland's southeast corner to Zermatt.

Trains run in both directions, leaving in the early morning and arriving in late afternoon. In their elegant dining cars a complete three-course lunch is served on the Chur-to-Andermatt leg. The meal costs approximately €30, excluding beverages, and reservations are required. (Your wine glass on the Glacier Express has a tilted base to keep the wine from spilling on the route's many steep turns and gradients—turn it now and then to keep it tilted in the right direction.)

Bernina Express: The Bernina Express, which crosses into Italy over the Alps in Switzerland's southeast corner, is Europe's highest transalpine railway. The train trip follows the same route as the Glacier Express from Chur to St. Moritz, then strikes southward for the Bernina Pass, Poschiavo and on to Tirano in Italy.

Along one eight-mile stretch the track passes through two straight tunnels, negotiates five corkscrew tunnels, and crosses eight viaducts. The train crosses the Bernina Pass at 7,405 feet, climbing the steepest gradient of any non-cogwheel train.

The Engadin Express: This train and postbus route connects St. Moritz with Innsbruck, Salzburg and Vienna. The trip from St. Moritz to Landeck, done mostly by post-bus, lasts almost three hours and is generally felt to be one of Europe's most romantic trips.

After leaving St. Moritz, the train chuffs alongside a beautiful Swiss national park, through the village of Scuol; then the postbus takes travelers past the famous castle of Tarasp and on to Vulpera. This is the home of the fourth language of Switzerland, Ladin. The express ends in Landeck, Austria, in the Tyrol district.

Making reservations: These train trips can be booked in the United States through the Swiss National Tourist Office (tel. (800) 223-0048; in New York (212) 757-5944); in Britain through the Swiss National Tourist Office (tel. (01) 734-1921); in St. Moritz at the Rhaetic Railway station; in Chur at the main train station; and in Zermatt at Zermatt-Tours.

The Swiss ski experience

The Swiss consider skiing more as an enjoyable cultural endeavor rather than a competitive race to measure vertical feet achieved in any certain day. They are fascinated and a bit amused by the high-tech watches that measure vertical feet skied worn by many aggresive North American skiers. The Swiss tend to measure skiing in terms of restaurants and chaise lounges, not numbers of fast runs.

Being in the mountains on vacation means enjoyment to these hard-working Swiss. They work hard and they take advantage of the sunshine and low-keyed atmosphere in the mountains to really give themselves a break.

The Swiss take advantage of sunshine by renting lounges on the mountain and enjoying the slow pace of a long, leisurely lunch. Lunch is their main daily meal and it is traditionally large and takes up to a couple of hours to consume. It might include numerous courses, beer, schnapps and coffees. They then take off to ski through the afternoon finally stopping on the trail back to the village for a late coffee and schnapps at one of the many private bistros and restaurants along the trail.

After skiing you won't find wild exuberance in the bars. The Swiss take their après-ski with restraint. Not that there's nothing going on, but the Austrian-style tea party drinking and dancing will be hard to find.

Swiss fondue and raclette

Fondue and raclette are cultural customs with an economic base. One of the Swiss mainstays is dairy farming and this country is home to some of the best cheeses that can be found. There are more than 100 different types of cheese.

Here in Switzerland, fondue and raclette are more than just a meal. They are part adventure and part ritual. They are quick meals that can be enjoyed by large groups of singing tourists or intimately by candlelight.

Raclette spread from the Valais canton of Switzerland and now can be found throughout the country. With raclette, cheese is melted in front of an open fire or under a broiler and then scraped off the wheel onto a plate. It is then served with potatoes and pickled onions and eaten immediately before the cheese sets.

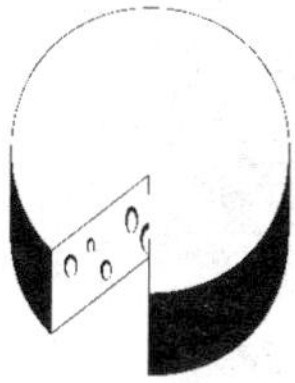

Cheese fondue can be considered by many to be the national dish of Switzerland. Emmentaler and Gruyère cheeses are melted in a big pot and combined with wine and various seasonings. Then hard-crust mountain bread is cut into squares and dunked into the melted cheese.

Two other fondues without a cheese base are relatively widespread and very popular. Fondue bourguignon is made with meat and vegetables which are speared on fondue forks and then cooked in oil at the table and served with various toppings. Fondue chinoise is created from thinly sliced beef that is cooked in a broth then dipped in Oriental sauces.

The wine of choice, and normally the most affordable on the menu is Fendant, a local light white wine. Trust us. It seems to go with everything. It is the wine to order when eating out. You can't go wrong.

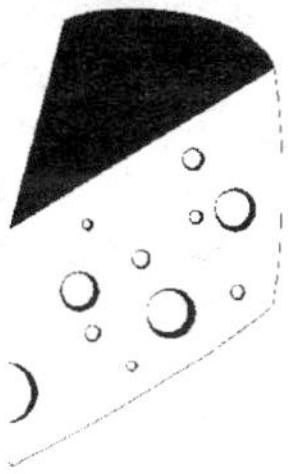

Traditional recipe for Swiss Fondue
2 to 3 large cloves of garlic
800 gr. or 20 oz. finely grated Switzerland cheese
(half Emmentaler, half Gruyère)
2+ cups dry white wine
1 to 2 jiggers of Kirsch Schnapps mixed with
1 teaspoon of cornstarch
dash of pepper
plenty of crusty, chewy one-inch bread cubes

Mince or crush garlic and rub the inside of your fondue pot. Leave remains in pot. Pour in white wine and 1/3 of the grated cheese. Place over medium heat on stove. Start stirring in a figure-8 motion, gradually adding the rest of the cheese. Cook over moderate heat, stirring all the time until the mixture starts to bubble. Add the cornstarch mixed with kirsch and bring once more to a boil. Season with pepper and bring to the table. Adjust the heating flame so that the fondue will simmer throughout the meal.

Spear a cube of bread and dip it into the pot, giving it a figure-8 stir each time. Serve with a dry white or sparkling white wine or tea. During the meal it is customary to drink a jigger of Kirsch Schnapps to help digestion.

Arosa

A long-established Swiss ski resort, Arosa played a part in the development of skiing as a popular winter sport. Today it is known for relatively easy, wide-open skiing and good off-slope activities. The town is tucked into a circle of mountains at the end of the Schanfigger valley, above Chur.

Everything in Arosa is within easy walking distance. If you drive a car to the resort, you can park it in the public area and forget it, unless you decide to escape to some other area during your stay.

Mountain layout

At 6,000 feet, Arosa's lifts fan out to reach the two major peaks in the area, the 8,241-foot-high Hörnli and the Weisshorn, at 8,704 feet. Although there are only 13 lifts, their combined capacity exceeds 21,000 skiers an hour. With the entire resort above the trees and some 43 miles of runs, long and spread out, there's plenty of wide-open skiing and perfect cruising. There are also nearly 16 miles of groomed cross-country trails.

Mountain rating

Arosa is Eden for beginners and intermediates because of its long, wide runs. When it hasn't snowed for several days, and skiers have broken new trails between the normally prepared runs, you can virtually ski across the entire mountain.

One run that does require an expert—sort of—is the descent from the top of the Weisshorn to the Carmennahütte. This very steep run is wide enough to allow a gutsy intermediate to traverse and make his way down the slope, but it also offers expert-level practice on the steeps with plenty of room for error.

Ski school (2003/04)

The Swiss Ski School in Arosa (081-3771150; fax 081-3771996) has more than 100 qualified instructors, most of whom speak English. The ski school has special courses for children, deep-snow skiers, snowboarders and telemarkers. The also organize other events, including torchlight descents accompanied by fireworks, descents by full moon and ski races.

Private lessons cost €93 for two hours, €233 for six hours per person.

Group lessons cost €27 for two hours (half day); €117 for five half days; €273 for five full days (Monday through Friday).

Note: Reductions for children are available.

Cross-country courses are also available. Private instruction is €47 for a 50-minute lesson for one person.

There are also three **snowboarding schools** in Arosa. The Bananas Swiss Snowboard School (081-3771150), ABC Snow Sports School (081-3565660) and Private Ski and Snowboard Instructors Arosa (081-3773448), all operate one set of courses for €27 per half day; €77 for three half days; and €117 for five half days.

Lift Tickets (2003/04 prices)

All lift tickets for seven days or more require photos that are taken by the ticket office.

	Adults	Children (to age 16)
one day	€36	€18
three days	€102	€51
six days	€168	€84
seven days	€181	€91

For the first week of December, lift tickets are reduced 15 percent. One-day tickets cost €14 for adults and €10 for children.

Accommodations

Arosa has a hotel for everyone—from the most luxurious to the bargain one-star. Price ranges noted for each hotel are per person based on double occupancy with half board (breakfast and dinner): €€€—€125+; €€—€75–€124; €—less than €74.

Recommended four-star hotels: **Kulm Hotel** (081-3788888; €€€); **Tschuggen Grand Hotel** (081-3789999; €€€).

Our recommended four-star hotels are: **Hohenfels** (081-3770101; €€); **Posthotel** (081-3785000; €€) right in the center of the town near the train station; **Sporthotel Valsana** (081-3770275; €€) by the lake, with a good restaurant and child care; **Waldhotel National** (081-3785555; €€€) a bit back in the woods, nevertheless considered excellent; **Hotel Eden** (081-3787100; €€€).

The three-star hotels most convenient to the lifts are: **Alpina** (081-377165; €) recently restored and beautiful; **Astoria** (081-3771313; €); **Hohe Promenade** (081-3787700; €); **Obersee** (081-3771216; €); **Arve Central** (081-3785252; €).

Our recommended two-star hotels: **Erzhorn** (081-3771526; €); the **Hold** (081-311408; €); or **Carmena** (081-3771766; €).

Apartments, condominiums, flats

Arosa is well organized to handle tourists who want to rent apartments during the ski season, normally for a minimum of one week, Saturday to Saturday. During the Christmas and Easter seasons a minimum two-week rental is required.

The tourist office keeps track of available apartments. When writing, include the number of beds required, the preferred number of rooms, and your planned vacation dates. You will receive a quick response that lists a selection of apartments and prices.

Pick your apartment and contact the owner.

Normally linen and kitchen utensils are provided. Other amenities, such as swimming pool, sauna, TV or room phone all add to the cost. Standard apartments rent for €35 to €60 per person a night. Prices vary significantly from low to high season.

Dining

The following restaurants come recommended by local Arosa residents: **Stüva, Säumerstube, Hotel Hof Maran Im Stübli, Hotel Central Arven-Restaurant, Locanda, Bajazzo, Chez André** and **Gspan**. For something different, take the sleigh ride up to the **Hotel Alpenblick** above Arosa and enjoy a special meat platter that is grilled at your table.

Après-ski/nightlife

Arosa is not the nightlife capital of Switzerland. The fun is where you make it, usually with groups that seem to form on their own on any ski trip. Arosa's après-ski activities center around the hotels in the evening. Here you'll find cozy bars with bands or piano players. There are approximately 20 such bars. Try the **Kitchen-Club** in an old hotel kitchen and **Nuts**—probably the hottest discos in town.

On the slopes the best spot to eat is the Carmennahütte beneath the Weisshorn. Get there early or late—it seems to always be crowded. The Weisshornsattelhütte is good as well with smaller crowds.

Child care (2003/04 prices)

There are two public kindergartens. For more information and rates contact the tourist office in Arosa.

Both the Bananas Swiss Snowboard School (081-3771150), ABC Snow Sports School (081-3565660) provide lessons for those 16 and younger. It costs €27 for a half day with lunch and five half days costs €118. A full day with lunch costs €44 and five full days cost €162.

If you want to leave your children at the school for a supervised lunch the cost is €17 per day or €84 for five days.

Other activities

Arosa is known for its off-slope activities. There are **indoor swimming pools, ice skating** on three open-air rinks and one covered rink, **curling, indoor golf, chess and bridge evenings**, more than 29 km. of **walking trails, squash and tennis courts** at Heidi's Parkhotel and the Robinson Club, **horse-drawn sleigh rides**, and **hot-air ballooning**. The town is also active in arts and entertainment.

For swimming expect to pay about €5.5–€7 for adults and €3.5–€4.5 for children.

For horse-drawn sleigh rides, contact J. Graber (081-3774716), or Weierhof Stables (081-3774196). Costs are from €55–€140 for four persons depending on the route.

Arosa offers organized curling lessons every Tuesday, starting in January, for €33 a lesson.

Hot-air ballooning is available. Call 081-3771843.

Getting there

The closest airport is Zürich; from there Arosa is less than three hours by train. Go first to Chur, where you catch a special train for Arosa just outside the main station entrance. The train ride from Chur to Arosa takes about one hour.

Driving from Zürich to Arosa will take about two-and-a-half hours in good weather. Follow the signs to Chur and after entering the city, follow the signs to Arosa. The road is steep and narrow and requires chains for most of the winter. Arosa has a car park for 460 cars. A free public bus in Arosa makes moving around the resort easier.

Tourist information

Arosa Tourism, CH-7050 Arosa, Switzerland; 081-3787020; fax 081-3787021). Hours: Monday–Friday 9 a.m.–6 p.m., Saturday 9 a.m.–5:30 p.m., Sunday 10 a.m.–noon and 16:00 p.m.–5:30 p.m.

Champéry

Portes du Soleil

The Portes du Soleil ski area, nestled just south of Lake Geneva and straddling Switzerland and France, claims to be Europe's biggest ski area. Though Trois Vallées makes a similar claim, the skiing in Portes du Soleil is more unrefined. Where a skier in the Trois Vallées may be able to transfer easily from valley to valley, transfers in the Portes du Soleil area take more time and effort. Where the lift system in the Trois Vallées forms a tight web linking miles of prepared slopes, the lifts through this region are gossamer strands linking far-flung pistes.

I remember breathing heavily after a long morning of continuous skiing from Champéry in Switzerland to Châtel in France. Jean, my guide, asked me, "Do you see that peak over to the right of the stand of trees?"

"Yes," I answered.

"Do you know where that is?"

"Somewhere in France? Is it Mont Blanc?" It looked far, far away.

He chuckled. "It's not that far away. That's where we started this morning."

"Oh, come on. There's no need to exaggerate. I'm already tired enough."

"No, no, no, I'm not making a joke. I just want you to know that we have a long way to get back."

I was incredulous and forgot any notions about a relaxed afternoon cruising home.

The Portes du Soleil area is made up of about a dozen different resorts. Four to six lie on the Swiss side of the border and the remaining eight or ten, depending on how one counts resorts, are in France. The key resorts are Champéry in Switzerland and Avoriaz in France. More than 50 mountain restaurants dot the slopes.

Champéry is a mountain village that is waking up to the fact that it has turned into an international resort. Les Dents du Midi majestically stand watch over the valley and provide dramatic views of jagged mountain peaks, but it isn't a polished recreation. The old chalets look lived in, the odor of cow manure wafts across the main street, a plucky kid (of the goat type) prances in the back of a station wagon, the discos look like a throwback to the 1950s, and no tour buses pack the center of town.

The other main Swiss towns that are a part of the Portes du Soleil don't measure up to Champéry. Les Croset is isolated and once held promise as a resort, but today, is more fit for a skiing recluse. In the future with more stability, it has a chance of becoming a very convenient station. Morgins is far too quiet and most lodging is not very close to the two lifts up to the region.

Mountain layout

This is a real skier's area—over 650 km. of ski trails. But not only is it challenging to ski the slopes; finding your way from resort to resort can test the skills of an Eagle Scout. The area does provide good maps outlining the 228 different lifts with suggested itineraries to make crisscrossing the region less difficult. (With such an expanse of skiing, no one map allows sufficient detail; when you arrive in a new section, stop and pick up the local lift map that shows runs in that area.)

NOTE: The lift system does not perfectly interconnect. In Châtel there is a shuttlebus between the Linga and the Super-Châtel cable car.

The Portes du Soleil benefits from the fact that most of the skiable terrain is pasture land during the summers rather than rocky mountainside. This allows excellent skiing without the deep snow depth resorts such as Chamonix require. The locals claim that with only few inches of snow they can be up and running.

Experts can strike out in any direction but will most enjoy the World Cup section of Avoriaz, yo-yoing through the Plaine Dranse and Linga, and daring the Swiss Wall. No expert will feel complacent after any of these experiences. There is unlimited untracked snow for those looking for that type of adventure. Locals swear that since most visiting skiers stick to the trails, they can find untracked snow up to four days after a storm.

Intermediates should be ready for an endurance test of the first order. Forget any idea of skiing every run on a week-long vacation; it is just not possible. There are plenty of intermediate circuits that will provide a very full day of skiing. Try from Champéry to Avoriaz and back, or vice versa; on another day, take intermediate runs from Avoriaz to Châtel and return.

Beginners will not have a chance to really enjoy the expansive skiing of Portes du Soleil, but they certainly will have a beautiful place to learn.

Mountain rating

Score this one as a test for any expert, extensive enough for every intermediate on your list, and more than any beginner can handle.

Beginners taking the tram up from Champéry have a limited area in which to ski. Champoussin may be a better bet for beginners, but then they lose the village atmosphere.

Intermediates will have a wonderful time criss-crossing the resorts on the Swiss side of the region, from Champéry to Champoussin to Le Crosets and down to Morgins.

Chavanette, also known as the Swiss Wall, between Avoriaz and Les Crosets, has lured experts for decades. Standing at the lip of the drop, skiers cannot see the slope that falls under the tips of their skis. Once dropping off the rim, it's a wide-open, expert steep with either ice or giant moguls, depending on the weather. Don't be ashamed to take the path around the Wall at this point—many skiers choose this option. The black runs above Avoriaz are good and new lifts have eliminated many of the bottlenecks.

One serious recommendation for intermediates or experts is to limit your range unless you are in good physical shape. If you are already exhausted and someone in your group points to a distant mountain and announces that you have to return to that point before quitting, you will arrive very, very tired. As we all know, that's when the snow snakes seem to strike. Be careful. This is one of the few areas in the world where you *can* ski too far to get back home.

Ski school (2002/03 prices)

The Swiss Ski School in Champéry (024-479-1615) and the Freeride Company (024-479-2029) offer downhill lessons.

Downhill group courses: half day costs €26 for adults or for kids age 3–7; full day costs €52 for adult or child; five half days, €97 for adults or €103 for kids; five full days cost €200 for adults and €206 for kids with lunch.

Private lessons (skiing and snowboarding): €77 per hour for one or two persons, €103 per hour for three or four. Half-day private lessons for groups of one or two cost €110, or €129 for three to four skiers. Full-day lessons for groups of one or two cost €206; groups of three or four cost €226.

Snowboarding group lessons cost €26 for a half day, and €97 for five half days.

A good way to get to know the area is through organized **Ski Excursions Portes du Soleil** groups of at least four skiers for €40 a day or €165 a five-day week. The groups, organized by the Swiss Ski School in Champéry, normally make a loop through Les Crosets, Champoussin, Morgins and Avoriaz, and then return to Champéry.

From Berra Sport in the center of town you can get ski rentals for about €120 (six days) and €125 (seven days). Snowboard rentals are about €30 (one day) and €110 (seven days). Rentals are also available from Holiday and Borgeat Sports.

Lift tickets (2003/04 prices)

The Portes du Soleil ski pass is for adults, age 19–59; children, age 5–15; youths, age 16-19 and students with proper identification age 24 and younger; and seniors, age 60 and older.

	Adults	Children	Youth	Seniors
One day	€34	€23	€28.50	€27
Three days	€93	€62	€79	€74
Six days	€162	€108.50	€137.50	€130
Fourteen days	€287	€192	€243	€229

Photos are required for passes of six days of more. Half-day passes start at noon and children younger than age 5 are free when accompanied by a paying adult.

Limited passes are available for each region in the Portes du Soleil.

The Portes du Soleil Family Ski Pass is a bargain for families with a minimum of four people. The pass covers two parents with children younger than age 20.

Accommodations

Champéry has only a handful of hotels but plenty of apartments. There is also an excellent weekly program called Ski Passion, which includes seven, five or four days accommodation with half board, six- or five-day lift tickets for the entire Portes du Soleil area, and free entry to the Sports Center.

Price ranges noted for each hotel are per person based on double occupancy high season with half board (breakfast and dinner): €€€—€125+; €€—€75–€125; €—less than €75.

Hotel Suisse (024-479-0707; fax 024-479-0709; €€). Hotel Suisse is in the center of the village. The hotel has been expanded and modernized. All the rooms are comfortable; however, they vary significantly in size. Ask for a big room when you make reservations or when you show up at the hotel. The hotel's subterranean jazz bar, Les Mines d'Or, is a popular late night watering-hole often featuring live music. The Bar des Guides has become the nightlife haven of choice for English speakers. The manager of the hotel was a member of the Swiss Olympic ski team. He makes an effort to ski with the guests whenever possible.

Hotel et Residence de Champéry (024-479-1071; fax 024-479-1402; €€). This hotel, 50 meters up the road from the Suisse, is the largest hotel in town. The hotel's piano 5bar is a popular haunt for regular visitors.

Hotel Beau-Séjour (024-479-5858; fax 024-479-5859; €€). A nice hotel with a good restaurant and reasonable prices.

Hotel des Alpes (024-479-1222; fax 024-479-1223; €). Good basic hotel with a fancy and expensive à la carte restaurant.

Hotel National (024-479-1130; fax 024-479-3155; €€) has an excellent restaurant with very affordable daily menus starting at about €13 for lunch without wine.

Hotel la Rose des Alpes (024-479-1218; fax 024-479-1774; €€) is full of mountain atmosphere and has a good restaurant as well.

Ski Chalet: Piste Artiste runs four of these chalets right in town and also has a program that provides guides for the chalet groups. Phone or fax 024-479-3344 in Champéry, or e-mail them at ski@pisteartiste.com.

Apartments

To reserve apartments write to the tourist office (details at the end of this chapter) or use its Web site, www.mychablais.com. You will receive a listing of available apartments, but you will have to make your reservations through a rental agency or directly with the owners. In Champéry the agencies are Agence Immobilière René Avanthay, (024-479-1444), Agence Mendes de Leon (024-479-1777) and Agence les Gaieuls (024-479-1885). Mendes de Leon seemed to be the most helpful.

Child care

The ski school (024-479-1615) has a special Mini-Club for children aged 3–7, open 9:30 a.m. to 4:30 p.m. daily. It includes ski lessons, games and lunch. Half-day cost is €26; five half days will cost €100. A full day with lunch costs €46 and five full days with lunch are €185.

There is a nanny service which must be booked before arrival. Approximate rates are €200 for a week, €35 for full-day service and €26 for a half day. Babysitting can also be arranged. The tourist office has phone numbers and information.

Dining

Location, location, location ... Champéry's cooking benefits from its proximity to France. For the best meals in town try the **Restaurant le Mazot** in the Hotel de Champéry (try their *Pierrade* where you cook your meat on a heated stone).

These other restaurants in town are all very agreeable.

Café du Nord at top of the High Street near Banque Cantonale. One of the more popular restaurants in the village, especially with families. Serving up an assortment of rösti, fondue, and raclette.

Restaurant le Sport has a famous pasta party and other specialties set in a nice atmosphere.

Restaurant National in the center of the village offers specials each day, has topnotch fish and a rustic atmosphere for very affordable prices.

La Vieux Chalet has lamb, fish, and meat dishes. Some nights offer music and dancing. Located at the end of High Street or top of the hill from the Téléphérique.

Le Gueullhi is next to the cable car.

Across the valley there is a raclette house called **Les Rives**. The raclette parties there are part of the resort's dining-around program for guests taking half-board at hotels or pensions. The raclette "wheel" is heated against an open fire by the chef.

Restaurant Grand Paradis in Grand Paradis is famous for its Raclette room.

Chez Coquoz at Planachaux is the best on the Swiss side of the region.

Chez Gabi, on the slopes above Champoussin, also has excellent food and makes a great midday stop or a good evening meal after a ride up on a snowcat.

See the Avoriaz chapter for restaurants on the French side.

Après-ski/nightlife

The best après-ski spot in town is **Bar des Guides** in the Hotel Suisse. There are good beers on tap and the place is packed with English speakers from the U.K., Canada, U.S.A., Holland and Scandinavia. **Mitchell's Bar** is also a favorite.

The English-style **La Crevasse Bar** run by Piste Artiste is right on the main street and has also become a focal point of English-speaking après-ski crowds until 3 a.m. **The Tarine Disco-Club** is also a popular hang-out for English-speaking après-skiers.

Café du Levant is the grunge and snowboarder hangout. Things sometimes get a little out of hand, which is this establishment's most redeeming value.

Other activities

Champéry is just over a half-hour winding drive up the mountain from Montreux and Lausanne. Monthey, in the valley, has a covered bridge and open-air market. The town is about two hours from the airport at Geneva.

The sports center has **ice skating**, **curling** and **swimming** as well as a **fitness center**, **sauna** and **massage**. Those staying in a participating hotel have free entrance. Adult entrance to the pool for those not staying in participating hotels is €4.30; for children €3. Ice skating costs a bit less. Skate rentals are €2.60. The sports center is undergoing renovations. Contact the tourist office for a list of available activities.

Paragliding costs €66 per flight. Contact Vincent Marclay at 479-2408. A visit to the thermal baths of Val-d'Illiez is a relaxing must with hourly train connection. Entrance is €6.

There is night skiing twice a week until 10 p.m. in Planachaux. Heliskiing and ski mountaineering is offered with qualified guides for €230 a day plus flight fees.

Getting there

The closest airport is Geneve. Champéry is less than 90 minutes from Geneva and only 45 minutes from Lausanne. Take the Lake Geneva motorway to Monthey, and follow the signs to Champéry. The road normally has good driving conditions year-round. Train service arrives in either Aigle or Monthey where travelers can transfer to a Postbus for the drive to the resort. The entire bus/train trip from Geneva will take approximtely three hours.

Tourist information

Champéry: Office du Tourisme, CH-1874 Champéry, Switzerland; Telephone: 024-479-2020, fax 024-479-2021.
Internet: www.champery.ch; www.mychablais.com
E-mail: info@champery.ch

Crans-Montana

Spread out on the high, broad Valais plateau 3,000 feet above the floor of the Rhone valley, the twin towns of Crans and Montana command a panoramic view of some of the most storied peaks in Alpine lore: Matterhorn, Mont-Blanc, the Weisshorn, and the Dent-Blanche. A little too large and too eclectic in its architecture to be called quaint, Crans-Montana is a modern luxury resort catering to the well-heeled, with more than 50 resort hotels and numerous boutiques sporting the haute couture of Paris and Milan. Visitors might well run into celebrity locals on the bustling shopping streets, such as former 007 Roger Moore, who has a residence slopeside.

Though little known to many American skiers, Crans-Montana has a rich skiing history and sits in the shadow of world-class ski mountains. In 1993 the resort celebrated its 100th anniversary, and in 1987 it hosted the prestigious World Alpine Ski Championships, where the Swiss swept the medals. In 1950, the first Swiss ski championships were held here. The new racing runs and ski-lift improvements made for the World Championships resulted in one of the most accessible skiing areas in the world. In 1911 the founder of downhill racing Sir Arnold Lunn organized a mass race from the highest point on the Plaine Morte glacier down to Montana. That race eventually developed into today's famous Kandahar downhill race, held alternately each year in St. Anton, Mürren, Chamonix, Sestriere and Garmisch.

Although the names are most often said in the same breath, Crans and Montana do have their differences. As mentioned, neither is a paragon of Alpine architecture; an architects' convention might have been given a free hand to erect as many kinds of buildings as possible. Unappealing square concrete boxes stand beside massive triangular Toblerone-box hotels, with a smattering of traditional chalets amidst the concrete and glass. Crans has the more concentrated city atmosphere. Not counting several fashion and souvenir shops and the occasional jewelry store, the shop signs in Montana read simply Cheese, Fondue, Real Estate, Restaurant. In Crans, the signs read Gucci, Louis Vuitton, Piaget, Cartier. Crans is chic and often crowded with furs; Montana is more for the family, where one is more at home in a ski outfit.

Be prepared to hike up and down hills, because both towns climb the side of the mountain from their plateau above the Rhone. But this slope, although many curse it by day, provides many hotels with spectacular views of the Alps in the south.

Mountain layout

The ski area above Crans-Montana-Aminona is reached from four major lifts. From Crans, an eight-passenger gondola goes from there to Cry d'Err (7,173 feet), the hub of the entire area. From Montana, a six-passenger gondola whisks skiers to Cry d'Err. At Les Barzettes, a five-minute bus ride from Crans or Montana, another fast gondola takes you to Les Violettes (7,176 feet). From the base again, five minutes on the bus takes the skier to Aminona, where a gondola goes on to Pt. Mont Bonvin (7,836 feet); here, a wide-open, above-treeline area provides fantastic uncrowded conditions.

The Cry d'Err sector of the mountain is the most crowded. Ten lifts go to Cry d'Err. After a long, flat traverse, the skier arrives on the Crans section of the mountain. From here the best bet is to take the Super-G/Slalom run into Crans, then catch the gondola back to Cry d'Err. The runs below Cry d'Err heading to Montana are intermediate playgrounds, but suffer from a serious bottleneck near Pas du Loup where the four trails merge through a narrow gap before widening on the way to town. At the end of the day, this bottleneck will be crowded—ski slowly and in control. From Cry d'Err another trail traverses to the right, leading you into the Violettes section. This area is separated from the Montana section by a sheer cliff whose edge is marked generally by the Piste Nationale run on the ski map. The Violettes area is a favorite of intermediates, featuring twisting runs down through the trees to the gondola midstation, and four other lifts opening great intermediate skiing.

Across the valley from Violettes is the Aminona area and the Toula lifts, a favorite section of the resort. La Toula offers challenging expert runs, and Aminona boasts wide-open, uncrowded cruising.The Plaine Morte trail starts atop the 9,843-foot-high Plaine Morte glacier, which also serves as a summer ski area. Sometime during your stay take the Funitel mountain subway up from Violettes and measure your time against the Kandahar ski pioneers, whose best time was just over one hour for the run. The run is a long nine miles of intermediate terrain with expert tendencies, thanks to the chance for frequent off-trail shortcuts. The trail down from Plaine Morte is closely controlled for avalanche danger. After even a relatively light snowfall, the run from the glacier back to Violettes is sometimes closed, but opened after the necessary precautions.

For beginners, there is a series of baby lifts and very mellow terrain surrounding the Le Signal area. Not only are there good areas to learn to ski and ride, but there is a clutch of three restaurants there for hot tea, coffee and meals. Beginners normally graduate to the easiest and widest intermediate trails up at Cry d'Err.

Snowboarders can find a 25 km. snowboard park in Arimona at La Tza. Once a week visitors can snowboard or ski at night at Cry d'Err and Verdetts.

Mountain rating

Intermediates will rate Crans-Montana one of the greatest places they've ever skied, with excellent variety. Indeed, for the intermediate skier, Crans-Montana may be heaven on the slopes. Long, challenging trails coupled with virtually no waiting at lifts make for a combination that most skiers will find hard to beat.

Beginners are relatively limited on this mountain. In Crans, absolute beginners should start on the golf course, which is perfect, but the next step – directly onto the mountain – is a big one. Montana beginners will likely opt for the Signal restaurant area. Fortunately, the slopes on the golf course and at Le Signal welcome beginners from both Crans and Montana. From Crans, take the bus and the cable car in Montana or Les Barzettas or Aminona. Instructors admit that the area is limited for beginners.

Try the blue run from the Chetzeron gondola first. In Violettes there are no beginner slopes, and the beginner sections of Aminona are for those who have been on skis at least three or four days—even then the gentle slopes are isolated in a sea of red-rated trails.

Only experts need to worry at all about whether there are enough challenges to keep things interesting. Experts will find only a few really steep sections, and there is plenty of off-trail and tree skiing. The championship runs are a good test. For steep, wide-open skiing try the run on the skier's left coming off the Les Violettes lift, or access this terrain while skiing down from the glacier. Though guides are suggested, there is also challenging off-trail skiing off the Petit Bonvin lift above Aminona.

Ski school

The Crans-Montana area has more ski instructors (about 200) than some Swiss ski villages have permanent residents. There's a lesson being given somewhere on the slopes from Crans to Aminona nearly every hour of the day. For information, call 027-485-9370 or 027-481-1480.

Unless otherwise stated the following prices are for ski or snowboarding lessons.

In the distant past, the Montana Ski School was more international, however, today both Crans and Montana Ski Schools are very international.

Private lessons cost €40 an hour for one, €54 for two students, €60 for three students, and €68 per hour for four people.

Group lessons (from age 7) in Crans and Montana a half-day (3 hours of lessons) are €33. Six half days (18 hours) is €123. For snowboarders, all half days or 2 hours, cost €33. A week of half-day lessons (12 hours) is €133.

Cross-country lessons are available, and six different trails with a total length of 40 km. of gliding and almost 30 km. of skating are prepared during the season.

Lift tickets (2003/04 prices)

The Crans-Montana area pass is available at the following rates:

	Adults	Children (6–15)
half day (from 12 p.m.)	€27	€16
one day	€36	€21
three days	€100	€60
six days	€175	€104
fourteen days	€307	€182

Note: The Plaine-Morte glacier at the upper reaches of the mountain is reached by a Funitel, or mountain subway running from Les Violettes. It is now included in the above prices.

A family of three people or more receives a 10% discount on any ski pass.

Accommodations

Crans-Montana can be very upscale. It doesn't claim many movie stars or much of the old rich, but it is an oasis for the corporate rich. The town boasts more five-star hotels than any other Swiss resort except St. Moritz, and a dazzling selection of prize-winning, expensive restaurants. Finding the ritziest isn't difficult—digging for the good solid values for the middle-of-the-road crowd takes a bit more time. Rates are per person based on high season (February), double occupancy with half board: €€€—€125+; €€—€75–€125; €—less than €75.

Crans Ambassador (027-485-4848, fax 027-485-4849; €€€) The best hotel on the Montana side of the town. Next to the cable cars, has good nightlife and a pool.

Royal (027-485-9595, fax 027-485-9595; €€€) in Crans is the most luxurious on this side of town offering the Ski Soleil program.

St-George (027-481-2414, fax 027-481-1670; €€€) More three than four stars but with an English-speaking staff and popular with the British.

Mont-Blanc (027-481-3143, fax 027-481-3146; €€€) High on the hill with great views, a favorite of English-speakers. This hotel has one of the top restaurants in town.

De la Forêt (027-480-2131, fax 027-481-3120; €€€) A bit of a walk to the downtown area but close to Les Violettes lift. Has a covered swimming pool.

The Best Western National (027-481-2681, fax 027-481-7381; €€€) This hotel is near the Crans lifts. It is used by British groups, but the owner can be cantankerous.

La Prairie (027-485-4141, fax 027-485-4142; €€€) A rustic chalet type of hotel only a few minutes outside of town. A low three-star with shuttle to the lifts.

Teleferique (027-481-3367, fax 027-481-3309; €€) At the base of Cry d'Err lifts.

Apartments, condominiums, flats

With 25 major rental agencies in Crans-Montana, apartment and chalet listings in Crans-Montana are overwhelming. Expect to pay €450–€550 per week for a two-bed studio in high season (Christmas, February and Easter); €625–€750 for a four-bed, two-room apartment; €1,200–€1,300 for a four-room, six- to eight-bed apartment.

Book an apartment online or write to or call the reservation office noted at the end of the chapter with details of what you want and the price range. You'll get a prompt reply.

Dining

This town, as noted above, has plenty of great eateries. These are some of our favorites—from expensive to moderate to inexpensive.

Head to **Nouvelle Rotisserie** (027-481-1885) for delicious food from its owner Mrs. France Massy who is renowned for her fresh food, and **Le Sporting** (027-481-1177) has top French and Italian food. **L'Hostellerie du Pas-de-l'Ours** (027-485-9333) in Crans has a Michelin star.

For more moderately priced meals try **Hotel Aida** (027-485-4111) with a beautiful rustic setting. Another is **Le Bistrot des Ours** (027-485-9333) in the L' Hostellerie du Pas-de-l'Ours mentioned above. If you have time, try the restaurant at **Miedzor** (027-485-9010) at the golf course. Hotel restaurants for affordable menus in Crans are **Eden** (027-480-1171), **Splendide** (027-481-2056) and **Des Alpes** (027-481-3754).

In Montana head to **de la Foret** (027-480-2131) for a good meal. In Montana try **Mont-Plaisible** (027-480-2161) or the mountain-styled **Colorado** (027-481-3271). The budget crowd should indulge at the **Brasserie "Le Green"** (027-485-8787). Almost all the pizzerias have good budget dining.

On the mountain at Plans Mayens for great meals stop at **Le Mont-Blanc** (027-481-3143) or **La Dent Blanche** (027-481-1179) which specializes in *raclette au feu de bois* (raclette in front of a fire). Make reservations to ensure a table. Rustic restaurant **Le Cervin** (027-481-2180) at Vermalla is excellent for fondue and raclette and has an atmosphere you can't beat. We liked the lunch menus at **Les Violettes, Bella-Lui** and **Chez Erwin**. The scenery from **La Plaine Morte** restaurant (027-481-3626) on the glacier and **Cry d'Err** (027-481-2410) is the stuff of which memories are made.

In the town of Bluche, just below Montana, try the small **Petit Paradis** (027-481-2148) that offers good basic meals at a great value.

Après-ski/nightlife

By United States and British standards, there isn't much. Immediately after the slopes close, the only bars with a crowd are in Montana—the small, smoky **La Grange** and **Amadeus**. **The Pub Georges & Dragon** in Crans is the top English-speaker après-ski spot with reasonable beer. **The New Pub**, with its electronic and lottery games, is also good for apres-ski and nightlife. If you have the urge to go out between 9 p.m. and midnight, try some of the normally quiet piano bars. Our favorite is the **Memphis Bar** in Crans with its blond wood decor and raucous piano jazz. The **Punch Bar** in Crans also features Cuban music and cigars until 2 a.m.

Discos don't get going until midnight to 1 a.m. If you're determined and well-heeled, head for **Absolut** and **Le Barocke** in Crans, but expect to pay a €13–€15 cover charge, which includes a drink. **Constellation,** which is only open until midnight is a bar packed with young snowboarders. **Zapata** and **Number Two,** which is popular for its karaoke, also have good recommendations.

Child care

The ski school for children (6–12) runs only half days. Costs are the same as for adults.

Crans-Montana has four nurseries which can handle children by the hour, for half days, or all day. Call the **Swiss Ski School** in Crans (027-485-9370), in Montana the **Swiss Ski School** (027-481-1480), **Fleurs des Champs** in Montana (027-481-2367), and **Zig-Zag** in Montana (027-481-2205).

The tourist office provides a list of babysitters.

Getting there

You'll most likely arrive at the Geneva airport. From there it's an uncomplicated car or train ride of a couple of hours around the lake and into the mountains. From Sierre, the bus departs directly in front of the railway station, the cable car from around the corner.

Crossair now flies from Zürich and London to nearby Sion, only a half hour from Crans-Montana by bus or taxi.

Other activities

Crans-Montana is a center for hot-air ballooning, paragliding and hang-gliding, with instruction in hang-gliding available. Call 027-485-0800 or 027-485-0404 for information about both. A winter meeting of hot-air balloon enthusiasts is held annually, usually in February. You can also find horseback riding, snowshoeing, snowmobiling, bowling, curling, tennis, squash and tobogganing (a 6 km. toboggan course runs from Petit Bonvin to Aminona). There's also a golf-simulator and fitness and wellness centers.

Tourist information

Crans-Montana Tourism, CH-3963 Crans-Montana, Switzerland; 027-485-0404 or 4850800; fax 027-485-0460 or 485-0810).
Central reservations for hotels or apartments is at the same address. Telephone: 027-485-0444, fax 027-485-0460.
Internet: www.crans-montana.ch
E-mail: reservation@crans-montana.ch; information@cransmontana.ch for general info.

Davos

Davos is not a small quaint Alpine resort. This is a ski city—the largest ski resort in Switzerland and the highest city in Europe. The year-round population is 13,000 and the town can fill up with an additional 23,000 tourists. Davos was one of the first ski resorts to be created and is still one of the world's best.

In the southeast corner of Switzerland, Davos sits dwarfed by mountains on both sides of the valley (Davos means "behind" or "beyond" in the Romansh language). Five separate ski areas have been developed, any one of which would be enough for a U.S. resort, ensuring diversity and skiing for every skier.

The main town, or should I say city, is split into two sections: Davos Dorf, where the Parsennbahn starts, and Davos Platz, beneath the Schatzalpbahn. These, with several other villages—Wolfgang, Laret and Glaris—make up greater Davos.

Instead of wooden chalets, for the most part, square concrete hotels line the streets. But Davos still maintains a sense of comfort. Traffic moves easily along the upper and lower main arteries without buildup. The hotels have a long and distinguished tradition for excellence, and practically every type of recreational activity is available. If you want to buy the latest in Gucci accessories, or the finest Atomic racing ski, you'll find them without any problem.

The town was founded in 1860 by Dr. Spengler, a German physician who recognized the benefits of the dry, healthy climate in treating tuberculosis, a scourge of the times. Huge balconies seen on older houses were for patients to lie out in the sunshine. This type of treatment continued until about 1930. Thomas Mann's wife was treated at Davos, from which came his novel *The Magic Mountain*.

Development of Davos as a sports region began in 1955. Davos and Klosters (see our Klosters chapter) combined offer 320 km. of runs, a variety of lodging, cable cars and even some yodeling accordion players. This resort was one of the first to turn skiing into a business with the construction of the Parsenn railway and the creation of the first drag lift.

At night the mix of people has unusual variety, from teenagers in town for the good skiing to elderly couples enjoying a walk in the crisp, clear mountain air and the restorative powers of an Alpine vacation. Nightlife is adequate, if restrained. Everything except the skiing seems to be done in moderation.

Mountain layout

The five ski areas of Davos are the Parsenn, the Schatzalp/Strela, Jakobshorn, Rinerhorn and Pischa.

The Parsenn: This is the best known area, almost the size of Manhattan and the major reason why Davos has become a premier European resort. The Parsennbahn, a cable railway, leaves every 15 to 20 minutes in ski season. It peaks at the Weissfluhjoch, the upper lift central of the Parsenn. Here the runs are wide open and offer beginners and intermediates a paradise for cruising. The Parsenn has 40 seemingly endless trails, including what was once Europe's longest: the 12-km. trail from Weissfluhjoch to Kublis. Experts will want to take the cable car which leaves the Weissfluhjoch and ascends to the Weissfluhgipfel, eventually arriving at 9,331 feet. From this point two expert runs drop to the spreading Parsenn. There are good restaurants at both the Weissfluhgipfel and Weissfluhjoch.

Lift improvements continue with high-speed chair lifts replacing many of the remaining drag lifts. A gondola stretching from the Weissfluhjoch over to the Schiflerhut allows skiers to cruise for 20 to 30 minutes and then zip back to the top of the Parsenn.

The toughest runs back into Davos are alongside the Parsennbahn, or down the Meierhofer Talli over moguls and advanced intermediate drops to Davos-Wolfgang, where you'll have to take a bus or train back into town.

Schatzalp/Strela: This area, just above Davos Platz, is the least challenging in the valley. It has finally been graced with a new chair lift replacing the ancient gondola. It is perfect for those searching for a day of cruising.

Jakobshorn: This is the second largest area in Davos, on the opposite side of the valley from the Parsenn. Here the trails have good pitch consistency and top-to-bottom skiing makes use of the entire vertical. It's called "The Fun Mountain," and is ideal for snowboarding.

A cable car rises from the town to the lower station of the Jakobshornbahn, which peaks at 8,497 feet. Here 14 marked trails will keep a skier busy for at least a day. The area is more challenging than the Parsenn, but trails are shorter and more limited.

You reach the Jakobshorn from Davos-Platz with a two-stage cable car or with a high-speed double chair lift. Then six more lifts open up the entire side of the mountain—2,140 feet of wide-open vertical, all above treeline, with another 1,200 feet of trails through the trees (only one or two U.S. resorts have more vertical). Obviously, there is plenty to ski on this side of the valley.

If you are an expert, you have the option of off-piste and dropping into the Dischma Valley to Teufi, where a bus will pick you up and take you back to Davos-Platz.

Rinerhorn: The next area is the Rinerhorn area at Glaris, just up the valley from the main town, with 13 runs and several good advanced intermediate descents. These slopes are normally uncrowded except for the ski schools, which use the wide-open slopes for classes. This is where most of the locals ski, especially on weekends—they can do the Parsenn during the week and would rather ski than wait in line.

You'll arrive at the area first by train or bus from Davos-Platz. Take the Rinerhornbahn up 1,900 feet and take your choice of three more lifts reaching up another 1,446 feet. This area, with its children's facilities, is perfect for families.

Experts can drop down the 4.5-km. run back down to Glaris. Intermediates and beginners will have the entire upper reaches to practice and play in.

Pischa: This area, reached by a short bus ride from Davos, offers uncrowded runs down a 2,230-foot vertical. There isn't a lot for an expert here, but how many of us are that expert? Virtually everyone will enjoy skiing this area with its super-sunny slopes.

Mountain rating

Davos earns an A-plus when it comes to beginners and intermediates. This is perhaps the ideal terrain for learning to ski and for perfecting your technique. For experts, the upper Parsenn terrain may become a little boring (Ah, to be so jaded!), and they might ask where the most challenging skiing—normally off the Parsenn—can be found.

Locals might suggest runs on the Parsenn from the top of the Weissfluhgipfel, the trails that drop into town alongside the Parsennbahn, or the Drostobel-to-Klosters run, which is narrow and sometimes steep. Rinerhorn has great tree skiing and good off-piste as well. The Jakobshorn has bumps and moguls to wear out any skier.

On days with good powder, it pays to hire an instructor for the morning who will take you to the special spots (off-trail) for thrills.

Snowboarding

This resort has become one of the top snowboard destinations in the world. Jakobshorn is the center for snowboard action with plenty of other action in each of the areas. There are halfpipes (one for night boarding) at the Jakobshorn as well as a boardercross park. The Jakobhorn boarderpass is only €33. The normal meeting spots for boarders are Bolgenschanze, Jatzhütte, Fuxägufer, and Chalet Güggel.

Boarders congregate at the Mammut-Bar at the Jochexpress lift or at the New Bar at the middle station of the Höhenweg. The Pischa sector has a fun park near the Mittaltälli lift. And the Rinerhorn has a fun park near the training lift.

Cross-country

Davos has great cross-country skiing—the second largest cross country ski area in Switzerland—with 75 km. of groomed trails.

Ski school (2003/04 prices)

The Davos ski school has more than 200 instructors for skiing and snowboarding. Almost all of them speak some English. There are reductions for groups of senior citizens and for children. Inquire at the ski school to see whether such a group has been organized (081-4162454). There is a lot of off-piste skiing in good winters and many skiers come for that experience. A guide at private instruction rates is the way to go.

Private lessons: half day, €126 (2-1/2 hours); one day, €207 (approximately six hours); ten consecutive days cost €193 per day.

Group lessons	**Adults & Children**
one half-day	€27 (2-1/2 hours)
one day	€40
five half-days (x-c)	€113
five full days	€160

Lift tickets (2003/04 prices)

Separate passes are sold for each of the areas.

The most convenient pass to use is the Klosters/Davos all-inclusive pass (REGA). It includes the Madrisa side of the valley, plus use of the train that runs between Davos and Klosters and as far down the valley as Kublis. It is also good on local buses in Davos and Klosters. The tickets are available only for periods of two days or more.

There are 10 percent discounts for REGA passes purchased for three days or more before the Christmas season, (Nov. 15–Dec. 19).

	Adults	Youth (13–17)	Children (6-12)
two days	€81	€55	€37
three days	€111	€75	€40
six days	€186	€125	€62
fourteen days	€331	€222	€109

NOTE: Day ticket for the Parsenn area costs €40; for Rinerhorn and Pischa, €31; for Jakobshorn, €37.

Important transportation note: The shuttlebuses that carry you from your hotel to the Parsennbahn, or down to the Jakobshornbahn, ply a route up and down the *same* one-way street. If you are in Platz and want to take the shuttlebus to the Parsennbahn, go to the main street, Promenade, which is one-way in the opposite direction. Your bus will come down Promenade in a special lane—against traffic—to take you to the lifts. If you logically head down to Talstrasse, you will have to climb back up to Promenade.

Overall, the bus system has been significantly expanded in the past seasons. Nearly all the outlying lodging is now accessible by bus. The entire system, as well as the train between Davos and the outlying villages, is free to those with guest cards.

Accommodations

Davos hotels range from plush to plain. The following are our top recommendations in each category. The general location—Davos Dorf, Davos Platz an so on—is noted. Price ranges noted for each hotel are per person based on double occupancy high season with half board (breakfast and dinner): €€€—€125+; €€—€75–€125; €—less than €75.

Our recommended five-star hotels are:

Steigenberger Belvedere (081-415-6000, fax 081-415-6001; €€€). This is one of the grand old Alpine hotels in Davos-Platz. The view from the rooms facing the valley will beg for photography. Service cannot be topped anywhere else in town. The hotel restaurant, Romeo and Julia can be excellent and expensive. We enjoyed a superb medallions of reindeer on sautéed forest mushrooms, a Norwegian salmon appetizer was dinner-sized and the cranberry sorbet with fresh cranberries sublime. The indoor pool and spa, with steam and sauna, are very comforting. Complimentary transfers to the train station. In the U.S. call (800) 223-5652.

Hotel Flüela (081-410-1717, fax 081-410-1718; €€€). A family-run hotel conveniently located by the Davos-Dorf station with easy access to all ski areas. A lounge with hardwood floors, comfy chairs and fireplace welcomes you, and the restaurant has beautifully painted ceilings. The rooms are all different.

Morosani Post Hotel (081-415-4500, fax 081-415-4501; €€€). This hotel in Davos Platz is especially popular with Swiss visitors, which speaks well of its quality, service and prices. Rooms are furnished in light pine and the interior is beautifully Alpine, even if the exterior appears cold and square.

Turmhotel Victoria (081-417-5366, fax 081-417-5380; €€€) was formerly the Hotel Cristiana. It re-opened in 1999 and is now a four-star hotel. In Davos-Dorf, it is a bit out of the way from nightlife and restaurants.

The Arabella Sheraton (081-416-1212, fax 081-416-6110; €€€), formerly the Hotel Seehof, is a renovated hotel in Davos Dorf next to the mountain railway and within walking distance of the train station.

Central Hotel (081-415-8200; €€€). An excellent hotel with pool and sauna in Davos-Platz. It has a cozy piano bar.

Meierhof (081-416-8285, fax 081-416-3982; €€+). This is a hotel with a large Swiss clientele in Davos Dorf. The rooms are beautiful and the food exceptional.

Hotel Ochsen (081-415-4444, fax 081-415-4445; €) This hotel is rustic and in the center of the action with an excellent restaurant.

Edelweiss (081-416-1033, fax 081-416-1130; €). B&B. A quaint hotel with private baths. The **Sports Center** in the middle of town offers budget dormitory accommodations for €50–€58 a night with half-board.

The most popular, inexpensive snowboard lodgings are the **Bolgenschanze, Snowboarder's Palace, Bolgenhof and Guesthaus Suvretta** near the Jacobshorn. Near the Rinerhorn most boarders stay at the **RinerLodge**.

Apartments, condominiums, flats

Rental apartments are well organized and bookings can be arranged through the tourist office (see Tourist Information). Write and provide details—when you plan to arrive, how many people will be sharing the apartment and what facilities you desire. They will respond quickly with several choices. The reservations number is 081-415-2121.

It is more convenient to stay in Davos-Platz or Davos-Dorf—Davos-Laret and Davos-Wolfgang are further out of the way. Make your selection and notify the tourist office or the individual owner, depending on the instructions from the tourist office.

Normally, linen and kitchen utensils are included in every apartment. Taxes and cleaning may be extra. Expect to pay €20–€30 per person a night, depending on the number sharing the apartment, its location and its relative position on the luxury scale.

Dining

Davos has scores of restaurants. They are all relatively good. This is a town where taking half-board can be a good idea, at least when it comes to saving money. The finest restaurants here are expensive, but moderate restaurants and most listed here except for Hubli's are far more reasonable.

Hubli's Landhaus in Laret (081-417-1010; fax 081-417-1011) is a local nouvelle cuisine shrine adorned with a Michelin star. Make reservations early. Dinner will end up costing about €65.

Vinikus (081-416-5979) serves in a French bistro atmosphere for €40–€80.

The **Arabello Sheraton** (081-416-3131) is another serving excellent nouvelle cuisine dinners in Davos. Other hotel restaurants that are excellent with reasonable daily menus for €20–€29 are **Flüela** and **Meierhof** in Davos-Dorf, **Ochsen** in Davos-Platz (see the hotel section for their phone numbers) and the **Crystal** (081-414-0101, fax 081-414-0100) also in Davos-Platz.

The **Pöstli** in the Morisani Posthotel has good local fare, and **Al Ponte** serves Italian meals. The **Bündnerstübli** at Dischmastrasse in Dorf is very local, very crowded and very reasonable. Just outside the town, try the **Gasthof Landhaus** in Frauenkirch (081-413-6335) for typical Swiss specialties.

For fondue head to **Bistro Gentiana** (081-413-5649).

The best pizza in town is found at **Al Ponte** or **Il Padrino** in Platz. **Zum Goldenen Drachen** (081-413-2525) in Terminus Hotel and **Zauberberg** (081-415-4141) in the Hotel Europe are the best spots for Chinese food.

Après-ski/nightlife

Davos-Platz is the place to be for any nightlife. For dancing the slightly older groups head to the **Pöstli Club**, open every evening from 8:30 p.m. The younger set meets at the **Cabanna Club**, which gets started at 9 p.m., or the

Cava Grischa. Expect to hear lots of techno rock and to pay about €4.50 for a Coke, more for mixed drinks and beer. The **Ex-Bar** also hops but has a strange period around midnight where they close to change crowds it seems.

The **Chämi Bar** on Promenade is where folk gather to see and be seen, drink, and little else. Immediate après-ski with a bit of class is found at the **Café Schneider** in Davos-Platz or **Café Weber** in Davos-Dorf. These are more coffee and cake spots.

Piano Bar in the Hotel Europe offers changing entertainment. During our last visit a blind black piano player and singer from Atlanta turned out cool tunes for a middle-aged comfortable crowd, some leaning on the piano, some at the bar, others in overstuffed chairs.

Child care (2003/04 prices)

Bobo Club (081-416-2454), is open Monday to Friday. Costs are: one half day, €27; five half days, €113; five consecutive days including lunch, €160. Lunch is served from noon until 2 p.m. and babysitting service during lunch will cost €13. Advanced booking is required.

Other activities

The sports center next to the ice stadium has a public indoor swimming pool, saunas and a solarium. **Pool** and **sauna** cost €8.50 a visit. Swim only is €4.30 a session.

There is **tennis** and **squash** in Davos-Platz with indoor courts (081-413-3131).

Europe's largest natural **ice skating** rink is open, and rentals are available. Entry for adults is €2.60 and for children, €1.70 (415-3604).

Hang-gliding courses are taught by Paragliding Davos (079-237-7500), Flugcenter Grischa (081-422-2070) and Christian Sprecher (401-1414).

There is also a **toboggan run** down the Schatzalp with banked turns and a total drop of over 750 feet. There is no charge for admission. Toboggans are available for rental at the base of the Schatzalp Funicular. Call 081-415-9280.

A **casino** operates in the Europa Hotel.

Getting there

The closest airport is Zürich, nearly three hours away by train. You must change trains in Landquart.

By car, follow the signs to Chur on an excellent superhighway until you get to the Landquart/Davos exit. The drive from Landquart to Davos is through a narrow valley and passes through Kublis and Klosters before arriving at Davos-Platz. The distance from Zürich to Davos is just less than 100 miles.

Tourist information

The tourist information office is open Monday–Saturday, 9 a.m.–6:30 p.m.; Sunday, 10 a.m.–noon and 4:30 p.m to 6 p.m.
Davos Tourism, 7270 Davos-Platz, Switzerland;
Telephone: 081-415-2121, fax 081-415-2100.
Internet: www.davos.ch/
Email: info@davos.ch

Engelberg

This resort is one of the closest to Zürich. It has both challenging skiing and mellow stuff. You can find crowds on the weekends and empty runs during the week. You can come here and ski for a day or an afternoon from Zürich or Lucerne, or you can stay for a week or longer enjoying the scenery.

The region is blessed by a natural beauty found in few places. You have the meeting of three mountain ranges as well as spectacular views of Lake Lucerne on clear days. There are 25 hotels and 250 vacation homes.

Mountain layout

When you ski at Engelberg in central Switzerland, just remember that the Gerschnialp is for beginners and the Titlis is for the advanced. This will save you a few difficult moments if you're wary of the ski school of hard knocks.

At Engelberg there are two major areas. The Brunni is on the sunny side of the valley, with slopes all the way up to the Schonegg, at 6,691 feet. From Schonegg it's an intermediate cruise down to the village.

The finest beginner and lower intermediate skiing is on the opposite mountain, below the Titlis glacier on Gerschnialp. Ski out the doorway of the six-person gondola station at Trübsee and down to the Gerschnialp lifts.

Because it is central Switzerland's major resort, Engelberg is crowded on weekends. During the week things are far less hectic. Everyone but the beginner eventually makes it up to the 10,624-foot-high summit of Titlis. This is where the best skiers sharpen their skills. To join them, take the gondola from the valley floor to Trübsee and then the unique two-section rotating cable car the rest of the way up to Klein-Titlis, at 9,908 feet. You've spent over 40 minutes getting here, so enjoy the view all the way to the St. Gotthard Pass off to the south, and from Lucerne to the north past Interlaken to the Bernese Oberland in one grand sweep to the west.

From the Kleine Titlis there is a memorable run all the way to Trübsee from what seems (on clear days) like the roof of Europe. The run crosses the snowfields below Titlis peak toward the Rotegg lift, then becomes a black trail, dripping steeply for most of the 2,500-foot drop to Stand. After Stand, the run mellows a bit as it tracks down to the base of the cable car. Take it easy the first time down. The glacial ice, sharp turns, and steepness of the slope can be treacherous. Don't let the nets, set out at the worst places, break your concentration.

After one run some intermediates choose to stay on the wider red run from Stand down to Trübsee. If you make this decision, take the horizontal T-bar across the frozen lake to Alpstübli, where you can go up to the 8,474-foot-high Jochstock. The red run down to Jochpass and Alpstübli is a good warmup for the Kanonenrohr.

The Kanonenrohr (cannon barrel) section is only a few hundred meters long, but you'll turn enough to keep your thighs burning for a while. Lower intermediates should opt for the blue trail to the left of the toughest section. To repeat the best part of the run, stop at the Untertrübsee cable car station and go back up. From Jochstock down to the ground station is about six miles, and it's about eight miles from the Titlis peak.

The best off-trail skiing is on the Laub above the Ritz restaurant and below Titlis. The 1,000-meter vertical drop is a challenge for even experienced skiers, and a guide (for about €80) is recommended.

Mountain rating

For beginners, the slopes of the Gerschnialp and Untertrübsee are best. Intermediates will be challenged on both sides of the valley, particularly up on the glacier which tops Titlis. Experts will discover whether they really merit that classification after several runs down from the glacier summit. In short, Engelberg is an excellent ski destination for the broadest range of skiers.

Snowboarding

Engelberg is somewhat of a snowboarders' hill. Thousands of local Swiss kids come here to learn tricks and turns. There is excellent riding on the glacier at 10,000 feet. The 12 km.-long drop down from the summit of Titlis to town is one of the great Swiss snowboard adventures. There is a snowpark and a halfpipe in the Jochberg section.

Ski school (2003/04 prices)

Two schools (for information, call 041-637-3040) with 65 instructors offer group and private lessons for skiers and snowboarders.

Private lessons cost €87 for two hours; €120 for a half day (three hours); and €190 for a full day (five hours).

Group lessons are offered in full-day blocks. The ski schools offer four hours of instruction a day. The following rates include lifts as well. An adult full day, €37; two days, €70; three days, €103; four days, €123; five days, €137.

Cross-country lessons are all private.

Lift tickets (2003/04 prices)

The Engelberg ticket is good for all 25 lifts in the area, opening about 62 miles of trails. There are discounts for children, senior citizens and families. Day ticket prices drop a few euros per hour after 10 a.m.

	Adults	Children(6–15)	Youth (16–20)
one day (Mon. - Fri.)	€35	€21	€28
one day (Sat. - Sun.)	€39	€23	€31
two days	€65	€38	€52
three days	€93	€56	€75
six days	€167	€100	€133

Lift tickets four days or more are discounted 10% for skiers with an Engelberg guest card.

Accommodations

Engelberg is a relatively small town (3,300 residents) with a major tourist capacity. There are nearly 10,000 beds available in hotels, guest houses and pensions, plus another 6,500 in private homes and apartments. Check with the Tourist Center for all reservations. Call 041-639-7777 or fax 041-639-7766. Price ranges noted for each hotel are per person based on double occupancy with half board (breakfast and dinner): €€€—€125+; €€—€75–€124; €—less than €75.

The all-inclusive plan offers dramatic savings for a week's accommodation and buffet breakfast, six-day ski pass, ski bus and other extras, starting at around €500 a week during most of January in a two-star hotel; €550 a week during most of January in a three-star hotel; €600 a week during most of January in a four-star hotel;. The following hotels offer excellent accommodations:

Berghotel Trübsee (041-637-1371, fax 041-637-3720; €€€) hotel has a phenomenal setting halfway up the Titlisbahn. The panoramas are unparalleled and the meals are fantastic. The cafeteria is open to the public during the day, but the wonderful dinners are for hotel guests only.

Hotel Regina Titlis (041-637-2828, fax 041-637-2392; €€€) is one of our favorite hotels in town. It is considered the best.

Hotel Schweitzerhof (041-637-1105; €€) has a covered pool and is in the middle of town. Guest can only have half-pension because the kitchen is closed for lunch.

Hotel Engelberg (041-637-1168, fax 041-637-3235; €€) is an affordable, pleasant hotel in the city center with an excellent restaurant.

Garni Sunmatt (637-2045, fax 041-637-1533; €) is B&B only but a delight.

Hotel Crystal (041-637-2122, fax 041-637-2979; €) has an exceptional kitchen with very pleasant rooms at bargain prices.

Hotel Central (041-637-3232, fax 041-637-3233; €€) Ideal spot for all activities in town with its own pool and sauna.

Hotel Europe (041-637-0094, fax 041-637-2255; €–€€).

If the hotels in Engelberg are fully booked, as they often are in peak season, the lakeside city of Lucerne is a good alternative. It is only 30 minutes from the slopes by car. It is a perfect arrangement for the non-skier/rider traveling with a skier/rider.

Apartments, condominiums, flats

Engelberg has much to offer the skier seeking apartment accommodations. Prices start at €250 a week for a one-bedroom apartment. The average apartment for four costs in January about €410, and in February about €475. These prices include cleaning and bed linens.

The tourist office (041-639-7777 or fax 041-639-7766) has a computerized listing of available apartments, and an inquiry will be answered by mail the same day.

Dining

The **Dorfstübli** on the first floor of the Hotel Engelberg is highly recommended. The menu of the day will run about €22 and ordering à la carte can cost twice as much. Other excellent eateries are **Restaurant Spannort** (041-637-2626) for local fare, **Maro** (041-637-1076) has good reports, and **Restaurant La Strega** (041-637-2828) in the Hotel Regina Titlis has great Italian meals, but at a price—daily menu runs around €40. As mentioned in the hotel section, Hotel Crystal has an excellent and affordable restaurant.

Après-ski/nightlife

Drop into the **Spindle** in the cellar of the Alpenclub Hotel. It's crowded with the 18- to 25-year-old set, as is the nearby **Casino**. Our favorites were **Dream Life**, an English pub at the Central Hotel. The **Bierlialp Chalet** disco has dancing in the center of town. Try **Yucatan** in Hotel Bellevue.

Child care (2003/04 prices)

The ski school (041-637-1074 or 041-637-3040) operates a ski kindergarten for kids ages 3–5, from 2 p.m.–5 p.m.

For kids 3 to 5 years of age who ski, rates are: full day, €40; two days, €77: three days, €113; five days, €163. These rates include four hours of lessons, supervision during lunch, lift tickets and ski test. Lunch costs €7 per day.

Group lessons for kids ages 6–15 are: full day, €47; two days, €93: four days, €167; five days, €183. These rates include four hours of lessons, supervision during lunch, lift tickets and ski test. For kids who don't ski the rates are significantly lower. Lunch costs €8 per day.

Other activities

Engelberg is sunny most of the year. The biggest non-skiing pursuits are **hiking** and **sightseeing**.

Engelberg has a sports center with indoor and outdoor **ice skating**, **indoor tennis courts**, a **fitness center**, a **curling** competition area, **billiards**, **darts** and **table tennis**.

Horse-drawn sleigh rides are available throughout the winter; on Fridays, January through March, nighttime sleigh rides are a tradition.

Visit the beautiful twelvth-century Benedictine abbey at the edge of town. For more extensive touring, take the train for a tour of Lucerne and the four lakes area.

The **Engelberg Talmuseum** has been set up in the Wappenhaus. Visitors will get a good idea of what life is and was like in these high Alpine valleys.

Courses in **trick skiing** are offered (041-637-1074).

The most scenic local excursions other than the ride up the Titlisbahn, is **a trip to Schwand**, about five miles away, where from a vantage point above the church, you get the best view of the ring of mountains.

Getting there

The main international airport is Zürich, and transfers are by train or automobile. Driving time from Zürich is about one-and-a-half hours. If possible, make a sightseeing stop in Lucerne along the way.

Tourist information

Contact the Tourist Center, CH-6390 Engelberg, Switzerland.
Telephone 041-639-7777, fax 041-639-7766.
For hotel and apartment reservations call the tourist center.
Internet: www.engelberg.ch. E-mail: welcome@engelberg.ch.

Flims Laax Falera

Flims Laax Falera, the Alpen Arena, is still one of the undiscovered ski areas in Switzerland as far as American and British skiers are concerned, even with excellent ski club patronage. Unlike the best-known Swiss ski resorts, which were patronized by English visitors, Flims Laax Falera were discovered by the Swiss and the Germans, who know a good area when they see it. The ski area is in the southeast part of Switzerland across the valley from Arosa.

Flims is a small village in the traditional sense. The ski lifts start from the village center (about 3,600 feet altitude) and the major hotels are spread throughout the village. Laax, a couple of kilometers down the road, as far as skiers are concerned, is limited to the new hotels and apartments, purpose-built at the base of the Crap Sogn Gion cable car. Not only are the major hotels centered here but also the major nightlife. Flims is perhaps the more Swiss; Laax is a purer ski vacation experience.

It is hard to describe the incredible expanse of ski area that surrounds a skier as he or she gazes from the station at the top of the Crap Sogn Gion cable car that rises from Laax. This is a wide-open area that cries out for all-day skiing.

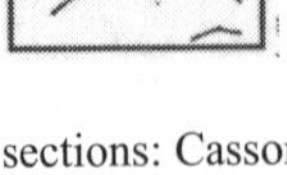

Mountain layout

One major lift from each town carries skiers to the snowfields, which are in turn linked by an extensive far-flung lift system. These lifts are not tightly packed, but they service the trails belonging to four major sections: Cassons Grat, La Siala, Crap Sogn Gion and Vorab.

Above Laax the cable car reaches the Crap Sogn Gion, at 7,283 feet, and a second continues to Crap Masegn, 650 feet higher. From here, skiers can shoot back into the valley toward Falera or to the lower cable car station. Other runs drop into the opposite valley, where more lifts bring skiers up to the La Siala area above Flims. High-altitude buffs head to the Vorab area, which at 9,842 feet presents great panoramas and skiing.

Snowboarders will find a boarder park and halfpipe on the Crap Sogn Gion with Café No Name. There are also two halfpipes and a snow park on the Vorab glacier.

Mountain rating

The beginner will find the best areas on Nagens and on Crap Sogn Gion and on Foppa, the first stage of the way up the Cassons Grat.

Intermediates will be overjoyed with the Crap Sogn Gion section and can find more than enough challenging runs anywhere in the resort area.

The expert skiers can stay busy when the mood strikes them, especially beneath the Crap Sogn Gion cable car, the back side of the Vorab and through the Cassons Grat powder and trails. But they will have to pick their spots.

Ski school (2002/03 prices)

Swiss Ski School Flims Laax Falera has classes in all the villages. **Private instruction** costs €132 for a half day (two hours), €229 for a full day (four hours).

Group lessons for adults are €132 for three full days; €188 for five full days.

Group lessons for children are €32 for a half day; €132 for five half days.

The ski school offers a special Carving Academy to help intermediate skiers improve their technique with shaped skis. A half-day lesson with skis provided is €45.

Snowboard lessons are available throught the Snowboard Fahrschule in Laax-Murschetg (081-9277155). Group lessons are €36 for a half-day course, €59.25 for a full day. Private lessons are €100 for one boarder for a half day. Full-day lessons for one boarder is €131. Extra boarders cost €28.

Lift tickets (2003/04 prices)

A combination ticket that allows unlimited skiing in the Flims Laax Falera area costs as follows (a photo, which they take at the lift station, is required for lift passes of six days or more):

	Adults	Children & Youth	Seniors
one day	€41.40	€20.70	€41.40
two days	€82.80	€41.40	€82.80
six days	€207.60	€103.80	€166

Children are ages 6–12; youth are 13–17; Seniors are males 65+ and females 62+.

Discount cards: With a Jackdaw Youth Card, kids ages 13–17 receive a 50 percent reduction on the basic adult price. Senior citizens, who have the Pioneer Card and are skiing for six days or more, get 20 percent off the basic price for adults . Check out www.alpenarena.ch/clubcard/eng/ to see how you can get these discount cards by registering on the Internet.

Accommodations

Rates noted below are based on double occupancy during the high-season (February) with half pension:

€€€—€125+; €€—€75–€124; €—less than €75.

Prices are around 20 percent less in low season. All-inclusive White Week packages are available during special weeks throughout the winter season. They include seven nights accommodation, six days of lifts and five days of lessons.

Park Hotel Waldhaus (081-9284848; fax 081-9284858; €€€) The best hotel in Flims. A beautiful hotel that is almost its own small village. The buildings are interconnected by covered paths and underground walkways. You can be elegant and formal or casual in this complex in the woods.

Adula (081-9282828; fax 081-9282829; €€€) In Flims, this runs a close second to the Park Hotel Waldhaus. In fact, many people prefer it because it is cozier and smaller. It has an indoor pool, sauna, fitness room and a new spa. Its Barga restaurant is considered one of the best in the region. The Italian restaurant La Clav costs about half as much.

Albana Sporthotel (081-9112333; fax 081-9113109; €€) is right next to the lifts.

Hotel Curtgin (081-9113566; fax 081-9113455; €€–€€€), an exceptional hotel, is also near the lifts and features light, modern cuisine.

Hotel Bellevue (081-9113131; fax 081-9111232; €€-) is only about 150 yards from the lifts and has one of the best traditional Swiss restaurants in town, Bundnerstube, nestled in the hotel's four-century-old cellar.

Hotel Meiler-Prau da Monis (081-9209393; fax 081-9209394; €€) In Flims and close to everything.

Alpenhotel Flims (081-9279800; fax 081-9279801; €€) Ten minutes from the lift in Flims Dorf. Enjoy a cozy atmosphere in the Tschuetta Bar.

Arvenhotel Waldeck (081-9281414; fax 081- 9281415; €€) In Flims/Waldhaus this hotel is known for its restaurant that features very affordable daily menus. Rooms are done in knotty pine and the ambiance is casual.

Hotel Grischuna (081-911-1139; fax 081-911412; €€) is 50 yards from the lifts.

Alte Säge (081-9112807; fax 081-9112841; €), only a five-minute walk from the lifts, is packed with boarders paying only €23 with breakfast in dormitory rooms. Dinners cost about €13.

In Laax the best places to stay are up at Laax-Murschetg near the lifts. Try the surprisingly affordable **Hotel Laaxerhof** (081-9208200; fax 081-9208210; €€) and **Sporthotel Signina** (081-9279000; fax 081-9279001; €€). The Laaxerhof has an indoor pool. The Sporthotel Signina has indoor tennis.

Hotel Rancho Laax (081-9271800; fax 081-9271899; €€) is, for lack of a better description, a condo-hotel. Some apartments are rented out with half-pension, others are rented as simply self-catered condos. This complex has an indoor swimming pool, fitness center and covered parking.

Garni Casa Selva (081-9212829; fax 081-9212827; €€) is a B&B near the lifts.

Budget boarders and skiers can check out dormitory beds at the **Riders Palace** (081-9279700, fax 081-9279701; €) where bunks can go for only €20.

Down in the village of Laax-Dorf, stay in either **Arena Alva** (081-9272727; fax 081-9272700; €€) or **Hotel Bellaval** (081-9214700; fax 081-9214855; €€).

For a unique experience you can stay at the highest hotel in the Alps, **Crap Sogn,Gion Mountain Hostel** (081-9277373; fax 081-9277374; €€€). Sleep at an altitude of 7,309 feet in the summit station of the cable car.

Apartments, condominiums, flats

Flims, Laax and Falera are well organized to handle apartment rentals. Apartments are normally rented out for a minimum stay of one week, Saturday to Saturday; in the Christmas and Easter seasons a minimum two-week rental is often required.

The tourist office keeps a computerized, updated listing of available apartments. When writing, include the number of beds required, the preferred number of rooms, and your planned vacation dates. You will receive a quick response that lists a selection of apartments and prices. Select your apartment and contact Flims Tourism.

Normally, linen and kitchen utensils are provided. Other communal or private amenities, such as swimming pool, sauna, TV or room phone all add to the cost. Apartments rent for €26–€197 per person a night.

Dining

Area restaurants are reasonably priced and most feature a good selection of international and regional specialties with some exceptionally fine dining available in both valleys.

The best in Flims, according to Gault Millau, is the **Restaurant Barga** (081-9282828) in the Hotel Adula. The **Fidazerhof** (081-9113503), filled with Swiss tradition, is rated by Michelin as the best in Flims.

In Laax, the **Posta Veglia** (081-9214466) is highly recommended for traditional Swiss cooking and has a two-Michelin-fork rating. The restaurant at the **Hotel Des Alpes** (081-9110101) comes highly recommended with affordable daily menus starting some days at less than €10 for three courses. For pizza try **Pizzeria Pomodoro**.

From Laax head directly to Sagogn about two-and-a-half km. from the village, for a dining treat at **Da Veraguth Carnetg** (081-9276464; fax 081-9213698). This place rates one Michelin star and dining is in an elegant rustic setting. Try the special ravioli, meatcakes and lobster with fennel. This is a gourmet treat that will cost about €65–€85. Make reservations early.

Other excellent restaurants in Laax-Murschetg are those at the **Hotel Laaxerhof** (081-9208200) and **Sporthotel Signina** (081-9279000) where both restaurants feature very affordable daily menus starting at about €13.

Après-ski/nightlife

The best meeting spot in the area is the **Iglu Bar** in Flims that caters to a younger crowd earlier in the evening. An older crowd congregates for the special shows that start around midnight. The **Argel Flims** next to the Iglu also has good après-ski for the younger set.

In Laax, the **Red Cat** offers action reminiscent of big city discos. The **Casa Veglia** in Laax has a somewhat older crowd and is more sedate. You'll pay about €7 for a beer and €10 for a mixed drink.

The **Crap Bar** and the **Granite Bar** are hotspots for snowboarders.

Child care (2003/04 prices)

Kindergartens associated with the famous Swiss Ski School operate in the area. In Flims and Laax, the children's ski school and kindergarten is open from 8:30 a.m. until 4 p.m.

Rates are €34.50 for a half day; €62.50 for a full day; €139 for five half days; and €243 for five full days. Lunch is served, but must be requested at the time of booking.

Other activities

Ice skating is €4 a half day (€8 including skate rental). Play **tennis** in the Park Hotel Waldhaus in Flims and in the Hotel Signina in Laax. There are varying court prices for guests and non-guests depending on the time of day, ranging from €13–€26 per hour.

Six heated hotel pools are open to the public—Park Hotel Waldhaus, Schweitzerhof and Adula in Flims, and the Laaxerhof and Signina in Laax.

A public swimming pool is open in Laax Monday to Thursday from 13:30 p.m. to 9:30 p.m. On Friday it closes at 8 p.m. and on Saturday and Sunday it closes at 6 p.m. It is also open 9:30 a.m. to noon on Sunday. Entrance is €5 for adults and €3 for children.

Getting there

The closest airport is Zürich. From there you can take a train to Chur, where you must change for a postbus to Flims, Laax or Falera. The entire trip takes about three hours.

If driving, take the main road to Chur and continue until you see signs for Flims to the right. Driving time is about two hours. Do not try to approach Laax, Falera and Flims from the west—the Oberalp pass is closed in winter.

Tourist information

Office Flims, Alpenarena.ch, CH-7017 Flims, Switzerland; tel. 081-920-9200; fax 081-920-9201. Hotel and apartment booking: tel. 081-920-9202.

Office Laax, Alpenarena.ch, CH-7031 Laax, Switzerland; tel. 081-920-8181; fax 081-920-8182.

Office Falera, Alpenarena.ch, CH-7153 Falera, Switzerland; tel. 081-921-3030; fax 081-921-4830.

Internet: www.alpenarena.ch

E-mail: tourismus@alpenarena.ch

Gstaad-Saanenland Super Ski Region

People associate Gstaad more with the jet set than with good skiing, and that's a mistake, because it has outstanding slopes for beginners and intermediates.

This Alpine village tucked into a scenic valley just east of Lac Leman (Lake Geneva), two hours from Geneva and 90 minutes from Interlaken, is part of a thriving ski circuit called Ski Gstaad. When you buy a lift ticket in Gstaad, or at one of the ten smaller resorts in the area, you can use any of 69 lifts opening up about 250 km. of prepared trails. The other villages lie stretched along the railway line (from east to west): St. Stephan, Zweisimmen, Saanenmöser, Schönried, Gstaad, Saanen, Rougemont, Chateau d'Oex, Les Moulins-with Lauenen, Gsteig and Reusch accessible by bus up the valleys fanning from Gstaad.

Mountain layout

The skiing in the immediate area of Gstaad is fragmented. The relatively low Eggli (5,494 feet) is the largest area, interconnected with the peak of Videmanette and the towns of Saanen and Rougemont.

The Wasserngrat (6,365 feet) and the Wispile (6,397 feet) are the two other totally separated areas. The Wasserngrat is the most challenging of the three areas, but is limited to two lifts. However, the skiing is superb and there is hardly ever a line. If the Eggli is crowded, this area offers skiing with no waiting. (It should be noted that beginners and lower intermediates may be slightly out of their league here.)

The Wispile is not as difficult as the Wasserngrat and is closer to town.

This is a good intermediate area with limited lifts but long, enjoyable runs; wide stretches of the slopes are left unprepared for powder hounds. It also has short lines and is within walking distance of the Eggli lifts. The Swiss Ski School is located at its base and the drag lift is used mainly by the ski school.

The Eggli shows one black run and an intermediate should seldom feel anxiety here. The run through the trees from the chair lift at Eggli Stand to the ground T-bar station in neighboring Saanen has enough moguls and turns for an expert.

There is some genuine skiing adventure above Gstaad. The finest is La Videmanette. Ski over the Eggli and down to the Pra Cluen chair lift to reach the area above neighboring Rougemont, or drive there. From Rougemont, four-passenger gondolas ascend past rocky pinnacles to the La Videmanette summit at 7,071 feet. The run down through the rocks off the back side is strictly for experts.

On the Videmanette front side, the first 300 meters straight over the edge is also an eye-opener (skittish types can take the traverse around the rim of the bowl). There's a difficult mogul field to negotiate before beginning the remainder of the 3.5-mile intermediate run to Rougemont. Alternatively, ski around the corner to the top of the Pra Cluen lift and cruise the 3.5-mile-long schuss into the valley.

There is summer glacier skiing at Les Diablerets (10,637 feet), reached by a Glacier 3000 Col du Pillon cable car at the end of the valley. This glacier has also become a favorite of snowboarders.

The Hornberg section is the largest interconnected grouping of lifts in the region. It is not directly connected with Gstaad, but is easily reached by bus or train (both included with your ski pass). Take either the Horneggli lift from Schönried or the Saanerslochgrat gondola from Sannenmöser. Both lifts are opposite the respective railway stations, making it impossible to get lost. This area, a lower-intermediate paradise, is served by 14 lifts, which keeps waiting time to less than five minutes.

For more challenging runs, head for the St. Stephan lifts connected with Hornberg. Take the Saanerslochgrat gondola and ski down to Chaltebrunne.

Then take the chair lift up to the Gandlouenegrat, which sits at the top of the St. Stephan section. The face of the mountain from Gandlouenegrat down to Chaltebrunne is an enjoyable wide-open slope. There is something for everyone, from advanced beginner to expert. Playing here can take up half the day. Time it right for lunch and eat at the Chemi Hütte at Lengebrand on the slopes above St. Stephan, at the top of the chair lift from town.

Opposite the Hornberg section is the Rellerligrat (6,285 feet) with what many claim is the most beautiful view of Gstaad. The slopes face the sun, and so are the first to lose snow. Mornings can be icy and afternoons slushy, but skiing here on sunny days is a joy. The restaurant at the top is one of the best in the area. The runs back into the valley are long cruising trails, with a long black run under the gondola for experts.

Zweisimmen offers a relatively isolated ski area flanked on the left by St. Stephan and on the right by the Hornberg lifts. A new lift from Rinderberg to Saanersloch now connects this area with the rest of the trails. The gondola from town to the Rinderberg opens up seven prepared runs served by five lifts. It is pleasant for a day's skiing. Most of the people who stay in Zweisimmen take the train to ski the Hornberg section.

Chateau d'Oex is another area included in the regional ski pass. Here the La Braye gondola lifts skiers over a ridge behind the town to a mellow area of about a dozen runs.

Despite the relatively low-lying intermediate slopes, Gstaad enjoys good snow most years from late December to mid-April, with skiing available on the glacier through the end of April.

Mountain rating

If you are a beginner, Gstaad is an excellent destination. There are plenty of gentle inclines to practice snowplows and turns. The finest beginner run is the 1.253-km.-long Skilift Schopfen slope from the gondola station on the Eggli.

Intermediates will be overjoyed at the variety. Just when you think you've mastered it all, you can cut through the woods or go over the edge of a mogul field you've been bypassing and suddenly realize you have more to learn.

Experts can enjoy Gstaad if they place more emphasis on technique than thrills.

Ski school (2002/03 prices)

Gstaad, with more than 100 instructors, has a good reputation for English-speaking ski instructors and for private lessons. It is open 8:30 a.m.-noon and 2:30 p.m.-6 p.m. The Saanenland region has four ski schools in various towns.

Private lesson rates: one hour (one to four persons), €50; all day, €185.

Group lesson rates: full day, €31.50; five consecutive days, €130.

Ski classes meet directly on the Wispile slope or at the entrance to the Wispile gondola station. Call 744-1865 for information and bookings for Gstaad Ski School.

Lessons are available for cross-country and snowboarding.

Snowboarding lessons cost €28 per lesson and €112 for five days of lessons.

Lift tickets (2003/04 prices) .

These multiday tickets are good for the entire Gstaad Super Ski Region area covering 69 lifts and 250 km. of runs for all lift tickets purchased for at least two days.The one-day tickets are good in the particular sector where they are purchased. They cover every town and slope mentioned in this chapter.

Lift tickets are also are good on the railroad, on buses and for entrance to the covered pool in Gstaad.

	Adults	**children (6-15)**
one day (per region)	€19.50–€36	€19.50–€22
two days	€68.50	€42
six days	€177	€120.50

Accommodations

All hotels in the region offer special weekly programs running throughout the season except for holiday periods. These packages include seven nights accommodation with half board, a six-day ski pass, cross-country or snowboarding pass, plus entrance into the indoor swimming pool and local transportation.

Price ranges noted for each hotel are per person based on double occupancy high season with half board (breakfast and dinner): €€€–€125+; €€–€75–€124; €–less than €75. For information call 748-8181.

Gstaad Palace (033-748-5000, fax 033-748-5001; €€€) The best in town. A chance to rub shoulders with the best of the movie, fashion and jet-set world if you can afford the entrance.

Grand Hotel Park (033-748-9800, fax 033-748-9808; €€€) New hotel with indoor salt-water pool, heated outdoor pool, fitness center, squash and tennis, greenhouse coffee shop, elegant and rustic restaurants only two minutes' walk from the center of Gstaad.

Le Grand Chalet (033-748-7676, fax 033-748-7677; €€€) A small, charming hotel on the hill with a magnificent view of Gstaad.

Bernerhof (033-748-8844, fax 033-748-8840; €€€) Centrally located with swimming pool. Spacious rooms, great restaurant, good service with good kindergarten.

Hotel Arc-en-Ciel (033-748-4343, fax 033-748-4353; €) Best location for skiing the Eggli. Opposite the gondola station and near a ski rental shop. Quiet, with a good restaurant.

Christiania (033-744-5121, fax 033-744-7109; €€) is small with an Egyptian restaurant.

Hotel Gstaaderhof (033-748-6363, fax 033-748-6360; €) Good location relatively near lifts, station and downtown. It is known for good, affordable meals.

Hotel Alphorn (033-748-4545, fax 033-748-4546; €) Good for skiers; near the lift for the Wispile (across the highway from the Eggli gondola). It is a good place for meals.

Posthotel Rössli (033-748-4242, fax 033-748-4243; €) This is one of the hotel prizes in Gstaad, but is small and booked very early. The restaurant is one of the best in town.

Sporthotel Victoria (033-748-4422, fax 033-748-4420; €) Excellent food; has two restaurants and a pizzeria. The most reasonable hotel in town.

Saanen

Hotel Steigenberger in Gstaad/Saanen (033-748-6464, fax 033-748-6466; €€€) Deluxe hotel with pool, sauna, good disco and two restaurants.

Landhaus (748-4040, fax 748-4049; €€) Good, middle-priced hotel in town center with a well-respected restaurant.

Saanerhof (033-744-1515, fax 033-744-1323; €€) is a 23-room hotel with a noted restaurant that offers affordable daily menus.

Alpine Lodge (033-748-4151, fax 033-748-4152; €€) features a Salomon rental shop, computers in every room, 24-hour Internet access, pool and fitness room.

Saanenmöser

Hotel Hornberg (033-748-6688, fax 033-748-6689; €€€) Everything a good ski hotel should be: near the lifts, pool and sauna and an owner who helps his clients.

Schönried

Hotel Alpenrose (033-744-6767, fax 033-744-6712; €€€) This is a Relais et Châteaux property. Many claim the hotel restaurant is the best in the area.

Hotel Alpin Nova (033-748-6767, fax 033-748-6768; €€-€€€) Centrally located with a traditional mountain atmosphere.

Hotel Bahnhof (033-744-4242; fax 033-744-6142; €€) Includes ski school. The lowest priced major hotel in town with nice rooms and close to the station.

Chateau d'Oex

This town down the tracks toward Montreux from Gstaad is significantly less expensive than the Saanenmöser-Gstaad-Saanen area. The town is in the French part of Switzerland. It is not as charming nor as "Alpine" as Gstaad.

But for overall savings of about 25 percent, this might be the place to stay if you don't mind the half-hour train ride to the major slopes above Gstaad and Schönried. Good English spoken at both.

Hostellerie Bon Accueil (026-924-6320, fax 026-924-5126; €€), built in an 18th-century chalet, is considered the best in town.

Residence La Rocaille (026-924-6215, fax 026-924-5249) is a tiny nine-room hotel with a wonderful restaurant that serves affordable meals daily.

Hotel de Ville (026-942-7477, fax 026-924-4121; €) is one of Switzerland's bargains with good meals thrown in for good measure.

Hotel Beau-Sejour (026-924-7423, fax 026-924-5806; €) This hotel is very convenient, across from the train station and the cable car to the Chateau d'Oex area.

Hotel Ours (026-9242279, fax 026-9242270; €) In the center of town about three minutes from the lift and train station.

Apartments, condominiums, flats

Vacation apartment rentals are available in every village. Information on rentals is provided by the tourist offices. In middle season an apartment with one bedroom, living room and furnished kitchen costs approximately €450–€900 a week. Ample room for four people is typical. Call 033-748-8184 for reservations.

Dining

Even with Gstaad's jet-set reputation, the best restaurants are just outside town. Naturally, the Palace has several world-class restaurants, but then again most of us are not up to Palace prices. **The Cave** in the Olden Hotel (033-744-3444) in the center of town has excellent dining by anyone's standards. Expect to pay top price, but you'll never know who you're going to rub shoulders with.

Always vying for best gourmet restaurant in town, and winning according to Michelin, is the one-star **Chesery** (033-744-2451, fax 033-744-8947) serving phenomenal Asian-influenced cuisine.

By far the best Italian meal is found at **Rialto** (033-744-3474) where the daily menu will run about €27.

Considerably more reasonable is the **Rössli** across the main street from the Olden—typical Swiss cooking at its best. The **Arc-en-Ciel** opposite the Eggli gondola is stark but serves excellent Italian food at low prices.

The **Sonnenhof** (033-744-1023) in Saanen-Unterbord has mouthwatering meals with vistas that are hard to beat. You must call for reservations.

Out-of-Gstaad Places

Schönried has the **Alpenrose** (033-744-6767) with a Relais et Châteaux gourmet restaurant. This small nouvelle cuisine restaurant is one of the tops in Switzerland. An exceptional traditional Swiss restaurant is the **Bären** (033-755-1033) in Gsteig on the road from Gstaad to Les Diablerets.

Down the road from Gsteig try the **Rössli** in Feutersoey (033-755-1012). In tiny Lauenen enjoy a meal at the **Wildhorn** (033-7653012). Finally, don't miss the 17th-century **Restaurant Chlösterli** (033-755-1912) outside town on the road to Les Diablerets.

On the slopes

The best mountain restaurants above Gstaad are at the Eggli and Kalberhöni. Above Schönried, try the **Hornberg** restaurants—one is slightly more upscale, the other has wonderful *rösti* and plenty of pasta. Both have great terraces to enjoy the sun. **The Rellerli Mountain Restaurant** on the opposite side of the valley from Hornberg enjoys a storybook view of Gstaad. Try the **Chemi Hütte** at Lengebrand above St. Stephan.

In Château-d'Oex make sure to stop at **Chamois** for a wonderful meal and a panorama from 3,753 feet.

Après-ski/nightlife

The place for après-ski just off the slopes is the **Olden Bar**. It's normally packed. Otherwise, even on Friday night, this town snoozes until midnight.

The **Chesery Bar** and the **Stöckli Bar** in the Bernerhof were recommended as the best places to have a beer or drink, but both are very quiet. **Club 95** in the Hotel Victoria is a popular disco with a young crowd. **The Grotte** in the Hotel Alpinnova is a good disco.

The well-heeled enjoy an après-ski drink in the **Palace Hotel** lounge above the city. Take money if you want to join them. For starters, the Palace disco cover is €6.

After dark there's a lively crowd and live music at the Chlösterli disco outside town. Also try the **GreenGo** at the Palace Hotel for dancing.

Gstaad has a new casino where the rich can strut their stuff and gamble away some of their earnings or inheritances.

Child care

The Gstaad Tourist Office can help with child care arrangements. Call 033-748-8181. The ski schools all have programs – call 033-744-1865 in Gstaad or 033-748-8160 in Saanen.

In Chateau d'Oex, call Mme. Blati at Les Clematites, 026-924-7351. She takes children from 2 months old. The ski school has children's lessons, 026-924-6848.

Other activities

Gstaad has an excellent covered **swimming** pool.

Gstaad is in a good location for train or auto **excursions** to Montreux, Geneva, Lausanne, Interlaken and Bern, all within approximately two hours by train.

There are world-class **toboggan runs** here. Eggli-Grund is 6 km. Turbach is 2 km. and Chinnetritt-Gsteig is 6 km. That's a long way to slide.

Ballooning over the Alps provides a once-in-a-lifetime thrill. Balloon rides can be arranged through the tourist office (033-748-8181). The price is €325–€350 per person for about two hours. **Paragliding** is also available.

Ice skating, **curling** and **horseback riding** are available (033-744-4368).

Getting there

The most popular international airport is Zürich. From there, it is about three-and-a-half hours by train to Gstaad. Rental cars are also available in Zürich. You may also arrive in Geneva which doesn't have as convenient train connections, but is closer by rental car.

Tourist information

Information on the Ski Gstaad Region is through Gstaad Saanenland Tourist Association, CH-3780 Gstaad, Switzerland.
Telephone 033-748-8181; fax 033-7488133.
Tourist Office Chateau d'Oex: 026-9242525.
Internet: www.gstaad.ch
E-mail: gst@gstaad.ch

Jungfrau Region

Grindelwald, Wengen, Mürren

The spectacular and far-flung Jungfrau region is near Interlaken on the map; for intermediate skiers it is at the end of the Alpine rainbow. A network of 188 km. of trails spreads over a vast expanse of slopes, set in two majestic valleys about an hour's drive from Bern, the Swiss capital. The backdrop created by the Jungfrau, Mönch and Eiger mountains is one you see on posters the world over. This series of valleys is the definition of picture-postcard beautiful.

The Jungfrau region has three major ski areas accessible from its twin-valley towns. For many Americans, the Jungfraujoch is best known for the Eiger, a 13,026-foot peak made famous by Clint Eastwood's movie, *The Eiger Sanction,* that came out in 1975. Although the movie is over 25 years old, the view hasn't changed.

The best-known resort is Grindelwald, a picture-postcard settlement nestled at the foot of 10,000-foot peaks about 30 minutes by train or car from Interlaken. Wengen is a car-free resort, reached only by cog railway from Lauterbrunnen, that shares many of Grindelwald's ski areas. And Mürren is another car-free town on the opposite side of the Lauterbrunnen Valley nestled beneath the Schilthorn.

Skiing is more or less divided into three regions. Grindelwald has skiing at Grindelwald First (First, in this case, means peak), which in its day had Europe's oldest operating chair lift. Ironically, this is also the location of the first chair lift in Switzerland.

The second area (actually two well-connected areas), Kleine Scheidegg and Männlichen, is effectively shared between Grindelwald and Wengen lying just beneath the brooding Eiger. Kleine Scheidegg, the train junction with a hotel, restaurant and dormitory, serves as the hub of the this area.

The third ski area, Mürren/Schilthorn, is across the Lauterbrunnen Valley and is also reached only by cog train or cable car. Mürren is a tiny village, as perfect as a movie set. In fact it was, for James Bond in *On Her Majesty's Secret Service.*

Mountain layout

The Jungfrau Winter Region has scores of lifts including railway routes up the mountain. Grindelwald and its surrounding hills and mountainsides are divided into seven pie-slice pieces radiating out from the center of town. Each forms a co-op for business purposes: by a plan set up in 1402, people clustered near the center have land-use rights to any land and pasture in their slice.

The ski lifts are owned by the individual co-ops. Since there is no one ski company, every time you use one of the lifts, your ski ticket is read by a scanner so that each region's ski income can be calculated. (Many of the lift attendants farm the ski runs in the summer; it is told that one farmer, many years ago, decided he'd had enough of winter and spread manure on the ski run to hasten the spring melt.)

The 9,609-foot Schwarzhorn, on your left as you enter town from Interlaken, is the backdrop for the **Grindelwald First** slopes. It used to be a real pain to reach even for those staying in Grindelwald. However, the creaky chair lift sideways ride was an experience. Alas, no more. Or should I say, Hooray! A gondola now leaves from the city core of Grindelwald, about 50 yards off the main street, taking skiers to the upper reaches of the area that is a beginner and intermediate playground. Grindelwald First did have its fair share of drag lifts, but currently all but one drag lift has been replaced. And beginning skiers no longer have to take the long and dramatic drag lift, but are now whisked up to Oberjoch's wide, groomed runs by a quad chair.

This region has become somewhat of a snowboarders' hangout with a snowpark and a halfpipe together with some good off-piste trails from the Oberjoch.

For some, First is a place to work out those kinks before moving over to tackle the runs on the Kleine Scheidegg side of the valley. But First offers plenty of great skiing on its own. In the U.S. any resort would be overjoyed to have this much terrain and vertical drop (4,705 feet—more than any resort in the United States). There are 50 km. of prepared trails here, with good limitless off-piste runs.

Most skiers stay at the higher altitudes, on the runs under the Oberjoch and the trails served by the Schilt and Grindel chair lifts. This area is shielded from the wind and provides the most varied skiing.

Kleine Scheidegg is reached by taking the cog train from Grindelwald. It takes about 45 minutes to reach Kleine Scheidegg, a bit of an Alpine ski village trisected by railway tracks. Across from the parking lot of the Grund station is the Männlichenbahn, a gondola lift.

If you take the cog train you can yo-yo your way across towards Männlichen on the Arven, Honegg, Gummi, Tschuggen and Läger lifts. The skiing gets progressively more difficult as you work your way across, until you arrive at the wide-open Männlichen area.

From the Kleine Scheidegg station you can take the lift to the top of the Lauberhorn and then either ski back toward Kleine Scheidegg or loop around to the Wixi lift and Wengen, more or less following the famous Lauberhorn downhill race course. The World Cup is held there every January. It's a delightful ski experience, with a seemingly endless variety of dips, turns, mogul fields and occasional ice patches—perfect territory for the advanced intermediate. Try the run from the Lauberhorn to the Wixi chair lift, picking your way through the mogul fields. When the snow is good, this run is exceptional.

You can also take the cog train up to the next stop, Eigergletscher, where several steep runs drop back down toward Wixi and Wengen and over-the-ridge runs also descend toward Grindelwald alongside the Salzegg lift.

At the end of your day, you'll have a marvelous 30-minute run to Grindelwald, passing the Arvengarten lift base before reaching a network of intermediate trails that offer a touch of adventure—there is always an easier way around the tough places for the less advanced. This 30-minute run to the car park of the Männlichen gondola or to the Grund cog train station may be the highlight of your stay in the Jungfrau region, unless you're counting the chills of Mürren's 007 Run as a fun experience.

Männlichen is reached by taking the gondola from Grund directly to Männlichen. You will rise 4,223 feet of vertical, which can be skied in one long expert run or one long intermediate run. In 25 minutes the gondola takes you to the Männlichen summit.

Most skiers remain at the upper level of the Männlichen and play on the wide-open slopes served by the Männlichen and Läger chair lifts. From the Läger chair skiers drop down to the Gummi chair lift and yo-yo their way over to Kleine Scheidegg. These runs between Männlichen and Kleine Scheidegg are a delight for all skiers.

Wengen: The town sits at the base of the cliff dropping from the Männlichen and the Lauberhorn areas. There is a choice of taking either the cable car from town to the Männlichen area, or the cog train around the Lauberhorn to the Kleine Scheidegg area. The only way back to town without parachute or hang-glider is around the Lauberhorn under the Wixi lift, down to the Bumps T-bar, then along the trails to the town.

Mürren: For ski challenges in this region, savvy downhillers head for the Schilthorn, the mountain above Mürren, across the gorge from Wengen. Take the cog train from Lauterbrunnen to Mürren and then go by cable car the rest of the way; or take a direct cable car from Stechelberg, outside Lauterbrunnen.

There is less good skiing but more challenges on the Schilthorn than at any of the other locations. Overall, there are 18 slopes with about 48 km. of runs. The eye-opener is the black run from the 9,748-foot Schilthorn. Start by quaffing an extra-strong cup of espresso or have lunch in the Piz Gloria revolving restaurant atop the Schilthorn, then tackle the famed Inferno, also called the 007 Run. The lower section, called the Kanonenrohr (Cannon Barrel), sends you hurtling down a series of narrow, steep, bumped-up, rutted and often icy trails. Actually, good intermediates can make it haltingly down the entire run. The Engetal area, approximately a third of the way down from the Schilthorn, offers plenty of wide-open skiing, with the option to take the last stage of the Schilthorn cable car up to the top for another chance to carve your way down the face of the mountain. It's below the Engetal area that the series of narrow and steep spots come into play.

If you visit in mid-to-late January, watch at least a part of the Inferno-Rennen, the traditional (since 1928) Schilthorn race that pits nearly 1,500 (as many as 4,000 apply) would-be champions against the clock and the 15.8-km. course. It takes a world-class skier almost 15 minutes. The race is normally scheduled in mid January.

Adventurous skiers also tackle the black runs from the 7,035-foot Schiltgrat. This area has excellent bumps and some super-steep off-piste skiing. Intermediates stay on the flat top of the ridge. Connecting lifts take you to the Winteregg and Allmendhubel, the mountain's other two ski areas, where intermediate skiing—with an occasional black run—is the rule. The best intermediate run leads down to the base of the Winteregg chair, where you can lunch at an excellent restaurant.

If you are coming up from Lauterbrunnen on the train for Mürren, there is a stop at the Winteregg chair where you can start and work your way to Allmendhubel and over to the Schiltgrat and the Schilthorn.

Mountain rating

Grindelwald First: This is an intermediate and beginner playground with some expert flashes. The panoramas across the valley to the Eiger and the Schilthorn are spectacular.

Kleine Scheidegg: Working one's way around the mountain toward Männlichen from Kleine Scheidegg requires good skills, but can be handled by most intermediates.

The Lauberhorn can get bumped up, but still can be skied by any intermediate. The Wengen side with the Lauberhorn run is perhaps the most challenging. The runs dropping from the Eigergletscher down to the Wixi are expert territory, and intermediates can also make the drop down the Salzegg side.

Männlichen: The wide-open area at the top of the gondola is perfect for every level of skier. Intermediates and experts will have a blast playing on the trails that wend over to Kleine Scheidegg. The long run to the base of the gondola is a joy.

Wengen: The nursery slopes surrounding this town are the best in the valley. If you are a beginner or traveling with a beginner, Wengen is the best village to stay in. It's also the sunniest of the ski areas.

Mürren: Don't plan to ski Mürren extensively if you're a beginner. There are some intermediate slopes that the absolute beginner may be able to handle after a few days, but just barely. Lower intermediates will have their hands full, but strong intermediates will have a field day. Experts will find that the slopes of the Schilthorn and the Schiltgrat are the most challenging in the entire Jungfrau area.

Ski school (2003/04 prices)

All major resorts in the region have ski schools offering downhill, snowboarding and cross-country instruction.

More than 80 ski instructors are available daily for individual and group lessons in Wengen (033-855-2022) and Grindelwald (033-854-1280). Mürren (033-855-1247) ski school has 25 instructors giving group and private lessons.

Prices are within in the same range in all three ski areas. These prices are for the Grindelwald Ski School:

Private lessons	
one hour	€52
half-day (2 hours)	€130 (a.m.) €110 (p.m.)
full day (5 hours)	€207
Group lessons	
full day (4 hours)	€49
three days (12 hours)	€120
five days (20 hours)	€172

Cross-country instruction is available. There is a seven-mile loop around the outskirts of Lauterbrunnen. Grindelwald has 35 km. of trails. Wengen does not have a cross-country run, but Mürren has a simple 2-km. circuit.

Lift tickets (2003/04 prices)

The Jungfrau Winter Region ticket for a two-day minimum includes Mürren, Schilthorn, Männlichen, Kleine Scheidegg and Grindelwald First, as well as all cog trains and ski buses. Tickets good only for individual areas and group passes are also available.

Jungfrau region	**Adults**	**Teenagers (16–19)**	**Children (6–15)**	**Seniors (62+)**
two days	€80.40	€64	€40.20	€72.20
three days	€110.20	€88.40	€55.20	€99.40
six days	€191.80	€153.80	€96	€172.80
fourteen days – (with photo)	€317	€253.80	€156.60	€285

Grindelwald/Wengen	**Adults**	**Teenagers (16–19)**	**Children (6–15)**	**Seniors (62+)**
one day	€37.40	€30	€19.20	€34
two days	€69.40	€55.80	€34.60	€62.60
six days	€172.80	€136.20	€127	€155.80

Mürren/Schilthorn	**Adults**	**Teenagers (16–19)**	**Children (6–15)**	**Seniors (62+)**
one day	€37.40	€30	€19.20	€34
two days	€68	€54.40	€34	€61.20
six days	€162.60	€130	€81.60	€146.20

Accommodations

Price ranges noted for each hotel are high season (February) per person based on double occupancy with half board (breakfast and dinner): €€€—€125+; €€—€75–€124; €—less than €75.

Grindelwald

Grindelwald has 49 hotels, and 45 of them are owned and managed by families. Many of the hotels are 100 years old, and most are smaller than 100 beds.

Grand Regina Alpine Wellfit Hotel (033-854-8600, fax 033-854-8688; €€€) Grindelwald's only five-star hotel, with excellent location by the Jungfrau cog railway station is as luxurious as it gets in this town. Jacket and tie worn in the candlelit dining rooms. Old-World elegance. Has a new wellness center.

Hotel Schweizerhof (033-853-2202, fax 033-853-2004; €€€) A chalet-style hotel with downtown location near the Jungfrau cog railway station.

Sunstar Hotel and Sunstar-Adler (033-854-7777, fax 033-854-7770; €€–€€€) This is a modern hotel in chalet style across from the Grindelwald-First lifts. One side faces First; the other side faces the Eiger and Kleine Scheidegg.

Hotel Spinne (033-854-8888; fax 033-854-8889; €€).

Derby Bahnhof Hotel (033-854-5461; fax 033-854-2426; €€) Hotel with an excellent location handy to the Jungfrau cog railway station.

These hotels (with 25 or fewer rooms) are recommended—**Bodmi** (033-853-1220, fax 033-853-1353; €€€), **Caprice** (033-854-3818, fax 033-8543819; €€), **Fiescherblick** (033-854-5353, fax 033-854-5350; €–€€), **Glacier** (033-853-1004, fax 033-853-5004; €–€€), and **Alpenhof** (033-853-5270, fax 033-853-1915; €€–€€€). The following Garni or B&Bs are also recommended—**Grindelwalderhof** (033-854-4010, fax 033-854-4019; €€–€€€), **Cabana** (033-854-5070, fax 033-854-5077; €–€€), **Hotel Bernerhof** (853-1021, fax 853-4646; €€) and **Bellevue Garni** (tel/fax 033-853-1234; €) in the middle of town—ask for a room with bath.

Wengen

Beausite Park Hotel (033-856-5161, fax 033-855-3010; €€) This is now the most elegant and upscale hotel in Wengen. It has indoor pool and sauna. It overlooks the wide-open beginner slopes and is near the Männlichen cable car. With good snow, you can ski right back to the front door.

Sunstar Hotel (033-856-5200, fax 033-856-5300; €€–€€€) A hotel with an excellent location between the station and the lifts.

Hotel Silberhorn (033-855-5131, fax 033-855-5132; €€–€€€) One of the first hotels in Wengen, directly across the street from the station. Recent renovations have all rooms with light pine furniture, sauna and whirlpool. Known for healthy servings at the dinner table—you can choose from four different dining rooms.

Wengener Hof (033-856-6969, fax 033-856-6970; €€) Popular with ski racers, particularly during Lauberhorn race week, but a bit out of the center of town.

Hotel Eiger (033-856-0505, fax 033-856-0506; €€) By the station, this is a locals' place too, not as Alpine-looking on the inside as it seems from the outside.

Hotel Berghaus (033-855-2151, fax 033-855-3820; €) A very pleasant hotel next to the Beausite Park and the Männlichen lift. All rooms have TV.

Alpenrose (033-855-3216, fax 033-855-1518; €–€€) Noted for its setting and traditional meals.

Hotel Hirschen (033-855-1544, fax 033-855-3044; €–€€) This is a charming mountain inn with one of the best kitchens in Wengen. The rooms are small, but each has a modern shower and toilet squeezed in.

Ski Chalets: available through Crystal (see page 20 for contact information).

Staying on the mountain above Grindelwald and Wengen

Scheidegg Hotel (033-855-1212; fax 033-8551294; €€+) is a bit worn, but for overall experience, the finest lodging in the area for the skier; overlooks Kleine Scheidegg station in the shadow of the Eiger. Thirty minutes by train into the mountains from Grindelwald. Reserve well ahead. *BARGAIN NOTE: Skiers looking for very basic accommodation can stay in a dorm above Scheidegg train station, Silvi's Mountain Lodge, for €20 per person €25 with breakfast or €36 with half-board. Rooms are €35 with breakfast and €47 with half-board.*

Hotel Jungfrau (033-855-1622, fax 033-855-3069; €€€) sits at 6,234 feet altitude, in Wengeneralb, with spectacular views of the Jungfrau massif. Reached by the cog railway, the hotel only has 22 rooms. Skiers can stop here for lunch, but dinner is only for residents.

Mürren

Hotel Eiger (033-856-5454, fax 033-856-5456; €€) This is the class act in Mürren as far as hotels go. The owner is delightful and the perfect hostess. This hotel can stand as a definition of excellent service. The restaurant is one of the best in town, and the bar is a gathering spot for locals.

Hotel Alpenruh (033-856-8800, fax 033-856-8888; €€) As close to the lifts as you can get. This is a restored chalet with great views and exceptional decor in the old Swiss style. The restaurant presents Mürren's best nouvelle cuisine.

Jungfrau (033-855-4545, fax 033-855-4549; €€) This hotel looks absolutely Gothic, with spires and peaked roof, but you step through the door into a time warp—everything is so modern, guests at first may have trouble finding the elevator button. Right in the center of town, near the sports center with its indoor pool.

Hotel Blumental (033-855-1826, fax 033-855-3686; €€) A three-star hotel not far from the center of the small town.

Hotel Alpina (033-855-1361, fax 033-855-1049; €–€€) Good hotel with family discounts. Excellent view and a quiet setting, but a long walk from the lifts.

Hotel Alpenblick (033-855-1327, fax 033-855-1391; €) Small hotel with great views, two minutes from the cog-train station but a long way to the Schilthorn lifts.

For unusual places to stay up on the mountain, Mürren has two guest houses in the middle of the slopes that get rave reviews from those who know them. These are the **Pension Flora-Suppenalp** (033-855-1726; €) and the **Pension Sonnenberg** (033-855-1127; €). Neither has private baths. They have only a handful of rooms, but both have dormitory space and are filled with atmosphere. Rates for rooms per person, double occupancy with half board, are €43 for the Flora-Suppenalp and €41 for the Sonnenberg. Dorm rates with half board are €30–€38 and €35 respectively.

Hotel Regina (033-855-4242, fax 033-855-2071; €–€€) The bargain hotel in town, in a majestic building but quite under-cared-for on the inside; it might be described as a skiers' commune. There are a handful of rooms with private bath. Everyone makes up his own room each day. Normally youngsters pack in here and share rooms, making the bargain a bit better. Food is simple and substantial.

Eiger Guesthouse (033-856-5460; fax 033-856-5461) Swiss-Scottish run, cozy and relaxed hotel near the BLM Train Station with splendid view of Eiger, Mönch and Jungfrau. Offers comfortable budget accommodation, restaurant, bar and gameroom.

Lauterbrunnen

Hotel Silberhorn (033-856-2210, fax 033-855-4213; €) Ten minutes' walk from the cog trains to Kleine Scheidegg and Mürren. Great views.

Hotel Schützen (033-855-3025, fax 033-855-2950; €) Comfortable and only eight minutes' walk from the cog train.

Staying in Interlaken

Interlaken has begun to emerge as a hotel center for skiers planning to ski the Jungfrau area. It is only a 45-minute bus ride from the lower lift stations and as a relatively large city it has nightlife and good dining. Two reasons for staying in Interlaken may be persuasive for some visitors.

First: Interlaken hotels and ski packages are much less expensive than those of Wengen, Mürren and Grindelwald. In general, Interlaken menu prices are about one-quarter less than Grindelwald's. (**Piz Paz** is a satisfying Italian restaurant, in the medium price zone. At **Yelp Beers & Comics** on Centralstrasse, 400 brands of beers are available.) Second: If you are traveling with a non-skier, Interlaken has more to offer than the liveliest Jungfrau resort, Grindelwald, and is in a perfect position for day trips to many Swiss cities such as Bern, Lucerne, Zürich and even Zermatt.

If neither of these considerations applies, then head into the mountains. If you are a real skier, this city is probably too far from the mountains to keep you happy. If you're sharing a vacation with a non-skier, it's perfect.

Apartments, condominiums, flats

There are many apartments and chalets for rent in the Jungfrau region. The local tourist offices have prices and locations, and will assist in booking.

A typical apartment in Grindelwald, Wengen or Mürren with one bedroom for two, living room (with sleeping space for two more people), kitchen and all utensils costs about €800 a week in high season; €600 in midseason. The only extra is tax.

Dining

Grindelwald

In Grindelwald you can choose from more than 50 restaurants. For a very special (and expensive) meal, try the dining room, **Pendule d'Or**, in the **Grand Hotel Regina** (033-854-8600); it may serve the best meals in town. Chateaubriand for two costs about €85. The **Hotel Spinne** restaurant has good Swiss and international specialties, and a full wine cellar. The most crowded eatery in town is normally the **Swiss Chalet** (033-854-3131) which has Swiss and new cuisine. **Ristorante Mercato** has a good Spaghetti Rustico for €12. A Hopfenperle Bier brings the minimal meal to €15. Pastas, usually Bolognese or Milanese, and pizzas are the best dining value in local restaurants. The pastas are about €8–€12. A decent wine will cost at least €12.

At the Hotel Schweizerhof, the **Schmitte Restaurant** (033-853-2202) is highly recommended and has surprisingly affordable specials of the day. **La Marmitte** and **Hilty-Stübli** at the Hotel Kirchbühl (033-853-3553) has excellent affordable meals.

The restaurant at Fiescherblick, **Swiss Bistro** (033-854-5353), has daily menus for about €23.

Other good affordable spots are the **Adlerstube** (033-854-7777) in the Hotel Sunstar, the restaurant in the **Eiger** (033-854-3131), the **Kreuz und Post** restaurant (033-854-5492), the **Alpina** (033-853-3333) and the **Glacier** (033-853-1004).

Wengen

The best restaurant town is **Chez Meyer's** (033-856-5858) in the Hotel Regina. Call for reservations. One of the best typical meals and excellent fondue *chinoise* is found at the **Hirschen** (033-855-1544). The best fondue and raclette can be found in the **Bernerhof**. **Restaurant Eiger** in the Hotel Eiger (033-856-0505) serves good fare with a nice outdoor dining area for sunny days. The **Bären** (033-855-1419), **Sunstar** (033-856-5111), **Schönegg** (033-855-3422) all have Michelin recommended affordable menus in ascending order of cost. Some of the best fish dishes are found at **Berghaus**. **Sina's** has good pizza.

Mürren

In town the **Alpenruh** (033-856-8800) serves the best nouvelle cuisine in a beautifully rustic setting. The **Edelweiss** (033-856-5600) is also recommended for an affordable daily menu. The **Eiger** (033-856-5454) has excellent traditional Swiss fare, real U.S. cut steaks, and the best fondue—either Chinoise or Bourguignonne—in town. The **Palace Hotel Mürren** and the **Stägerstubli** both have excellent cheese fondue. The restaurant in the **Hotel Blumental** is perhaps the most rustic and atmospheric spot to enjoy Swiss specialties. The **Eiger Guesthouse** (033-856-5460) offers good moderate meals at similar prices. For Italian meals try **Peppino** at the Hotel Palace or **Taverna**.

Lauterbrunnen

A meal at the **Silberhorn** (033-856-2210) is excellent and won't break the bank.

On the slopes

Enjoy at least one midday meal inside the **Piz Gloria**, a revolving restaurant (033-8552141) on the Schilthorn. Lower down stop in at **Restaurant Allmendhubel**, tiny, cute and filled with locals; or at the new **Winteregg Restaurant**, which has great lunches and excellent après-ski. The **Flora-Suppenalp** or the **Sonnenberg** also serve excellent mountain meals.

At the **Berghotel Männlichen**, even the cafeteria fare is served on china plates. For sun worshipping, a lounge chair and blanket rent for €3.50. **Mary's Cafe** on the trail down to Wengen has a great raclette at lunch. The restaurant at the railway station at Kleine Scheidegg has excellent meals at good prices.

Interlaken

This is an international tourist center and starting point for excursions in the Bernese Oberland, one of Switzerland's most beautiful regions. No-smoking restaurants are an extreme rarity in Switzerland, and McDonald's in Interlaken is one of the few.

Après-ski/nightlife

Grindelwald

The **Gepsi-Bar** and **Plaza Club** are the singles meat market and the hottest immediate après-ski hangouts, where folk squeeze in and stay for the duration. **Le Plaza Club** disco in the Sunstar Hotel is the hottest spot for nightlife and gets crowded. **Mescalero** in the cellar of the Hotel Spinne is not as packed but gets interesting, depending on which groups are in town. For Country & Western music try the **Challi Bar** in the basement of the Kreuz & Post Hotel. The **Bodenwald** and the **Glacier** have traditional music and entertainment. For quieter conditions, try the **Espresso**

Bar—have Kaffe Fertig with Schnapps—the **Alte Post Bar**, the **Hotel Wolter Terrace** or the **Hotel Kreuz Terrace**.

Live music or a DJ for dancing and listening are offered nightly in the **Hotel Grand Regina** and the **Challi Bar**. The **Cava Bar/Spaghetti Factory**, under the Derby Hotel, has a local band for music and dancing from 9 p.m. It's closed Sundays.

The **Mescalero Club** under the Hotel Spinne and the **Plaza Club** under the Hotel Sunstar are both open to 2:45 a.m.

A nighttime adventure you will remember is sledding from the tiny Gasthaus at **Bussalp** back into Grindelwald. A bus will take you up and sleds will be waiting after a fondue or other Swiss dinner. Call the tourist office for prices and to make your sled and dinner reservations. (033-854-1212).

We've been told that the **Down Town Village** is quite unique with bars in a glass globe and a tepee.

Wengen

Check out the Eiger Hotel's **Pickel Bar,** the **Tanne Bar, Hot Chili Peppers** and the **Silberhorn** terrace on sunny days for good après-ski. Nightlife is more limited here, since after dark only the group staying on the mountain will usually be around, although trains run until late evening. Try the **Tiffany Disco** in the Silberhorn, or **Carrousel** in Hotel Regina for dancing or head to piano bars for a quiet evening. The Tanne Bar and Rocks Cafè and Bar are good late night get-together spots.

Mürren

For immediate après-ski, head to the base of the **Winteregg**, to the old and rustic **Stägerstübli** filled with grizzled locals and a handful of tourists, the **Bellevue** across from the ski school, the pub in the **Eiger Guesthouse** for socializing, or hang out on the terrace of the **Jungfrau Bar.** For later nightlife in Mürren, head to the Hotel Eiger's **Tächi-Bar**. This bar gets a crowd aged around 27 and up. The **Inferno Disco** has a mixed clientele ranging from age 18 to 27. The **Bliemlichäller** in the cellar of the Hotel Blumental, with video games, attracts a younger, virtually all-teenage crowd.

Child care (2003/04 prices)

Grindelwald offers ski kindergarten from ages 3–7. The Grindelwald Bodmi school begins at 9:30 a.m. and lasts until 4 p.m. The cost for one day is €60, including meals. A morning session costs is €20 without lunch; an afternoon session, €25. In Grindelwald look for the Kinderclub Bodmi which is open from 9:15 am. to 3:30 pm. and costs €20 for a morning; €25 for an afternoon; €50 for a full day; and €18 for a lunch.

The Grindelwald ski school will take care of and feed kids at lunch for €10.

In **Wengen** head for the Sport Pavilion where school begins at 8:45 a.m. and lasts until 4:30 p.m. Children from 18 months old are accepted. Cost in Wengen is based by the hour on a sliding scale. €15 gets five hours. Lunch is €18. Wengen, with its no-traffic environment, is one of the premier resorts for families with children. It has good nursery slopes and plenty of easy tracks back to the town.

Mürren: The Snowgarden for Children takes little ones from 9:30 am.–4 pm. They provide a pick-up service, lunch and a full day's care for €35; pick-up service and lunch for five days costs €149. A half day without lunch is €14. One hour's care is €6.50: two hours or more costs €6 per hour. Lunch is from noon to 1 pm. and costs €9. Call the tourist office for more information.

Private babysitters are also available call 033-855-3706 or check with the tourist office or your hotel for assistance.

Other activities

Fully 30 percent of winter visitors to Grindelwald are non-skiers, and there is plenty for them to do. Hikers, skinny skiers and snowshoers have their own trails throughout and around the ski areas. They're even groomed, to a width of about eight feet, and good for sledding. You can hike or ride a lift up. There is even a restaurant above First, to which the lifts don't even come close—you'll have to walk, but as Mark Twain said in *A Tramp Abroad,* "There is no opiate like Alpine pedestrianism."

The smart shops in Bern and the really charming Old-World center of the capital city merit a side trip.

Grindelwald offers the widest range of non-skiing activities such as ice skating, curling, hang-gliding, sledding, swimming and hiking.

The Grindelwald Winter Festival in mid-January has snow sculpture contests feature four-member teams from around the world.

The sports center, on the main street of Grindelwald, is excellent, with swimming, fitness rooms and ice skating.

There are great toboggan runs from Bussalp—Bussalp to Grindelwald is eight km., the race course is 4.5 km. and Faulhorn to Bussalp to Grindelwald is 16.5 km. The postbus connects Grindelwald with Bussalp. Bus fare is €16.

The Jungfraubahn cog railway

The Jungfraubahn that takes skiers up the mountain is also a delightful outing for the non-skier. It bores through the Eiger's north face to the Jungfrau slopes. The entire route through the mountain took 14 years to build and was finished in 1912.

A stop inside the mountain allows passengers to look through windows at the precipitous mountain face. At the top, the train arrives at 11,333 feet, the highest railway station in Europe. A spectacular building houses a restaurant, an ice palace carved into the glacier and outdoor observation platforms with views down over the glacier.

Be careful navigating your next path if you're in ski boots! It's an entanglement of pathways carved through an ice tunnel. Glittering passages, mysterious niches and stairways pass ice sculptures sprinkled along the route and end up at an ice bar where typical Swiss ice wine is served to giddy singing, playful children in adult bodies.

Piz Gloria

Piz Gloria and its revolving restaurant were chosen as the villain's lair in the James Bond movie, *On Her Majesty's Secret Service*. The movie features a wild chase on skis from the restaurant to the car-less village of Murren below.

A series of cable cars and cog trains haul you up to the Schilthorn, a 9,748-foot-tall peak surrounded by a sea of 200 spectacular snow-covered Alps with a view of France, Germany, and of course, much of Switzerland. Along with a 200-mile radius view on a clear day, the Piz Gloria restaurant offers a special local dish: rare, local mountain mushrooms or "steinpilz" over pasta. It's as fabulous as the vista.

Getting there

The most frequently used international airports are Geneva and Zürich. Rail connections are frequent and excellent to Interlaken and on to Grindelwald, Wengen or Mürren.

Tourist information

Wengen Tourismus, CH-3823 Wengen, Switzerland;
Telephone (033) 855-1414, fax (033) 855-3060.
Email: info@wengen.ch Internet: www.wengen-muerren.ch

Grindelwald Tourist Center, CH-3818 Grindelwald, Switzerland;
Telephone (033) 854-1212, fax (033) 854-1210;
Email: touristcenter@grindelwald.ch.
Internet: www.grindelwald.com.

Mürren Tourismus, CH-3825 Mürren, Switzerland;
Telephone (033) 856 8686, fax (033) 856 8696.
Email: info@muerren.ch Internet: www.wengen-muerren.ch.

Jungfrau Winter Region, CH-3800 Interlaken, Switzerland;
Telephone (033) 828-7233, Fax (033) 828-7260;
Email: info@jungfrau.ch. Internet: www.jungfrau.ch.

Klosters

A small and traditional village, Klosters offers the low-key atmosphere and relative obscurity that make it the perfect hideaway. The English royal family, most notably Prince Charles, has chosen Klosters as their winter ski center for several years. They come for the excellent skiing and the relaxed elegant atmosphere—you will probably like Klosters for the same reasons. The houses surrounding the town proper are a bit more elaborate than most other places you'll visit, giving an immediate tipoff that Klosters is a cut above. The central town area is small and quaint, but packed with specialty stores.

Think of Klosters, little more than a suburb of Davos, as Davos' little sister resort, the beauty of the family who has been kept hidden. Both resorts share the Manhattan-sized, wide-open expanse of the Parsenn, but Klosters has the more challenging runs into town. Klosters also has its own ski runs and lift system in the Madrisa area, on the opposite side of the valley from the Parsenn. The entire Klosters-Davos ski area offers 200 miles of runs served by more than 50 lifts.

Mountain layout

From the village center, 3,937 feet high, the lift system takes you to 9,330 feet on the Parsenn side at the Weissfluhgipfel, and up to about 7,874 feet on the upper lift of the Madrisa.

The Parsenn is the best-known area and is reached by the Gotschna cable car, which leaves every 15 to 20 minutes in ski season. The cable car lets you off at the Gotschnagrat, where you can either traverse to the Parsenn or ski under the cable car to a T-bar and chair lift. The Parsenn reaches its peak at the Weissfluhgipfel (9,330 feet) where it drops with two expert runs. Here it is wide open, offering both beginners and intermediates a paradise for cruising. The Parsenn has 40 seemingly endless runs, including what was once Europe's longest—from Weissfluhjoch to Kublis. If you like carefree cruising, you will love the Parsenn.

The Madrisa area is much smaller: some 30 miles of runs served by seven lifts. The area is reached by cable car from Klosters-Dorf, an outlying hamlet, which is a hike from the center of town. The area runs are mostly beginner and intermediate. When the sun is out, the Madrisa slopes are bathed with warming rays the entire day, something to remember when it's cold but sunny. The longest and most scenic Madrisa run is from Glatteggen, 8,340 feet down to the Schlappin overlook, then down to the Madrisa cable car.

For the jaded, Madrisa is a springboard for an exciting ski mountaineering trek to Austria, which combines both skiing and climbing. The Swiss Ski School can line you up with a guide for this adventure if the snow quality is good.

Mountain rating

Klosters earns an A-plus from beginning and intermediate skiers. The Parsenn is perhaps the ideal terrain for learning to ski and perfecting your technique.

Experts may find the Parsenn terrain somewhat boring and should ask instructors where the most challenging skiing can be found. The best expert runs on the Parsenn are from the top of the Weissfluhgipfel. Otherwise, stick to the trails that drop into town alongside the Parsennbahn, or take the Drostobel-to-Klosters run, which is narrow and sometimes steep. The Wang trail, which runs directly under the Gotschna cable car, is one of the toughest expert runs in Europe. Unfortunately it seems to be closed more often than open, but if it's open and there is no avalanche danger, you're in for an experience. Watch yourself here: this is the spot where Prince Charles narrowly escaped an avalanche and his aide was killed while skiing out of bounds.

The Madrisa area is strictly for intermediates, beginners and sun-worshippers.

Ski school (2003/04 prices)

The Klosters ski and snowboarding school is divided into six levels, and also offers special children's courses and cross-country instruction. Classes meet either on the Madrisa or near the Gotschna. Check with the Swiss Ski and Snowboard School Klosters (081-4102828) for lesson times. There is the Ski and Snowboard School Saas in Klosters Dorf (081-4202233). Bananas Swiss Snowboard School Klosters offers extreme snowboarding, freestyle and racing lessons (081-4226660).

Private lessons for one to two skiers or boarders cost €221 for a full day or €143 for a half day. There is an additional fee of €14 for each extra skier or boarder.

Group lessons are €26 for a half day, €80 for three half days, €146 for six half days.

Lift tickets (2002/03 prices)

Daily lift passes for the Gotschna, Parsenn are €39; for the Madrisa, €31.

The most convenient pass to use is the Klosters/Davos all-inclusive pass (REGA). It includes the Madrisa side of the valley, plus use of the train that runs between Davos and Klosters and as far down the valley as Kublis. It is also good on local buses in Davos and Klosters. The tickets are available only for periods of two days or more.

There are 10 percent discounts for REGA passes purchased for three days or more before Christmas season.

	Adults	Children (6-12)	Teen (13-17)
two days	€82	€27	€55
three days	€113	€38	€76
six days	€189	€63	€126
fourteen days	€335	€111	€225

Lift tickets for Gotschna/Parsenn and Madrisa for one day adult cost €41; child, €14; teen, €28. Two-day adult lift ticket is €82; child, €27; teen, €55.

Children younger than 5 years old ski free.

Accommodations

The best time to ski Klosters is during one of its special organized Ski Weeks. These weeks are normally held in early December, the last three weeks of January and first week of February, and late March through April. Contact the tourist office for the special rates, which include lift tickets together with room and board.

These hotels are all recommended. Based on per person, double occupancy with half-pension in February are €€€—€125+; €€—€75–€124; €—less than €75.

The **Hotel Alpina** (081-4102424, fax 081-4102425; €€€) has a great location, indoor pool, nice staff, and reservations through Best Western.

Perhaps the most traditional hotel is the **Chesa Grischuna** (081-4222222, fax 081-4222225; €€€). It is part of the Romantic Hotel chain, but though it has ambiance, the rooms are small and there is no pool.

At the upper end of the scale is the four-star **Hotel Pardenn** (081-4232020, fax 081-4232021; €€€+). A hike from the ski shuttlebus and 10 minutes walk from town, but with plenty of five-star comfort—pool, sauna and fitness room. The **Albeina** (081-4232100; fax 081-4232121; €€) is recommended by Michelin and is a bit less expensive than the Pardenn. Other recommended hotels are the **Steinbock** (081-4224545; €€) and **Silveretta Park** (081-423-3435; €€€) only a short walk from the lifts.

The tiny, 11-room **Hotel Rustico** (081-4221212; fax 081-4225355; €€–€€€) is only steps from the lifts and downtown. It gets rave reviews from locals and tourist press for meals and comfort. **Sporthotel Kurhaus** (081-4224441; fax 081-4224609; €–€€) with 30 rooms is highly recommended for both meals and rooms. The **Cresta** (081-4222525; fax 081-422-4169; €€+) also has a very good restaurant.

Sonne (081-4221349; €), a traditional B&B, is inexpensive and convenient.

The less expensive lodging is in Klosters-Dorf, near the lifts for the Madrisa area but a hike or shuttlebus ride from the Parsenn lifts. Try **Büel** (081-4222669; €), **Casa Erla** (081-3225275; €) a group of condos with kitchenettes for only €34 a night per person, and **Jost** (081-4223344; €).

Apartments, condominiums, flats

Apartments are normally rented out for a minimum of one week, Saturday to Saturday; in the Christmas holiday season a two-week minimum rental is required.

The tourist office keeps track of available apartments. Write and let them know the number of beds required, preferred number of rooms and dates of your stay. You'll get an immediate response from apartment owners with a choice of apartments and prices. Select the apartment you want and return their forms.

Normally, linen and kitchen utensils are provided, while extras, such as swimming pool, sauna, TV or room phone all add to the cost. Standard units rent for €22 to €39 per person a night.

Dining

The **Walserhof** (081-4102929; fax 081-4102939) is in a class by itself with two Michelin stars. If you want to eat here, make reservations early, very early. Expect to pay €50–€100 for your meal.

Highly recommended and much more traditional and rustic with quite affordable fixed-price menus are **Chesa Grischuna** (081-4222222), **Hotel Alpina** (081-4102424), and **Restaurant Steinbock** (081-4224545), **Rustico** (081-4221212), **Sporthotel Kurhaus** (081-422-4441) and **Cresta** (081-4222525). The **Alte Post Aeuja** (081-4221716) for lamb specialties and a very rustic setting is in the same category. Full meals can be enjoyed at all these restaurants for as little as €15.

A bit out of town by taxi or sleigh ride is **Höhwald** in Monbiel (081-4223045) with a wonderful rustic setting. The **Hotel Wynegg** (open only during the winter season) also has a good restaurant with reasonable prices and is packed with Brits. In Madrisa head to **Bahnhof Restaurant** or **Pizzeria Al Berto**. Also try the new **Pizzera Fellini** (081-422221) in Klosters Platz.

Après-ski/nightlife

On the way off the slopes stop at the **Serneuser Schwendi Hut** for a great time. Ski down to **Gaudi's Grasträchni** at the end of the slope for après-ski.

Klosters' nightlife centers around its major hotels. For discos, there are **Casa Antica** and **Kir Royal** in the Silveretta Park. In Klosters-Dorf head to **Rufinis** or **Mountain Pub**.

Pizzera Fellini has a fabulous après-ski tea as does the **Chesa Grischuna**. The bar in the **Pardenn** for a late evening visit is intimate and relaxing, but a bit stuffy. Better still is the bar of the Chesa Grischuna where there is quiet piano entertainment.

Also recommended: **Rossli Bar** in Klosters Center and **Brasserie** in Hotel Vereina.

Child care

Babysitting service in town can be arranged for around €10 per hour by calling 081-4102020.

There is also child care (2 years and older) on Madrisa near the gondola, open every day 10 a.m. to 4 p.m.. Cost is €6 per hour or €32 per day, without lunch. Telephone 410-2028.

Other activities

Klosters is rather quiet. Visitors looking for other activities should take the train to Davos, only 15 minutes away. Klosters has an open-air skating rink, cross-country skiing, horse-drawn sleighs and tobogganing. There are four covered hotel pools in town; check with the hotel for the facility rates.

Getting there

The closest airport is Zürich. Klosters is two-and-a-half hours by train, with a change in Landquart.

If you decide to rent a car, take the Zürich-Chur road as far as the Landquart/Davos exit. The drive from Landquart to Klosters is through the narrow valley and passes through Kublis before arriving at Klosters Dorf and then Klosters. The distance from Zürich is about 90 miles.

Tourist information

Tourist Office, CH-7250 Klosters; Monday–Saturday, 8 a.m.–noon and 2:30 p.m.–18:30 p.m. It is also open 9:30 a.m.–noon and 3:30 p.m.–6:30 p.m. on Sundays. Telephone 081-4102020, fax 081-4102010.
E-mail: info@klosters.ch.
Internet: www.klosters.ch

Saas-Fee

Saas-Fee is a village of very narrow streets, wooden chalets, small hotels and year-round skiing. It's for serious skiers—the ones who care more about the number of black-rated runs on the mountain than the number of discos in the village. Nestled in the next valley from Zermatt, Saas-Fee allows no private cars in town; you park on the outskirts and take public transportation.

The town occupies a magnificent site at 5,904 feet, ringed by 13 separate peaks of 13,000 feet or more. Snowcaps on these mountains are permanent, as is skiing on the 9,840-foot-high Felskinn. Saas-Fee also has its own snowmaking equipment on the beginner slopes below. That, combined with the glacier runs above, means that your vacation will never be in danger from poor snowfall.

Mountain layout

Saas-Fee's nearly 50 miles of downhill trails are superbly divided between beginner, intermediate and expert. Absolute beginners start on the Saas-Fee town lifts, where they usually stay for about three days. Later they ski either the Plattjen lift or the Felskinn.

The first area to get the morning sun is the Spielboden/Längfluh. These runs are on good intermediate to expert terrain. From Längfluh down to the chair lift is intermediate country. If you ski past this middle station, get ready for the steep and narrow.

From the top of the Längfluh cable car there is a drag lift right on the glacier. This Feekatz lift connects the two main ski areas of Längfluh and Felskinn/Mittelallalin.

The Felskinn/Mittelallalin area is the most popular section of Saas-Fee's trails. Two small lifts tow skiers from town to the lower station of the Felskinn cable car.

Once at the top of the Felskinn cable car, you're whisked up another 1,600 feet on the underground Metro Alpin to Mittelallalin. Here, stop to enjoy the magnificent panorama of dozens of 13,000-foot peaks. Intermediates, and beginners brave enough to come this far, should traverse to the left, and experts should cross to the right, in front of the revolving restaurant. Skiers have a choice of doing several runs or heading back to the Metro Alpin underground and the Felskinn area.

To the left of the Felskinn cable car, a drag lift opens to a delightful smaller area—the Egginer. Strong intermediates will be satisfied with the Egginerjoch lift.

The rest of the Felskinn runs crisscross under the cable car back toward town. The area between the middle station and the top of the Felskinn is a beginner and intermediate playground. The drop back into the village steepens considerably, and experts have a challenge on the Kanonenrohr and Bach trails.

The final section of Saas-Fee's ski domain, the Plattjen, catches the last of the day's sunshine. This area is served by a long top-to-bottom six-person gondola. The gondola takes skiers up from town (5,910 feet) to Plattjen (8,430 feet), resulting in a run with a little more than a 2,500-foot vertical drop. There are uncrowded trails for all abilities.

One interesting point for anyone searching for a place to go summer skiing, the new lifts have opened glaciers at 11,811 feet above sea level. Saas-Fee has constructed a year-round snowboarding park on its glacier complete with halfpipes, quarterpipes, rails, tables, gaps and a high jump for professionals.

Snowboarding

Snowboarders have a snow park with jumps, 5 rails, a halfpipe and a triple kicker line. There are four snowboard schools as well with lessons covering all aspects of the sport.

Mountain rating

Experts will never complain about the runs at Saas-Fee. There's enough black to make things interesting.

Intermediates may think that the lift network and trails were laid out with them in mind: most trails above Saas-Fee start with a red or blue leg, often with the option of taking a black-rated stretch.

Beginners can work toward becoming advanced beginners on the Saas-Fee town slopes; then the slopes above the valley beckon.

Ski school (2003/04 prices)

The Saas-Fee school (027-957-2438) has approximately 100 instructors. English is no problem.

Private lessons cost €40.50 an hour for one or two persons, €47.50 an hour for three or four people, €204 for a full day.

Group lessons (three hours a day) are €31.50 for a day. Group and private lessons for children are the same prices.

Snowboarding: Groups cost €104–€112 a week. Privates lessons are €40.50 an hour for one or two people; €47.50 an hour for three or four people.

Special ski mountaineering off-trail adventures have been organized in the past for climbs to the top of the Alphubel and Allalin. These treks start with a two- to four-hour climb on skins and end with long, high-altitude powder cruises through virtually virgin snow. Tours are limited by both the weather and the availability of qualified instructors. From mid-February through the end of the season the treks depart approximately once a week.

"The Haute Route" is a classic ski adventure tour between Saas-Fee, Zermatt, Courmayeur and Chamonix. These trips are organized from mid-April to the end of May. For this tough, physical trek participants should be in good shape and must be able to ski in deep snow. The mountain climbing school conducts a different special tour from early May until the first week in June. Contact: Bergsteigerschule Saastal, CH-3906 Saas-Fee; (027-957-4464, or the tourist office at 027-958-1858). The classic "Haute Route" costs approximately €1,000, including guides, accommodations in mountain huts, meals, hotel expenses during the tour, and mountain railway and bus.

Lift tickets (2003/04 prices)

	Adult	Child (6–16)
one day	€41.50	€25
three days	€111.50	€67
six days	€203	€121.50
fourteen days	€358.50	€215

The resort also offers a ticket for five of seven days costing €185 for adult; and ten of fourteen days for €315, adults and €189 children.

Beginners can purchase tickets for only the village lifts at €10.50 for an adult half day and €5.50 for a child's half day; €15 for adult full day and €11 for child's full day.

Children younger than 6 ski free.

Accommodations

Price ranges noted for each hotel are per person based on double occupancy during February with half board (breakfast and dinner): €€€—€125+; €€—€75–€124; €—less than €75.

Ferienart Resort and Spa (027-958-1900, fax 027-958-1905; €€€) The best hotel in town. For a splurge, try the suite with round bed, white marble bath and sauna.

Ambassador (027-957-1905; €€€) Renovated with new pine furniture. In town near the ski school.

Allalin (027-957-1815, fax 027-957-3115; €€) This three-star hotel is really four-star quality with hand-carved wooden furniture. It is at the far end of town from the lifts, but has ski storage facilities at the lifts. They have some of the best food in town.

Mischabel (027-957-2118, fax 027-957-2461; €€€) At the entrance of the town, about a seven-minute walk to most lifts.

Chalet Cairn (027-957-1550; fax 027-957-3380; €€€) A rustic gem with only 16 rooms and a traditional atmosphere.

Hotel Waldesruh (027-958-6464, fax 027-958-6465; €€) Near the Plattjen and Längfluh gondola ground stations. Caters to families and has a wonderful, affordable restaurant.

Hotel Marmotte (027-957-2852, fax 027-957-1987; €–€€) This hotel shines because of its owner, Karl Dreier, who makes everyone feel at home. Karl, who doubles as the chef, cooks some of the best hotel food we've eaten. There is a free ski storage arrangement with the Waldesruh Hotel opposite the Felskinn lift, and a free baby sitting arrangement with Hotel Alphubel, a good hotel for children.

Derby (027-957-2345, fax 027-9571246; €€) for families near Felskinn or Plattjen.

Hotel Europa (027-957-3191; fax 027-957-2018; €) Small hotel for those planning to do some hiking on the Hannig.

Mühle (027-957-2676, fax 027-957-2677; €) Small basic hotel.

Feehof (027-957-2308; fax 027-957-2309; €) (Garni only) Inexpensive. No telephone, no public restaurant and no credit cards accepted.

Ski Chalets: Crystal, Inghams/Bladon (see page 20 for phone, fax and internet addresses).

Apartments, condominiums, flats

Apartments are the way to go if you really want to save money. Saas-Fee has about 1,500 chalets and apartments for rent. Write to the tourist office and ask for apartments that will be available when you plan to be in Saas-Fee. Include details on the number of people in your party. The office will send a list of available apartments and a map showing locations. Select the apartment you want and write to the tourist board or to the owner. The reservation line for apartments is 027-958-1868.

The apartments normally include linen and kitchen utensils. You will be charged a visitor's tax, and there may be an extra charge for the electricity and heat you use.

Expect to pay €20–€35 per person per night, based on location and the number of people sharing the apartment.

Dining

The best restaurant in the region is the **Fletschhorn** (027-957-2131; fax 027-957-2187), a 30-minute walk from town or a 10-minute taxi ride. It is considered one of the best in Switzerland and features nouvelle cuisine. It has one Michelin star. Make reservations early. Meals will range from €85–€115.

Perhaps the second-best eatery is the **Hohnegg** (027-957-2268), just about a 10-minute walk above the town (or call for its taxi service). Also nouvelle cuisine in a Swiss country atmosphere. It features a daily menu selection starting at less than €15.

The **Swiss Châlet** (027-957-3535) is considered another of the top gourmet spots with nouvelle cuisine. Its normal fixed-price menu is €60.

Le Mandarin Thai restaurant in the Ferienart Resort and Spa (027-958-1903) serves Asian cuisine for €30–€60. The Italian restaurant in the same hotel, **Del Ponte** is highly recommended with meals from €25–€55 and pizzas for only €10–€13.

For excellent traditional local Walliser food, try the **Golfhotel Saaserhof** and the **Schäferstube**. For cheese and Swiss specialties the top recommendations are the **Käse-Keller** (027-957-2120) and the **Arvu Stuba** (027-957-2747).

For good, less expensive meals, try the **Hotel Allalin** (027-957-1815)—a rebuilt 300-year-old room with wooden beams and hand-carved chairs that make it magical by candlelight; **Hotel Dom** (027-957-5101) for great *rösti*. **La Gorge** (027-958-1680) and the **Robinson Club** (027-958-1600) also has excellent fondue and raclette.

For pizza, try the restaurant **La Ferme** under the Hotel Beau-Site, or the **Boccalino**, in front of the Saaserhof. Pizza or pasta is €10–€13.

On the slopes have at least one lunch in the revolving restaurant at the top of the **Metro Alpin** lift, the world's highest such restaurant. The prices are down to earth. The mountain restaurant **Berghaus Plattjen**, a third of the way down the National run from the top of the Plattjen lift, is great for a late lunch when the area catches the sun. It has great *rösti*.

On the opposite side along the Längfluh run, where it meets the Gletschergrotte trail cutting off from the Kanonenrohr, is the **Gletscher-Grotte**, which catches sun most of the day.

A good lunch with beer and coffee at most spots on the mountain costs €15–€18. Fondue is about €24 and a normal three-course dinner will be about €24.

In Saas Grund try the **Hotel Dom** (027-957-5101) for magical setting and very affordable meals.

Après-ski/nightlife

Saas-Fee is known as a town for young skiers and those who think young. The **Crazy Night** in the Metropol has good music with a crowd aged 18–25. **Pic Pic** is a Swiss locals' spot; the **Alpen Pub** and the **Popcorn** (young crowd and snowboarders) normally have a good crowd; **Feeloch** under the Robinson Club and the **Go-Inn Bar** (young crowd) near the Hotel Beau Site are lively.

Après-ski, as the slopes close, is an early affair because the sun drops behind the mountains quickly. If you're off the mountain at around 3 p.m., the terrace bars at the **Derby, Mühle, Rendezvous** and **Christiana** do a great business. After 4 p.m., when the sun drops out of sight, the crowd evaporates. Most gather in bars like **Chemi Stube** in the Christiana, the **Saaserhof, Nesti's,** the **Black Bull** or the **Rendezvous**.

Child care (2003/04 prices)

The ski school (027-957-2348) takes children from age 4 to 6, with a day fee of €51.50 plus a lunch fee.

A guest kindergarten is run in the Hotel Garni Berghof (957-2484). A full day costs €41.50 including lunch and a half day is €20 without lunch.

Other activities

The Hannig area is now closed to skiers. It gets good early morning sun and is now the location of a 5-km. **toboggan** run. Tobaggans can be rented from the sports shops or at the Hannig cable car station.

Visit the **Saaser Museum**, packed with photographs of the old Saas valley, and old tools, kitchen utensils and furniture of mountain people. Open from 2–6 p.m., the museum charges €3.50 for adults, €1.50 for children to age 16.

The **Bielen sports and leisure center** has been newly renovated. It offers an 25-meter, heated indoor swimming pool, an indoor tennis court, billiards and table tennis, exercise room, whirlpools, steam bath and coed sauna. Tennis court should be reserved. Open all week from 10 a.m. to 9 p.m. The indoor pool costs €8.50 for adults and €5 for children. The sauna area costs €13 for adults.

Getting there

By train: From Zürich airport via Bern, Spiez, through the Lötschberg tunnel to Brig. From Geneva, trains run directly to Brig. Travelers by rail reach the Saas valley via Brig or Visp, and change into the post-car with direct destination "Saas Fee." There are connections every hour until 8:15 p.m. from Brig or 8:30 p.m. from Visp.

By car: Private car travelers from the north approach via through Bern through the Lötschberg (railway car ferry). Trains transit the tunnel every half-hour from 5:35 a.m. to 11:05 p.m. The trip takes only 15 minutes. Cost per car (including nine-seat vans) is €16–€18. From Goppenstein, drive to Visp, then on to Saas-Fee.

From the east and south via the Furkaand Simpion.

From western Switzerland you reach Saas-Fee via Lausanne, and along the Rhone valley to Visp. Motorway until Sierra-East.

Park in the public lot at the town entrance. Call your hotel for pickup, or take a taxi. Taxis from the parking lot and bus station to town cost about €10.

Tourist information

Write Tourist Office Saas-Fee, CH-3906 Saas-Fee, Switzerland
Telephone 027-958-1858; fax 027-958-1860.
Reservations: 027-957-1868.
Internet: www.saas-fee.ch or www.saastal.ch
E-mail: to@saas-fee.ch

St. Moritz

Yes, when you have visited all the other great resorts, when you have enjoyed the other hotels claiming to pamper guests to the extreme, when you've seen all the mountains said to be grand and great, then and only then: journey to St. Moritz. You'll find that though there is elegance and Alpine beauty everywhere in Switzerland, nowhere is it concentrated in such huge amounts as here on the rooftop of Europe, St. Moritz, the original Swiss winter resort. Each night at dinner at the Hotel Schweizerhof it is great theater to observe the maitre d'hotel greet guests in German, French and English. After speaking with you once, he always addresses you in your native language.

In winter the great expanses of snow-covered lake provide a massive, scenic foreground for the celebrated town whose name is a synonym for quality and luxury. The most elegant aspect of St. Moritz—the great hotels—are expensive, but everything else, restaurants included, is there for nearly everyone.

The tourist office claims the sun shines 322 days a year in St. Moritz; in the winter this sunlight brightens some 250 miles of downhill ski runs, 100 miles of cross-country ski trails, 30 curling rinks, horse races, polo and cricket on the frozen lake, the Cresta and bobsled runs, an Olympic ski jumping hill and much more.

The central area, St. Moritz Dorf, is compact, really only two main streets with a few side streets and a single small main square. Movies are up-to-date, nightlife superb, moonlight strolls on the lake wonderful. The entertainment fits every pocketbook and taste. St. Moritz Bad, the less built-up section and ancient health spa, curls around the western end of the frozen lake.

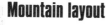

Mountain layout

Until you have experienced St. Moritz, your education in Swiss skiing is incomplete. Exclusive, exciting, this two-time winter Olympic site—1928 and 1948—is home to some of the finest intermediate skiing anywhere. St. Moritz was one of the first to embrace ego snow for the rich and famous.

Altogether there are 250 miles of groomed trails. The setting is stunning: 6,000 feet high in the southeastern corner of Switzerland, near the border with Italy in the twin shadows of the 9,270-foot Piz Nair and the 10,833-foot Piz Corvatsch.

The main runs are clustered around the summits of the three main mountains. The Corviglia runs finish near St. Moritz-Dorf, the Corvatsch Hahnensee run drops into St. Moritz-Bad and Diavolezza drops into a nearby valley.

The finest run is the Hahnensee, a black-rated trail that is intermediate for most of the five-mile length. It boasts a vertical drop of more than 4,900 feet. It's a five-minute walk from the end of the Hahnensee run to the Signalbahn cable car, which takes you up to Corviglia.

On the second run down the Hahnensee, break off at the Mandras T-bar and climb to the Murtèl cable midstation. Here the run down the Surlej is peppered with moguls and dips, while the panorama includes the frozen lakes of Champfèr and Silvaplana. Adventurous folk work their way along the slopes via the T-bars at Alp Margun to the 9,186-foot-high Culöz de las Furtschellas. From here there is an interesting run to Sils-Maria on the Silvaplana lake shore.

The longest and favorite run of many is from Piz Nair, either down the front side to St. Moritz or over the ridge at the 8,154-foot level at the cable car station in Corviglia and down to Marguns. For the greatest length along an intermediate trail, climb to the top of the Fuorcia Grischa chair lift, behind Piz Nair, for the run to the valley floor.

The single most challenging run in the valley is "Il Muro," a chilling drop from the top at Lagalb on the Bernina Pass. On the other side of the pass is Diavolezza. The skiing there is good, but the Diavolezza to Morteratsch run is wonderful. A stunning glacier ski trek awaits after a 25-minute walk on skis to the mountain bar run by Islas Pers. On full-moon nights glacier skiing is a unique Alpine experience.

Snowboarding

St. Moritz has taken to snowboarding unconditionally. Every section of the mountains has a hidden gem for riders. The Corvatsch is favored for racing. The Furtschellas has a hidden freestyle snowpark with jumps, windlips and powder. On the Corviglia section there is a halfpipe near the Signal lift. In Diavolezza-Lagalb there is a natural halfpipe.

Mountain rating

Beginners will start to feel at home after several runs on one of the longer trails. But this is not the best spot to learn to ski. Beginner skiers will feel limited with not too many slopes to take them from absolute beginner to lower intermediate.

Eighty percent of the slopes in the St. Moritz area are for intermediates. Corvatsch has plenty of ego-boosting trails that catch lots of sun. The Diavolezza-Langalb has some of the best intermediate trails with the thinnest crowds. When in doubt, tag behind the advanced beginners of a St. Moritz ski class for the best slope that day.

Experts will head for the toughest parts of the back side of the Piz Nair, as well as Corvatsch summit and the super challenge of the black run at Lagalb. If you are in the Diavolezza sector head to the Schwarzer Hang for some steep skiing. To ski off-piste from Corviglia or Corvatsch a guide is required for many of the itineraries.

Ski schools (2003/04 prices)

St. Moritz area ski schools employ up to 350 instructors. In 1927 the world's first ski school was established here. The main ski school (081-8300101) is in the center of town next to the public parking.

Private lessons cost €213 for a full day. A half day costs €120.

Group lessons are €30 for a half day and €47 for a full day.

Snowboard private lessons cost €126 for two hours (half day) and €220 for five hours (full day). Each extra person must pay €6.

Snowboard group lessons are €29 for a day, €122 for three days and €155 for five days.

Cross-country lessons are extremely popular thanks to nearly 121 km. of well-maintained trails in the valley. Cross-country buffs will probably want to participate in the Engadin Marathon course, a 26-mile cross-country circuit. Come in March and take part along with 12,000 others in one of the world's great cross-country races.

Private cross-country lessons are €55 per hour for one or two skiers or and €181 for a full day, plus €6 for each additional person.

Group cross-country lesson rates are €23 for a day and €84 for five days.

Lift tickets (2003/04 prices)

The Engadin regional pass includes St. Moritz and Corviglia, Sils Maria, Silvaplana, Surlej, Champfer, Celerina, Samedan, Pontresina and Zuoz. The pass serves 55 lifts covering 350 km. of prepared trails as well as buses, some train links and entrance to the swimming pool. These prices are for holiday and February seasons. January lift ticket prices are about five percent less.

	Adults	Youth (16–20)	Children (6–16)
one day	€68	€61	€34
three days	€178	€161	€80
six days	€322	€290	€151
fourteen days	€556	€500	€278

Accommodations

Over half of the hotels in St. Moritz are four- and five-star, the highest concentration of quality hotels in Switzerland.

Price ranges noted for each hotel are per person based on double occupancy with half board (breakfast and dinner): €€€—€125+; €€—€75–€124; €—less than €75.

The Engadin region also organizes special all-inclusive Holiday Active Weeks that include seven days half-board, six days of lifts and six days of instruction or a ski guide. Contact the tourist office for details and prices.

The best of the best is the **Suvretta** (081-836-3636, fax 081-836-3737; €€€) in neighboring Champfèr. This wonderful monument to Swiss hotel expertise is a model of understatement, a great hotel with its own lift connection to Corviglia.

Second in our ranking of the five five-star hotels in St. Moritz is the **Kulm** (081-836-8000, fax 081-836-8001; €€€), on the road to the bobsled and Cresta runs. The Kulm seems more welcoming than the Palace; it's also a center for sports, its trophy cases brimming with awards for curling, skiing, golf, tennis, and the famous Cresta run. The hotel sits high on a hill overlooking the frozen lake and offers a commanding view of the valley. Afternoon tea here with this vista is highly recommended.

Badrutt's Palace (081-837-1000, fax 081-837-2999; €€€) the place to stay if you want to be seen. It is one of the most famous and elegant hotels in the world, where if you have to ask the price you should be staying somewhere else. Coat and tie required in public areas after 7 p.m.

Hotel Albana, (081-836-6161, fax 081-836-6162; €€€) is an excellent downtown lodging with four-star staff and an excellent kitchen. The walls are hung with a private hunting trophy exposition amassed by the safari-loving owner. Along with these animals is a collection of armor, antiques and Middle Age pieces. The best restaurant is the **Grill** that is not included in the half board.

Schweizerhof (081-837-0707; fax 081-837-0700; €€€) The food is very good and the staff friendly and efficient. Four-star and one of the most comfortable hotels in town, the Schweizerhof is well located a few blocks up from the Palace on Via dal Bagn, along with Bulgari, Bugatti, Vuitton, Armani, Cartier and Versace. If you think these are ski instructors, you're in the wrong neighborhood.

Posthotel (081-832-2121, fax 081-833-8973; €€€) looks like a castle set right between the Palace and the Schweizerhof.

Hotel Steffani (081-836-9696, fax 081-836-9717; €€€) is comfortable, right in midtown near the parking garage. **Hotel Bären** (081-833-5656; fax 081-833-8022; €€€) is a bit of distance from Dorf central. **Hotel Steinbock** (081-833-6035; fax 081-833-8747; €€€) is a small three-star hotel (30 beds) with a good restaurant and a reputation for making guests comfortable.

Hotel Nolda (081-833-0575, fax 081-833-8751; €€€), in a charming Swiss chalet, is a family hotel at the end of the Corviglia run and close to the Signal cable car; it has sauna, swimming pool, solarium and whirlpool. The lobby is full of Swiss mountain atmosphere with leather couches surrounding a fireplace.

Hotel Bellaval (081-833-3245; fax 081-833-0406; €) is a B&B minutes from St. Moritz-Dorf center and the train station. **National Hotel** (081-833-3274; 081-833-3275; €€-) is another good bargain choice.

The **Youth Hostel** (081-833-3969; fax 081-833-8046) has bunks for €22 a night with breakfast. Some of the more inexpensive hotels frequented by snowboarders are **Hotel Inn Lodge** (081-834-4795; €) in Celerina, **Hotel Julier Palace** (081-828-9644; €) in Silvaplana, and **Hotel Saratz** (081-839-4000; €) in Pontresina.

A bit outside of the center of town is **Waldhaus am See** (081-836-6000, fax 081-836-6060; €€) a three-star 85-room hotel in quiet location on the shore of St. Moritz lake; only three minutes' walk from the train station. It has the largest whiskey bar in the world according to Guinness and has been rated the best three-star hotel in Switzerland.

Champfèr, about three km. away, is home to **Chesa Guardalej** (081-836-6300, fax 081-836-6301; €€€) a spectacular hotel consisting of a village of small buildings connected by underground passages. The rooms are excellent. There are several different dining areas and restaurants, and the hotel has a full exercise room and swimming pool. The restaurant offers very affordable menu meals starting at around €12.

Albana (081-828-9292, fax 081-828-8181; €€€) in Silvas plana, about six km. from St. Moritz, features an award-winning restaurant. Also in Silvaplana the 12-room Garni/B&B **Chesa Silva** (081-838-6100; fax 838-6199; €€) is delightful.

Apartments, condominiums, flats

The apartment business is well organized and bookings can be arranged through the Interent, the Internet or the tourist office. Rentals are from Saturday to Saturday. Give them details about when you plan to arrive, how many people will be sharing the apartment, and what facilities you desire; they will respond quickly with several apartment choices.

There are about 6,500 apartment beds, but only about 2,900 are rentals. Interhome operates an office from Via dal Bagn 21, 7500 St. Moritz (081-833-1520, fax 081-833-0440) or contact the Tourist Office (081-837-3399, fax 081-837-3366).

Dining

One dining experience you should enjoy is the excursion to **Muottas Muragl**, a mountain hotel restaurant near Pontresina and Samedan on the way to the Bernina Pass. You take a funicular up to the hotel, which has a truly spectacular location overlooking the valley. Take the funicular just before sunset (it runs every half hour, 8 a.m.–11 p.m.) and watch the lights come on in the valley. Reserve in advance (081-842-8232) and get a window seat.

The great hotels of St. Moritz boast equally famous dining rooms. The Palace owns the ancient **Chesa Veglia** (081-837-1000) standing in an original Engadine farmhouse dating back to 1658. The real draw here is the ambiance. Dine in the Chadafö Grill where your meal will be cooked over fire. Be ready to leave around €80–€100 apiece for your meal if you have a starter, grilled meat or fish and flaming dessert.

The Italian specialties in the pizzeria at the **Chesa Veglia** are served at down-to-earth prices. **Trattoria** there is also superb but expensive. (Have lunch for the same great food without the high costs.)

For one of the area's top gourmet spots try **Jöhri's Talvò** (081-833-4455), a Relais & Chateaux restaurant in nearby Champfèr. The owner, Roland Jöhri-Tanner, is one of Switzerland's best cooks. Reservations are necessary and plan on spending €60–€120.

The restaurant at the Steinbock hotel has tasty, reasonably priced Swiss cuisine. The **Soldanella** hotel also has good meals and prices.

To demolish your budget and add an unforgettable dining experience, lunch at **La Marmite** (reservations required for noon and 2 p.m. seatings; 833-6355), a gourmet restaurant atop Corviglia. Meals will set you back €45–€130. It's in the funicular station near the self-service restaurant. **Brasserie**, run by the same owner in the same place, costs half as much.

The Hotel Steffani (081-836-9696) has its **Le Lapin Bleu** where the daily menu can be very affordable—between €20 at lunch and €30 for dinner. It also houses the top Chinese restaurants in town, **Le Mandarin,** open for dinner only where the daily menu costs €30–€60.

The **Stüvetta**, a cozy corner of the restaurant building at the Marguns lift station, is great for lunches, particularly pasta dishes. And the last stop of the day should be the **Alpina Hütte**, the St. Moritz ski club hut in the shadow of Piz Nair where you should order a Café Grischa, a traditional hot coffee and liqueur-filled pot with drinking spouts for four. One of the most reasonably priced restaurants in the area is **Veltlinerkeller** (833-4009), downhill from Dorf toward Bad, serves wonderful local dishes.

The acclaimed Italian restaurant, **Grissini** (081-836-2626) in Hotel Crystal, is very affordable for lunches. The daily lunch menu is between €12 and €15. Dinner is much more expensive heading up to €52.

Dinner at **Meierei** (081-833-3242; fax 081-833-8838), looking across the lake to the town, is very romantic. Ask for a table with a view. The restaurant is in an old farmhouse about a 20-minute walk from town (or take a horse-drawn sleigh). The daily menu starts at only €15 and *al la carte* can range up to €60.

Another excellent restaurant is **Chasellas** (081-833-3858) about a mile-and-a-half out of town. The daily menu is set at about €65. Call for reservations.

Après-ski/nightlife

At 1 a.m. most nights, many visitors are still sampling St. Moritz's great nightlife. The most famous address is the **King's Club** disco at the Palace where €20 gets you in (men, bring a tie) and buys one drink. The most fun we had, by far, was at the **Stübli**, the typical Swiss wood-paneled bar in the lower level of the Schweizerhof. The ski instructors come early and stay late. There's usually so little room you are crowded, shoved and shuffled from one spot to another. The **Cava Bar** at the Hotel Steffani is the same style as the Stübli, but in a cave. It's open from 5 p.m. to midnight.

The **Cresta Bar** in the Steffani is a good meeting place after the walk down the hill from the Corviglia funicular, but from there you might move on after 10 p.m. to the nearby **Vivai,** a disco with a young following. Nearby also is **Cascade**, a sort of combination bar and pub you'll like almost as much as the Stübli. The younger set heads to **Pit Stop** in an old garage near the Kulm. For a quiet drink try the bar-sitting room in the **Albana** after a day on Corviglia.

It's chic in the late afternoon to order a hot chocolate and whipped cream-covered slice of Black Forest cake at **Hanselmann**, the famed chocolate specialist near the Hotel Albana in the center of town.

Child care (2003/04 prices)

The ski school has a child care program for those age 4 to 12. The program provides child pickup. During the day the children have lunch, a horse-drawn sleigh ride to the ski school and ski lessons. Child care, pickup and lunch costs €16 per day. The price of the normal ski school lessons is additional.

There are supervised classes for children age 3 to 6 at the Suvretta Ski School. Rates are: €44 for a full day and €110 for three full days. Lunch is €9 per day.

Child-care programs are available at the Parkhotel Kurhaus and the Schweizerhof (in ascending order of prices). At the Parkhotel (081-836-2111) a full day is €23 with lunch. At the Schweizerhof (081-837-0707) the full-day cost with lunch included is €22. You can take kids to either the Parkhotel or the Schweizerhof for €4 per hour.

Other activities

If you have the time, ride the **Glacier Express**, a 150-mile crossing of the ice-covered landscape between St. Moritz and Zermatt. Or take the Bernina Express on the scenic mountain rails to Tirano in Italy.

A **horse-drawn sleigh ride** along the lake costs about €29 per person for an hour or €16 for a half hour. A trip in the Roseg Valley is around €16 per person or €84 per carriage.

"Skijöring" races, with horses pulling skiers on the frozen lake racetrack, started in 1907. The competition continues on the first three Sundays in February.

Bobsledding is available for €142 per run with a photo and certificate.

For information on **hang-gliding** instruction, call 081-833-2416. You can go airborne for €142. Five lessons cost €516.

Excursions to Italy are easy, and bus tours are available if you are not driving.

St. Moritz has two **museums**, the Engadine, filled with local history, and the Segantini, an art museum.

The public **swimming pool** entrance fees are €5 per adult or €3 per child. There are discount booklets for repeated visits. You will also find a sauna at the pool.

Getting there

You'll normally fly into Zürich and then catch a train to St. Moritz.

If you are driving, the easiest route is Zürich-Chur-Thusis, then a 30-mile stretch over the Julierpass (chains needed only in the worst weather) or through the Thusis-Samedan car-train tunnel when the pass is closed or the new Klosters-Susch Vereina.

If you stay in St. Moritz and not in one of the outlying towns, you'll pay a stiff fee for parking, about €9 a day unless you are staying for more than a week. In that case, there is a discount card available. The main garage is centrally located, however, two minutes down the hill from the Corviglia funicular.

Tourist information

Kur-und-Verkehrsverein, CH-7500 St. Moritz, Switzerland.
Tel. 081-837-3333, fax 081-837-3366.
Internet: www.stmoritz.ch
Email: information@stmoritz.ch
In neighboring Pontresina, the address is Verkehrsverein, CH-7505 Pontresina, Switzerland; tel. 081-838-8300, fax 081-838-8310.

Verbier

Seen from below in the fading day, the flickering lights of Verbier beckon as if from Olympus, the quaint Swiss town resting in the saddle of majestic mountains nearly 5,000 feet above the valley floor. This is the crux of Switzerland's renowned "4 Valleys," a vast, interconnected web of Alpine valleys and towns that comprises over 402 km. of ski runs and 94 individual ski-lifts. With some of the most challenging ski terrain and scenic vistas in the Alps, a southwesterly orientation that maximizes sun exposure, and the 850-year history of the surrounding "Val de Bagnes" region, Verbier epitomizes the kind of adventure unique to the European "superski" networks.

Though sizable at nearly 15,000 beds, Verbier is dominated by chalet-style houses and mid-size hotels, giving it a traditional Swiss feel that is at odds with the multi-story hotel blocks and modern atmosphere typical of many major French resorts. This is the French-speaking region of Switzerland, but thanks to its standing as one of the most popular Alpine destinations for British tourists, Verbier also hangs out an "English is spoken" plaque for its visitors.

Though quaint in appearance, Verbier offers all the amenities of the major destination ski resort. There are one five-star hotel, five four-star hotels, three relatively affordable pensions, and much in between. There are a number of gourmet restaurants offering regional specialties such as raclette and fondue – including the noted restaurant Le Rosalp, run by Roland Pierroz, who was voted "1992 Gault Millau Cook of the Year" – and numerous inexpensive pizzerias. There is raucous après-ski (more on this later) and varied nightlife and dance clubs catering to all ages. Most of all, however, Verbier is renowned for its mountains and the skiing.

Mountain layout

This resort is at one end of the Four Valleys area. It links with Thyon, Veysonnaz and Nendaz. Verbier has the best skiing for experts and advanced skiers, a decent beginner area, but limited intermediate trails.

The Savoleyres area is the smallest of the Verbier sectors. A gondola takes skiers up to mellow trails. This area doesn't get too many crowds, is full of sunshine all day long, and the lift lines stay manageable for the most part. During the early season, skiing back to Verbier is relatively easy, however during the late season the snow coverage requires most skiers to download on the gondola.

The main Verbier area is on the north-facing slopes with the main lifts rising to Ruinettes and Attelas. This section gets crowded and at the lower levels skiers don't only have to watch out for each other, but deal with walkers, dogs and kids on sleds.

From the Attelas upper station, cable cars rise to the Mont Gelé glacier. The problems here are weather, which closes the area many days, and the lift lines which can be a pain.

One intermediate secret is the Bruson area. It is connected with the rest of the Four Valleys by a 15-minute bus trip from the lower station of the Châble cable car. The trails here are far from the maddening crowds. On powder days this is a wonderful spot to practice turns and perfect technique.

Experts and advanced skiers will have the time of their lives with virtually limitless off-piste possibilities. Many of the formerly black runs have been redefined as itineraries. They are not groomed or marked, but have so much traffic, they may as well have been marked by the resort as they once were. A guide is highly recommended in this area to get the most out of the mountain.

Snowboarding

Like some other mecca's of free ride, Verbier's snowboarding depends heavily on snow conditions. If it hasn't snowed in more than a few days, boarders will find themselves faced with crowded groomed slopes due to the disappeal of the chopped up and moguled off-piste. Especially during the high seasons, you will find all the best descents from Mont Gelé and Mont-Fort totally covered with moguls. After a good dump of snow, though, be ready for extraordinary powder rides that can take you from the 10,925 foot peak of Mont-Fort all the way down to Verbier at 4,921 feet, with a few cuts of tree-boarding around the gondola line of Médran 1&2. On good snow days, the Bruson area can also host good tree-boarding and off-piste terrain.

The other three valleys connected to Verbier have good variety and nice slopes, but getting there and back on a snowboard is not only a pain, but also dangerous; if you don't make it up the lifts back to Verbier in time, you're stuck. In general, the lifts at Verbier are faster and of better quality than in the other parts of the four Valleys, so you aren't missing anything by spending most of your time just in the Verbier section.

Unfortunately, the main Verbier ski area offers little haven to never-ever and beginner boarders. If you fall in to one of these categories, stick to either the Bruson or Savoleyres areas, which are excellently connected to the Verbier village; Savoleyres by a bus ride from either Médran or la place centrale, Bruson by a gondola ride down the valley and then a free shuttle to the slopes.

Intermediate snowboarders will be able to find slopes matching their abilities all over the mountain except from Mont-Fort and Mont-Gelé. For the most variety and best scenery, we recommend hitting the lifts set around La Chaux, Les Ruinettes, and Attelas. From here you'll be able to challenge yourself on a steeper run, or take a break on a nice easy run.

Advanced and expert riders will have a ball hitting the challenging slopes of Mont Fort and Mont Gelé. After a good snow, the itineraries from either peak all the way down to Tortin can keep you happy all day long.

The snow park at La Chaux, depending on snow conditions, is comprised of many table tops, rails, and one big-air jump sure to test your guts. On sunny days the park can be a nice place to hang out, take some jumps, and listen to some new french and swiss music.

Mountain rating

Verbier enjoys a well-deserved reputation as the Promised Land for advanced and expert skiers. The twin and only runs down the Mont-Fort Gondola—steep, mogully, and … did we say steep already? — make this among the most difficult marked descents from a gondola station (10,925 feet) in all of the Alps. The Tortin descent from either Col des Gentianes or Chassoure is also renowned for its steepness: if you fall, as we have learned from personal experience, you can slide as far as 328 feet. All of the areas beneath Mont Fort and Mont Gele above Verbier – Attelas, Le Chaux, Les Ruinettes – offer challenging runs for experts as well as good terrain from advanced and intermediate skiers.

In truth, any area this large offers something for every skier. Intermediate skiers who want to combine skiing and a ski-touring adventure will greatly enjoy the top-to-bottom runs down to towns such as Nendaz, Veysonnaz, or Les Collons: all are long, well-groomed trails with good pitch. Be forewarned, however, that you must time your touring to reach the Tortin lift back to Verbier before it closes at the end of the day, or you could be stuck on the wrong side of the mountain ridge and facing a bus ride of many hours.

Advanced beginners will prefer the La Tzoumaz/Savoleyres area just above Verbier. The slopes on this side of the mountain tend to be wide-open and well-groomed. There are also many gentler slopes across the valley at Mayens-de-Bruson.

Cross-country

There are 4 km. of cross-country skiing near the Sports Center, and another 5 km. at 2,200 meters at Les Ruinettes/Le Chaux. We recommend, however, taking the gondola down and accessing the 45 km. of cross-country trails in the Valley de Bagnes below.

Ski school (2003/04 prices)

There are four ski schools in the town. The Swiss ski school has 1,705 instructors and is in the Chalet Orny (027-7753363). Le Fantastique can be reached at 027-7714241. For Adrenaline, call 027-7717459 and for Altitude call 027-7716006.

Private lessons	
one or two persons (2 hours)	€95.36 (Swiss Ski School)
one or two skiers for a half day	€127 per person (Le Fantastique)
one or two skiers for a full day	€237 per person (Le Fantastique)
Group lessons Lessons run from 9:15 a.m. to 11:45 a.m.	
five consecutive days (adults)	€170.29 (Adrenaline)
five consecutive days (child)	€149 (Le Fantastique)

Five full-day ski seminars or weekend seminars let skiers tour the area trails, honing their skills at the same time. The instructor takes the skiers over mountain runs within their ability. It's a great way to spend a week, ski the entire mountain, and leave a much better skier.

There are freestyle classes that average about €97 per day.

Snowboarding group lessons meet from Monday through Saturday from 9:45 a.m. to noon. Lessons are approximately €140 for three half-day lessons.

Lift tickets (2003/04 prices)

Family vacationers should be sure to ask about discounts, because the formula that is used may result in a healthy discount for them. Similar discounts apply to single parents.

These lift ticket prices are for the entire Four-valley area with Mont-Fort and only Verbier.

	Four-Valley	Verbier
half-day	€36	€32
one day	€40	€35
two days	€78	€68
six days	€207	€180
fourteen days	€386	€336

Note: Ski passes for three days or more are issued on computer-chip cards. These rechargeable cards cost approximately €3.50 each and are non-returnable.

Thirty percent-off tickets are available for skiers older than age 65 and for children age 6 to 15. Youth age 16–20 receive a 15 percent discount. Lift tickets are discounted further in certain low-season periods. Family and group rates are also available.

Accommodations

Special weekly programs cost €935–€1,705 per person depending on the hotel for a full week from the middle of March to the beginning of April with half board, six-day lift pass and free entry to the sports center.

The approximate daily high-season rate with half pension, based on double occupancy, is noted after each hotel. €€€—€125+; €€—€75–€125; €—€74-.

Four-star hotels:

Rosalp (027 771 63 23; fax 027 771 10 59; €€€).

Vanessa (027 775 28 00; fax 027 775 28 28; €€€).

Montpelier (027 771 61 31; fax 027 771 46 89; €€€).

Three-star hotels:

Bristol (027 771 65 77; fax 027 771 51 50; €€–€€€).

Golf Hotel (027 771 65 15; fax 027 771 14 88; €€).

Rhodania (027 771 61 21; fax 027 771 52 54; €€–€€€).

Les Chamois (027 771 64 02; fax 027 771 27 12; €€–€€€).

De la Poste (027 771 66 81; fax 027 771 34 01; €€€).

La Rotonde (027 771 65 25; fax 027 771 33 31; €€€).

Au Vieux-Valais (027 775 35 20; fax 027 775 35 35; €€€).

Two-star hotels:

Garbo (027 771 62 72; fax 027 771 62 71; €€).

Bed & Breakfasts: (the *** note how many stars each B&B has)

Les 4 Vallées****** (027 775 33 44; fax 027 775 33 45; €€).

Rois Mages (027 771 63 64; fax 027 771 33 19; €€€).

Bristol***** (027 771 65 77; fax 027 771 51 50; €€).

Ermitage***** (027 771 64 77; fax 027 771 52 64; €€).

Farinet***** (027 771 66 26; fax 027 771 38 55; €€).

Mirabeau***** (027 771 63 35; fax 027 771 63 30; €€).

Verbier***** (027 775 21 21; fax 027 775 21 20; €€).

There is a Bomb shelter turned cheap hotel called **The Bunker** (027 771 66 02, fax 027 771 66 03), located inside the sports center with rates of about €30 per night for bed; breakfast and dinner; whirlpool, ice-rink and pool access; digital TV and video; showers; and locker. A nearby public bus stop takes you to the ski area. Bring your own sleeping bag and for a few euros more you can also have access to a sauna; tennis and squash; public telephone; internet access; and the bar.

Ski Chalets: Crystal, Inghams/Bladon, Simply Ski, Chalet World, Thomas (go to page 20 for phone, fax and Internet addresses).

Apartments, condominiums, flats

The tourist office keeps track of apartment availability. Send details on the number of beds required, the preferred number of rooms, and the dates you plan to be there. An immediate response with a selection of apartments and prices will follow. Select the apartment you want and contact the owner directly. Minimum stays are normally one week, Saturday to Saturday (in Christmas season the minimum is two weeks).

Bed linen and kitchen utensils are usually provided. Other communal or private amenities, such as swimming pool, sauna, TV or room phone, all add to the cost. Apartments rent for €510 per person per week in high season. Prices vary significantly by season.

Dining

Given the strong French influence and regional culinary traditions in Verbier and the surrounding Val de Bagnes region, it is difficult to find a poorly prepared meal. Prices, of course, will depend on the establishment's relative position on the luxury scale. Be sure to try the local raclette, a soft, melted cheese that is continually replenished on your plate, and typically served with potatoes, pickles, vegetables and assorted meats. Raclette is especially nice when accompanied by one of the crisp, dry white wines of the local Val de Bagnes region.

For a special splurge, try the restaurant **Rosalp** (027 771 63 23) in the four-star Rosalp Hotel. Award-winning chef Roland Pierroz is a culinary celebrity in Verbier. **Au Vieux Verbier** (027 771 16 68) you'll find good service, exquisite food, and a unique mountain class; just be sure that you know what you're getting your wallet in to before you sit down. The **Vanessa** (027 775 28 00) is also excellent. We especially liked the relatively new **The King's Restaurant** (027 775 20 35), a trendy restaurant with stuffed leather couches, roaring fireplace and arched windows. The candle-lit atmosphere matches its sophisticated menu of game, fish and innovative salads. Excellent raclette with all the fixings is served up in a comfortable, woodsy atmosphere at the **La Channe Valaisanne** restaurant in the Hotel Bristol. Other restaurants recommended by the locals include the **Au Vieux Valais** (027 775 35 20) and **Le Mazot**. The **Toro Negro** (027 771 99 01) features excellent steaks and game (try the excellent rabbit in wine sauce) in a warm atmosphere.

Barsalino's Pizzeria (027 771 17 50) across from the Hotel Bristol near the central round-about is also very good and reasonable, with excellent pizzas cooked in a wood-burning oven. The food in **Le Fer à Cheval** (027 771 26 69) is inexpensive and good, with a lively atmosphere where English is usually the common language. If you're looking for a cheap burger, head to **Harold's Hamburger** (027 771 62 43), where you can check your email while you wait for your order.

In terms of on-mountain dining during the day, Verbier offers the wide variety typical in Europe. Gondola-station buffets share duty with numerous private restaurants dotted about the slopes. At least two restaurants, however, merit a special mention. At the **Chez Dany** (027 771 25 24) chalet just above Verbier, visitors enjoy unsurpassed vistas of the valley below from the outside deck. Try the "Croute au Fromage," a piece of locally baked bread topped with ham and smothered in melted Swiss cheese, with a fried egg on top. Those skiing the Savoleyres area should try lunch at the **Le Sonalon** restaurant halfway down the slope. The specialty-of-the-day pastas are excellent and reasonable, and the view from the outside deck is equally rewarding.

Après-ski/nightlife

With 12 bars and discotheques, Verbier boasts some of the best après-ski and nightlife in the Swiss Alps. Immediately after stepping out of your boards, stop at The **Pub Mont-Fort** near the gondola. This pub is a favorite of the British crowd, and there is more English spoken than any other language. The music system is excellent and the selection is generally good, the bartenders are friendly, and the crowd raucous and eclectic. If you're staying in the center of town, however, remember it's a long, wavering walk down with skis and ski boots. The English accent is carried over at the **Big Ben** pub nearer to the gondola station, and down in the center of town near the round-about at **The Nelson Pub**. **Le Fer a' Cheval** (the "horseshoe") halfway between the center of town and the gondola also rocks after the lifts close, and you can pass the time checking out the endless license plates from all over the world that are plastered on the wall. The **Offshore** has a funky, well, right off the shore theme, and serves mostly as a before dinner après-ski hang-out. Other bars favored before hitting the discos are **Aristo**, the **New Club** and **Jacky's Bar**.

When dinner is done and the leg-strong still have dancing on the mind, Verbier is ready to accommodate. The **Marshall Club** and **Club Taratata** in the Bristol Hotel play techno-music, largely for a younger crowd of 20- somethings. The **Farm Club** in the Hotel Rhodania caters to an older, more sophisticated crowd, many of them up from Geneva to visit their chalets. The scores of vodka bottles on the wall with names on them are for the regulars who come back every weekend. The atmosphere is nice, with stuffed couches and a smallish dance floor, but the prices will make your eyes roll. The **Scotch Club** is also popular with a slightly older, local crowd sprinkled with British visitors. Expect to pay about €13–€15 for entry to most clubs, with drinks at the more swanky spots costing roughly the same.

Child care (2003/04 prices)

The ski kindergarten that was in Chalet Lesberty, just a short distance from the tourist office, has been closed. The ski kindergarten is scheduled to re-open in a new building at the beginning of the winter season. Call the tourist office for more information.

The ski school runs a ski nursery (027 771 44 69), which offers ski lessons for children from 3 years of age. These lessons cost €33 for a half day; €59 for a full day; and €238 for six days. Prices do not include lift tickets. Lunch is €10.

A children's ski program for good skiers age 3–12 runs Monday–Friday from 9 a.m.–4:30 p.m. Rates are abour €107 for five days.

Other activities

Verbier has an extensive sports center, which features an **indoor swimming pool, ice rink, curling rinks, squash courts, whirlpools, saunas,** and **solariums**. Pool entry is about €4.75 for guests staying in a hotel in Verbier. An hour of tennis costs €15.50. Ice skating is €4 and squash courts cost €8–€10 per half-hour. There are also **tandem paragliding** flights offered at Verbier (call the Centre de Parapente, 027 771 68 18).

Getting there

The closest airport is Geneva. Train service runs from Martigny on the Simplon. Then you must take a small train to Le Chable, where you can either take the cable car to Verbier or a direct bus from the station in the winter. The drive from Geneva takes about two hours. Follow the signs to the St. Bernard Pass (home of the famous St. Bernard dogs) until Sembrancher; turn left there, up the hill to Verbier.

Tourist information

Tourist office, CH-1936 Verbier, Switzerland; tel. 027 775 38 88; fax 027 775 38 89.
Internet: www.verbier.ch
E-mail: info@verbier.ch

Zermatt

Zermatt, Switzerland's best-known ski resort, was the base for the famous first assaults on the Matterhorn in the 1860s (prior to that villagers only climbed as high as their cattle). Finally, in 1865, a Brit named Edward Whymper conquered the "Mother Horn" but lost four of his party on the descent. Winter sports enthusiasts started skiing under the shadow of the killer mountain in 1933, and now the storybook village has become one of Europe's premier winter playgrounds.

Thanks to strict town zoning, almost every structure in town is a quaint Swiss chalet less than four stories high. This fairy-tale setting is augmented by a babbling stream running through the middle of town. And, as if that is not enough, transportation is by horse drawn sleighs or electric taxis. Only the doctor is allowed to have a car in Zermatt! Everyone else, since 1891, arrives by train. Unfortunately, the horse-drawn sleighs that used to carry tourists and townsfolk through the village, along with bags of groceries or ski equipment, have been largely replaced with speeding electric trucks and carts; when you hear a ringing bell, get to the side of the street.

But Zermatt is no small Alpine town. It is home to 5,500 permanent residents and swells to more than 20,000 on busy holidays. Fortunately, Zermatt is a destination resort; that is, the village is difficult enough for weekend skiers to reach to keep most of them away, and the vast terrain—more than 155 miles of marked ski trails (including Breuil-Cervinia) and a resort lift capacity over 38,800 people per hour—easily absorbs this many people. Even in the busiest seasons lift lines are not impossibly long and uncrowded slopes can be found.

Despite constant development, new hotels and apartments, Zermatt remains the world's most quintessential ski resort. No matter how many times you come here you are always charmed and amazed that the village remains part of the real world.

Mountain layout

Unlike many other fashionable ski resorts around the world, most people who come to Zermatt actually ski! There are about 2250 km. of pistes and 71 lifts covering three separate (though partially connected) areas and the Italian resort of Breuil-Cervinia with a lift capacity of 75,180 skiers per hour. There are numerous cross-country trails between the mountain villages. All the areas have runs for beginners, intermediates and advanced skiers, though in all fairness, Zermatt is not the perfect place to come as an absolute first-time skier. Intermediates should also realize that the trails will not all be groomed as they are in the States, though there are plenty of them and there should be no problem skiing anywhere.

Zermatt sits at the end of a long valley and is bounded by three major skiing areas. Each area will keep skiers busy for at least two days' worth of thrills. The three lift areas branch out from different sections of Zermatt and all are within walking distance depending on where you are staying. There is a free ski bus connecting the three areas and taxis can take up to six passengers to any of the lifts in town for €2 per person.

The Sunnegga-Blauherd area (7,506 feet) is quickly reached by an underground cable railway and has ski lifts that reach the Rothorn at 10,180 feet. This area is the least time-consuming to reach; the cable railway leaves once every 10-20 minutes on its four-minute journey to Sunnegga. This area also gets the most sun in the valley and has recently been equipped with snowmaking facilities that stretch from the top station down to National. A quad chair now whisks skiers from National up to Blauherd, eliminating what was one of the worst lift lines in the area, and cable car from Sunnegga to Blauherd, added in 1996, eases what was often quite a bottleneck. If you want the quintessential Swiss experience, you can have your picture taken with Dixie, a wonderful drooling St. Bernard, who hangs out just above Sunnegga. Each picture costs €10 and can be purchased at Foto Fast in the train station plaza.

From Blauherd there are numerous ways down. Or another cable car takes you still higher up to Rothorn with its own intermediate runs and a triple chair lift to service them. Long runs back down to Tuftern will keep advanced skiers and intermediates happy. The Sunnegga-Blauherd area is also where locals ski when visibility is poor; trees lining the lower trails help improve depth perception in flat light.

The Fluhalp trail from Sunnegga down to the lower station of Gant initially has good skiing but long flat runouts at the lower levels. For those planning to hook up with Gornergrat, it's the only connection, but it is not recommended for anyone below advanced intermediate. A new cable car from Gant to Hohtälli lifts skiers and riders almost 3,500 feet and accesses the Gornergrat area more easily than the two steep T-bars that are still in place. Or you can return to Blauherd via a double chair lift.

The **Gornergrat** area is served by a cog railway that has been expanded in recent years with additional cars. It leaves from the center of town, and the ride to the upper station takes about 40 minutes. The wait in line at the Gornergrat station in town can be up to a half hour in high season. Normally, however, when the line at Gornergrat is long, walk over to Sunnegga and head up the mountain—there's almost no wait.

From Gornergrat there are a variety of fun rolling intermediate runs, many of which are covered by snowmaking now. There are several ways of skiing down to Riffelberg where you can get back on the train or take the T-bar back to the top. Beginners can get off on the way up at Riffelberg, where there is a platter lift with its own trails to the right of the big hotel.

Conditions permitting, and usually after the Christmas season, there is also a cable car that continues from Gornergrat to Stockhorn and opens a whole new area of expert terrain served by its own T-bars and the new Gant-Hohtälli cable car.

From Gornergrat, you can ski almost 3,400 feet down to the train station at Landtunnel, taking the train to the top again. Alternatively you can ski from here to both of the other areas in Zermatt—Sunnegga and Klein Matterhorn (note, you can not get back to Gornergrat from Klein Matterhorn). The ski route from Gornergrat down to Furi where you get the cable car up to either Furgg or Trockener Steg is quite scenic and great fun for any good intermediate skier and is highlighted by several mountain chalets where you can stop for lunch or a drink. From Furi, the route continues right into the center of Zermatt if you don't choose to take the lifts to Klein Matterhorn.

The third ski area of Zermatt is **Klein Matterhorn** (Little Matterhorn) or **Trockener Steg** area. This is the largest area and it is here that you connect with the ultimate intermediate skiing experience in the world: cross-border skiing to Cervinia!! This sector is reached by a series of cable cars. It is slightly out of town and up-hill; unless you are staying at this end of town, take the bus or a taxi to get here. The bus drops you at the bottom of a slippery hill, but a taxi will take you directly to the lift.

It can easily take 45 minutes to an hour to reach Klein Matterhorn's upper stations, but once you are there, skiing on the glacier is good throughout the summer. Snowmaking facilities have been installed below Trockener Steg down to Zermatt in order to keep the lower sections of the ski area open in the warmer months. But unless it's a good snow year, you will likely have to take the cable car or gondola back to Zermatt at day's end.

From Trockener Steg you are again confronted with one of skiing's engineering marvels, the cable car to the Klein Matterhorn. If your heart can take it, try and stand in the front of the cabin and watch as you approach the top station (the highest cable car in Europe). Try and imagine building this thing! Once you arrive, you walk through a tunnel of about 100 yards. If you are in the mood for a diversion, visit the ice cave that's accessible from the tunnel. Or continue down the tunnel and come out on what is certainly the single most breathtaking view in skiing. Unfortunately the conditions here can be cold and windy, since you are on top of the world at about 12,746 feet. The ski down is not at all difficult and any budding intermediate can handle it. This is the glacier area that is open all summer and serviced additionally by three T-bars.

WARNING: This glacier area is very dangerous if you decide to ski off-piste (off the marked and groomed trail). The stories people tell about crevasses swallowing up skiers are painfully true. I have received e-mail and letters from skiers and family members who have been lost on this glacier. Some of the stories have happy endings where the friends are rescued. Most stories are tragic. A friend of mine died falling into one of these crevasses. A mother died when she fell as she tried to climb out of a crevasse, while her son tried to get the ski patrol to go and search for her. Be careful and **ALWAYS SKI WITH A BUDDY ON THE GLACIER**. If someone falls into a crevasse stay with them. Get someone else to go for help.

Unfortunately, the ski patrols, in Italy and in Switzerland, have received too many false reports of missing skiers. These "missing skiers" normally are found in a bar drinking or back in their hotel room.

From the glacier you can ski back down to Trockener Steg or head over to the Italian ski resort of Cervinia. There is a restaurant right on the border at the top – a great place to stop and enjoy the view if the wind isn't blowing.

Going down to Trockener Steg opens up another area of skiing. There are several T-bars and a Poma lift back up, and if you continue down to Furgg on the steep intermediate run, you can take the cable car back. One of our favorite runs is from Furgg back down to Furi—an expert run that may make you feel as if you are Robert Redford in *Downhill Racer*.

Or from Furgg, you can take a gondola up to Schwarzsee. Schwarzee is a great place to end your day as it marks the beginning of a very scenic run, easily handled by below average intermediates, down to Furi.

Over to Italy: Skiers shouldn't miss the opportunity for a special adventure: skiing over to the Italian side of the mountain and visiting Cervinia. Don't expect a picturesque Florence-style Italian town—Cervinia has all the architectural flavor of frozen pizza. Fortunately, the cooking in Cervinia is excellent. After the hour-long ascent and the long run into Cervinia, you'll be ready to have a good Italian meal. This is an experience not to be missed by anyone with modest intermediate skills or better. The entire day can be taken up with two cruises down the Cervinia trails and a sumptuous full Italian lunch.

Always make sure you come with the idea in mind that you may have to spend the night if the weather changes and they are forced to close the lift. In 13 years this has only happened once to one of our staff, but the warning to bring your passport is probably a good idea.

Change your money before you strike out for Italy—the rates for changing Swiss Francs into euros are better on the Swiss side of the mountain. However, Swiss Francs are accepted freely in Italy, albeit at poor exchange rates. Remember to buy the pass that is good in Italy as well as in Zermatt.

The last lift leaves at 3 p.m. There are gondolas all the way to Testa Grigia, so lift lines for getting back to the Zermatt side are not too bad, but they can take a while to negotiate.

New 2003/04: Zermatt is planning to build three new chair lifts that will replace three existing drag lifts. Construction has already begun on the 6-person covered chair lift, the Furggsattel-Express, that will connect Trockener Steg to Furggsattel. There will also be another 6-person covered chair lift connecting Riffelberg to Fifthittli. Zermatt is also seeking permission to build a four-person covered chair lift from Haubennest to the ridge above Schwarzsee during the 2004/05 season.

Also new for 2003/04, both the Gandegg and Theodulpass drag lifts will be replaced by one drag lift and the Testa lift will be moved.

Mountain rating

Skiers of every level will find thrills in Zermatt. Each area has some runs to make beginners feel like experts, and some to make experts wonder just how expert they really are.

When there is enough snow, advanced skiers will enjoy the Kumme side of the Rothorn and some of the steeps drop back into the village from the Sunnegga area. There are a half-dozen steep, bumpy and exciting runs in the Gornergrat section from Stockhorn, Rote Nase and Hohtälli down to Gant into the valley between Sunnegga and Gornergrat. And although the Klein Matterhorn area is wide open with gentle slopes, some of the runs from Schwarzsee back into town can be testing. Experts also have almost unlimited opportunities for off-trail skiing, but given the dangers of glacier skiing, we recommend hiring a guide at the Alpine Center.

Intermediate skiers can be happy in any area, but should avoid many of the black runs, which are really for experts. Plus, many of the trails are not groomed. If you take the cable car over to the Stockhorn, Rote Nase and Hohtälli, be aware that there is no easy escape from the steep and bumpy.

Beginners will find easy slopes on the Gornergrat area and on the Klein Matterhorn glacier. Also, the Sunnegga area has a good long beginner/lower intermediate trail network from Blauherd into town.

Ski school (2003/04 prices)

The Zermatt ski and snowboard school (966-2466; fax 966-2464) has more than 175 qualified instructors and mountain guides who teach in the traditional Swiss ski school system.

Individual lessons	**Adults & Children**	
one day (1–2 skiers)	€204–€210.60	
each additional person	€13	
two hours	€98.70	
three hours	€138	
Group lessons	**Adults**	**Children** (with lunch)
one day	€33	€46–€52.60
two days	€59	€79–€85.50
three days	€138	€144.70–€164.40
five days	€184	€217–€243

Children are those ages 4–12 and their lessons include lunch.

Zermatt also offers a special Matterhorn Ski Week. The course includes a seven-day international ski pass and an instructor for six full days (Sunday to Friday), lodging with half-board and seven days of ski rental. The major difference between this program and standard group lessons is that the instructor stays with the group for the entire day instead of only four hours a day, and takes the group down almost every run within the skiers' abilities. Cross-country classes are also available.

To enroll in one of the Matterhorn Weeks, write in advance to the tourist office and request enrollment forms. The price (including five-day ski pass) is €673–€1,580 with accommodations.

There are many off-piste ski programs for better skiers, for further information contact the Alpine Center (027-966-2460; fax 027-966-2469).

"The Haute Route" is a classic ski adventure tour between Saas-Fee, Zermatt, Courmayeur and Chamonix. These trips are organized from mid-April through the end of May. These are tough, physical treks, and participants should be in good shape for high-altitude ski-climbing and must be able to ski in deep snow. The tour is normally conducted from mid-May to the first week in June. Cost is approximately €987.40, which includes guides, accommodation in mountain huts, meals, hotel expenses and mountain railway and bus fares. Contact: Franz Schwery, mountain guide, CH-3920 Zermatt, Switzerland; (027-967-2880), or the Alpine Center in Zermatt (027-966-2460).

Tour Monte Rosa is two to five days of skiing from Grachen to Zermatt. These trips start in the middle fo June and end in September. Price ranges from €72–€327 and includes accommodations and luggage transportation. For more information contact Zermatt Tourism.

Lift tickets (2003/04 prices)

There are two basic lift tickets —Zermatt only; Zermatt and Cervinia. (The Matterhorn-Cervinia Pass is no longer offered.) The prices are:

	Zermatt	**Zermatt/Cervinia**
one day	€42	€48
three days	€118	€134
five of seven days	€202	€228
six days	€208	€236
fourteen days	€378	€428

Children age 10–16 ski for half price. Those age 9 and younger ski free.

Seniors: Men age 65+ and women age 62+ get 25 percent discount.

Note: If you plan to ski to Cervinia and you do not have the Zermatt-only pass, you must pay a surcharge to use Cervinia's uphill lift system. The surcharge for the combination ticket is €21.

Also note that Zermatt still publishes their original prices in Swiss Francs and prices in Euros are not guaranteed.

Accommodations

Do yourself a favor when requesting a room and ask for one that doesn't face the main street. For some reason the disco denizens feel compelled to yell and sing at the top of their lungs as they stagger down the main street from the music-filled cellars from one to three o'clock in the morning. Price ranges noted for each hotel are per person based on double occupancy with half board (breakfast and dinner): €€€—€125+; €€—€75–€124; €—less than €75.

You almost can't go wrong picking a hotel; the only thing to consider is location. The closer you are to the center of town, the easier it is to get home at night.

For the best Zermatt has to offer, head for the **Zermatterhof** (027-966-6600; fax 027-966-6699; €€€), the **Mont Cervin und Residence** (027-966-8888; fax 027-966-2878; €€€) or the **Riffelalp Resort 2222** (027-966-0555; fax 027-966-0550; €€€). All with most facilities one can think of including health clubs, sauna, Jacuzzi and indoor swimming pools.

The most charming is **Hotel Monte Rosa** (027-966-0333; fax 027-966-0330; €€€), one of the grand hotels in the center with access to one of the best pools in town.

The second group and slightly less expensive includes the **Hotel Nicoletta** (027-966-0777; fax 027-966-0788; €€–€€€) with its roof-top bar, the **Schweizerhof** (027-966-0000; fax 027-966-0066; €€–€€€) with numerous restaurants and a night club and the **Hotel Alex** (027-966-7070; fax 027-966-7090; €€–€€€). The Alex is a favorite with its indoor swimming pool, indoor tennis, squash, health club, sauna, grill room and one of the most interesting discos you'll find anywhere for the 30–60 set; actually if you didn't ski you wouldn't have to leave the Alex!

The next group includes:

Hotel Walliserhof (027-966-6555; fax027- 966-6550; €€) First-class rustic lodgings with top restaurant.

Hotel Butterfly (027-966-4166; fax 027-966-4165; €€) In the center of town, whirlpool and fitness room.

Hotel Simi (027-966-4600; fax 027-966-4605; €) Same owner as the restaurant at Furi.

Hotel de la Poste (967-1932; fax 967-4114; €–€€) If you can stand the activity and noise, the funkiest hotel in Zermatt (if not the whole ski universe) which really deserves a chapter to itself.

Hotel Gornergrat (027-966-3920; fax 027-966-3925; €) A fairly modern hotel in the heart of Zermatt across the street from the train station and next to the Gornergrat terminus.

Hotel Alpenhof (027-966-5555; fax 027-966-5556; €€) By all reports one of the best hotels in town. A chalet-style hotel just across from the main Sunnegga lift and only minutes from the center of town.

Hotel Admiral (027-966-9000; fax 027-966-9004; €€) Shares the pool with the nearby Christiania. Most who have stayed here have nothing but praise for the place.

Alphubel (027-967-3003; fax 027-967-6684; €) A relatively small, two-star hotel in the middle of Zermatt.

Hotel Biner (027-966-5666; fax 027-966-5667; €) Two-year renovation concluded in 1997. Biner now sets the pace for home-style comfort. Downstairs you can pamper yourself in a heated pool, jacuzzi and sauna.

More economical:

Burgener Pensione (027-967-1020; fax 027-967-5579; €) Traditional and rustic.

Testa Grigia (027-966-7900; fax 027-966-7908; €) This is a bed & breakfast.

There are countless hotels in Zermatt and there are not any bad choices. Check out the B&B rate since one of the highlights of visiting Zermatt is the restaurants. This insures you won't be tied down to eating dinner every night in the same hotel.

Ski Chalets: Inghams/Bladon, Total Ski and Crystal (see end of page 20 for phone, fax and Internet addresses).

Apartments, condominiums, flats

Apartments are the best choice if you really want to save money in Zermatt. Not only will it cost substantially less but you will have room to spread out, the facilities of a kitchen and the option of staying home for dinner and relaxing.

A well-organized rental system offers apartments for more than 6,500 people a night. Write to the tourist office and ask for a list of apartments available when you plan to be in Zermatt. Include your needs, such as the number of people in your party. The office will send a listing of available apartments and a map showing their locations. Select the apartment you want and correspond directly with the apartment owner.

The apartments normally include bed linen and cooking utensils. You will be charged a visitor's tax, and there may be an extra charge for the electricity and heat you use during your stay.

Expect to pay €23 to €43 per person a night, depending on the number of people sharing the apartment and its location.

Dining

On the mountain: Here Zermatt excels with an incredible selection of charming and wonderful restaurants. There are 38 different mountain restaurants in Zermatt. We start with the Sunnegga area.

One of the highlights of the Sunnegga area, and of all of Zermatt, is lunch. Few other ski areas have such a variety of Hansel & Gretel chalet restaurants and bars. Sunnegga and Rothorn both have great restaurants with large terraces (Rothorn also has an outdoor bar with music where you'll see people sipping wine even in the morning hours) and Blauherd has a large cafeteria. But the most charming are the restaurants in little mountain villages, and we recommend hunting these out rather than eating in the self-serve cafeterias. Skiing down from Blauherd to the National quad is **Tuftern**—a simple place serving hearty soups, sausages, cheeses, etc. Further down and impossible to find is **Othmar's Hutte in Ried** (027-967-1761).

Down from Sunnegga or Rothorn on the other side is Findeln, a collection of wooden huts housing several restaurants that give new meaning to the word cozy, including **Findlerhof** (027-967-2588) the most elegant of the group, **Paradies** (027-967-3451), **Franz & Heidi** (027-967-2588) and **Chez Vrony** (027-967-2552), which is so quaint, you won't want to leave (the clean and well-appointed bathroom is also well worth a visit). Make reservations if you expect tables at any of these restaurants. These are not cheap, quick lunch meals—the lunch menu can cost from €25–€50. There is a chair lift back up to Sunnegga from Findeln.

In the Gornergrat section, **Hotel Restaurant Riffelberg** has a cafeteria restaurant with a large terrace and a wonderful hotel restaurant with a spectacular view. (Spending a night or two here can be a very romantic experience!—027-966-6500; fax 027-966-6505.) The hotel restaurant is quite affordable with a lunch menu less than €15.

The **Kleiner Matterhorn/Trokener Steg** has a self-service cafeteria and pizzeria worth skipping. Farther down the mountain, past Furgg, is one of the post popular lunch and après-ski spots—**Restaurant Simi** (027-967-2695), an institution in Zermatt. It is also where you end up if you ski down from the Gornergrat area. There are many different restaurants as you ski down to Furi, but try Simi at least once if you can get in. Don't be alarmed if you open the front door and find yourself face to face with an accordion player. Just laugh with him and move into the restaurant. Another excellent and affordable restaurant in Furi is the **Silvana** (027-966-2800)

Heading down to the village is a long exciting trail with great views. Past Furi, you will ski by the village and restaurant of **Zum See** (027-967-2045)—another must on the charm list for Zermatt and the quintessential après-ski stop. The restaurant is famous for Café Grolla. The tradition started in the Aosta Valley of Italy on the other side of the Matterhorn. Café Grolla is served in a wooden pot (certainly not legal in the U.S.) with four, six or eight spouts. It is a steaming a concoction of coffee, grappa, Cointreau, fruit and who knows what else that is passed around the table. The ritual is to light up the alcohol and serve the drink piping hot. It goes down easy as skiers and boarders pass the wooden bowl. Just remember you still have to ski down to town.

In town:

Three restaurants battle to be the best in Zermatt. The **Rôtisserie La Broche** in the Zermatterhof (027-966-6600; fax 027-966-6699) is the most elegant, however Michelin has bestowed a star on **Le Gourmet** in the Hotel Alpenhof (027-966-5555; fax 027-966-5556). The third top spot is **Le Corbeau d'Or** in the Hotel Mirabeau (027-966-2660; fax 027-966-2665. A full meal costs between €50 and €70.

Experience dining in Zermatt by sampling the different types of restaurants hidden around town. Here are some of our recommendations.

For excellent meat dishes, try **Le Mazot** (027-967-2777) in a charming old farm house by the river and where even normally taciturn Germans go out of their way to compliment the owner on great food and service. Try the lamb served in the evenings and make sure to call far in advance for reservations. Expect to pay about €30–€60.

Try the **Grill at the Alex Schlosshotel Tenne** (027-966-4400). The **Stockhorn Grill Room** (027-967-1747) also serves excellent lamb in a cozy, romantic atmosphere (the cutlets are from the owner's lambs). Service is polite and efficient, and the prices are reasonable. One of the most romantic restaurants is the **Spycher** (027-967-7741) on the other side of the river; perfect for that intimate rendezvous.

Don't miss the Swiss fondue. You can have either meat or cheese (or chocolate for desert). For meat fondue, which can be either Bourguignon (chunks of beef dipped in boiling oil) or Chinoise (thin slices of veal cooked in consumé), head to the **Stockhorn Grill Room** (027-967-1747). For cheese fondue and *Raclette* (melted cheese served with potatoes, onions and pickles) you should end up in a *Stübli,* which will be downstairs in a sort of cave-like setting. Two favorites are downstairs at the **Stockhorn** or the popular **Whymperstube** (027-967-2296) below the Monte Rosa hotel. The **Café DuPont**, a rustic spot on the south end of the main street, is a local favorite for fondue.

For a variety of Swiss specialties, including the local trout, try **Old Zermatt** (027-967-6111) with views of the river and the cemetery. For seafood go to the **Boat-House** (027-967-1932) in the Hotel de la Poste.

Another "in" place to have dinner is **Restaurant Chez Heini** (027-967-1630). It specializes in succulent home-grown lamb prepared by their singing chef, Dan Daniell, the Don Ho of Zermatt. He'll even autograph his CD for you.

The meals served at the train station are amazingly good! And better yet, inexpensive, if you have the menu of the day. Try the **Bahnhofbuffet-Panorama** (027-968-1968) and have the buffet menu of the day for about €14 or so. Ordering à la carte can shoot the price up to €20–€40.

For Italian the best is **Hotel Derby** (027-966-3999) or **Casa Rustica** (027-967-4858) across from the train station. The Derby is open from 11:30 a.m. to 10:30 p.m., so when you first stagger into town jet-lagged and hungry, this is the place to go for an early dinner (most restaurants in Zermatt don't open for dinner until 6 p.m.—a problem for weary U.S. travelers who typically arrive around mid-afternoon).

The most fun Italian restaurant is the **Spaghetti Factory** downstairs in the Hotel de la Poste (027-967-1932); go for the 9 p.m. sitting. You will overlook the disco and be ready to go when it starts to fill up after 11 p.m. You can also venture further down into the labyrinth of the Post to the **Pizza Factory** or leave this craziness and go across the river to **Pizzeria Roma** (027-967-3229) or **Da Mario** (027-966-0000) in the Schweizerhof. At the corner of Kirshstrasse, the **Pizzeria Papperla Pub** (027-967-4040) serves good everyday lasagna and cannelloni. Don't miss the crêperie on Bahnhof-strasse opposite the Mont Cervin.

Make sure you try the various specialties of the region. We have mentioned the fondues and raclette and at lunch you will find almost everything comes with rösti, the Swiss version of hash brown potatoes. There is also käse-schnitte, bread with melted cheese and sometimes ham and/or an egg on top—delicious but not on the Slim-Fast diet. The mixed salads are great and come with all kinds of things in them including a special dressing. Bundnerfleisch is a regional specialty consisting of air-dried beef.

Après-ski/nightlife

The fun starts even before the lifts close. In addition to stopping on the way down for a schnapps, Glühwein (hot spiced red wine), and so on, and assuming you can still make it down, from 4–6 p.m., stop at the **Olympia Stübli** on the way to town from the Sunnegga area. On the way down from Furi, **Zum See** is also a good after-ski watering hole, as is the **Simi**.

In Zermatt, try the **Papperla Pub** (younger crowd), **Old Zermatt** (slightly older and quieter) and **Elsie's Bar** (most pretentious) where the upscale crowd meets for oysters and serious, cramped mingling. The **Myako** further on along Bahnhofstrasse is slightly less packed, though not so the bar of the **Hotel de la Poste** across the street.

Tea rooms along Bahnhofstrasse have fantastic pastries and hot chocolate. And the **Café in the Walliserhof** fits somewhere between bar and tea room and has great Glühwein and Café Fertig (the Swiss version of Irish Coffee or Austrian Jägertee).

Before and after dinner there are numerous bars worth checking out. Walk to those of the **Mont Cervin**, **Zermatterhof** and **Monte Rosa** Hotels, the **Schweizerhof** with its fireplace or the bar at the **Tenne Grill**. Still going strong will be the **Papperla Pub**, the **Myako** and the bars of the **Hotel de la Poste**. For a view of Zermatt try the **Panorama Bar** on the top of the Nicoletta Hotel. There is no shortage of bars, and you will find your favorite tucked away in some hidden alley.

For dancing or listening to music, the undisputed place to go is the **Hotel de la Poste**; if it sounds like you don't have to leave the Post Hotel, you are right. Owned by an eccentric American, it is a totally unique concept in the ski (and perhaps any other) world. It resembles an underground jumble of something Hieronymous Bosch might have concocted—it is THE hot spot of Zermatt. Just go, you'll understand. The disco downstairs is so confusing that on one trip we found friends thought lost years ago. The 2nd floor **Boat-House** (mentioned under restaurants) also has a great bar with less noise and on the ground floor in the back is the **Elephant Bar**—Zermatt's premier jazz address. The **Moby Dick** in the Schweizerhof also gets a slightly older (late 20s–30s) dancing crowd, while the **Pollux** is for the younger set.

GramPi's Pub needs a warning—if you close this place, you're well on your way to missing tomorrow's skiing. English-speakers are as much a part of GramPi's as is the decor (you might even feel as if you haven't left home). GramPi's is easy to find right on the Bahnhofstrasse.

A perfect disco for anyone older than age 30, is in the **Alex Hotel**. There are posh banquets, a great bar and numerous rooms in which to get lost; don't miss it even if only for a drink. It is perfect for finding a romantic corner with someone special; and if you are alone, the bar always seems to be a happening place.

Finally, and not to be missed, is the movie house: This multi-level combination of bars, art galleries and a movie theater (showing first-run movies) is unique. The lower level has a theater set up more or less like some Hollywood mogul's screening room, complete with a bar and lounge chairs. Grab a drink and make yourself at home. Like so many things in this town, you have to see it to believe it.

In the end Zermatt offers an incredible number of bars and restaurants; if you just follow the narrow, winding streets you will discover your own favorite. And remember, you can have one for the road—you're not driving!

Child care

At the Kinderclub Pumuckel in Hotel La Ginabella (027-967-4535) nurses take care of children age 2-1/2 to 6 years of age. A ski instructor gives lessons to those four years and older. Prices: Full day with lunch and snack, €59; half day with lunch included, €36. Prices change based on the age of the child. Open 9 a.m. to 5 p.m. except Saturdays.

Seiler's Paradies (027-966-0777) for children is at the Hotel Nicoletta. It accepts children 2 to 8; the hours are 9 a.m. to 5 p.m. Closed Saturday and Sunday.

The ski school Pingu kindergarten costs about €56 per day; €164.50 for three days; and €243.50 for five days—all prices include lessons, lunch and beverages.

Kinderparadies in Zermatt takes care of children aged 3 months and older. A full day including lunch is €66; half day with lunch, €39.50; three days, €184 and five days, €296.

Other activities

Zermatt is up to handling non-skiers on vacation, although activities are much more limited owing to its distance from other tourist destinations and its dedication to skiing. For a mountain thrill off skis, rent a **sled** for €3. Either take the gondola to Furi and fly down one of the hiking trails, or hike up and zing down. Most hotels have sleds for rent (though oddly not helmets). Or hike on the many "winterwanderwegen"—**winter hiking paths**.

The town has seven indoor **swimming pools** at various hotels; most can be used by non-guests for a small fee. Also available are 17 saunas, a salt-water swimming pool, two **ice skating** rinks (free for children younger than age 9), **curling rinks, covered tennis and squash courts, indoor golfing,** 19 miles of marked **walking** trails, **helicopter rides, hang-gliding** and cross-country ski circuits. There are also many **art** and **cultural exhibitions**.

Zermatt **walking tours**, in English, leave from the front of the tourist office several times a week, contact them for times and dates. The **Alpine Museum**, one block off the main street across from the Mont Cervin, has a fascinating mountaineering exhibit. In winter, the museum is open 4:30 p.m.–6:30 p.m. Cost is €3 for adults, €0.66 for children.

The other great activity is **shopping**—Zermatt has one of the best collections of shops of any ski resort. Not just great ski clothes, but fine jewelry, watches, linens and wonderful local artifacts, wood carvings, pewter, etc.. For many, this is where the real après-ski takes place.

Air Zermatt (027-966-8686; fax 027-966-8685) offers **sightseeing** and **heliskiing**. Tours are about 20 minutes with the option of landing on Theodul glacier, the Rothon or Testa Orgia (skiers only). There is a minimum of four people and costs €128.

Heliskiing, sleighrides and **dogsledding** available through Gorge Adventure Passenger Flights.

Getting there

By train: From Zürich airport via Bern, Spiez, through the Lötschberg tunnel to Brig. At Brig you change to the special Zermatt train at the front of the Brig station. Travel time from Zürich to Brig is about three-and-a-half hours, Brig to Zermatt an hour and 20 minutes. Trains run from the Geneva airport to Brig in two hours. You can purchase tickets on the Swiss Rail's Web site: www.rail.ch/pv/index_e.htm.

Note: You can check your bags through to Zermatt from the airport, but cost is €13 per bag, and they might not arrive for three days.

The trip from Milan is slightly shorter and less expensive, but the ride in from the airport to the train station adds easily another 60–90 minutes to the trip.

By car: From Montreux, go up the Valais pass through Sion to Visp, where you turn south and follow signs to Zermatt. The car park, just outside the village of Täsch, is about three miles from Zermatt. Buses and trains connect Täsch with Zermatt approximately every 20 minutes; the ride takes eleven minutes. Parking costs €4.60–€7 per day.

If you are driving from Zürich or Basel, you can also take the Lötschberg tunnel from Kandersteg to Goppenstein, above Brig and Visp. Trains, with your car aboard, transit the tunnel every half hour from 5:10 a.m. to 11:10 p.m.; the trip takes only 15 minutes. Cost per car, including nine-seat vans, is €16.50. From Goppenstein, continue your drive to Visp, then on to Täsch. If you choose you can park you car for free in Visp and take the train to Zermatt.

Upon arriving in the village take a taxi to your hotel or apartment or take the luggage trolleys to your hotel if it is not very far away. The more upscale hotels usually have their own electric taxis or horse drawn carriages waiting for guests. There are plenty of electric taxis and sleighs for hire. The taxis charge by number of people and luggage, but other than going to and from the train station you can survive without ever using one. Taxi charges range from normally from €8–€12 and the sleighs about €13. For taxis call 027-967-3030, 027-967-6060 or 027-967-7777.

Air Zermatt Helicopters can be called at 027-966-8686.

Tourist information

Tourist Office, CH-3920 Zermatt, Switzerland;
Telephone: 027-966-8100; fax 027-966-8101.
E-mail: zermatt@wallis.ch;
Internet: www.zermatt.ch or www.ski-zermatt.com.

Andorra

Valls de Canillo —

Canillo, Soldeu El Tarter, Pas de la Casa - Grau Roig

A surprising haven for skiers and smugglers lies along the border of France and Spain. This tiny country, Andorra, a leftover from the glory days of the Catholic Church and nobility, has survived for centuries as an independent state wedged between two of Europe's largest powers. This is the country that has been the home of the Catalan language over the centuries when it was suppressed by Spain and France. Today it still uses Catalan as its official language, but with French and Spanish spoken liberally in every valley.

For years, beneath jagged mountain peaks and between narrow passes, Andorra has thrived as a smuggling and shopping mecca. This is the original duty-free store. The entire country is a duty-free store. Thousands of Europeans come here to purchase much less expensive cigarettes, cigars, whiskeys, jewelry and virtually every luxury that is faced with high taxes in their homelands. Andorra, faced with a new unified European Community, has been forced to begin to find alternative economic activities to smuggling.

Many years ago, Andorrans also realized that they had an abundance of snow. In the 1930s they were some of the first developers of ski areas in Europe. However, these resorts remained relatively small and were not interconnected because of small-country politics. Recently, some of the logjam regarding linking of resorts has broken free. A group of lifts serving the Valls de Canillo, the original Andorran ski resort, has linked up and more interconnections are on the way.

Today Valls de Canillo can compete with virtually any ski area in Europe. Millions have been invested in new hotels, gondolas, high speed lifts, grooming machines and facilities to make Andorra a true world-class destination.

It is still dependent on much group tourism. However, in a revolutionary move, the country is developing areas of the valleys that will not cater to group tourism and that have semi-private ski areas and private upscale restaurants. It is a daring move, but should play well with the upscale skiers from around the world and from Barcelona and Toulouse that flock to here on weekends and holidays.

Andorra already has a reputation for world-class, upscale shopping. Now, it is adding the element of extensive snowmaking, rustic restaurants, topnotch lodging and modern lifts.

This section focuses on the Valls de Canillo where we spent most of our time. We have included a short section on the other major ski and snowboard areas closest to Andorra la Vella, Pal-Arinsal, starting on page 341. These areas offer another interconnected collection of trails with a slightly different experience.

At the risk of generalizing, Canillo and El Tarter are visited by more Spanish skiers; Soldeu is packed with British skiers; and Pas de la Casa/Grau Roig has more of a French flair.

Mountain layout

Closest to the capital city of Andorra la Vella is the enclave of Canillo that provides the name for the main valley. Canillo is being developed for individual tourism and has established a club concept that limits the number of skiers on their section of the mountain. A massive and modern base lodge/gondola station is the portal for this section of the resort. The slopes of Canillo can also be reached from the main Soldeu-El Tarter ski area via a drag lift. Canillo has newly cut swooping trails slicing through thick forests and provides an excellent place to ski when visibility is poor. The trails offer something for everyone and were designed by the same resort architects who have created many of the trails in Courchevel, France. Here at Canillo there is also a dedicated ski school with a magic carpet and individualized instruction.

After the village of Canillo the road winds upward to El Tarter, which together with the next town up valley, Soldeu, anchor the main ski area. El Tarter is filled mainly with Spanish visitors and has two chair lifts taking skiers above treeline to the Pla Riba Escorxada hub. From this hub, lifts rise to Cap de Clots. From Cap de Clots a snowcat (included in the lift ticket price) takes skiers to off-piste adventures down ungroomed vertical. Also from Cap de Clots a drag lift links El Tarter with Canillo. One new six-seater chair lift brings skiers from the Riba Escorxada hub to the top of the resort at 8,398 feet where the entire Soldeu El Tarter area spreads beneath the summit.

Soldeu is the main group tourist town and is invaded by British skiers during much of the season. From January through March there is a better chance of hearing English spoken than Spanish, French or Catalan. Gondolas depart directly from the rear of hotel and apartment complexes and other older chair lifts rise as well to Pla dels Espiolets that serves as the hub of the Soldeu section. From Pla dels Espiolets several high-speed chair lifts take skiers to an elevation of more than 9,186 feet and serve almost 850 meters of vertical drop in virtually any direction. The fields of snow are dramatic when viewed from the peak of Alt del Griu.

At the French extreme of this region lies the town of Pas de la Casa with its linked lift hub of Grau Roig. The Pas de la Casa/Grau Roig area has a total of 100 km. of terrain and are linked by a gondola from the village of Encamp. Despite the fact that Pas de la Casa/Grau Roig and Soldeu El Tarter are adjacent and seemingly have interconnected lifts that would make transfer between Pas de la Casa/Grau Roig and Soldeu El Tarter relatively easy, they are separate areas that require separate lift tickets. Before you plop yourself on a lift, check to make sure your lift ticket is valid for the area.

Mountain rating

Canillo/Soldeu-El Tarter/Pas de la Casa has a bit of something for every skier or boarder. Beginners have an excellent learning area near the main restaurants with a long looping trail back to the base area that can be negotiated with difficulty because of zigzagging skiers barreling down the same trails. A safer bet may be to download on the gondola. In Canillo return to the base area is via gondola for most skiers.

Intermediates have the entire mountain. There are only a few off-piste areas where they can get into trouble and most intermediates won't venture that far off the trails. Experts can push themselves as far as they want to go.

In an area this large, any expert worth his or her salt can find challenges. Next to the lift connecting Soldeu with Canillo there is a free snowcat that carries off advanced and expert skiers and boarders for excellent off-piste adventures dropping down from Pic d'Encampandana to Pla Riba Escorxada above El Tarter.

Cross-country

The main cross-country center for Andorra is La Rabassa in Sant Julià de Lòria (759798) south of Andorra la Vella. Cross-country skiing trail fees are €7 for adults and €4.50 for children. Tobogganing is available for a fee of €1.80 per run and €8 for six runs down a prepared run. Cross-country lessons are €15 per person per hour and €30 for two to five persons per hour.

Ski school (2003/04 prices)

Excellent ski and snowboard schools are available at every resort center, however, the Soldeu El Tarter ski school naturally has the most English-speaking ski instructors. For reservations call (376) 890501. Lesson costs are almost identical between Pas de la Casa and Soldeu El Tarter.

These prices are for Soldeu El Tarter.

Private lessons for one or two skiers cost €31.50 per hour during high season and €29.50 per hour during low season.

Group lessons for adults, based on 15 hours of lessons, cost €92.50 during high season and €84 during low season. Fifteen hours of children's lessons cost €88 for high season and €79 for low season.

Lift tickets (2003/04 prices)

These are prices for Soldeu El Tarter.

High season is Christmas/New Years, most of February, Easter week and all the weekends.

Low season is most of December other than holidays, January after New Years and most of March and April other than holidays.

high/mid-season prices	**Adults**	**Children**
half day (from 13:00 p.m.)	€22.50/€20.50	€18/€19
one day	€31.50/€29	€24.50/€22
three days	€80.25/€74.25	€63/€54
five days	€125/€116.25	€97.50/€90

There is also a **Ski Andorra ski pass** that is good for five days at all resorts in Andorra including Soldeu El Tarter, Pas de la Casa/Grau Roig, Pas-Arinsal and Ordino-Arcalis. You can only ski one resort per day. The high season cost is €144 for adult and €116 for children for five of six days. The low season cost is €127 for adults and €100 for children for five consecutive days.

Children younger than age 6 and adults older than age 70 ski free at all Andorra resorts. Adult from ages 65–70 pay €12 per day for lift tickets anywhere in Andorra.

Accommodations

Canillo

Hotel Ski Plaza (739444; fax 739445) is a new luxury hotel five minutes from the lifts in quaint and traditional Canillo. It is dedicated to high standards and will focus on individual clients rather than groups.

Hotel Bonavida (851300; fax 851722) An excellent hotel undergoing renovation floor by floor. Rooms are large and the location across the street from the gondola building is hard to beat.

Roc de Castell (851825; fax 851707) Very simple accommodation but clean and modern with a good location only about five minutes' walk from the gondola in Canillo.

Tarter

Hotel Llop Gris (851559; fax 851229) is a large hotel right at the base of the lifts with excellent spa facilities and a fine swimming pool. The owner's wife used to work with a circus. They purchased the circus wagon where she once lived and turned it into a special spot for a quiet drink and a cigar.

Hotel del Clos (851500; fax 851554) is in a good location across the main road from the lifts. It is modern with blond wood features, good sized rooms and a good buffet dinner each evening.

Hotel del Tarter (802080; fax 802081) is good for families away from drunken pub crawlers and the disco crowd.

Soldeu

Sport Hotel (870600; fax 870666) is filled with group tours but it is quite nice. One of the main pubs in town is here, so crawling home is no problem. This together with the Sport Hotel Village are probably as good as group tour accommodations get in Andorra.

Sport Hotel Village (870533; fax 870533) across the road from the Sport Hotel this place is bigger, more luxurious, with a massive lobby and direct access to the lifts.

Hotel Xalet Montana (739333; fax 739331) on the opposite side of the street from the lifts and catering to more and more individual skiers. It is new and modern.

Hotel Naudi (739300; fax 852022) is a small family-run hotel that caters to individual tourists. The building has been constructed in the old valley style with lots of stone and wood.

Piolets (871787; fax 871788) is a run-of-the-mill group hotel with some good meeting facilities. If price is a consideration, this will offer adequate accommodations right in the middle of the nightlife action and direct access to the lifts.

Austria Hotel (735555; fax 735556) is a small place right on the main road. It is one of the less expensive hotels in town but a long walk from Soldeu if you are planning on heading home late and not staying in this hotel. It has one of the more popular discos in town.

Pas de la Casa/Grau Roig

Grau Roig (755556; fax 755557) is as beautiful as a mountain hotel gets. This hotel is nestled in a hollow in the mountains that also serves as one of the main lift junctions for the region. The location is ideal and romantic, rooms are dramatic, the main restaurant is excellent, the lifts are steps outside your door, the pool and spa sparkling, parking is plentiful and the hotel works exclusively with individual tourists and has a long list of return visitors. Make reservations early. Full board here runs approximately €100 a day.

Other recommended hotels (that we did not have the opportunity to visit) over the pass in Pas de la Casa are **Font d'Argent (**739739; fax 739800) and **Guineu** (856661; fax 856662).

Apartments

Condos and flats are available throughout Andorra for weekly rentals. The normal rentals take place from Sunday through Saturday. Prices range from €200 per person for a studio for a week in low season to €450 a person in high season. Pricing, naturally, depends on location and level of luxury.

Dining

Soldeu/El Tarter/Canillo Pas de la Casa/Grau Roig

Borda de l'Horto (851622) in Canillo is a rustic spot just outside of the village. On a nice night it is about a 20 minute walk from the gondola building, otherwise call a cab.

Cort del Popaire (851211) in Soldeu is built in an old barn and is as rustic and full of atmosphere as it gets. The grilled meats are exceptional. The owner tells great jokes as well.

Cantina dels Racons (852607), in Canillo just down the road from the village, has good grilled meats on the main road.

Sangria in Meritxell (851327) is quite touristy but has excellent grilled meats.

Canut in Escaldes has excellent cooking.

Can Manel (822397), in Andorra la Vella, is very typical with excellent snails.

L'Ermita in Meritxell (852500) is a typical restaurant in the same town as the church dedicated to the patron saint of Andorra.

Try pizza and other Italian fare at **la Fontanella** (871787) in the Hotel Piolet.

On the slopes

There is a new group of mountain restaurants above Canillo. One serves traditional Andorran meals, the second is a gourmet restaurant, and the third has cafeteria service.

Gall de Bosc (890500), right on the slopes, can't be beat on a sunny day when you dine on the deck with great food and fine wines.

Espiolet (851176) above Soldeu and **Riba Escorxada** (852900) are both good sit-down restaurants where you can linger over a meal.

Hotel Grau Roig's **La Marmita** is one of the best restaurants in the region. It is perfect for a long lunch prepared from local fresh produce and game.

Other recommended mountain restaurants are **Llac dels Pessons** (321683), **Solanellas** (344017) at the top of the Encamp gondola, and **Costa Rodona** above Pas de la Casa/Grau Roig ski area open for lunch only (800870). There is also a **Pizza Hut** at the Grau Roig ski lift hub.

Dining – Pas de la Casa

Restaurant **Marisqueria Campistrano** (856488) is the place to head for the most upscale gourmet dining. Expect to pay about €40-50 for a meal.

Dining – Arinsal/Pal

Borda Raubert (835420) is a very rustic, cozy and traditional restaurant in la Massana where a meal will be about €25 with wine.

El Rusc (838200), also in la Massana, is an upscale gourmet restaurant where meals will run about €40. It specializes in Basque cooking with lots of fish and lamb cooked on the grill.

El Surf, in Arinsal, serves Argentinean beef.

Après-ski/nightlife

In Soldeu: The scene is virtually all English-speaking. **Aspen** and **Piccadilly** are wild pub scenes packed with Brits and Irish drinking pints as quickly as they can. The disco **Capital** in the Hotel Piolet and **Pussycat** up the hill behind Aspen have loud, loud music and late night/early morning dancing.

In Bordes d'Envalira: Bar Cheyenne is a place where drinks are mixed with table soccer and pool. It is more of a family and hotel guest atmosphere.

In Tarter: Disco Arthur's is the place to go for much of the same, however the crowd here is Spanish-speaking. Many of the ski instructors go here for their nightlife.

In Canillo: The place to see and be seen is the unassuming **Pub Camping Pia**. This bar has great music and good drinks. Open from 8:30 p.m. to 4 a.m., it fills up around midnight with Spanish speakers. English is occasionally heard. The other watering hole in Canillo is **Pub la Roda** that doesn't generate the same energy. It opens from 5 to 8 p.m. for après-ski, then reopens at 10:30 p.m. and closes around 4 a.m.

Down in **Andorra la Vella** the largest nightlife venues pump out dancing and music until the early morning hours. The languages are mainly Catalan, Spanish and French and the experience is different from that of Soldeu. The best according to locals are **Satellit Pub, Chic, Borsa Pub** and **Festa Andorra**.

In Arinsal: Head to the **El Surf** or to the **Rocky Mountains** for nightlife and disco action.

Child care (2003/04 prices)

Child care and nursery facilities are also provided at every resort in the valley.

In the Soldeu El Tarter Ski Station, there are three nurseries which welcome children age 2 and older in the Canillo and Soldeu areas and children age 3 and older in the El Tarter area. There are also three snow kindergartens in Pla dels Espiolets, Riba Escorxada and El Forn in Canillo.

Prices for the nursery in Soldeu El Tarter are €6 per hour; €18 for a half day; €28 for a full day; €50 for five half days; and €80 for five full days.

The snow kindergarten is available on a group basis for 15 hours a week for a charge of €88 during high season and €79 during low season.

Other activities

Palau de Gel (800840) in Canillo has ice skating, hockey, an Olympic swimming pool, fitness rooms, indoor tennis, squash courts and classes in everything from aerobics to skating to stretch to swimming. On Fridays, they offer carting on ice on the hockey rink.

Caldea (800995) is a the largest thermal spa in Europe. The stunning glass building rises dramatically between the cliffs and apartments of Andorra la Vella. It houses a spectacular collection of lagoons and pools of differing temperatures, an outdoor thermal pool, suspended Jacuzzi tubs, baths, saunas, steam rooms, relaxation centers, massage rooms, and more. Entrance is €24.50 for three hours; €65.50 for three three-hour days; and €98 for five three-hour sessions. This entrance includes use of the pools, Jacuzzis and most common areas. Bring your own swim suit and robe. Spa treatments and massages are extra. The Caldea also houses a series of upscale shops and a simulated helicopter ride over Andorra that shows off the landscape and elicits laughs, oos and aaahs from the audience.

Shopping: The entire country is a duty-free shop. The main shopping streets are those of Andorra la Vella, the capital. You'll find every kind of luxury item as well as excellent deals on electronics and computer products.

Skidoos/snowmobiling: There are snowmobile rental shops in Port d'Envalira, between Pas de la Casa and Grau Roig, that also offer guided snowmobile excursions through the Pas de la Casa region and into Soldeu El Tarter. Call 324010 or 327220 for information and reservations.

The Automobile Museum (832266) is exceptional. Anyone who loves automobiles will have a blast. This museum houses one of the best and most complete collections of antique cars in the world.

Getting there

The best way to come to Andorra is to drive from either France or Spain. From Toulouse, France the driving distance is 181 km. From Barcelona airport to Andorra is 200 km. It will take about three hours traveling in either direction if all goes well. There are bus transfers directly from the airport to Andorra, however they are very cumbersome. Tour groups normally use buses from Toulouse airport passing through Pas de la Casa and then down to Soldeu.

Once in Andorra, there is a ski bus that runs between the resorts Canillo and Bordes d'Envalira that is free with your lift pass or skating rink ticket, or €1 if you have no lift pass or rink entrance ticket. It leaves every hour on the hour from Canillo and leaves Bordes d'Envalira at 20 after the hour for the return trip.

The normal Andorran bus line links Andorra la Vella and Soldeu every hour as well. The bus passes through Canillo on the way up the mountain about 20 minutes past the hour and then returns on the hour from Soldeu. It costs €2.50 for each ride. This is the best way to head into Andorra la Vella for shopping or going to the Caldea hot springs.

For local taxis call 863000.

Tourist information

Officina de Turisme Valls de Canillo, Avenida San Joan de Caselles, Canillo, Principat d'Andorra.
Telephone (376) 851002. Fax (376) 851139.
Email: vdc@andorra.ad. Internet: www.vdc.ad

Ski Andorra offices are at Av. Tarronga 58–70 Edifici les Columnes, Despatx 14 Andorra la Vella, Principat d'Andorra.

Telephone (376) 864389. Fax (376) 865910.

Email: skiandorra@skiandorra.ad.
Internet: www.skiandorra.ad.

Andorra, Pal/Arinsal

These two resorts are interconnected and offer a bit of a contrast. Arinsal is built-up, hodgepodge and still growing. Pal isn't even a real town, the name has more to do with the mountain. Arinsal's trails are long on treeless open slopes. Pal's runs are much shorter and wind through the woods. New lifts have breathed new lift into these resorts whose slopes once were inconvenient and now are much more accessible.

Mountain layout

For skiing Arinsal is limited to a narrow east-facing mellow slopes that get lots of morning sun. Trees are nowhere to be found until you get below the midstation. A gondola takes everyone up to the midstation, that is the only hub of the mountain. It is hard to get lost here, since all trails lead back to the midstation. If skiers or riders are looking for thrills and challenge, they should head elsewhere. After one or two runs, everything difficult can be covered.

For those searching for a good place to learn to ski, this is a good spot—the learning trails are out-of-the-way and have good snowmaking.

Arinsal and Pal are connected by a cable car.

Experts will head into the trees at Pal. With a new, deep snowfall, these woods are lots of fun. In fact, the tree skiing here in Pal is relatively unusual in all of Europe which has above-treeline skiing for the most part.

Intermediates will have a blast on these trails dropping from the summit to La Caubella, El Fontanal, or down to the cable car station.

Beginners have a good learning area in front of the base lodge with easy trails for progression.

Lift tickets (2002/03 prices)

high/low-season prices	**Adults**	**Children**
half day (from 13:00 p.m.)	€20.50/€17	€15/€12.50
one day	€26.50/€22	€20/€17
three days	€68/€57	€51/€43
five days	€100/€84	€75/€63

Accommodations

Most of the lodging is in Arinsal. Pal, doesn't really have accommodations. The other places to stay would be in the villages of Erts or Sispony.

Princesa Parc (736500) is a total leisure complex just 50 meters from the lifts. Rooms have satellite TV. The hotel provides private parking, bowling, gym, therapeutic center, sauna, sport and relaxation massages, and a disco.

Hotel Solana (835127) is a modern place with the basic amenities and the obilgatory disco.

Aparthotel Crest (835866) is an impressive building with good lift access. This place is packed with tour groups and you get the basics, but no pool.

The hotel **Roca Blanca** (836336) is

Telephone country code and prefix: 00376

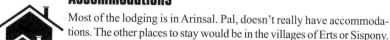

Coma Pedrosa Hotel (835123) is very basic and a bargain.

Hotel Micolau (835052) is an exceptional place. It is a departure from the over-built, modern hotels that dominate here. This rustic, stone place has only 11 rooms and is known for its wonderful cooking.

In the village of Erts, **Hotel Daina** (836005) is small with only 20 rooms but has the basics plus a small pool. A shuttle will be needed to get to the lifts. Also in Erts, the associated and sprawling **Hotel St. Gothard** (836005) has exceptional hotel food, hot tubs and a sauna.

Dining

Most of the dining in town is in the hotels where most guests have either full or half board. For a special meal head down the moutain road to La Massana and try a traditional meal at **Borda de L'Avi** (835154) where meat is grilled over glowing embers in a restored barn. The nearby, more traditionally elegant **Restaurant El Rusc** (838200) serves Basque cuisine with wonderful grilled fish and meat.

Après-ski/nightlife

There is plenty of après action at the base of the gondola in Arinsal. The bars are crammed during the high season. **Red X** has videos taken on the slopes with hilarious falls and gales of laughter from the drunk crowd. **Darby O'Gills** is local Irish pub, but there are no Irish, only Brits. **Rocky Mountain Bar**, **Quo Vadis**, **Surf Bar**, **Boro Calista** and **El Cau** are legendary in the town's après-ski lore.

Tourist information

Estació de Muntanya Pal-Arinsal
Ed. El Planell, Pal-LaMassana, Principat d'Andorra.
Telephone Arinsal (376) 737020, Fax (376) 836242
Telephone Pal (376) 737000, Fax (376) 835904.
Email: pal@arinsal.ad. Internet: www.vdc.ad

Ski Andorra offices are at Av. Tarronga 58–70 Edifici les Columnes, Despatx 14 Andorra la Vella, Principat d'Andorra.

Telephone (376) 864389. Fax (376) 865910.

Email: skiandorra@skiandorra.ad.
Internet: www.skiandorra.ad.

Spain

The ski scene in Spain is split between the north and the south. In the north, the rugged Pyrenees provide an effective border with France and very good skiing. The resort of Baqueira-Beret in the Valle de Arán, in the midst of these mountain, anchors the northern resorts. It is well-run with good snow conditions and acres of snowmaking coverage. The valley it calls home preserves one of the most fascinating cultures still existing in Spain. Other Pyrenees resorts such as formidable Formigal, traditional Panticosa, extensive La Molina and purpose-built Supermolina all provide good, if limited, skiing.

In the south, Sierra Nevada, rising above the town of Granada, provides a study in contrasts. Within an hour of the snow-covered slopes, swimming in the Mediterranean is possible and verdant golf courses beckon.

Spain has come a long way in the last decade in terms of skiing. The biggest change is the installation of snowmaking equipment that has provided much more of a guarantee of acceptable conditions for skiing.

Spain has always provided excellent value for money. Lift tickets are reasonable, the ski schools (when English-speaking instructors can be found) are a bargain, and it is hard to beat the values to be found in Spain for dining and enjoying excellent Spanish wines.

One of the biggest changes for U.S., Canadian and British skiers is the change in time zones. I'm not speaking about normal time zones, but the shift in dining and après-ski/nightlife timing. Dinner doesn't start until 9 p.m. and can easily last past midnight. And nightlife doesn't even start to flicker until at least midnight, normally by about 1 a.m. and can last until 4 or 5 a.m.

The Spanish Internet web site for tourism information is: www.spain.info.

Baqueira/Beret

The Spanish Pyrenees

The remote Valle d'Arán lies tucked hard against the French border in the rugged Pyrenees range midway between the Atlantic and the Mediterranean. This Spanish valley is virtually cut off from the rest of the country by jagged mountains. In fact, geographically it should be part of France since it lies on the northern side of the Pyrenees' tallest peaks. It is accessible only by bus or car along a winding road dwarfed by waterfalls and narrow canyons watched over by grazing goats and shaggy cattle.

The drive is arduous, but beauty unfolds with every turn as you pass a string of timeless villages and Romanesque churches. The surrounding peaks are the tallest in the Pyrenees. In the eastern section of the valley, ski lifts rise to a spreading series of runs with ridges and spines traced by trails and off-piste opportunities. The original village is starkly modern, but the newer developments echo the old Pyrenee stone architecture.

The valley oozes with wood and stone charm and the restaurants are among the best in Spain, even Europe. This is a valley that has developed in a cocoon of sorts—nestled between Spain and France over centuries. The first automobile road was only cut over the Bonaigua Pass in 1925 and a tunnel connecting the valley with the south was completed in 1948. Until those developments, Valle d'Arán was self-governing and isolated from Spain with better connections to France.

Val d'Arán has its own language, Aranés with connections to Ladin, spoken in parts of southern France and Switzerland and the Dolomites in Italy. Its traditional cuisine borrows from both the French and the Spanish.

Christmas/New Year, Easter and San José are super high season. January is low season. The first week of February is middle season. The remainder of February and early March is high season. The rest of March is low season.

Any time, prices are a bargain here, compared to the rest of Europe. Lift lines are few and far between. Extensive snowmaking, with more than 500 snow cannons, insures excellent terrain coverage. This is a resort that simply put, works well.

Mountain layout

Baqueira/Beret, covering 4,270 acres, is an expansive series of trails with four main access points. The vertical drop in this resort is 3,282 feet. The trails are served by 30 lifts inlcuding two new high-speed six-person chairs. More than 500 snow cannons provide dependable snow coverage on 35 km. of the trails even when faced with poor natural snow cover.

The village center of Baqueira is the main center with a high-speed quad lifting skiers from nearby hotels up to the 5,000-foot level where the ski school operates and the main beginner slopes welcome those starting with the sport. Beret is a cluster of facilities—ticket offices, restaurant, day care and ski school that anchors what is considered the wide open area of the resort. Between Baqueira and Beret, a new development of apartments and hotels, Tanau, is served by an old double chair that reaches the Altitude 1800 area as well. At the far eastern edge of the valley, a small building at the top of the Bonaigua Pass sells tickets and has parking, day care, restaurants and rentals.

The network of lifts and runs above Baqueira is dense and should keep most intermediates busy for days. The runs in the Beret section are much more widespread with lots of off-piste possibilities. The Bonaigua sector runs are well marked, and even without a map it is fairly easy to navigate.

Altitude 1800 above Baqueira is reached by the Bosque Lift, a detachable quad, from the edge of town. This brings skiers to a lower plateau where beginners learn on what are called the "pastures" and four more lifts take skiers to the upper reaches of the mountain. Head to the left of the restaurant and take the detachable quad lift. This allows experts and good intermediates the option of dropping down to the new six-passenger chair or heading to the Luis Arlas lift that will bring them back up to the Cap de Baqueira peak. Intermediates can enjoy the Isards and Mirador runs back to the lower plateau or all the way into the valley to the De la Choza chair lift. There is also an exciting off-piste itinerary, called Escornacrabes, off the back side of the Cap de Baqueira that loops back to the front side of the mountain and eventually back to the village. Beginners should stay to the right side of the restaurant, where a chair lift and a drag lift open up a practice area.

In December 2003, Baqueira will open a new area, Vall d'Aneu, which will extend Baqueira toward Bonaigua with a new access from Alt Aneu. Vall d'Aneu will have three new chairlifts, one of which will replace the old Bonaigua two-seater ski lift, and three new runs.

The Bonaigua area is really an extension of the Baqueira section that drops down to the Bonaigua pass. This is for the most part intermediate terrain with expert touches. Baqueira and Bonaigua share the steep Manaud trail from the top of the Manaud lift.

To get to the Beret section of the resort take the connecting Vista Beret lift. It is slow but well worth the ride. When you get off the lift stay high on the trail and ski over toward Beret. If you begin to drop down the trail, you arrive back at the base of the lift and will have to take the lift again to connect with Beret. Once in Beret get ready to cruise almost anywhere.

The Beret area is served by five lifts, but its terrain allows skiers to ski virtually anywhere and choose from beginner to expert. The trails here are an intermediate heaven with good beginner terrain laced throughout. Further to the left two triple chairs open more difficult terrain with the most difficult trails dropping from the top of the Dossau lift. The high-speed quad lift, Blanhiblar, opens up all-new terrain on the opposite side of the valley below Cap de Blanhiblar and Tuc de Costarjàs. A small drag lift links with this chair and opens extensive off-piste opportunities down into the valley.

Country code: 0034

The link from Beret back to Baqueira is made by using the high-speed six-person chair. From the top of this lift the long trail takes skiers back to either Tanau or Baqueira.

Mountain rating

For intermediates, there is plenty of skiing and enough challenge to leave you feeling pushed beyond your normal limits. Every lift has good intermediate skiing. Absolute beginners have plenty of area to practice their turns, then strike out for long easy trails. With good snow, experts will find plenty to keep them busy. With powder in the bowls, the slopes beneath Costarjas, the off-piste itineraries and the chutes dropping off the ridges running through the Baqueira and Bonaigua sections of the resort provide more than enough challenge. With poor snow, experts will be left wanting.

Ski school (2002/03 prices)

Baqueira/Beret has more than 200 ski teachers, about 10 of whom speak English. Be sure to request an English-speaking instructor if you don't speak Spanish. Ski lessons start for children who are age 3 and older. Discounts for children apply to those 11 years and younger.

Private lessons for one person cost about €30–€40 for one hour.

Group ski lessons for one person cost about €92–€120 for six days and €88–€109 for five days.

There are different **ski/snowboarding schools** in the area with similar prices. Check with them for the availability of English-speaking instructors.

Era Escuola (973-645126) has offices in Baqueira, Beret and Salardu.

Escuola Snowboard Val d'Aran (973-645881) focuses only on snowboarding.

Lift tickets (2003/04 prices)

	Adults	Children
one day	€34.50	€22
two days	€66	€40
five days	€152	€94

Accommodations

Lodges are spread throughout the valley. This may appear inconvenient at first, but staying in such a beautiful valley is arguably a plus.

The most convenient place to stay for skiing is, of course, in Baqueira or in Tanau right next to the slopes, but nightlife and restaurants are, for the most part, a drive away. Arties offers the best concentration of restaurants and nightlife and has exceptional hotels. Vielha has the valley's largest pool and skating complex, excellent après-ski and restaurants but is short on late nightlife. Otherwise stay along the road linking Vielha and Baqueira. With a car, the valley facilities can be easily reached. Rates are per person, double occupancy, in February with half board.

€€€—€125 per double room; €€—€75–124; €—less than €75.

Lodging at the slopes:

In the resort of Baqueira there are three hotels, all clustered at the base of the runs and the lifts. The most sought-after rooms are in the **Val de Ruda** (973-645258; €€), a small three-star hotel with heavy wood accents and lots of mountain atmosphere. The **Tuc Blanc** (973-644350; €€) is a big modern hotel and is closest to the lifts. It has the only covered swimming pool in the village as well as a steamroom. It seems like Grand Central Station when the lifts close at the end of the day. **Montarto** (973-639001; €€) has rooms that are quite small by modern standards but the service is first class and you'll have a short shuttle ride to the lifts or a 10-minute uphill walk. However, it is very convenient to the discos and the restaurants.

A small village of hotels and condos, Tanau has been built above Baquiera with a dedicated lift. Here you'll find the **Hotel Melia Royal Tanau** (973-644446; €€€) and its associated apartments. This is a full facility establishment, complete with fine restaurant, gymnasium, spa , pool facilities, a lovely view of the ski station and a location steps from the Esquiro chair lift. The nearby **Hotel Chalet Bassibe** (973-645152; €€) has pool, sauna and Jacuzzis. **Rafael Hoteles La Pleta** (973-645550; €€€) is in the same Tanau cluster, but about a 200 meter walk from the lift.

Lodging in Arties (7 km. from the slopes**):**

Parador Nacional Don Gaspar de Portola, Arties (973-640801; €€€) is a four-star parador (government-run country hotel). The town of Arties is the gourmet center of the valley, with some of Spain's top restaurants within a five-minute walk of the parador. This parador has been completely renovated over the past three years. **Hotel Valarties** (973-644364; €€) is the lodging arm of Restaurant Casa Irene. Half-board here means you dine on award-winning meals every day of the week. **Hotel Besiberri** (973-640829; €€) tucked into the back of the village is tiny, comfortable and cozy.

In Vielha (14 km. from the ski area):

Vielha, has come a long way in the past three years. The old town is being renovated and once-decrepit buildings house small restaurants and bars. The town now has two new four-star lodges— **Hotel Sol Vielha** (973-638000; €€) and **Hotel Val d'Aran** (973-643233; €€). We also recommend four smaller, recently renovated hotels tucked into the narrow streets of the old town only steps from good restaurants and packed tapas bars—**Hotel Fonfreda** (973-640486; €€) and **Hotel Riu Nere** (973-640150; €€), **Hotel Ribaeta** (973-642036; €) and **Hotel Orla** (973-642260; €).

Parador Nacional Valle de Arán, Vielha (973-640100; €€) is an impressive four-star hotel overlooking Vielha at the entrance to the tunnel leading south. Unfortunately, it is a long, inconvenient walk from the town.

Hotel HUSA Tuca (973-640700; €€) at the edge of Vielha, is convenient to Vielha and 13 km. from the Baqueira slopes.

Along the main road from Veilha to Baqueira:

The **Hotel de Tredos** (973-644014; €€) has a cozy atmosphere and is just down from the ski village. In Salardù, other small family-run, atmospheric hotels are **Hotel Lacreu** (973-644222; € half-board only), **Hotel Deth Pais** (973-645836; €) and **Hotel Mont Romies** (973-645820; €). **Garòs Ostau** (973-642378; €€) is very rustic and very small with only eight rooms.

Apartments, condominiums,flats

Baqueira/Beret has thousands of apartment beds. These places are small, built along the French style. We recommend two people take an apartment rated for four people and four sign up for a place for six in order to have adequate space. The rental folk here count the foldout couch as one of the normal sleeping places. For a one-bedroom unit in Baqueira, considered by the rental company to fit four, the special five-day rate in middle season with lifts tickets, is about €350–450, or €70–90 per person per day based on only two people sharing the unit.

In Viehla, at the other end of the valley, the new **Aparthotel Eth Refugi d'Aran** (973-643002; €€) and **Aparthotel La Vall Blanca** (973-643024; €€) in Vielha offer half-board and breakfast-only packages. **Aparthotel Eth Palai** (973-343220; €) only has condos without meals. These properties are within an easy walk of the old town.

For reservations call the tourist office in Baqueira/Beret.

Country code: 0034

Dining

If you enjoy fine food, coming to this valley will be like finding Shangra-La. The blend of French and Spanish cooking together with the mountain basics of the Valle de Arán has resulted in a unique cuisine (Aránes) praised across Europe. This cuisine has been complimented by other regional restaurants such as Basque. The valley also has a collection of gourmet restaurants that rival anything found at even top French resorts. With the highest-priced restaurants topping out at around €55 per person with wine, the best food in the world is within most skiers' budgets. Most full meals, with starter, main course and desert, will end up costing between €20 and €26. Pizza and wine ends up being around €12. Even without skiing, the trip to this valley would be worth the effort for only the food.

The restaurants are spread all through the valley. However most of the restaurants covered here are scattered between the main city, Vielha and the ski resort.

Start with the food on the mountain. Baqueira/Beret has an exceptional full-service restaurant, **Altitude 1800** (973-645202; €25+), at the top of the Bosque lift (the main lift out of town). The red beans were some of the best I have ever eaten and red peppers stuffed with ears and lips sound horrible, but taste heavenly; and excellent game and fish. In the Beret sector, the **Cafeteria Beret** (973-645227; €20) serves an excellent sit-down lunch as well. Call for reservations at both restaurants.

The restaurants in Baqueira are also part of the mountain eating since they are only a couple of minutes walk from the base of the lifts. The three best are **Ticolet** (973-645477; €15–25) with fine cuisine next to the Montarto Hotel and **La Borda de Lobato** (973-645708; €15–25) where more traditional meats and fish prepared on an open grill are served in a barn atmosphere oozing with rustic charm. **Esquiró** (973-645430; €€) serves what some say is the best fish in the valley.

Cap del Port (973-250082; €15–25) is in a castlelike building at the crest of the Port de la Bonaigua pass. This unique spot serves high altitude meals such as medalions of goat, deer fillets and mountain mushrooms. All these restaurants are open during the evening as well except the Altitude 1800 and Cafeteria Beret.

The town of Arties would be considered the cuisine capital of the region. Here you'll find **Casa Irene** (973-644-364; €35+) where the King and Queen of Spain often dine. Casa Irene still takes orders and chats with customers and her son, Andreas runs the kitchen. They normally serve a selection of three fixed-price menus ranging from €35 to €55, each with a half-dozen selections.

Also in Arties: **Eth Taro** (973-642558; €15–25) and **Candelaria** (973-642024; €€€) serve regional and international cuisine. The **Parador** (973-641103; €25) has an excellent restaurant but is rather stuffy and formal. **Restaurant Urtau** (973-640926; €€) borders on gourmet with more reasonable prices. **Mas Pasta** (973-641619; €15-) serves Italian food ranging from pizzas to pasta in a very romantic, rustic converted barn. **La Sal Gorda** (973-645431; €15–25) serves Basque cuisine.

If you are in Vielha try to visit **Era Coquèla de Vielha** (973-642915: €€) for an excellent meal (don't miss the chocolate soufflé for dessert). **Era Mola** (973-640868; €15–25) has gourmet flavors applied to some local favorites such as rabbit and duck. Two Basque style restaurants, **Sidreria Era Bruisha-Sorgiña** (973-642976; €15–25) and **Eth Baserri d'Aran** (973-642044; €15–25) serve excellent grilled meats and fish.

Three small spots are within steps of each other in Vielha on Carrer Mayor. **All i Oli** (973-641757; €) is cozy and serves family-made healthy Catalan meals. This is the perfect spot for vegetarians as well as those looking for barbecued meat. **Restaurant Eth Tidon** (973-640363; €) is a place for meat. There's no menu, just lots of meat fired over glowing coals sold by the kilo. **Restaurant Basteret** (973-640714; €) has a major

French clientele with delicious and reasonable food. During the day **La Lluna** has pastries, sandwiches and pizza.

Just outside of Vielha tucked on a narrow street of Betren (the village across from the Tuca Hotel) is **Era Borda de Betren** (973-640032; €15–25), a small restaurant that serves Aránese meals such as trout and lamb in a very cozy atmosphere .

Casa Carmela (973-645751; €15–25) in the tiny village of Unha, has grown from a small dining room that was packed night after night into a restaurant empire with three different levels for dining and lodging. It is listed as **Es de Don Joan Casa Carmela.** Her *cordero lechal* is exceptional as is her local soup, Olla Aranese. Her son runs a nearby wine shop with one of the region's best selections.

For good typical regional Aránese food are **Casa Turnay** (973-64092; €15–25), **El Niu** (973-641406; €15–25), **Es Pletieus** (973-640709) and **Casa Estampa** (973-640048; €15–25) in Escunhau, **Et Restrille** (973-641539; €15–25) in Garos, and the very reasonable **Borda de Benjamin** (973-645113; €15–25) in Salardu. **Zurbaran** (973-647710; €€) in Bossost is recommended for Basque cuisine with mountain touches.

You can find plenty of inexpensive pizza and Italian restaurants as well as some "combination plate" restaurants throughout the valley if you want to save money.

The bottom line here is that you can't go wrong when it comes to dining. Dining here is a passion. Lunch starts at about 2 p.m. and continues until at least 4 p.m. when skiers head out to catch the last half-hour of skiing before the slopes close at 4:30 p.m.

Here, as in the rest of Spain, the dinner is served late by English or American standards but not as late as in Andalusia. Restaurants open around 8 p.m. and most patrons show up between 9 and 10 p.m. Reservations, several days in advance, are necessary for many of them. Don't wait till the last minute.

Après-ski/nightlife

Après-ski here means tapas. Skiers meet in the hotel bars and in some of the bars in town from around 6 p.m. to 9 p.m. Vielha has a dozen excellent tapas bars that can be packed shoulder to shoulder. **Bar Neguri** and **Dues Portes** are right on the main road through town. **Bar Era Plaça**, on the town square, fills with skiers going over the day's adventures. In a cluster of recently restored ancient buildings on Carrer Mayor and nearby alleys try **Eth Petit Basteret**, **Eth Paer** and **Era Canaula** (ask for directions, it's tucked away).

In Arties the best tapas are at **Bar Urtau**—an experience that shouldn't be missed.

There is just not overwhelming late nightlife to choose from. The major discos at the resort are **Tiffany** and **Pacha**. They attract an older crowd (25 and up) with Pacha tending toward the younger set. The **Vielha** and **Elurra** discos in Vielha have a younger crew. Eth Clot is a music bar that gets packed on weekends.

There are four late-night music spots in Arties—**La Luna, Millenium, Devino** and **1844**. No one really shows up until midnight or later and the gyrations continue until three or four in the morning.

Child care (2003/04 prices)

There is babysitting service starting from 3 months old.

The resort has four child care centers accepting children from 3 to 8 years of age. One is at the 1500-meter level in the town which will also take infants from 3 months, and there is a children's snow park at the 1800-meter level near the restaurant with supervisory personnel and others in Beret and Bonaigua. Children can learn to ski or just play in the snow and watch movies.

For children from 2 to 6 years, five full days of care with lunch is €144.20 and six full days of care with lunch is €173.

Babysitting for infants from 3 months to 2 years is available. Call the tourist office for more information.

Other activities

Cross-country skiing is limited. There is a 7 km. loop in Beret and other cross-country opportunities in Ruda and Aiguamoix. The ski school has guides and lessons. **Helicopter skiing** (973-645797 and 619-847077), guided excursions with **dog sled** (630-882706 and 670-536654), and **paraskiing** (608-998711) are all offered at Baqueira/Beret. Two heated **swimming pools** and an **ice skating** rink are open at the Palau de Gel (973-642864) in Vielha; hours vary with skating every evening and swimming in the mornings and evenings. There are **thermal baths** origianlly discovered by the Romans about 35 minutes away at the end of Val Tredos (973-253003), accessible only by four-wheel drive in the winter, and towards France in Les (973-648717).

The **Aran Valley Museum** in Vielha, a collection of romanesque churches and unspoiled villages provide a glimpse of valley history. The restored Joanchiquet farmhouse in Vilamòs (normally closed in winter but open by appointment) is fascinating. Contact the valley tourist office (973-642915) for information and reservations.

Getting there & getting around

This is not one of the easier spots on the earth to reach. There are no trains or planes. That means bus or rental car. The nearest airports are Toulouse in France 166 km. away, and San Sebastian and Barcelona in Spain, about 250 km. and 350 km. respectively. From Toulouse take the autoroute west and exit at Montrejeau then follow signs to St. Beat and Val d'Arán. From Barcelona take the autopista to Lleida and then head north through Pont de Suert to Val d'Arán.

The bus ride between Vielha and Barcelona is about six hours with departures three times a day. It is not recommended.

The new Autoroute across southern France connecting Bayonne and the Mediterranean coast is also an excellent alternative to beating your way through the Spanish mountains. The airport in Biarritz or San Sebastian ends up being closer in driving time than Barcelona. The drive from Toulouse, France, is less than two hours.

Once in the valley, a car is the best way to move throughout the area. However, there is a bus system that links Baqueira and Veilha with buses heading to the resort hourly in the mornings and returning about every half hour starting from about 4 p.m. Tickets cost €0.75 per ride or €6 for ten rides. Gas is cheaper in Spain than France.

Tourist information

Oficina de Turismo de Baqueira/Beret, Apartado 60, 25530 Vielha-Lleida, Spain; information is open 9 a.m.–7 p.m. reservations is open 9 a.m.–1 p.m. and 3 p.m.–7 p.m.
Telephone 973-639000, fax 973-644488,
E-mail viajes@baqueira.es Internet: www.baqueira.es.
Snow reports (in Spanish) 973-639025.

☎ *When calling from outside Spain dial the country code then the phone number. From within Spain you must always dial 973 even for local calls.*

Sierra Nevada, Spain

Hard to believe, but there is skiing in southern Spain, about a half-hour drive from Granada. The Sierra Nevada resort has skiing at an altitude of over 10,000 feet and brilliant sunshine most of the winter. When storms arrive, life at the top of this treeless mountain top stops and visitors either drop down to Granada or curl up with a good book. With good weather the views are spectacular—almost unbelievable. From the top of the Veleta peak, skiers can see across the Mediterranean to the Atlas Mountains of Morocco.

The resort town itself, basically a sparse cluster of hotels and apartments at the base of the first series of lifts, is modern with a hint of traditional charm. It is purpose-built. It is here only for skiing and has been well located for that pursuit. It is not a traditionally Spanish enclave, nor does it appear in any sense Alpine; however, if you want to find snow in southern Spain, this is the place to be. When it does snow, it comes down light and dry because of the low humidity in Southern Spain. When it doesn't snow, Sierra Nevada has one of Europe's most advanced snowmaking systems.

What Sierra Nevada does exude is the intoxicating Spanish love of the good life. There are lively tapas bars, quaint shops and elegant hotels climbing the mountainside. After skiing no one here forgets good food and spirited nightlife.

In preparation for the the 1996 World Cup, Spain improved virtually every aspect of the village including the access road from Grenada. Even the old original hotels have been given a facelift and more of an Andalusian facade.

Mountain layout

To be honest, it would be hard to get lost on this mountain unless faced with white-out conditions. The skiing range is not that extensive, but it is wide open, and the runs are long and gentle. This is a true cruisers' delight. The resort boasts an above-treeline vertical of 3,757 feet.

The first lifts take all skiers to the main hub, Borreguiles, about 1,500 feet above the main village. Borreguiles is surrounded by beginner terrain and teaching slopes.

The resort has just undergone a major series of improvements that has added new lifts and other amenities in preparation for the 2003/04 Europe Cup Final. High-speed quad chairs serve every major section of the mountain, limiting lift lines. In total, 22 lifts open this mellow mountain to skiers. Intermediates can have fun in every fold of the resort, beginners have plenty of space and only experts will find the resort limited.

At Borreguiles, the mid-station of the cablecar rising from the town, the restaurant, café and the main ski school are grouped together. The restaurant has recently been expanded to handle the midday crowds. The beginner area surrounds this midmountain station and the ski school.

If you take the Veleta lift and ski back down towards Borreguiles, you cruise through an intermediate bowl. This route takes skiers past the World Cup race course and the snowboard park. A far traverse to the right will swing you along a ridge that offers some fancy off-piste runs into the Valle de San Juan. But don't drop too far, you'll have to get back over the ridge to descend some wide-open faces back to Borreguiles or right back into the main village. Choose your line. If you can see it, you can ski it.

However the more spectacular trails are reached by a traverse a little to your right toward the Olimpica run that slices down the Laguna de Yeguas bowl. Here, 2,300 vertical feet of more challenging intermediate terrain and wide-open snowfields beckon. The visuals are dramatic with the cliffs ringing the bowl and the stunning snow. There are trails packed by snowcats, but the real dream is diving into the ungroomed powder. This is an excellent off-piste itinerary called Tajos de Virgen that provides great views and challenge.

Below Borreguiles, when the snow is good, better skiers can drop down the Loma Dilar section of the resort and find some acceptable steeps or search for short steeps below the Borreguiles midstation.

Snowboarding

Snowboarding is allowed on the entire mountain, but limited in the designated beginner ski area. There is a snowboard school and plenty of snowboard rentals. There is a snowboard park above Borreguiles that can be fun, but the real riders strike out for the Laguna de Yeguas to head off-piste and play on the ridges and natural banked sides. After cruising down Laguna de Yeguas take the Dilar chair lift to the ridge and choose your spot to drop back into the bowl carving beneath the chair you just rode.

Mountain rating

As always, experts can find the tough stuff anywhere. Sierra Nevada has some good challenges in the far bowls and is delightful for strong skiers in the ungroomed areas. Intermediates will be ecstatic. For the most part, this is a mellow beginning and intermediate paradise when sticking to groomed trails. If you enjoy long mellow cruising carving big giant-slalom turns, you will think you are in heaven. You'll quickly discover that the object here is pure enjoyment, so relax and enjoy the sun.

High season in Spain occurs at Christmas/New Year, mid February, and Easter. Middle season is late January, early and late February, and March (except for Easter week). Low season is early December and most of January. In addition, Saturdays, Sundays and holidays draw premium rates.

Ski school (2002/03 prices)

There are few places that are this perfect for learning to ski. The Spanish temperament makes for great initial instruction. What's more, most of the mountain can be handled by beginners after three or four days of instruction. There are three ski schools (958-480168, 958-480011 or 958-480142) that have more than 100 instructors and have offices in the main square of the town and at Borreguiles at midmountain. About a quarter of the instructors speak English.

Private lesson for one adult costs €26 and an additional €6 per additional person up to a maximum of four.

Group ski lessons for adults cost €105for five days during high season and €99 during mid-season. Classes area held three hours each day in groups of eight to 10 skiers or riders. Children pay around €115 for five days.

Saturday/Sunday courses are available for €55 with three hours of instruction each day, or for €29 for two hours of teaching.

There are different ski/snowboarding schools in the area with similar prices: Spanish Ski School (958-480168); Official Ski School (958-480011); and the International Ski School (958-480142). Check with them for the availability of English-speaking instructors.

Lift tickets (2002/03 prices)

high/mid-season prices	Adults	Children
one day	€31.50/€28	€20/€17
three days	€88.80/€79	€51/€43
five days	€133.90/€119	€75/€63

Night skiing costs €10 a day.

The high season here is every weekend as well as the Christmas and Easter holiday periods. Mid-season is Monday through Friday, except during holidays. There is also an early and late season, but snow conditions should be carefully checked when coming to Sierra Nevada in the shoulder season.

Accommodations

All the hotels are relatively new. Add 12 percent value-added tax to each of these rates.

All these hotels have good rooms with bath. They are listed in descending order of luxury. Rates are per person, double occupancy with half board in February. €€€—€125+; €€—€75–€124; €—less than €75.

Hotel Maribel (958-249111, fax 958-249146) is a small place with only 31 rooms and is considered the best place to stay on the mountain with quiet luxury.

El Lodge (958-480600, fax 958-481314; €€€) is one of the top spots, right on the slopes with ski-in/ski-out.

Hotel Kenia Nevada (958-480911, fax 958-480807; €€€) This four-star hotel provides some of the town's best accommodations in a rustic Alpine style, all within walking distance of the slopes and most shops and restaurants.

Hotel Melia Sierra Nevada (958-480400; fax 958-480458; €€€) This four-star hotel is located at the Plaza Pradollano and only steps away from shopping, restaurants and the ski slopes. The lobby is cozy with heavy wooden beams and a stone floor gives it a Nordic atmosphere.

Hotel Ziryab (958-480512, fax 958-481415; €€) is center-village and has impressive rooms. The hotel meals are all buffet-style and it still is rated by Michelin!

Hotel Melia-Sol y Nieve (958-480300, fax 958-480458; €€€) is one of the original standbys with all the basics and a great location.

Hotel GHM Monachil (958-481450 or 902-481100, fax 958-48101; €€–€€€), formerly Hotel La General. This hotel right on the main town square -- 30 meters from the first stop of the Parador chairlift and 40 meters from the Maribel slope -- has a restaurant with a solarium.

Other hotels to consider in descending order of luxury are: **Rumaykiyya** (958-481400, fax 958-480032; €€), **Hotel Nevasur** (958-480350, fax 958-480365; €€), **Casa Alpina** (958-480600, fax 958-480506; €€), **Mont Blanc** (958-481212 fax 958-481358; €€) and a B&B named **El Ciervo** (958-249409, fax 958-249461; €€).

There are also a series of Apartment-Hotels. These are basically condos with cleaning service. The two most luxurious are **Aparthotel Cumbres Blancas** and **Aparthotel Ginebra** (958-480456, fax 958-480438).

Cheap student lodging can be found at **Albergue Universitario** (958-480122), **Albergue Juvenil Sierra Nevada** (958-480305), **Albergue Militar** (958-481227) or **Residencia Pradollano** (958-480114).

Accommodations in Granada

Granada is only about a half-hour drive away from the resort, assuming no traffic and no bad weather. On most days, the commute to ski is not bad. It is recommended that skiers planning on staying in Granada rent a car and try to stay outside of the warren of narrow streets that make up the center of town. Also, try to stay in a place that has parking, since it comes at a premium in this city. €€€—€125+; €€—€75–€124; €—less than €75.

The weather in Granada can be 65 degrees while it is freezing up at Sierra Nevada. Staying here is perfect when coming for late-season skiing.

Hotel Kenia (958-227506; €€) is built in an old manor building furnished with antiques and with a nice garden. It is only a short walk to the Campo de Principe, one of the tapas, dining and nightlife centers.

Hostal Suecia (958-225044 fax 958-227781; €) is a small place near the Hotel Kenia. Make sure to ask for a room with private bath—some rooms have shared baths.

Hotel Guadalupe (958-223423 fax 958-223798; €€) is up behind the Alhambra with almost a country feeling. It is easy to head to the slopes here, but it is a long walk or a bus ride to any restaurants or nightlife.

Los Alixares (958-225575 fax 958-224102; €€) is another hotel behind the Alhambra. It is modern and without much charm, and it is a bus ride out of downtown. But, it is convenient to the back way out of town.

To have a different, luxurious, Old World experience, stay at the **Alhambra Palace** (958-221468, fax 958-226404; €€€). The views from the high-ceiling rooms over the town are wonderful. The back road out to the highway avoids much of the town traffic. It has convenient bus transport to the center of town.

Dining

This tiny village has plenty of restaurants that put on a good meal. Make reservations if you are planning to eat anywhere between 10 p.m. and midnight—these places can get packed.

Ruta del Veleta (958-486134) is a favorite of Spain's King Juan Carlos and features excellent Andalusian cuisine. Michelin rates this place with three fork—almost a star. Call for reservations and expect to pay about €35-€40.

Traditional Spanish cooking can be found at **Casablanca** (958-480830), **Rincón de Pepe Reyes** (958-480394), and **Mesón Alcazaba** (958-480129). **Restaurant La Bodega** (958-249133) serves an excellent paella and other good rice dishes.

Restaurant la Carihuela, named after the old fishermen's district of Torremolinos, in the Edelweiss building is considered to serve the town's best fish dishes.

Tito Luigi (958-480882) serves excellent pizza and inexpensive Italian cooking. **Andalusi** (958-480206) is a pizza joint with other pasta as well. **Creperie La Gauffre** (958-480445) has a Spanish version of French crêpes. For Chinese food try **Restaurante Chinatown** (958 480433).

A great place for breakfast or a sweet is the **Croisanteria La Gauffre** where there are wonderful breads, rolls and pastries.

On the slopes, the best place to head for an excellent sit-down lunch is **Restaurant Tia Maria** (958-340432) in the Borreguiles building. Call for reservations. A good place for fast food is the **Burguer Alpino** in the same complex.

Après-ski/nightlife

This is a small resort, so you should be able to find out if anything is going on rather quickly. Though the village may be small, the nightlife is charged with that special Spanish spirit that takes advantage of the moment and normally stretches that moment into the wee hours of the morning.

El Golpe and **Soho Bar de Copas** both have hot action immediately after skiing. These are the spots to make contacts with other tourists that you can follow up on later in the night. Try **Mango** and **Sitcky Fingers** as well. Any place surrounding the main square will be packed as skiers come off the mountain. On a sunny day, the après-ski is wonderful.

The discos start pumping around midnight but may only get crowded around 1 or 2 a.m. Try **Nevada 53** in the Hotel Meliá Sierra Nevada, **La Chimenea** in Edificio Primaverall and **La Chicle** where the younger crowd gathers in Edificio Bulgaria. **Mango** has good disco action when the resort is packed. The older nightlife crowd tends to congregate in the **Sala Muley,** at the Hotel Meliá Sierra Nevada, or at **Crescendo** in the Telecabina building.

Expect to pay hefty cover charges, but remember these cover charges normally include one or two drinks. You'll quickly learn why party folk here don't swig down drinks at a fast pace. Most nurse their drink for the entire evening.

In Granada, the nightlife centers around tapas. The discos are expensive and filled with youth and blaring music. For a great evening of tapa-hopping try the Calle Navas right in the middle of town or head to Campo de Principe about a 15-minute walk from Navas.

Child care

Spanish culture revels in children—you can be sure children will be well cared for here. Child care is available at Guarderia Infantil in the new village area next to the Telecabina Al-Andalus. The facility is well-equipped and staffed by certified care providers. The guarderia has plenty of toys and videos with activities planned throughout the day. Children from 3 years of age are accepted. Hours are 10 a.m.–4 p.m. Children are accepted for a half day as well. Prices are about €25 for a half day, €32 per day, €115 for five full days or €85 for five a.m. or p.m. sessons.

Other activities

Snowtubing is available for €10 for three rides. Dogsledding can be arranged at a cost of €36 for a half-hour trip. Snowmobiling is also possible for €40 for a 20-minute jaunt on your own, or €30 if you go with a guided group.

The location is what makes this resort so special. Within an hour you can reach Granada and visit the fabulous Alhambra and the old center of the city. Malaga is only about two hours away, and the Costa del Sol—its chalk-white towns like Salobrena clutching small hilltops—is even closer. Excursions can be made to Jaen, with its massive cathedral and Moorish baths, or Gaudix and Purullena with their troglodyte villages. At nearby Lacalahorra castle you will have to find the gate-keeper in the town below the castle before heading up the hill.

During the spring, golf is one of the major activities of this area. There are more than 30 courses lining the Costa del Sol within a two-hour drive.

Getting there

Granada is 31 km. away. There is only one road from the city to the ski area that will take about a half-hour to drive. Traveling by car is highly recommended—it gives you much more freedom and allows exploration of Granada and the surrounding towns. Buses leave Granada from the Station Buses of Granada each morning at 9:00 a.m. and return at 17:00 p.m.

The airport is 17 km. from Granada. It has flights to Madrid, Barcelona, Valencia, Palma de Mallorca, Tenerife and the Canary Islands. Taxis are available from the airport to Sierra Nevada. Call Tele Taxi at 958-280654 or Radio Taxi at 958-151461. Expect to pay €45–€55 for a taxi from the airport to the resort.

Tourist information

For reservation center and information contact
Cetursa Sierra Nevada, Plaza de Andalucia, 4, Sierra Nevada, Monachil-Grenada. Telephone 902-708090; fax 958-249181
Internet: www.sierranevadaski.com
The provincial tourist office in Granada has responsibility for the resort. Write Patronato Provincial de Turismo de Granada, Pl. Mariana Pineda, 10-2, Granada, Spain (958-223527).
The telephone country code for Spain is 34.